FREE Test Taking Tips Video/DVD Offer

To better serve you, we created videos covering test taking tips that we want to give you for FREE. **These videos cover world-class tips that will help you succeed on your test.**

We just ask that you send us feedback about this product. Please let us know what you thought about it—whether good, bad, or indifferent.

To get your **FREE videos**, you can use the QR code below or email freevideos@studyguideteam.com with "Free Videos" in the subject line and the following information in the body of the email:

a. The title of your product

b. Your product rating on a scale of 1-5, with 5 being the highest

c. Your feedback about the product

If you have any questions or concerns, please don't hesitate to contact us at info@studyguideteam.com.

Thank you!

SCAN HERE

CSCS Study Guide 2024-2025

5 Practice Tests and CSCS Exam Prep Book for the NSCA Certification [6th Edition]

Lydia Morrison

Written and edited by TPB Publishing.

ISBN 13: 9781637755358

Table of Contents

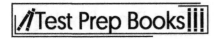

Welcome

Dear Reader,

Welcome to your new Test Prep Books study guide! We are pleased that you chose us to help you prepare for your exam. There are many study options to choose from, and we appreciate you choosing us. Studying can be a daunting task, but we have designed a smart, effective study guide to help prepare you for what lies ahead.

Whether you're a parent helping your child learn and grow, a high school student working hard to get into your dream college, or a nursing student studying for a complex exam, we want to help give you the tools you need to succeed. We hope this study guide gives you the skills and the confidence to thrive, and we can't thank you enough for allowing us to be part of your journey.

In an effort to continue to improve our products, we welcome feedback from our customers. We look forward to hearing from you. Suggestions, success stories, and criticisms can all be communicated by emailing us at info@studyguideteam.com.

Sincerely,
Test Prep Books Team

FREE Videos/DVD OFFER

Doing well on your exam requires both knowing the test content and understanding how to use that knowledge to do well on the test. We offer completely FREE test taking tip videos. **These videos cover world-class tips that you can use to succeed on your test.**

To get your **FREE videos**, you can use the QR code below or email freevideos@studyguideteam.com with "Free Videos" in the subject line and the following information in the body of the email:

a. The title of your product
b. Your product rating on a scale of 1-5, with 5 being the highest
c. Your feedback about the product

If you have any questions or concerns, please don't hesitate to contact us at info@studyguideteam.com.

SCAN HERE

Quick Overview

As you draw closer to taking your exam, effective preparation becomes more and more important. Thankfully, you have this study guide to help you get ready. Use this guide to help keep your studying on track and refer to it often.

This study guide contains several key sections that will help you be successful on your exam. The guide contains tips for what you should do the night before and the day of the test. Also included are test-taking tips. Knowing the right information is not always enough. Many well-prepared test takers struggle with exams. These tips will help equip you to accurately read, assess, and answer test questions.

A large part of the guide is devoted to showing you what content to expect on the exam and to helping you better understand that content. In this guide are practice test questions so that you can see how well you have grasped the content. Then, answer explanations are provided so that you can understand why you missed certain questions.

Don't try to cram the night before you take your exam. This is not a wise strategy for a few reasons. First, your retention of the information will be low. Your time would be better used by reviewing information you already know rather than trying to learn a lot of new information. Second, you will likely become stressed as you try to gain a large amount of knowledge in a short amount of time. Third, you will be depriving yourself of sleep. So be sure to go to bed at a reasonable time the night before. Being well-rested helps you focus and remain calm.

Be sure to eat a substantial breakfast the morning of the exam. If you are taking the exam in the afternoon, be sure to have a good lunch as well. Being hungry is distracting and can make it difficult to focus. You have hopefully spent lots of time preparing for the exam. Don't let an empty stomach get in the way of success!

When travelling to the testing center, leave earlier than needed. That way, you have a buffer in case you experience any delays. This will help you remain calm and will keep you from missing your appointment time at the testing center.

Be sure to pace yourself during the exam. Don't try to rush through the exam. There is no need to risk performing poorly on the exam just so you can leave the testing center early. Allow yourself to use all of the allotted time if needed.

Remain positive while taking the exam even if you feel like you are performing poorly. Thinking about the content you should have mastered will not help you perform better on the exam.

Once the exam is complete, take some time to relax. Even if you feel that you need to take the exam again, you will be well served by some down time before you begin studying again. It's often easier to convince yourself to study if you know that it will come with a reward!

Test-Taking Strategies

1. Predicting the Answer

When you feel confident in your preparation for a multiple-choice test, try predicting the answer before reading the answer choices. This is especially useful on questions that test objective factual knowledge. By predicting the answer before reading the available choices, you eliminate the possibility that you will be distracted or led astray by an incorrect answer choice. You will feel more confident in your selection if you read the question, predict the answer, and then find your prediction among the answer choices. After using this strategy, be sure to still read all of the answer choices carefully and completely. If you feel unprepared, you should not attempt to predict the answers. This would be a waste of time and an opportunity for your mind to wander in the wrong direction.

2. Reading the Whole Question

Too often, test takers scan a multiple-choice question, recognize a few familiar words, and immediately jump to the answer choices. Test authors are aware of this common impatience, and they will sometimes prey upon it. For instance, a test author might subtly turn the question into a negative, or he or she might redirect the focus of the question right at the end. The only way to avoid falling into these traps is to read the entirety of the question carefully before reading the answer choices.

3. Looking for Wrong Answers

Long and complicated multiple-choice questions can be intimidating. One way to simplify a difficult multiple-choice question is to eliminate all of the answer choices that are clearly wrong. In most sets of answers, there will be at least one selection that can be dismissed right away. If the test is administered on paper, the test taker could draw a line through it to indicate that it may be ignored; otherwise, the test taker will have to perform this operation mentally or on scratch paper. In either case, once the obviously incorrect answers have been eliminated, the remaining choices may be considered. Sometimes identifying the clearly wrong answers will give the test taker some information about the correct answer. For instance, if one of the remaining answer choices is a direct opposite of one of the eliminated answer choices, it may well be the correct answer. The opposite of obviously wrong is obviously right! Of course, this is not always the case. Some answers are obviously incorrect simply because they are irrelevant to the question being asked. Still, identifying and eliminating some incorrect answer choices is a good way to simplify a multiple-choice question.

4. Don't Overanalyze

Anxious test takers often overanalyze questions. When you are nervous, your brain will often run wild, causing you to make associations and discover clues that don't actually exist. If you feel that this may be a problem for you, do whatever you can to slow down during the test. Try taking a deep breath or counting to ten. As you read and consider the question, restrict yourself to the particular words used by the author. Avoid thought tangents about what the author *really* meant, or what he or she was *trying* to say. The only things that matter on a multiple-choice test are the words that are actually in the question. You must avoid reading too much into a multiple-choice question, or supposing that the writer meant something other than what he or she wrote.

5. No Need for Panic

It is wise to learn as many strategies as possible before taking a multiple-choice test, but it is likely that you will come across a few questions for which you simply don't know the answer. In this situation, avoid panicking. Because most multiple-choice tests include dozens of questions, the relative value of a single wrong answer is small. As much as possible, you should compartmentalize each question on a multiple-choice test. In other words, you should not allow your feelings about one question to affect your success on the others. When you find a question that you either don't understand or don't know how to answer, just take a deep breath and do your best. Read the entire question slowly and carefully. Try rephrasing the question a couple of different ways. Then, read all of the answer choices carefully. After eliminating obviously wrong answers, make a selection and move on to the next question.

6. Confusing Answer Choices

When working on a difficult multiple-choice question, there may be a tendency to focus on the answer choices that are the easiest to understand. Many people, whether consciously or not, gravitate to the answer choices that require the least concentration, knowledge, and memory. This is a mistake. When you come across an answer choice that is confusing, you should give it extra attention. A question might be confusing because you do not know the subject matter to which it refers. If this is the case, don't eliminate the answer before you have affirmatively settled on another. When you come across an answer choice of this type, set it aside as you look at the remaining choices. If you can confidently assert that one of the other choices is correct, you can leave the confusing answer aside. Otherwise, you will need to take a moment to try to better understand the confusing answer choice. Rephrasing is one way to tease out the sense of a confusing answer choice.

7. Your First Instinct

Many people struggle with multiple-choice tests because they overthink the questions. If you have studied sufficiently for the test, you should be prepared to trust your first instinct once you have carefully and completely read the question and all of the answer choices. There is a great deal of research suggesting that the mind can come to the correct conclusion very quickly once it has obtained all of the relevant information. At times, it may seem to you as if your intuition is working faster even than your reasoning mind. This may in fact be true. The knowledge you obtain while studying may be retrieved from your subconscious before you have a chance to work out the associations that support it. Verify your instinct by working out the reasons that it should be trusted.

8. Key Words

Many test takers struggle with multiple-choice questions because they have poor reading comprehension skills. Quickly reading and understanding a multiple-choice question requires a mixture of skill and experience. To help with this, try jotting down a few key words and phrases on a piece of scrap paper. Doing this concentrates the process of reading and forces the mind to weigh the relative importance of the question's parts. In selecting words and phrases to write down, the test taker thinks about the question more deeply and carefully. This is especially true for multiple-choice questions that are preceded by a long prompt.

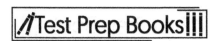

9. Subtle Negatives

One of the oldest tricks in the multiple-choice test writer's book is to subtly reverse the meaning of a question with a word like *not* or *except*. If you are not paying attention to each word in the question, you can easily be led astray by this trick. For instance, a common question format is, "Which of the following is...?" Obviously, if the question instead is, "Which of the following is not...?," then the answer will be quite different. Even worse, the test makers are aware of the potential for this mistake and will include one answer choice that would be correct if the question were not negated or reversed. A test taker who misses the reversal will find what he or she believes to be a correct answer and will be so confident that he or she will fail to reread the question and discover the original error. The only way to avoid this is to practice a wide variety of multiple-choice questions and to pay close attention to each and every word.

10. Reading Every Answer Choice

It may seem obvious, but you should always read every one of the answer choices! Too many test takers fall into the habit of scanning the question and assuming that they understand the question because they recognize a few key words. From there, they pick the first answer choice that answers the question they believe they have read. Test takers who read all of the answer choices might discover that one of the latter answer choices is actually *more* correct. Moreover, reading all of the answer choices can remind you of facts related to the question that can help you arrive at the correct answer. Sometimes, a misstatement or incorrect detail in one of the latter answer choices will trigger your memory of the subject and will enable you to find the right answer. Failing to read all of the answer choices is like not reading all of the items on a restaurant menu: you might miss out on the perfect choice.

11. Spot the Hedges

One of the keys to success on multiple-choice tests is paying close attention to every word. This is never truer than with words like *almost*, *most*, *some*, and *sometimes*. These words are called "hedges" because they indicate that a statement is not totally true or not true in every place and time. An absolute statement will contain no hedges, but in many subjects, the answers are not always straightforward or absolute. There are always exceptions to the rules in these subjects. For this reason, you should favor those multiple-choice questions that contain hedging language. The presence of qualifying words indicates that the author is taking special care with his or her words, which is certainly important when composing the right answer. After all, there are many ways to be wrong, but there is only one way to be right! For this reason, it is wise to avoid answers that are absolute when taking a multiple-choice test. An absolute answer is one that says things are either all one way or all another. They often include words like *every*, *always*, *best*, and *never*. If you are taking a multiple-choice test in a subject that doesn't lend itself to absolute answers, be on your guard if you see any of these words.

12. Long Answers

In many subject areas, the answers are not simple. As already mentioned, the right answer often requires hedges. Another common feature of the answers to a complex or subjective question are qualifying clauses, which are groups of words that subtly modify the meaning of the sentence. If the question or answer choice describes a rule to which there are exceptions or the subject matter is complicated, ambiguous, or confusing, the correct answer will require many words in order to be expressed clearly and accurately. In essence, you should not be deterred by answer choices that seem excessively long. Oftentimes, the author of the text will not be able to write the correct answer without offering some qualifications and modifications. Your job is to read the answer choices thoroughly and completely and to select the one that most accurately and precisely answers the question.

13. Restating to Understand

Sometimes, a question on a multiple-choice test is difficult not because of what it asks but because of how it is written. If this is the case, restate the question or answer choice in different words. This process serves a couple of important purposes. First, it forces you to concentrate on the core of the question. In order to rephrase the question accurately, you have to understand it well. Rephrasing the question will concentrate your mind on the key words and ideas. Second, it will present the information to your mind in a fresh way. This process may trigger your memory and render some useful scrap of information picked up while studying.

14. True Statements

Sometimes an answer choice will be true in itself, but it does not answer the question. This is one of the main reasons why it is essential to read the question carefully and completely before proceeding to the answer choices. Too often, test takers skip ahead to the answer choices and look for true statements. Having found one of these, they are content to select it without reference to the question above. The savvy test taker will always read the entire question before turning to the answer choices. Then, having settled on a correct answer choice, he or she will refer to the original question and ensure that the selected answer is relevant. The mistake of choosing a correct-but-irrelevant answer choice is especially common on questions related to specific pieces of objective knowledge.

15. No Patterns

One of the more dangerous ideas that circulates about multiple-choice tests is that the correct answers tend to fall into patterns. These erroneous ideas range from a belief that B and C are the most common right answers, to the idea that an unprepared test-taker should answer "A-B-A-C-A-D-A-B-A." It cannot be emphasized enough that pattern-seeking of this type is exactly the WRONG way to approach a multiple-choice test. To begin with, it is highly unlikely that the test maker will plot the correct answers according to some predetermined pattern. The questions are scrambled and delivered in a random order. Furthermore, even if the test maker was following a pattern in the assignation of correct answers, there is no reason why the test taker would know which pattern he or she was using. Any attempt to discern a pattern in the answer choices is a waste of time and a distraction from the real work of taking the test. A test taker would be much better served by extra preparation before the test than by reliance on a pattern in the answers.

Bonus Content & Audiobook

We host multiple bonus items online, including all 5 practice tests in digital format and our audiobook. Scan the QR code or go to this link to access this content:

testprepbooks.com/bonus/cscs

SCAN ME

The first time you access the page, you will need to register as a "new user" and verify your email address.

If you have any issues, please email support@testprepbooks.com.

Introduction to the CSCS Exam

Function of the Test

The CSCS exam is a two-part test required to receive qualification as a Certified Strength and Conditioning Specialist (CSCS). The role of CSCS experts is to help improve the physical performance of athletes of all ages and abilities, from beginner to professional, while minimizing the risk of injury. The exam measures candidates' aptitude regarding the scientific foundations and practical applications of strength training and conditioning. Exams are held in test centers around the world.

CSCS exam candidates residing in the U.S. must have a bachelor's degree or be current registered college seniors at an accredited school. In addition, candidates must have Cardiopulmonary Resuscitation (CPR) and Automated External Defibrillator (AED) certification cards from an accepted association, such as the American Heart Association or the Red Cross. Those living outside the United States and Canada must have a bachelor's degree recognized by U.S. educational standards or confirm enrollment as a college senior at an institution acknowledged by that nation as a degree-granting college or university.

Candidates typically have educational or professional experience in one of the following specialties: exercise science/physiology, strength training and conditioning, kinesiology and biomechanics, or physical therapy and athletic training. According to the National Strength and Conditioning Association (NSCA), the organization that develops and administers the examination, 6,196 candidates took the CSCS in 2018. The current pass rate for the CSCS exam is 55%.

Test Administration

CSCS exams are offered throughout the year at Pearson VUE test locations worldwide. There are separate fees for NSCA members and non-members. Full-time college students can obtain a NSCA student membership; alternatively, professional memberships are also available. First-time test takers need to register and take both sections (Scientific Foundations and Practical/Applied). Examinees who achieve a passing grade on both test sections receive CSCS accreditation. However, if a candidate receives a passing score on just one section, he or she may retake the failed section and thus obtain certification upon receipt of a passing grade. There are applicable fees to retake the entire exam or just one section.

Although there are no restrictions on the number of times a candidate may retake the CSCS exam, he or she must wait 90 days to retest. Eligibility requirements do not need to be resubmitted unless prior CPR/AED certification has expired. Pearson VUE will honor special test arrangements for examinees with disabilities upon request.

Test Format

There are two parts of the CSCS exam: Scientific Foundations and Practical/Applied.

The Scientific Foundations section has a total of 95 multiple-choice questions – 80 that are scored and 15 that are not scored. The Practical/Applied exam incudes 125 multiple-choice questions – 110 that are scored and 15 that are not scored. The total time to take both sections is about 4 hours. There is a break between the two parts that is not included in this time estimation.

The non-scored questions are distributed throughout the exam so that individuals will give them the same amount of attention as the scored questions. Under evaluation by the CSCS Exam Development Committee for potential future use, these pretest questions may be included on forthcoming CSCS exams as scored questions. These non-scored questions are not included in a candidate's official score and do not impact pass/fail status.

Scientific Foundations Section

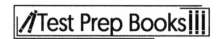

The Scientific Foundations section of the CSCS exam is meant to measure a candidate's exercise science skills, specifically in areas such as anatomy, exercise physiology, biomechanics, and nutrition. The length of time given to take this section is 1.5 hours. New in 2020, this section now includes Sports Psychology, in addition to Exercise Science and Nutrition, which used to constitute the entire section.

Total time = 1.5 hours

Field	Percent of Section	Number of Questions
Exercise Science	55%	44
Sports Psychology	24%	19
Nutrition	21%	17
Non-scored Questions		15
Total	**100%**	**95**

Practical/Applied Section

The Practical/Applied section focuses on Exercise Technique; Program Design; Organization and Administration; and Testing, Ongoing Monitoring, and Data Evaluation. The length of time given to take this section is 2.5 hours. This section includes thirty to forty electronic and/or visual prompts that measure knowledge in the areas of exercise techniques, functional anatomy, and testing procedures.

Total Time = 2.5 hours

Field	Percent of Section	Number of Questions
Exercise Technique	36%	40
Program Design	35%	38
Organization and Administration	11%	12
Testing, Ongoing Monitoring, and Data Evaluation	18%	20
Non-scored Questions		15
Total	**100%**	**125**

Scoring

Each part of the CSCS exam is graded on a point scale of 1 to 99, with 70 considered a passing score. Scaled scores can be compared across the various exam formulations, which may have somewhat different levels of complexity. For example, a scaled score of 75 received in 2014 is equal to a scaled score of 75 received in 2016, even though the two exams may have contained slightly different questions. Statistical techniques to equalize the CSCS exams are used to make sure the different exam formulations maintain the same standard of difficulty. A candidate's strong and weak points are depicted as raw (unscaled) domain scores. Raw scores cannot be directly associated to scaled scores.

Recent Updates

The CSCS exam outline and test were updated in January 2020. It now includes a separate and more-involved domain called Sports Psychology under the Scientific Foundation section. There are a variety of changes in the Practical/Applied section, including a greater emphasis on recovery techniques, teaching and evaluating movement preparation, and monitoring and ongoing evaluation.

Study Prep Plan for the CSCS Exam

1 **Schedule** - Use one of our study schedules below or come up with one of your own.

2 **Relax** - Test anxiety can hurt even the best students. There are many ways to reduce stress. Find the one that works best for you.

3 **Execute** - Once you have a good plan in place, be sure to stick to it.

One Week Study Schedule

Day 1	Exercise Sciences
Day 2	Nutrition
Day 3	Organization and Administration
Day 4	Practice Tests #1 & #2
Day 5	Practice Tests #3 & #4
Day 6	Practice Test #5
Day 7	Take Your Exam!

Two Week Study Schedule

Day 1	Exercise Sciences	Day 8	Organization and Administration
Day 2	Bioenergetics and Metabolism	Day 9	Practice Test #1
Day 3	Sport Psychology	Day 10	Practice Test #2
Day 4	Nutrition	Day 11	Practice Test #3
Day 5	Exercise Technique	Day 12	Practice Test #4
Day 6	Program Design	Day 13	Practice Test #5
Day 7	Determining and Assigning Training...	Day 14	Take Your Exam!

One Month Study Schedule

Day 1	Exercise Sciences	Day 11	Olympic Lifting and Plyometric Exercise...	Day 21	Answer Explanations #1
Day 2	Muscular Dynamics Involved During...	Day 12	Energy Systems Development	Day 22	Practice Test #2
Day 3	Basic Principles of Biomechanics	Day 13	Program Design	Day 23	Answer Explanations #2
Day 4	Bioenergetics and Metabolism	Day 14	Selecting Exercises	Day 24	Practice Test #3
Day 5	Physiological Adaptations...	Day 15	Principles of Exercise Order	Day 25	Answer Explanations #3
Day 6	Sport Psychology	Day 16	Determining and Assigning Training...	Day 26	Practice Test #4
Day 7	Mental Health Issues in Athletes	Day 17	Periodization Models	Day 27	Answer Explanations #4
Day 8	Nutrition	Day 18	Organization and Administration	Day 28	Practice Test #5
Day 9	Effects, Risks, and Alternatives...	Day 19	Testing, Ongoing Monitoring...	Day 29	Answer Explanations #5
Day 10	Exercise Technique	Day 20	Practice Test #1	Day 30	Take Your Exam!

Build your own prep plan by visiting:
testprepbooks.com/prep

Exercise Sciences

Muscle Anatomy and Physiology

Muscle Anatomy

Types of Muscle

Smooth Muscle has spindle-shaped fibers that are shorter and narrower than skeletal muscle fibers. Smooth muscle fibers only contain one nucleus and do not have striations. Sheets of these muscle fibers form the walls of blood vessels and the hollow organs of the urinary, digestive, respiratory, and reproductive tracts. The contraction and relaxation of smooth muscle is responsible for peristalsis, which moves substances through the digestive tract.

Cardiac Muscle is only located in the wall of the heart. The contraction of this muscle pumps blood through the heart and the body's blood vessels.

Skeletal Muscle is primarily used in the movement of bones at joints and for maintaining posture.

Muscle Fiber Types

Type I muscle fibers: Also known as slow-twitch muscle fibers (slow-oxidative fibers), metabolically, these fibers have a large capacity for aerobic energy supply and are relatively resistant to fatigue. Type I fibers have a limited ability to rapidly generate force because of their low anaerobic capacity and low myosin ATPase activity. Compared to type II fibers, type I muscle fibers have slower calcium-handling abilities, contract more slowly, have reduced glycolytic capacity, and they have numerous and relatively large mitochondria. Type I muscle fibers play an important role in endurance sports that rely on a sustained energy supply, such as long-distance running (e.g., 5000 meters, marathon), soccer, cross-country skiing, and distance cycling and swimming.

Type IIa muscle fibers: Also known as fast-twitch muscle fibers, these fibers are energy inefficient, easily fatigable, and have low aerobic power. Type IIa fibers have a moderate capacity for both anaerobic and aerobic energy production. These fibers can be classified as fast-oxidative/glycolytic fibers, and they can rapidly generate force due to high myosin ATPase activity and anaerobic power. Type IIa fibers are surrounded by a greater number of capillaries than type IIx fibers, allowing for greater aerobic metabolism.

Type IIx muscle fibers: Also a type of fast-twitch muscle fiber (sometimes called type IIb fibers), type IIx fibers have less capacity for aerobic energy production, making them more fatigable than type IIa fibers. Type IIx fibers, considered to be fast-glycolytic (FG) fibers, have the greatest capacity for anaerobic energy production and the fastest shortening velocity, so they can generate significant force.

Note that many sports (e.g., rowing, tennis, boxing, wrestling, soccer) require both type I and type II muscle fibers.

Muscle Groups by Region

There are over 500 skeletal muscles in the body, so muscles are often grouped together in various ways to simplify learning and to enhance application of muscular knowledge for practical purposes. For resistance training programs, muscles are often grouped by body region or movement. By considering muscles by groups, it is easier to develop a targeted resistance training program or implement split routine workouts. For example, thirteen muscle groups associated with individual body regions can be broken into two or three training groups that are rotated during a week of training.

Upper body: biceps (front of upper arms), rectus and transverse abdominus (stomach), deltoids (top of shoulders), latissimus dorsi and rhomboids (back and between shoulder blades), pectoralis major and minor (front of upper chest), obliques (side of torso), trapezius (upper/mid back), triceps (back of upper arms), etc.

Lower body: quadriceps (front of thighs), erector spinae (lower back), gastrocnemius and soleus (back of lower legs), gluteus major and minor (buttocks), hamstrings (back of thighs), adductors (inner thigh), etc.

Muscle Groups by Function

Muscles are also frequently grouped according to the movements they help produce or control. This is often called functional anatomy and is particularly important when assessing an athlete's movement dysfunction, imbalance, or injury pattern. The typical functional groups include muscles for 1) facial expression, 2) mastication, 3) head and vertebral column movement, 4) pectoral girdle movement, 5) arm movement, 6) forearm movement, 7) hand movement, 8) abdominal wall movement, 9) pelvic outlet movement, 10) thigh movement, 11) leg movement, and 12) foot movement.

Muscles Involved in Arm, Forearm, and Hand Movement

There are four primary actions associated with arm movement. Arm (humerus) or shoulder flexion is carried out by pectoralis major, the anterior fibers of the deltoid, and coracobrachialis. Teres major, latissimus dorsi, and the posterior fibers of the deltoid are the muscles that are responsible for arm or shoulder extension. The supraspinatus and deltoid muscles are responsible for arm abduction, and the subscapularis, infraspinatus, and teres minor muscles rotate the arm.

The biceps brachii, brachialis, and brachioradialis muscles are responsible for elbow flexion, which lifts the forearm. The triceps brachii and the anconeus control elbow and forearm extension. The supinator, pronator teres, and pronator quadratus muscles rotate the forearm.

Compared to the arm and forearm, a greater number of muscles are responsible for the flexion and extension of the wrist, hand, and fingers. Flexion of the wrist and hand results from the actions of the flexor carpi radialis, flexor carpi ulnaris, palmaris longus, flexor digitorum profundus, and flexor digitorum superficialis muscles. There are even smaller muscles that control thumb and digit flexion. Wrist and hand extension results from the movements of the extensor carpi radialis longus, extensor carpi radialis brevis, extensor carpi ulnaris, and extensor digitorum muscles. In general, large gross movements are usually produced by stronger but fewer muscles, while fine, coordinated movements involve many small muscles working in concert with one another to execute precise actions.

Muscles Involved in Leg and Foot Movement

Knee flexion results from the hamstring group of muscles (biceps femoris, semitendinosus, semimembranosus) and the sartorius muscle. Knee extension is carried out by the quadriceps femoris group of muscles (rectus femoris, vastus lateralis, vastus medialis, and vastus intermedius).

Dorsiflexion (lifting the foot up) of the ankle results from the movement of the tibialis anterior, fibularis tertius, extensor digitorum longus, and extensor hallucis longus muscles. The gastrocnemius, soleus, plantaris, and flexor digitorum longus are responsible for ankle plantarflexion. Inversion (medial movement) and eversion (lateral movement) of the foot are controlled by the tibialis posterior and fibularis longus muscles, respectively.

Orientation/Directional/Regional Anatomical Terms

The following anatomical terms are commonly used in the description of muscle origins, insertions, and actions:

Superior (cranial): Near or toward the upper part of the body, i.e., toward the head. The clavicle is superior to the iliac crest.

Inferior (caudal): Toward the lower part of a structure or the body and away from the head. The talus is inferior to the patella.

Anterior (ventral): At or near the front of the body. The sternum is anterior to the spine.

Posterior (dorsal): At or near the back of the body. The spine is posterior to the sternum.

Medial: Near or at the body's midline. The nose is medial to the ears.

Lateral: Away from the body's midline. The ears are lateral to the nose.

Bilateral: On either side of a central axis or midline. The body has many bilateral (paired) structures including the legs, eyes, lungs, etc.

Ipsilateral: On or affecting the same side of the body. Ipsilateral appendages (e.g., hands and feet) are located on the same side of the body.

Contralateral: On or affecting the opposite sides of the body. A stroke that occurs on the right side of the brain may affect the function of the left arm.

Intermediate: Located between two structures—one that is medial and one that is lateral or one that is superior and one that is inferior. The knee is intermediate to the ankle and hip.

Proximal: Location of the origin or point of attachment of the body part towards the trunk and away from the appendages. The thigh is proximal to the ankle.

Distal: Location of the origin or point of attachment being away from the body. The ankle is distal to the knee.

Superficial (external): Near the outside or surface of an object or body.

Deep (internal): Inside, away from the surface of an object or body.

Axial: Associated with the center of the body. When considering the skeleton, the body's head, neck, and trunk make up the axial skeleton.

Appendicular: Refers to the body's appendages, such as the legs and arms.

Abduct: A movement away from the body's midline. When doing jumping jacks, the first phase of the arm movement abducts away from the side of the body en route to its position above the head.

Adduct: A movement toward the body's midline. The second phase of the arm movement during jumping jacks (returning them back in line with the trunk) demonstrates adduction.

Specific Muscle Names

One of the easiest ways to remember specific muscle names is to group the muscles by body regions. The following table of muscles, grouped by region, provides the name and action of the muscle as well as the origin (the anchoring end of the skeletal muscle, typically on a bone) and insertion (the end of the skeletal muscle that attaches to the bone or tissue that moves during the contraction). Muscles that are of primary relevance (e.g., muscles critical for sport/activity movements and muscles that aid respiration) to the strength and conditioning professional are included in this list. Examples of resistance exercises that target specific muscles are also provided. Please bear in mind that this is not an exhaustive list, but rather covers the most relevant muscles for coaches.

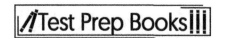

Muscle	Origin (immovable end of muscle)	Insertion (movable end of muscle)	Action	Resistance Exercise(s)
Erector spinae: iliocostalis (most lateral), longissimus (intermediate), spinalis (most medial)	Varies for each column	Varies for each column	Prime mover of back extension; each side consists of three columns (iliocostalis, longissimus, and spinalis muscles).	Seated rows Dumbbell rows Power jerk Stiff-leg dead lift Dead lifts Back extensions Lumbar extensions
Trapezius	Occipital bone, ligamentum nuchae, and spines of C7 and all thoracic vertebrae	A continuous insertion along acromion and spine of scapula and lateral third of clavicle	Stabilizes, raises, and rotates scapula; middle fibers retract (adduct) scapula; superior fibers elevate scapula (i.e., shrugging shoulders); inferior fibers depress scapula (and shoulder).	Back presses Bent-over lateral raises Arnold presses Lateral dumbbell raises Chin-ups Seated cable rows Dumbbell rows Dead lifts Power clean Power snatch Power jerk Lateral pull-downs Machine shoulder press Dumbbell prone posterior raise
Rhomboid major	Spinous processes of T2–T5	Medial (i.e., vertebral) border of scapula	Retracts, elevates, and rotates scapula	Dead lift Bent-over lateral raises Alternate front arm raises Dumbbell pull-overs Chin-ups Dumbbell one-arm row Seated cable rows Lateral pull-downs
Rhomboid minor	Spinous processes of C7–T1	Medial border of scapula	Retracts and elevates scapula	Dead lift Bent-over lateral raises Alternate front arm raises Dumbbell pull-overs Chin-ups Dumbbell one-arm row Lateral pull-downs Seated cable rows

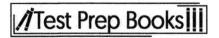

Muscle	Origin (immovable end of muscle)	Insertion (movable end of muscle)	Action	Resistance Exercise(s)
Levator scapulae	Transverse processes of C1–C4	Medial border of scapula	Elevates scapula; flexes neck to same side	Dead lifts
Serratus anterior	Series of muscle slips from ribs	Entire anterior (ventral) surface of vertebral border of scapula	Pulls scapula anteriorly and downward; abducts scapula	Back presses Arnold presses Alternate front arm raises Incline dumbbell press Dumbbell pull-overs Bench press, dumbbell Dumbbell fly Machine shoulder press
Pectoralis minor	Anterior surfaces of ribs three through five	Coracoid process of scapula	Abducts scapula, pulling it forward and downward; draws rib cage superiorly (raises ribs)	Incline dumbbell press Dumbbell pull-overs Bench press, dumbbell Bench press, barbell Incline press, dumbbell Dumbbell fly
Pectoralis major	Medial 1/2 of clavicle, sternum, and costal cartilages of ribs one through six	Greater tubercle of humerus	Prime mover of arm flexion; rotates arm medially, adducts humerus; pulls arm across chest	Triceps dips Arnold presses Alternate front arm raises Push-ups Barbell pull-overs Bench press, dumbbell Dumbbell fly
Teres major	Posterior surface of scapula at inferior angle	Intertubercular groove of humerus	Posteromedially extends, medially rotates, and adducts humerus; synergist of latissimus dorsi	Dumbbell pull-overs Barbell pull-overs Chin-ups Lateral pull-downs Dead lifts Dumbbell one-arm row Lateral pull-downs Seated cable rows
Latissimus dorsi	Spines of lower six thoracic vertebrae, lumbar vertebrae, lower three to four ribs, and iliac crest	Intertubercular groove of humerus	Prime mover of arm extension; arm adductor; medially rotates humerus at shoulder	Dumbbell pull-overs Barbell pull-overs Chin-ups Lateral pull-downs Seated rows Dead lifts Dumbbell one-arm row Seated cable rows

Muscle	Origin (immovable end of muscle)	Insertion (movable end of muscle)	Action	Resistance Exercise(s)
Deltoid	Spine of scapula, acromion, and lateral 1/3 of clavicle	Deltoid tuberosity of humerus	Prime mover of arm abduction (at shoulder); extends and flexes arm	Dead lift Triceps dips (anterior deltoid) Back presses Bent-over lateral raises Lateral dumbbell raises Alternate front arm raises Push-ups Seated cable rows Dumbbell rows Power clean Power snatch Power jerk Bench press, dumbbell Dumbbell fly Dumbbell one-arm row Lateral pull-downs Machine shoulder press Dumbbell prone posterior raise
Rotator cuff: supraspinatus, infraspinatus, teres minor, subscapularis	Varies for each muscle	Varies for each muscle	Medially or laterally rotates arm at shoulder; supraspinatus assists abduction; stabilizes shoulder joint, helping to prevent downward dislocation of humerus	Back presses Bent-over lateral raises Dumbbell rows Dumbbell prone posterior raise
Biceps brachii	Short head: coracoid process of scapula; long head: tubercle above glenoid cavity of scapula	Radial tuberosity of radius	Flexes elbow joint and supinates forearm and hand	Dumbbell curl Hammer curl Barbell curls Chin-ups Lateral pull-downs Dumbbell one-arm row Seated cable rows
Brachialis	Anterior, distal 1/2 of humerus	Coronoid process of ulna	Flexes elbow	Dumbbell curl Hammer curls Barbell curls Chin-ups Lateral pull-downs Dumbbell one-arm row Seated cable rows

Muscle	Origin (immovable end of muscle)	Insertion (movable end of muscle)	Action	Resistance Exercise(s)
Brachioradialis	Lateral supracondylar ridge at distal end of humerus	Base of styloid process of radius	Flexes forearm at elbow	Hammer curls Dumbbell curls Barbell curls Chin-ups Seated rows Dumbbell one-arm row Lateral pull-downs Seated cable rows
Triceps brachii	Long head: infraglenoid tubercle of scapula; lateral head: posterior humerus above radial groove; medial head: posterior humerus below radial groove	All three heads: olecranon process of ulna	Extends forearm at elbow	Push-downs Reverse push-downs Lying dumbbell triceps extensions Triceps kickbacks Seated dumbbell triceps extensions Triceps dips Back presses Arnold presses Push-ups Dumbbell pull-overs Power snatch Bench press, dumbbell Machine shoulder press
External oblique	Outer surfaces of lower eight ribs	Outer lip of iliac crest and linea alba	Tenses abdominal wall and compresses abdominal contents	Dead lifts Sit-ups Leg raises Dumbbell side bends Abdominal crunch
Internal oblique	Lumbar fascia, iliac crest, and inguinal ligament	Cartilages of lower ribs, linea alba, and crest of pubis	Tenses abdominal wall and compresses abdominal contents	Dumbbell side bends
Transverse abdominis	Inguinal ligament, lumbar fascia, cartilages of last six ribs, iliac crest	Linea alba and crest of pubis	Compresses abdominal components	Pelvic floor exercises Planks

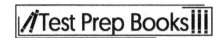

Muscle	Origin (immovable end of muscle)	Insertion (movable end of muscle)	Action	Resistance Exercise(s)
Rectus abdominis	Crest of pubis and symphysis pubis	Xiphoid process and costal cartilages of ribs five through seven	Flexes and rotates lumbar region of vertebral column; fixes and depresses ribs, stabilizes pelvis when walking; tenses abdominal wall, increases intra-abdominal pressure	Dead lifts Sit-ups Leg raises Dumbbell side bends Abdominal crunch
Psoas major (iliopsoas)	Lumbar intervertebral discs; bodies and transverse processes of lumbar vertebrae	Lesser trochanter of femur via iliopsoas tendon	Flexes thigh; also affects lateral flexion of vertebral column; important postural muscle	Leg raises Barbell lunge
Iliacus (iliopsoas)	Iliac fossa and crest, lateral sacrum	Femur on and immediately below lesser trochanter of femur via iliopsoas tendon	Prime mover for flexing thigh or for flexing trunk on thigh during a bow	Leg raises Barbell lunge
Gluteus maximus	Sacrum, coccyx, and posterior surface of ilium	Posterior surface of femur and fascia of thigh	Major extensor of thigh; generally inactive during standing and walking; laterally rotates and abducts thigh	Dead lifts Power clean Power snatch Power jerk Back squat Front squat Barbell lunge Stiff-leg dead lift Leg press Back extensions
Piriformis	Anterior surface of sacrum	Superior border of greater trochanter of femur	Abducts and rotates thigh laterally; stabilizes hip joint	Dead lifts

Muscle	Origin (immovable end of muscle)	Insertion (movable end of muscle)	Action	Resistance Exercise(s)
Hamstring group: biceps femoris, semitendinosus, semimembranosus	Ischial tuberosity (specifics vary on muscle)	Varies on muscle	Extends thigh and flexes knee; laterally or medially rotates leg, especially when knee is flexed	Dead lifts Standing leg curls Seated leg curls Power clean Power snatch Power jerk Back squat Front squat Barbell lunge Stiff-leg dead lift Leg press Leg curl Back extensions
Quadriceps group: vastus lateralis, medialis and intermedius, rectus femoris	Varies on specific muscle	Patellar ligament to tibial tuberosity	Extends and stabilizes knee	Dead lifts Leg extensions Power clean Power snatch Power jerk Back squat Front squat Barbell lunge Leg press
Gastrocnemius	Lateral and medial condyles of femur	Posterior surface of calcaneus	Plantar flexion of foot; flexes knee	Standing leg curls Seated leg curls Standing calf raises Power clean Power snatch Power jerk Barbell lunge Standing heel raise
Soleus	Head and shaft of fibula and posterior surface of tibia	Posterior surface of calcaneus	Plantar flexion of foot	Standing calf raises Power clean Power snatch Power jerk Barbell lunge

Muscle Belly Anatomy

Muscle fibers: Also called muscle cells or myocytes, muscle fibers are long, striated, cylindrical cells approximately the diameter of a human hair (50–100 micrometers). Many nuclei are dispersed throughout the cell, which is covered by a fibrous membrane called the sarcolemma. Up to 150 muscle fibers can be bundled together into parallel fasciculi, with each fasciculus covered by perimysium (i.e., connective tissue) and each muscle fiber covered by endomysium, another type of connective tissue.

Sarcolemma: The sarcolemma is a thin elastic membrane, surrounding each muscle fiber, that consists of a phospholipid bilayer (like eukaryotic cell membranes) and an outer membrane with collagen and other structural elements.

Sarcoplasm: Sarcoplasm is the special term for the cytoplasm of a muscle fiber. Sarcoplasm is filled with myofibrils and contains the components required for muscular contraction, including various proteins, protein filaments, mitochondria, the sarcoplasmic reticulum, stored glycogen, enzymes, and ions.

Sarcoplasmic reticulum: The sarcoplasmic reticulum is a network of tubular channels (i.e., transverse [T] tubule system) and vesicles, which together provide structural integrity to the muscle fiber. The sarcoplasmic reticulum also acts as a calcium ion (Ca^{2+}) pump, moving Ca^{2+} ions from the sarcoplasm into the muscle fiber. Influx of Ca^{2+} ions from the sarcoplasm into the muscle fiber results from an action potential in the sarcomere, causing the depolarization that initiates muscle movement.

Myofibril: Myofibrils consist of long, thin (approximately 1/1000 millimeter) chain proteins, such as actin, myosin, and titan. Bunches of myofibrils and nuclei together make a muscle fiber.

Myofilament: Myofilaments primarily consist of protein chains containing actin and myosin and are the smaller components of the myofibrils within striated muscle fibers. A sarcomere is composed of myofilaments.

Sarcomere: The smallest functional unit of a muscle fiber, a sarcomere contains the actin and myosin proteins responsible for the mechanical process of muscle contractions. Located between two Z-lines, actin and myosin filaments are configured in parallel, end to end, along the entire length of the myofibril. The varying arrangement of actin and myosin segments within the sarcomere causes the alternating light and dark pattern of skeletal muscle seen histologically. The sarcomere has four defined segments: A-band, H-zone, I-band, and Z-line. Each sarcomere is composed of a basic repeating unit between the Z-line located at each end of the sarcomere. The A-band contains both actin and myosin. The H-zone, a region located in the center of the sarcomere within the A-band, contains only myosin filaments. The I-band contains only actin filaments and consists of two connected sarcomeres on either side of the Z-line.

Transverse tubular system: The T-tubular system is perpendicular to the myofibril and two sarcoplasmic channels. The lateral end of each tubule channel terminates as a Ca^2 storing vesicle. Each Z-line region contains two vesicles and a T-tubule. T-tubules pass through the muscle cell, open externally from the inside of the cell, and touch the sarcolemma on the surface of the cell. The vesicles and T-tubules spread the action potential (i.e., wave of depolarization) from the surface of the cell's outer membrane to all inner regions of the cell. Depolarization releases Ca^{2+} from vesicles, initiating contractile motion.

Myosin: The interaction between myosin, the thick filament, and actin, the thin filament, causes the sarcomere to shorten as the muscle contracts. Myosin is often described as resembling a bunch of golf clubs, with the heads forming the attachment site along the actin myofilaments, which resemble a string of beads. Myosin is also responsible for splitting adenosine triphosphate (ATP). The phosphate released from ATP hydrolysis provides the energy required for myosin to produce the power stroke, causing the myosin head to grab onto the actin and pull the filaments closer together as muscle contraction occurs.

Actin: This is the protein that forms the thinner myofilament. The myofilament consists of two strands of actin in a double helix configuration. As mentioned, the sarcomere contracts when actin and myosin (the thick filament) bind together and complete a power stroke.

Troponin: Troponin, a protein located at regular intervals along the actin filament, binds with the Ca^{2+} released from the sarcoplasmic reticulum. This causes a conformational change in tropomyosin, exposing the binding site on the actin filaments for the myosin heads to form cross-bridges.

Tropomyosin: Tropomyosin is a protein in the I-band located along the actin filament in a groove formed by the double helix configuration of the two actin strands. The conformational change of troponin moves the tropomyosin deeper into the groove, allowing the actin and myosin cross-bridge to rapidly attach, pulling the actin toward the center of the sarcomere in a contractile action. When troponin is not affecting tropomyosin (i.e., no Ca^{2+} release), it inhibits actin and myosin bonding, which prevents a constant state of muscle contraction.

Acetylcholine (ACh): Vesicles located at the terminal end of motor neurons release the neurotransmitter ACh when an action potential arrives at the terminal end of a motor neuron. ACh diffuses across the synaptic space of the neuromuscular junction, and this excites the sarcolemma, initiating muscle contraction.

Types of Musculature Structures

Skeletal muscles vary in shape and function because of the various arrangements of the muscle fascicles. The table below provides the name of the fascicular arrangements, the structure of the fascicles, and an example of a muscle having each fascicular arrangement.

Name of Fascicular Arrangement	**Structure of Fascicular Arrangement**	**Muscle Example**
Circular	Fascicles are arranged in a concentric ring	Orbicularis oris (muscles surrounding mouth)
Convergent (sometimes called radiate)	Muscle has a broad origin and is fan- or triangular-shaped	Pectoralis major; gluteus medius
Parallel/longitudinal	Long axis of fascicles is parallel to long axis of muscle	Rectus abdominis
Unipennate	Short fascicles insert obliquely into only one side of tendon	Extensor digitorum longus; tibialis posterior
Bipennate	Fascicles insert into opposite sides of one central tendon	Rectus femoris
Multipennate	Tendon branches within the muscle	Deltoid
Fusiform	Spindle-shaped muscles	Biceps brachii

Here's an illustration of this:

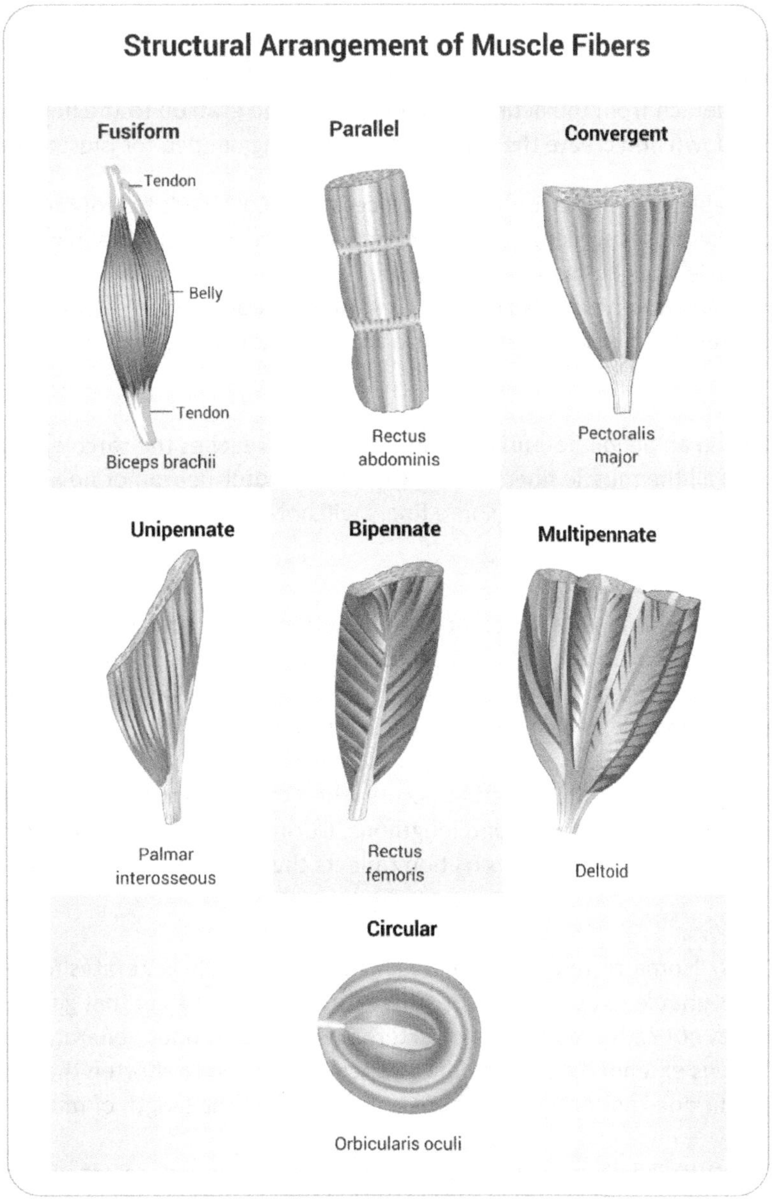

Muscular Dynamics Involved During Movement Patterns

Sliding Filament Theory

The sliding filament theory states that muscle shortening and lengthening is due to the movement of actin and myosin sliding past each other and reducing the distance between the Z-lines of the sarcomere because the overlap of the filaments increases. As the myosin cross-bridges attach and detach from actin filaments, the muscle fiber shortens due to the contractile action. Because minimal calcium is in the myofibril under resting conditions (during *resting phase*), very few myosin cross-bridges are bound with actin (i.e., actomyosin protein complex) because the binding sites are blocked. During the *excitation-contraction coupling phase*, the muscle releases an electrical discharge, and this starts a series of chemical events on the surface of the muscle cell, causing the release of calcium inside the muscle cell from the sarcoplasmic reticulum.

The Ca^{2+} binds with troponin, resulting in tropomyosin moving farther into the double helix groove, allowing rapid binding of actin and myosin filaments and the power stroke that pulls the actin toward the center of the sarcomere. During the contraction phase, the enzyme myosin adenosine triphosphatase (ATPase) breaks down ATP into adenosine diphosphate (ADP). The ADP on the myosin cross-bridge globular head is replaced with ATP so that the myosin head has energy to detach from the actin and then re-cock and grab on to the next binding spot on the actin filament, helping to "slide" down and create the sarcomere shortening needed for muscular contraction.

If ATP and Ca^{2+} are still available, the entire contraction process (i.e., Ca^{2+} binds to troponin, myosin cross-bridge binds with actin, power stroke causes sarcomere contraction, actin and myosin uncouple, myosin head position is reset) is repeated in the muscle fiber during the *recharge phase*. Relaxation occurs when Ca^{2+}, ATP, ADP, or ATPase is no longer available. The *relaxation phase* also occurs when motor neurons stop releasing ACh, the Ca^{2+} levels in the sarcoplasmic reticulum return to baseline, and myosin and actin uncouple.

All-or-None Principle

This principle states that when an action potential in a motor neuron reaches the sarcolemma, the action potential will either elicit activation of all the muscle fibers connected to the motor neuron or no activation of any of the muscle fibers will occur. Partial activation of just some fibers will not occur.

Types of Muscle Action

Concentric muscle action: This type of action occurs when the contraction force is greater than the resistive force (F_r), causing the muscle to shorten. The tension caused by the shortening of the muscle causes the joint to move. When an athlete is doing biceps curls, the elbow is initially extended. The concentric action of the biceps results in the shortening of the muscle, moving the elbow to a flexed position.

Eccentric muscle action: Eccentric muscle action occurs when the external resistance is greater than the muscle force (F_M). The muscle develops tension and lengthens. During a biceps curl, the lowering of the weight when moving the arm from a flexed to extended position reflects the lengthening of the muscle, resulting from eccentric action.

Isometric muscle action: Isometric muscle action results when a muscle generates force and attempts to contract concentrically but is unable to because the resistive force is greater than that generated by the muscle. In this situation, the action does not cause movement or external work, but it does generate force. If an athlete is holding a fixed bar with elbows extended and attempts a concentric action to shorten the biceps, the biceps produce force, but movement does not occur (i.e., there is no change in the length of muscle fibers).

Isokinetic muscle action: Isokinetic muscle actions result in a dynamic movement performed at a constant velocity. These actions do not occur naturally. For the muscle movement to occur at a constant velocity, a machine such as a dynamometer (a device that allows constant velocity movement regardless of the amount of torque) must be used.

Neuromuscular Anatomy and Physiology

Neuromuscular Anatomy

Motor Unit

This is the functional unit of the neuromotor system. It consists of the motor neuron and all of the muscle fibers it innervates. Motor unit function depends on the morphological and physiological characteristics of the muscle fibers innervated by the motor neuron.

Motor Neuron (Nerve Cell)

The motor neuron consists of an alpha motor neuron (cell body), axon, and dendrites. It transmits nerve impulses from the spinal cord to the muscle fiber. A myelin sheath surrounds the axon, with nodes interrupting the myelin every 1–2 millimeters. The alternation of myelin and nodes allows an electrical current (i.e., nerve impulse) to quickly move down the axon with impulses "jumping" from node to node. The terminal branches end at the neuromuscular junction.

Neuromuscular Junction (AKA Motor End Plate)

This is the functional connection (chemical synapse) between the end of the myelinated motor neuron and the muscle fiber. It transmits the nerve impulse from the motor neuron to the muscle fiber, initiating the stimulation of the nerve fiber by chemical transmission. The action potential reaches the terminal branches, and ACh is released across the synaptic space, stimulating the sarcolemma. When enough ACh is released, an action potential is generated and travels the length of the muscle fiber, causing it to contract.

Muscle Spindles

Muscle spindles are proprioceptors that sense the rate and magnitude of increases in muscle tension as the muscle lengthens with an eccentric muscle contraction. The spindles contain *intrafusal fibers* (modified muscle fibers) contained in a sheath of connective tissue that runs parallel to the normal *extrafusal muscle fibers*. As a muscle lengthens, the muscle spindles are stretched, activating a sensory neuron in the spindle that sends an impulse to the spinal cord. In the spinal cord, the signal coming from the sensory neuron synapses with motor neurons, which travel back to innervate the extrafusal muscle fibers. Motor neurons activate the muscle, causing a reflexive muscle action called the stretch reflex. This causes muscle contraction, the spindles shorten, and the sensory impulses stop. Increasing loads cause the spindles to stretch more. The muscle force (F_M) and power are potentiated by this reflexive contraction.

Golgi Tendon Organs (GTOs)

These mechanoreceptors lie parallel to extrafusal muscle fibers near the musculotendinous junction and act as feedback monitors by detecting tension changes in an active muscle. The increased tension caused by muscle shortening stimulates GTOs to relax the muscle via the inhibitory interneuron; this response is also called autogenic inhibition. Reciprocal inhibition occurs when a contracting muscle stimulates the GTOs, causing the opposing muscle to relax. The GTOs respond to muscle tension by sending impulses to the spinal cord to elicit reflex inhibition. Importantly, GTOs protect the muscle and tendon from injury caused by an excessive load by prohibiting excessive tension to build up in a muscle. Stimulation of GTOs is graded based on the amount of tension a muscle develops. At low forces, the effect of GTOs is minimal. With increasing loads, the GTOs mediate more significant reflexive inhibition.

Somatic Nervous System

The somatic nervous system innervates skeletal muscles and is responsible for conscious control of voluntary movements.

Autonomic nervous system (ANS): The ANS innervates smooth and cardiac muscles as well as glands. It is also responsible for visceral motor actions (e.g., pumping the heart, food movement through the digestive tract). The ANS, sometimes called the involuntary nervous system, is not under conscious control. It has two subdivisions: the sympathetic and parasympathetic nervous systems.

- Sympathetic nervous system (SNS): The SNS prepares the body for action and is sometimes called the fight-or-flight system. During exercise, the SNS is responsible for directing blood away from the digestive tract and skin and toward the skeletal muscles, heart, and brain. Physiological responses associated with the SNS

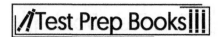

include increased blood pressure (BP), heart rate, and blood glucose levels; sweating; and dilation of the pupils and lung bronchioles.

- Parasympathetic nervous system (PNS): The PNS is considered the "resting and digestion system" because its primary function is conserving body energy by maintaining body activities at baseline levels. The PNS is responsible for digestive tract motility, smooth muscle activity associated with urination and defecation, pupil constriction, and gland secretion.

Neuromuscular Responses to Exercise

Motor Unit Recruitment Patterns

Motor units contain only one type of muscle fiber (i.e., type I, type IIa, type IIx). The ability to produce force is a requirement in all sport activities. There are two ways that motor units modulate force production: summation and size principle.

Summation

Summation is dependent upon how frequently motor units are activated. A single activation will cause a minimal muscle twitch with little force production, but if that motor unit continues to be activated at a greater frequency, there can be a summative effect of these twitches, resulting in greater force production.

Size Principle

The second method used to modulate force production is dependent upon how many motor units are activated. If greater force is needed for an activity, more motor units will be recruited. This phenomenon, called the *size principle*, describes the interrelationship between force, motor unit recruitment thresholds, and firing rates. The smallest motor units are recruited first, and as more force is needed, larger motor units (that innervate more muscle fibers) are activated. Ascending recruitment of smaller to larger motor units allows the continuum of low- to high-force production and smooth muscle movements when force changes, while conserving energy.

Selective Recruitment

This is an exception to the size principle. Under some circumstances, trained athletes can inhibit the activation of small motor units. This allows larger motor units to be activated immediately when rapid force production (e.g., vertical jump) is needed.

Nerve Conduction

When the electrical nerve impulse from the motor neuron arrives at the motor junction, ACh is released, converting the impulse into a chemical stimulus. This generates an action potential—a wave of depolarization—that travels the length of the muscle fiber through the T-tubules, causing the release of Ca^{2+}, which initiates the series of events leading to the contractile movement of the actin and myosin filaments.

Electromyography (EMG)

Surface and intramuscular EMG is used to assess the quality and quantity of the electrical activity within skeletal muscles resulting from neural activation by motor units. Greater neural activation is implicated when there is an increase in EMG signal.

Basic Principles of Biomechanics

Kinematic Principles of Movement

Anatomical Position

In the anatomical position, a person stands with their arms at their side and the palms of their hands facing forward. From this position, the body can be divided into three anatomical planes that cut the body into sections. These anatomical planes are important because they can be used to explain normal and athletic movements and the type of resistance exercises for training these movements.

Sagittal plane: This plane divides the body into right and left regions. Examples of body movements and related exercises that occur in the sagittal plane are provided below.

Body Movement	Example Sport/Activity That Utilizes the Movement	Related Exercise
Elbow extension	Shot put	Triceps push-down
Hip flexion	Football punter	Leg raises
Knee flexion	Diving (tuck dive)	Leg curl

Frontal plane: The frontal plane runs through the center of the body from side to side, dividing the body into front and back halves.

Body Movement	Example Sport/Activity That Utilizes the Movement	Related Exercise
Shoulder adduction	Swimming (breaststroke)	Wide-grip lateral pull-down
Ankle inversion	Resisted inversion	Soccer dribbling
Hip adduction	Standing adduction machine	Soccer side step

Transverse plane: The transverse plane is a horizontal plane that divides the body into upper and lower regions.

Body Movement	Example Sport/Activity That Utilizes the Movement	Related Exercise
Hip internal rotation	Basketball pivot movement	Resisted internal rotation
Lower back left rotation	Baseball batting	Medicine ball side toss
Lower back right rotation	Golf swing	Torso machine

Joint Angle

A joint angle is the angle, measured in degrees, between two body parts that are linked by a single joint. Body movements occur due to rotation around a single joint or multiple joints, with the force produced expressed as torque. Torque exerted varies by joint due to various characteristics of the joint (e.g., range of motion [ROM]; the relationship of muscle length versus force; leverage resulting from the use of joints as first-, second-, and third-class levers; and speed of contraction of muscles at the joint).

Velocity

Velocity is the rate of change of distance over time. Velocity and speed are often used interchangeably, but it is important for the strength and conditioning professional to separate the terms. Speed is the rate at which an object covers a distance, and velocity describes how fast and in what direction an object is moving. Velocity is calculated by dividing the distance traveled by the amount of time it took to cover that distance.

Kinetic Laws and Principles of Movement

Force

Force is best visualized as a push or pull exerted on one object by a second object. It is the interaction of two physical objects that have both size (magnitude) and direction. Force is measured in Newtons (N) and can be calculated using the formula: $F = m(a + g)$; where F is force, m is the mass of a dumbbell or other object, a is instantaneous acceleration, and g is acceleration resulting from gravity (9.81 meters/second/second). The number of cross-bridges formed between actin and myosin filaments determines the amount of force produced at any moment in time.

Force-Velocity Curve

The force-velocity curve graphically represents the relationship between velocity (meters/second), plotted on the x-axis, and force (N), plotted on the y-axis. The curve shows the inverse relationship between force and velocity, such that as force increases, velocity decreases, and vice versa. The strength and conditioning professional must understand this relationship when planning a training program. For example, if an athlete is strong but not fast, more time should be spent training at a lower force intensity (e.g., back squats at 30 percent of one-repetition maximum [1RM] instead of at 90 percent of 1RM) and a faster velocity in order to improve speed.

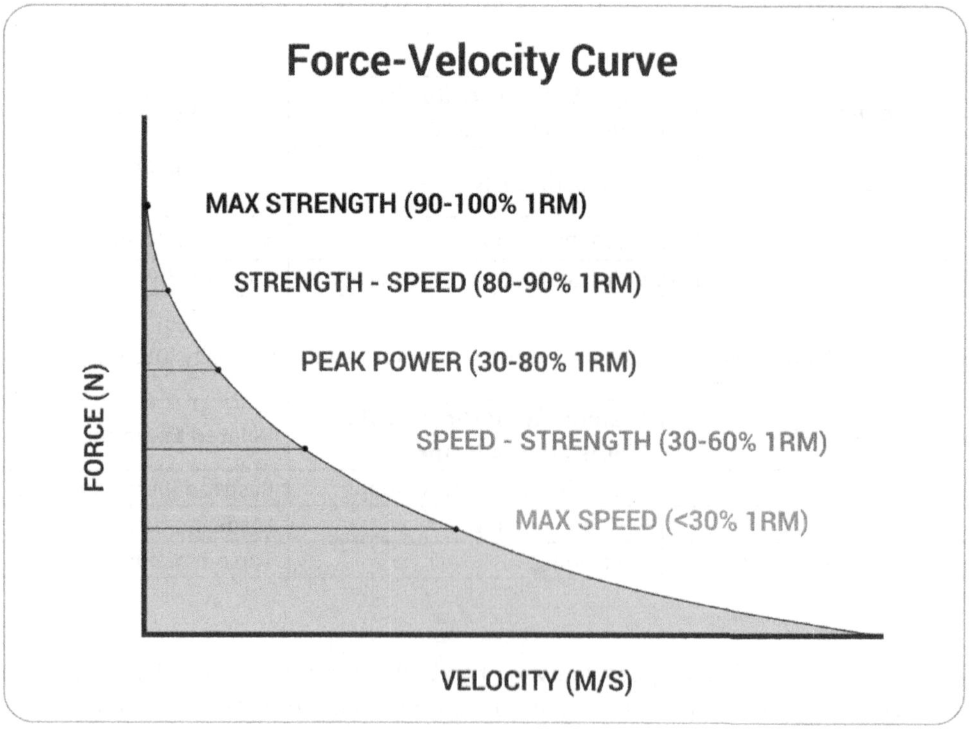

Force-Time Curve

The force-time curve graphically represents the relationship between time (milliseconds), plotted on the x-axis, and force, plotted on the y-axis.

Rate of force development (RFD): The RFD is the change in force divided by the change in time. It has significant relevance for sports where the timing of movements or explosiveness is critical. The generation of maximum force in minimum time is an index of explosive strength.

Momentum

Momentum is the amount of motion that an object has. It is calculated as the velocity multiplied by the object's mass, and like velocity, momentum is a vector quantity with a direction. Momentum is relevant to sports because it can be used for performance assessment. For example, an athlete having a mass of 125 kilograms and running at 10 meters/second will have more momentum than an athlete running at the same velocity who is 100 kilograms. Momentum can also play a role in injuries, particularly in collision sports (e.g., rugby, American football) because athletes having a large mass can hit or tackle another athlete with more momentum than athletes with less mass moving at the same speed.

Impulse

Impulse is the product of the time required to generate a force and the amount of the force. This quantity is represented as the area under the force-time curve. Impulse increases by improving the RFD, with the magnitude of change in the momentum of an object being contingent upon impulse.

Work

Work, measured in Joules [J], is calculated as the applied force on an object multiplied by the distance that the object is displaced (in the direction the force is applied). Quantifying work is useful for strength and conditioning programs because an athlete's training volume over the course of a training session, day, week, or the entire season can provide information about how well the athlete can handle varying amounts of training volume and intensity.

$$\text{Work} = \text{Force} \times \text{Displacement}$$

Power

Power is the rate that work is performed and it can be calculated as work divided by time. Power can also be calculated as the product of force applied to an object and velocity. Power is usually measured in watts (W), but it can also be measured in horsepower (hp). Power must be considered, in addition to work, when designing a strength and conditioning program. Training should consider the power associated with an athlete's sport or activity, and it should use various power outputs relevant to sport-specific movement velocities. Because power is the product of force and velocity, improving either of these components will improve the athlete's RFD and explosiveness.

$$\text{Power} = \frac{\text{Work}}{\text{Time}}$$

Center of Gravity (COG)

The balance point of an object when torque is equal on all sides is the COG. The COG is also the point where the planes of the body intersect. From a sports perspective, the lower an athlete's COG, the more stability he or she has. For example, hockey players skating with flexed knees low over the puck have increased stability, making it more difficult for opponents to get the player off of the puck.

Center of Pressure (COP)

COP refers to the point of application of ground reaction force, which is the force that is exerted by the supporting surface (e.g., ground) on the body. COP is relevant for postural control and gait and contributes to balance and stability. A tennis player may shift their COP medially and laterally as seen when the player moves from side to side before receiving a serve.

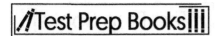

Musculoskeletal Lever Systems

Levers

Levers are rigid or semi-rigid bodies that pivot on a fixed point, or fulcrum, and when F_M is applied (i.e., effort), the lever moves a load (i.e., resistive force [F_r]). Joints act as the body's fulcrums when bones and muscle interact. Muscle contraction provides the force required to move an object against a resistive force. The load consists of the bone, the tissue over the bone, and whatever load is being moved. The three types of levers differ based on the relative position of three elements: F_M, F_r, and the fulcrum. Levers are relevant to sport activities because they allow a specific amount of effort to move a heavier load or to move a load farther or faster than would otherwise be possible. The majority of muscles in the body operate as third-class levers.

Joints

Joints are the junctions between bones that control movement. *Fibrous joints*, such as those in the skull, allow almost no movement, whereas *cartilaginous joints*, such as intervertebral joints, allow a limited amount of movement. *Synovial joints*, such as the elbow, allow the greatest amount of movement and ROM. Sport and exercise movements primarily occur around synovial joints (see the table below for specific synovial joints) because of the ROM and reduced friction that they afford.

Synovial Joint Type	Movements	Examples
Ball-and-socket	Rotation and movement in all planes	Hip, shoulder
Condylar	No rotation; variety of movements in different planes	Joints between phalanges and metacarpals
Plane	Twisting or sliding	Joints between various bones of the ankle and wrist
Hinge	Flexion and extension	Elbow
Pivot	Rotation	Joint between the proximal ends of the ulna and radius
Saddle	Variety of movements; primarily in two planes	Joint between carpal and metacarpal of thumb

Joints can also be classified based on the type of movement they allow, specifically, the number of directions that joint rotation can occur. A uniaxial joint, such as the elbow, rotates around only one axis and operates as a hinge. The wrist and ankle are examples of biaxial joints, which allow movement around two perpendicular axes. Multiaxial joints, such as the shoulder and hip joint, allow movement around three axes (any direction in space).

Fulcrum: The fixed pivot point of a lever.

Muscle force (FM): The force generated by the contraction of a muscle.

Resistive force (FR): An external source of resistance (e.g., gravity, friction, weights, inertia) that counters the action of the FM.

Torque: Also called moment, torque is the extent that a force tends to rotate an object around a specific fulcrum. Muscles pull on bones to create movement, maintain body position, and resist movement, and this force acts on the bones (levers) at the joints. Torque can be quantified as the magnitude of the force multiplied by the length of the moment arm and is measured in Newton meters (N·m).

Moment arm: Also called the lever arm, force arm, or torque arm, the moment arm is the perpendicular distance from the line of action (i.e., the long line that passes through the point where force is applied in the direction of the force exerted) of the force to the fulcrum.

Mechanical advantage: It is the trade-off of distance and force, because it is the ratio of the moment arm through which an applied force acts (i.e., F_M) through the F_r.

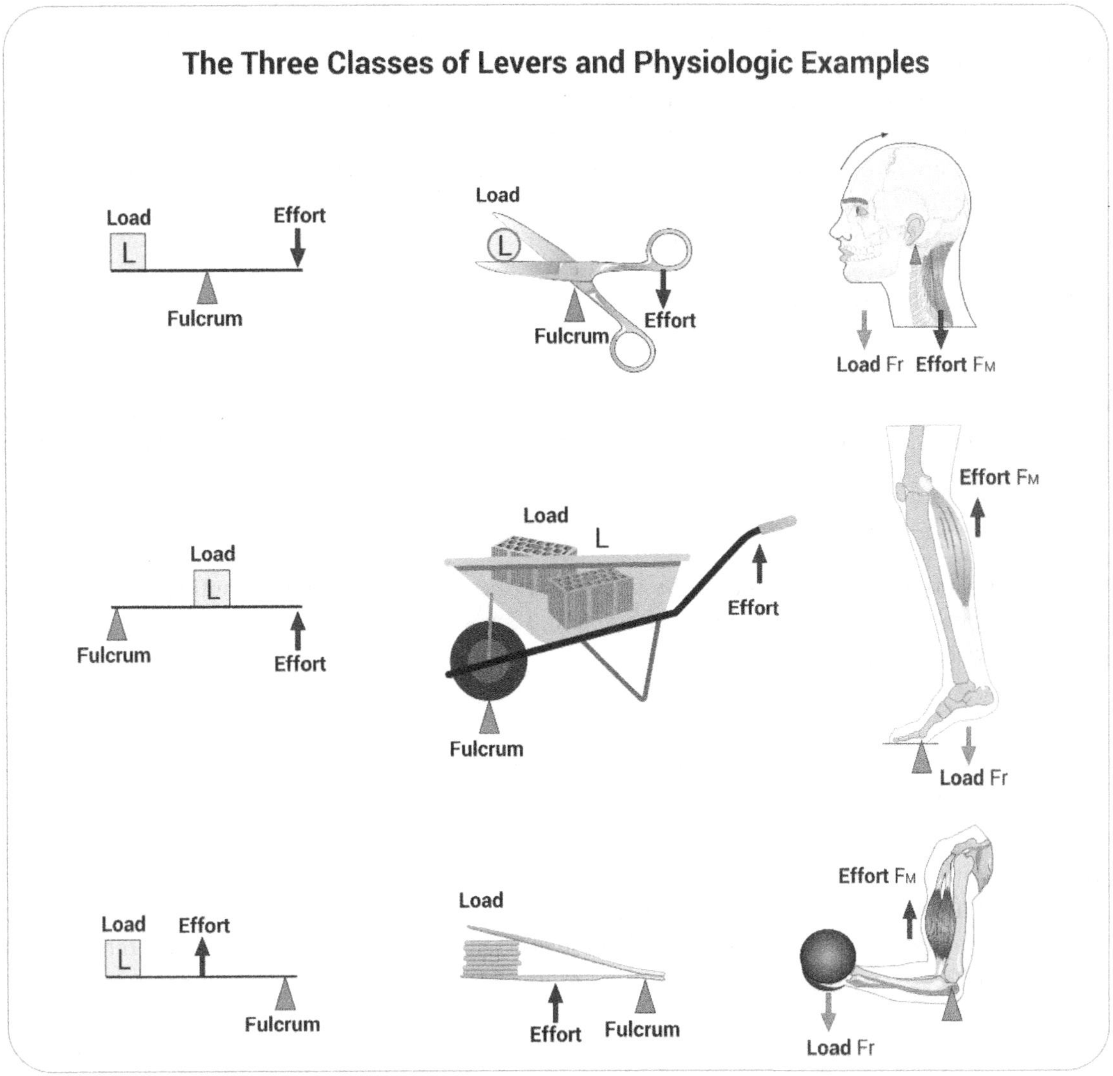

First-class lever: A first-class lever (e.g., a seesaw) has the F_M applied at one end of the lever; the F_r is at the other end, with the fulcrum located somewhere in the middle (i.e., $F_r \rightarrow$ fulcrum $\rightarrow F_M$). The forearm can serve as a first-class lever during triceps extension exercises. The fulcrum is the elbow joint; F_M comes from the contraction of the triceps, and the F_r is the weight machine.

Second-class lever: A second-class lever consists of a fulcrum at one end, the F_M is applied to the other end, and the F_r is between the ends (i.e., fulcrum $\rightarrow F_r \rightarrow F_M$). A wheelbarrow is a second-class lever. The wheel is the fulcrum, the F_r is the load in the wheelbarrow, and the F_M is applied to the handles. An example of a second-class lever in the body is standing on one's toes. The metatarsophalangeal joints act as the fulcrum, body weight is the load, and the calf muscle provides the effort as it pulls up on the heel.

Third-class lever: F_r is at one end of the lever, F_M is applied in the middle of the lever, and the fulcrum is at the other end (i.e., $F_r \rightarrow F_M \rightarrow$ fulcrum). A biceps curl is an example of a third-class lever; the F_r is the barbell, F_M is the contraction of the biceps, and the fulcrum is the elbow joint.

Isometric/Isotonic/Isokinetic Contractions

Isometric contractions occur when a muscle generates force and attempts to make a concentric contraction, but is unable to because the resistance force exceeds the force generated by the muscle. As a result, the muscle does not cause movement. Therefore, from a physics perspective, no "work" is done because work is force times distance ($W = F \times d$), and in this case, since no movement occurred, the distance is zero, so the work is zero. Isokinetic contractions are rare, but they involve muscle contractions that occur at a constant velocity. Isotonic contractions can be concentric or eccentric, in that the muscle can shorten or lengthen. However, the amount of tension generated stays the same during the contraction.

Role of Muscles in Movement

Agonist

An agonist is a muscle or group of muscles that is most directly responsible for generating the force to produce a movement; it is also called a prime mover. When lowering the body in the downward phase of a squat, the agonists are the gluteus maximus and the quadriceps group.

Antagonist

Antagonists generate a motion or force that is the opposite of the agonist's motion. Sometimes an antagonist is a muscle or a muscle group that performs a protective action, such as decelerating a force acting on the body or helping stabilize working joints.

Synergist

A synergist is a muscle that indirectly helps to generate force production during a movement or one that aids in stabilizing the agonist muscle as force is produced.

Neutralizer

Neutralizers prevent unwanted or extraneous movement by pulling against and canceling out the motion from the agonist. For example, when the elbow is flexed, supination is often undesirable, so the pronator teres counteracts the supination of the biceps so that only elbow flexion results.

Stabilizer

Also called a fixator, a muscle acting as a stabilizer muscle holds certain joints or body segments immobile, so that agonists can optimize movement and force production. For example, to do an abdominal exercise, the pelvis may be stabilized by the contraction of the muscles of the hip joint. It is often optimal to hold the insertion point or proximal joint stable, so that the working muscles have a more fixed end to pull from.

The muscles involved in the flexion of the forearm at the elbow joint and their roles in the movement are provided in the table below.

Muscle	Movement Role
Biceps brachii	Agonist (prime mover)
Triceps brachii	Antagonist
Deltoid	Stabilizer (fixator)
Brachioradialis	Neutralizer

Bone and Connective Tissue

Bone and Connective Tissue Anatomy

Bones

The human skeleton has approximately 206 bones and these bones provide protection and support for the body. Bones can be divided into the *axial* (skull, vertebral column, sternum, and ribs) and *appendicular* (the right and left clavicle and scapula and the left and right bones of the arm, forearm, and hand; the left and right coaxial and the left and right bones of the leg and foot) *skeletons.* Bones consist of varying amounts of spongy (*trabecular*) and compact (*cortical*) bone. A shell of dense cortical bone surrounds interlocking columns of trabecular bone called osteons. Bone marrow – composed of adipose tissue, vasculature, and the manufacturing site of blood vessels – occupies the space between the trabeculae and blood vessels and extends from the marrow cavity to cortical bone. *Bone periosteum*, connective tissue that covers all bones, is attached to tendons.

Collagen

Collagen is the primary structural component of all connective tissue. Bones, ligaments, and tendons are Type I collagen, and cartilage is composed of Type 2 collagen. Both types of collagen are formed from procollagen molecules, which consist of three protein strands in a triple helix formation. An enzyme produces active collagen, which aligns with other collagen molecules to form long filaments that are the components of microfibrils that form bundles as bone grows. The strength and durability of collagen stems from strong cross-linking bonds that are formed between adjacent collagen bundles. The longitudinal grouping of these bundles together forms ligaments and tendons. The bundles can also be arranged in layered sheets of varying directions, as found in fascia, bone, and cartilage.

Tendons and Ligaments

Tendons are fibrous connective tissue connecting muscle to the periosteum of bone. Muscle contractions pull the tendon, causing the attached bone to move. Ligaments are fibrous connective tissue connecting bone to bone. Ligaments contain elastin, a type of elastic protein that provides the stretch needed for normal joint movement. Tendons and ligaments contain relatively few cells that require little oxygen and nutrients for metabolic activity. Because of the limited vasculature and circulation in tendons, regeneration after injury takes a significant amount of time and is sometimes not possible without surgical intervention.

Bone and Connective Tissue Responses to Exercise and Training

Bone

Anaerobic Training

Minimal essential strain (MES) is the stimulus threshold required to initiate new bone growth. Anaerobic training can stimulate bone growth and should utilize specificity of loading and progressive overload to do so. Specificity of loading requires the use of specific movement patterns and exercises that directly load the targeted growth region of the athlete's skeleton. Exercises should involve multiple joints and apply increasingly heavier external loads. The anaerobic exercise components of mechanical load that stimulate bone growth are the intensity of the load, the speed of loading, the direction of the force, and the volume of the loading. Bone deposition follows Wolff's Law, which states that bone remodels according to the forces placed upon it; if forces are sufficient in intensity and frequency, bones become stronger, building additional matrix and mineralization. The inverse is also true that if there is not enough strain and physical resistance to bones, they atrophy and thin with disuse.

Aerobic Training

Aerobic programs that stimulate bone growth must be high-intensity weight-bearing activities (e.g., running, aerobics). The intensity of activity has to increase progressively to ensure continual overload of the bone. Because bone responds to the intensity and rate of external loading, when it is no longer possible to increase activity intensity, increasing the rate of the limb movement is required. This can be achieved with high-intensity interval training (HIIT).

Connective Tissue

Anaerobic Training

High-intensity anaerobic training causes connective tissue growth and structural changes. Increased enzyme activity due to anaerobic training results in the formation of collagen that aligns with other collagen molecules to form long filaments. Specific changes within a tendon include an increase in collagen fibril diameter, number, and packing density. These adaptations increase the tensional forces that the tendon can withstand. Anaerobic training increases tendon stiffness, which is directly associated with muscular recoil and power production—an important component of performance in some sports.

Aerobic Training

Aerobic exercise intensity that exceeds the strain put on connective tissue during normal activities is required for connective tissue changes to occur.

Bioenergetics and Metabolism

Characteristics of the Energy Systems

Bioenergetics

Bioenergetics refers to the flow of energy within a biological system and is primarily focused on how macronutrients, containing chemical energy, from food (i.e., carbohydrates, proteins, fats) are converted into biologically usable forms of energy to perform work.

Catabolism

Catabolism is the process of breaking large molecules into smaller molecules to make energy available to the organism. For example, carbohydrates are catabolized to provide fuel for exercise and normal physiological processes. Catabolism can also involve the breakdown of muscle tissue during periods of heavy training volume, low caloric intake, or high stress.

Anabolism

Anabolism is the process of restructuring or building larger compounds from catabolized materials, such as assembling amino acids into structural proteins, which are needed to maintain homeostasis and to generate new muscle tissue.

Exergonic Reaction

Exergonic reactions are chemical reactions that result in the release of energy from the system. The energy can then be used to perform work. These reactions are spontaneous and favorable.

Endergonic Reaction

An endergonic reaction is a type of chemical reaction that requires the input of energy. In the body, this energy comes in the form of adenosine triphosphate (ATP). These reactions are not spontaneous and are typically involved with anabolic processes.

Metabolism

Metabolism is the total of all catabolic and anabolic reactions occurring in the human body. Essential physiological processes such as muscle growth and hormone balance rely on these reactions and continually occur so that the body can maintain homeostasis. It is possible to evaluate an athlete's energy expenditure (metabolic rate) and fitness level using direct or indirect calorimetry.

Adenosine Triphosphate (ATP)

ATP is a high-energy molecule used for muscle contractions, movement, and other life-sustaining metabolic processes. ATP is an intermediate molecule (consisting of three primary parts—an adenine, a ribose, and three phosphates in a chain) that allows energy to transfer from exergonic to endergonic and catabolic to anabolic reactions. ATP is generated and replenished in skeletal muscles by three energy systems: phosphagen, glycolytic, and oxidative.

ATP Hydrolysis

Hydrolysis is a general term for any chemical reaction that breaks a chemical bond via the addition of water. ATP hydrolysis splits the ATP molecule into adenosine diphosphate (ADP) and usable energy. The enzyme adenosine triphosphatase (ATPase) is the catalyst for the hydrolysis of ATP. The following equation shows the reactants (left of arrow), enzyme (middle), and products (right of arrow) for ATP hydrolysis:

$$\text{ATP} + \text{H}_2\text{O} \leftarrow \text{ATPASE} \rightarrow \text{ADP} + \text{P}_\text{i} + \text{H}^+ + \text{Energy}$$

Adenosine Diphosphate (ADP)

When ATP undergoes hydrolysis, ADP (containing two phosphate groups), an inorganic phosphate molecule, a hydrogen ion, and free energy are produced.

ATPase

ATPase is the enzyme responsible for catalyzing the breakdown of ATP to ADP. The dephosphorylation reaction results in the release of energy used to carry out other chemical reactions.

Myosin ATPase

Myosin ATPase catalyzes ATP hydrolysis, providing the energy for cross-bridge recycling.

Calcium ATPase

Calcium ATPase is the enzyme that provides the energy used to regulate calcium movement by pumping it into the sarcoplasmic reticulum.

Sodium-Potassium ATPase

This enzyme controls the sodium potassium concentration gradient in the sarcolemma after depolarization to maintain the cellular resting potential. For every two K^+ ions pumped into the cell, there are three NA^+ ions pumped out.

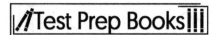

Adenosine Monophosphate (AMP)

AMP results from ADP hydrolysis, which cleaves the second phosphate group, leaving one.

Biological Energy Systems

There are several basic biological energy systems in muscle cells that replace ATP. The phosphagen and glycolytic systems occur in the sarcoplasm and are anaerobic mechanisms, which means that they do not require oxygen. The electron transport chain (ETC) and Krebs cycle are aerobic mechanisms that require oxygen and occur in the mitochondria. The cellular respiration systems act in concert, rather than individually, to provide all required energy during exercise or rest.

Phosphagen System (ATP-phosphocreatine [PC])

The phosphagen system utilizes ATP hydrolysis for high-intensity activities of short length (e.g., resistance training; short, intense sprints; other vigorous bouts up to about 10 seconds in duration) and is active at the start of all types of exercise of varying intensities until the other systems have had time to start producing energy. This system relies on the breakdown of creatine phosphate (CP) for energy. Because ATP stores are quickly depleted and ATP is required for cellular functions other than muscle contractions, the phosphagen system uses CP stores to maintain ATP concentrations. This system is rapidly depleted after about 10 seconds of maximal intensity work, so the glycolytic system starts to engage and contribute energy after this point. It takes longer for glycolysis, and especially oxidative energy systems, to generate energy, which is why the phosphagen system is the initial source.

Creatine Phosphate (CP), also called phosphocreatine (PC), concentrations in muscles are four to six times greater than ATP muscle stores, with higher CP concentrations in Type II muscle fibers. The phosphagen system uses creatine kinase in the chemical reaction that combines a phosphate group from CP with ADP to replenish ATP. CP is stored in small amounts, limiting the phosphagen system to supplying energy for intense, short bouts of exercise.

$$\text{ADP} + \text{CP} \leftarrow \text{Creatine kinase} \rightarrow \text{ATP} + \text{Creatine}$$

Creatine kinase is the enzyme required to catalyze the reaction that combines ADP and CP to form ATP and creatine. Elevated levels of creatine kinase in blood serum tests are an indicator of muscle damage (e.g., kidney failure, heart attack). In athletes, too much work performed in a training session (single or aggregate sessions) can cause rhabdomyolysis, the rapid breakdown of muscles, elevating levels of creatine kinase in blood serum.

Also called myokinase, adenylate kinase is the enzyme that catalyzes the reaction that replenishes ATP.

$$2\text{ADP} \leftarrow \text{adenylate kinase} \rightarrow \text{ATP} + \text{AMP}$$

Glycolytic System

Glycolysis is the breakdown of glucose to replenish ATP. Glucose either comes directly out of blood circulation, is broken down from glycogen stores in the muscles or liver, or is converted from other substrates. ATP replenished during glycolysis is slower than the replenishment provided by the single-step phosphagen system because glycolysis has ten steps and actually requires an investment of energy to drive some of the early steps in the energy pathway. The glycolytic system has an advantage, as it can produce significantly more ATP because of the relatively large supply of glucose and glycogen in the body versus the limited supply of CP.

In anaerobic glycolysis, also called fast glycolysis, ATP is produced by breaking down glucose without oxygen available during glycolysis. This process relies on converting pyruvate to lactate to replace ATP during short, high-intensity activity lasting 2 minutes or less. In the absence of oxygen, pyruvate does not get shuttled to the mitochondria for the Krebs Cycle. Instead, the lactate accumulates and must be broken down in the muscle or shuttled to the liver where it undergoes the Cori cycle.

Pyruvate is the result of anaerobic glycolysis; one glucose molecule produces two pyruvate molecules. Pyruvate can either be converted to lactate in the sarcoplasm or transported to the mitochondria for the Krebs cycle. Compared to pyruvate conversion to lactate, the Krebs cycle takes longer to replenish ATP because there are more steps required in the reaction series. However, the Krebs cycle can continue for a longer duration when exercise intensity is low. This process is aerobic glycolysis (also called slow glycolysis).

Pyruvate conversion to lactate: The enzyme *lactate dehydrogenase* catalyzes the reaction converting pyruvate to lactate. Lactate produced by anaerobic glycolysis can be cleared by oxidation within the muscle fiber, or it can be moved to the liver via the blood and converted into glucose. The process of the liver turning lactate to glucose is referred to as the *Cori cycle*.

The net reaction of glycolysis when pyruvate is converted to lactate:

$$\text{Glucose} + 2\text{P}_\text{i} + 2\text{ADP} \rightarrow 2\text{Lactate} + 2\text{ATP} + \text{H}_2\text{O}$$

Pyruvate transported to mitochondria for Krebs cycle: If oxygen is available, pyruvate and two molecules of nicotinamide adenine dinucleotide (NADH) will be transported to the mitochondria. Pyruvate is converted to acetyl-coenzyme A (acetyl-CoA) by pyruvate dehydrogenase, resulting in the loss of carbon (CO_2), and enters the Krebs cycle to resynthesize ATP. The Krebs cycle, a continuation of the substrate oxidation from glycolysis, is a series of reactions that results in the production of two ATP molecules.

The net reaction for glycolysis when pyruvate is transported to the mitochondria:

$$\text{Glucose} + 2\text{P}_\text{i} + 2\text{ADP} + 2\text{NAD}^+ \rightarrow 2\text{Pyruvate} + 2\text{ATP} + 2\text{NADH} + 2\text{H}_2\text{O}$$

Phosphorylation is the addition of an inorganic phosphate to a molecule. Phosphorylation of ADP to ATP occurs by adding a phosphoryl (PO_3) group to ADP. Substrate-level phosphorylation is a single enzyme-generated reaction that uses ADP to directly resynthesize ATP. It occurs during anaerobic glycolysis (fast phosphorylation) and can occur during both anaerobic and aerobic activities.

Oxidative System

During low-intensity activity and while the body is at rest, ATP is primarily supplied by the oxidative system, which utilizes carbohydrates and fats as substrates.

In addition to two pyruvate molecules produced by glycolysis, six molecules of NADH and two molecules of flavin adenine dinucleotide ($FADH_2$) are produced and used by the electron transport chain (ETC). Hydrogen atoms, transported by NADH and $FADH_2$ to the ETC, are used to produce ATP from ADP. The hydrogen atoms form a proton concentration gradient down the ETC that produces energy required to synthesize ATP. NADH and $FADH_2$ molecules rephosphorylate ADP to ATP via the ETC with each NADH molecule producing three ATP molecules and each $FADH_2$ producing two ATP molecules.

Oxidative phosphorylation is the process of ATP being resynthesized via the actions of the ETC. The oxidative system produces approximately thirty-eight ATP molecules when a molecule of glucose is processed all the way through glycolysis, the Krebs cycle, and the ETC. The oxidative system produces approximately 90 percent of the ATP yield while substrate-level phosphorylation accounts for approximately the remaining 10 percent.

Fats, compared to carbohydrates and proteins, have the greatest capacity for ATP production through their metabolism. The gross energy production of a molecule of glucose is 40 ATP and this number climbs to 463 ATP molecules for one 18-carbon triglyceride molecule. Protein is not a primary substrate and is only used for energy during long-duration exercise (more than 90 minutes) or times of starvation. During rest, approximately 70 percent of the ATP is produced from fat metabolism, and approximately 30 percent comes from the breakdown of carbohydrates. With the initiation of high-intensity activity, nearly 100 percent of ATP comes from carbohydrates metabolism. During long bouts of submaximal exercise, carbohydrates are used initially (due to their faster metabolism), but there is a slow shift back to using fats as glycogen stores deplete.

Net ATP Production

The net ATP production from the oxidation of one glucose molecule can be determined by adding the number of ATP molecules produced during each process. During glycolysis, substrate-level phosphorylation and oxidative phosphorylation produce four and six ATP molecules, respectively. During the Krebs cycle, substrate-level phosphorylation produces two ATP molecules, oxidative phosphorylation of eight NADH molecules produces twenty-four ATP molecules, and the two $FADH_2$ molecules produce four ATP. These processes combined yield a total of forty ATP molecules. Two ATP molecules are used by glycolysis, so the net ATP production is thirty-eight ATP molecules.

Law of Mass Action/Mass Action Effect

This law states that the concentration of reactants, products, or both in solution will influence the direction of the reactions. These are often referred to as near-equilibrium reactions because they continue in the given direction based on the concentration of available reactants. This equilibrium is specific to the amount of ATP needed for the specific work being completed by the athlete. The reactions will continue until the exercise intensity is low enough for another energy system to take over or the exercise ends.

Effects of Manipulating Training Variables to Target Specific Energy Systems

Interval training can be used to target any of the energy systems. To stress the *phosphagen system*, the maximum power should be 90–100 percent, with an exercise duration of 5–10 seconds and a work-to-rest ratio between 1:12 and 1:20. To emphasize the glycolytic pathway, 75–90 percent of maximum power is needed for 15–30 seconds with a work-to-rest ratio of 1:3 to 1:5. The combined targeting of the glycolytic and oxidative systems requires an exercise duration of 1–3 minutes at 30–75 percent of maximum power with a work-to-rest ratio of 1:3 to 1:4. To specifically target the oxidative system, a low percentage of maximal power (20–30 percent) is needed, but the duration of exercise needs to be greater than 3 minutes with a short work-to-rest ratio of 1:1 to 1:3.

Effect of Mode, Intensity, Duration, and Volume on Energy Systems

Strength and conditioning professionals must understand the activities required by an athlete to ensure the development of a training regimen that uses the appropriate mode, intensity, duration, and volume, while ultimately impacting energy system adaptations for specific sport activities. The use of relevant training intensities and rest intervals allows for the focus on a specific metabolic energy system during sessions to ultimately optimize performance.

The mode of exercise refers to the type of exercise being conducted. For example, running, jump roping, power lifting, calisthenics, and rowing are all different modes of exercise. The intensity of exercise refers to how rigorous the exercise is, or how much relative effort is being exerted to complete the exercise. Common ways that intensity is measured or reported are as a percentage of maximal heart rate, as a percentage of maximal oxygen uptake (VO_2 max), in METs, or as rate of perceived exertion (RPE), such as on the Borg scale.

Duration is simply the length of time the exercise is conducted. This may be measured in hours, minutes, or seconds, depending on the exercise. For example, if someone does a steady-state run at threshold pace for 45 minutes, the duration is 45 minutes. If someone completes single leg Romain deadlifts with a 15-kg kettlebell for 30 seconds per side, the duration is 30 seconds per side of the body. The volume refers to the amount of work done. This is usually quantified in sets and reps, such as 3 x 15 reps of shoulder press, but it can also be reported in the total weight lifted in a session.

High-intensity interval training (HIIT) uses brief bouts of high-intensity exercise followed by a recovery. HIIT typically uses running, cycling, resistance training, or calisthenics, and an HIIT program should be developed based on the specific goals of an individual athlete. Combining aerobic and anaerobic exercise is thought to enhance recovery.

Neuroendocrine Physiology

The organs and glands of the *endocrine system* release hormones that regulate physiological processes and maintain homeostasis when the body is confronted with external stimuli or environmental stressors such as altitude or exercise. The endocrine system releases hormones that regulate blood glucose levels, metabolism, tissue growth, recovery, reproduction, and mood. *Neuroendocrine physiology* refers to the interaction between the nervous and endocrine systems whereby hormones are released from glands receiving direct neural stimulation.

Functions of Hormones

Hormones are chemical messengers or signaling molecules produced by endocrine glands and other specific cells. They are created, stored, and released into the blood to stimulate specific physiological responses. Hormones are classified into three categories. Fat-soluble *steroid hormones* (e.g., cortisol, testosterone) passively diffuse across cell membranes. They are responsible for primary and secondary sex characteristics and are involved in metabolic control, immunity, fluid balance, and inflammation. *Polypeptide hormones* (e.g., insulin, growth hormones) are made of chains of amino acids inside the nucleus of cells. Because they are not fat-soluble, they serve as secondary messengers, signaling other hormones and hormonal cascades. *Amine hormones* consist of the amino acids tyrosine (e.g., dopamine, norepinephrine, epinephrine) and tryptophan (e.g., serotonin). Amine hormones bind to membrane receptors and work via secondary messengers. Hormones can be categorized as *anabolic* and *catabolic*. Anabolic hormones promote tissue building, and catabolic ones break down cellular components.

How Hormones Work

The *lock and key principle* refers to a binding mechanism of hormones and enzymes where the hormone receptor site has a specific structure that allows a single hormone to bind to the site, similar to a key fitting one specific lock. This principle is a simplistic view of hormone binding that does not take into account cross-reactivity, allosteric binding sites, or the need for the aggregation of several linked hormones to produce the optimal signal. *Cross-reactivity* occurs when a hormone fits the receptor but needs to interact with other hormones to produce a response. Some receptors have *allosteric binding sites* where substances other than the specific hormone can increase or decrease the response to the primary hormone via feedback loops.

Anabolic Hormones

Testosterone, growth hormone, and insulin-like growth factors are the primary anabolic hormones involved in muscle remodeling and growth.

Testosterone: Testosterone is the primary androgen (male sex hormone) in human physiology. Both males and females are affected by testosterone, although males have significantly higher levels of testosterone. Testosterone increases protein synthesis and the rate of cellular metabolism and red blood cell production. Testosterone is produced by the testes in males and the ovaries and adrenal glands in females.

Growth Hormone: The anterior pituitary gland secretes growth hormone, which has a significant influence on metabolism and energy availability. It is responsible for increasing the uptake of amino acids into skeletal muscle, and for increasing protein synthesis, facilitating the growth of Type I and Type II muscle fibers. Growth hormone has numerous other roles including decreasing glucose utilization and glycogen synthesis, increasing the availability of glucose and amino acids, increasing collagen synthesis and cartilage growth, and enhancing immune cell function.

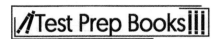

Insulin-Like Growth Factors (IGFs): The majority of the growth-promoting effects of growth hormone are indirectly controlled by IGFs. These growth-promoting proteins are produced by skeletal muscle, bone, the liver, and other tissues. IGFs stimulate the uptake of amino acids from the blood to be used for cellular proteins and the uptake of sulfur needed for the cartilage matrix.

Adrenal Hormones

Hormones produced by the adrenal gland play a critical role in the fight-or-flight response and are also responsive to exercise stress. Cortisol and catecholamines are the adrenal hormones that are most important in exercise training.

Cortisol: Cortisol, a glucocorticoid secreted by the adrenal cortex, is a catabolic hormone in skeletal muscle; however, its principal role is to ensure that energy is available. It is a primary signaling hormone for carbohydrate metabolism and is associated with the storage of glycogen in muscle tissue. Cortisol increases the production of glucose in the liver and glycogen production in skeletal muscles. Overtraining can cause chronically high levels of cortisol, which can result in loss of strength and lean muscle mass.

Catecholamines: Epinephrine, norepinephrine, and dopamine are secreted by the adrenal medulla and have a significant role in many physiological functions. In muscle, epinephrine and norepinephrine increase muscle blood flow due to vasodilation, elevate blood pressure (BP), increase the rate of muscle contraction, increase energy availability, enhance metabolic enzyme activity, and increase testosterone secretion rates.

Neuroendocrine Responses to Exercise and Training

Anaerobic Responses

During anaerobic training, hormones have a variety of regulatory roles that impact homeostatic mechanisms tasked with keeping functions of the body within normal ranges during exercise and rest. There are four primary endocrine responses to anaerobic training:

1. Acute anabolic hormone responses to anaerobic exercise are crucial for both exercise performance and the resultant training adaptations. For up to 30 minutes after anaerobic resistance training, testosterone, growth hormone, and cortisol concentrations are elevated. Such changes generally occur rapidly and are quickly stabilized as the body responds to the homeostatic challenges associated with acute and long-term exercise training. Hormone levels are elevated most with resistance exercises that utilize large muscle groups or with moderate- to high-volume and -intensity exercises that are combined with short rest intervals. The demands of acute anaerobic exercise cause increases in the concentration of catecholamines. Increased catecholamine concentrations are associated with the regulation of force production, energy availability, the rate of muscle contraction, and increased concentrations of testosterone and other hormones.

2. There are chronic changes in acute hormonal responses. When an athlete participates in a long-term resistance training program, changes in endocrine function correspond to the increased exercise stress that the body is capable of handling. It is thought that any chronic adaptations in hormonal response patterns to acute anaerobic exercise may enhance the athlete's ability to handle and maintain higher-resistance exercise intensities for longer time periods.

3. Chronic changes in resting hormone concentrations after anaerobic exercise have not consistently been found with growth hormone, testosterone, or insulin-like growth factor. Resting-state hormone concentrations likely reflect factors such as muscle tissue response to intensity or volume changes in the resistance training program. The elevated concentrations of hormones after resistance training are great enough to influence muscle tissue remodeling, so increased resting concentrations of hormones are not necessary to facilitate training adaptations.

Chronically high levels of anabolic steroids can be detrimental, causing downregulation (i.e., decreased number of receptors on target cell surface) of hormone receptors. Athletes using such performance enhancers try to combat this by cycling the drugs.

4. Hormone receptor changes have been shown to occur in response to resistance training. For example, androgen receptors seem to be upregulated within 48–72 hours after training. Changes in receptors mediate adaptations stimulated by hormonal responses.

Athletes can use resistance training to manipulate the endocrine system response and enhance training adaptations. For example, increasing the number of muscle fibers recruited for a resistance exercise increases the potential remodeling of the entire muscle.

Additionally, acute increases in serum testosterone concentrations can be achieved by using the following methods individually or in combination:

- Perform exercises such as squats, dead lift, and power clean, which target large muscles.
- Use heavy resistance loads that are 85–95 percent of one-repetition maximum (1RM).
- Perform multiple exercises or multiple sets to achieve moderate- to high-volume.
- Utilize short rest intervals of 30–60 seconds.

Growth hormone concentration levels can be increased acutely using one or both of the following training methods:

- Perform three sets of each exercise at high intensity with short (i.e., 1-minute) rest periods.
- Consume carbohydrates and protein before and after resistance training sessions.

Optimization of adrenal hormone responses can be achieved by the following method:

- Perform high-volume resistance exercises that utilize large muscles combined with short rest periods. This causes the body to experience adrenergic stress. Note that adequate rest and a varied training protocol should be utilized to avoid this stress leading to nonfunctional overreaching or overtraining.

Aerobic Responses

High-intensity aerobic training enhances the secretion of hormones in response to maximal aerobic exercise. This response likely improves the athlete's ability to handle and maintain high aerobic exercise intensities over long periods of time.

Cardiopulmonary Anatomy and Physiology

Cardiopulmonary Anatomy

Heart Structures

The *heart* is a muscle called the *myocardium*. It has a left and a right *atrium*, which deliver blood to the left and right *ventricles*, respectively. Ventricle contraction produces the force necessary to eject blood out of the heart into circulation. The *tricuspid valve* and *mitral valve* form the atrioventricular (AV) valves. During ventricular contraction (*systole*), the AV valves prevent blood from flowing back from the ventricles into the atria. The *aortic valve* and the *pulmonary valve* form the *semilunar valves*. During ventricular relaxation (*diastole*), the semilunar valves prevent backflow from the aorta and pulmonary arteries into the ventricles.

Blood Pressure (BP)

Systole is the highest pressure and top number recorded in a BP reading. It represents the pressure exerted by the blood on the walls of the blood vessels. Systole occurs during the contractile phase of the cardiac cycle, which forces oxygen-rich blood into the body and blood into the pulmonary arteries to be oxygenated in the lungs. During *diastole*, the heart chambers relax and fill with blood; this is the lowest pressure and bottom number in the BP measurement.

Electrical Conduction System

The mechanical contraction of the heart is controlled by an electrical conduction system. The conduction system has numerous components that are responsible for the transmission of the electrical impulse that causes the contraction and recovery of the atria and ventricles. The *sinoatrial (SA) node*, considered to be the intrinsic pacemaker, normally is the initiator of rhythmic electrical impulses. It consists of a small amount of specialized muscle tissue and is located in the upper wall of the right atrium. Internodal pathways conduct the electrical impulse between the SA node and *AV node*, which is the location where the electrical impulse is slightly delayed before it passes into the ventricles. The *AV bundle* conducts the electrical impulse to the ventricles, and it is divided into left and right bundle branches. The bundle branches are further divided into *Purkinje fibers*, which transmit the impulse throughout the ventricles.

Regulation of the Electrical Activity of the Heart

The autonomic nervous system (ANS) is responsible for the rhythmicity and conduction properties of the myocardium. The atria have both sympathetic and parasympathetic fibers, while the ventricles have mostly sympathetic fibers. Sympathetic fibers increase the speed at which the SA node depolarizes, resulting in a faster heart rate. Parasympathetic fibers decrease the speed of SA node depolarization, which decreases heart rate. The normal range for resting heart rate is 60–100 beats/minute. *Bradycardia* is an abnormally slow heart (less than 60 beats/minute), and *tachycardia* is an abnormally fast heart rate, defined as greater than 100 beats/minute.

Measuring the Electrical Activity of the Heart

An *electrocardiogram* (ECG) graphically represents the heart's electrical changes (recorded by electrodes on the skin) during the cardiac cycle. The cardiac cycle consists of several waves that represent depolarization and repolarization of the atria and ventricles. The first wave is the *P-wave*. This corresponds to atrial depolarization, which causes the contraction of the atria and the movement of blood down to the ventricles. The depolarization of the ventricles during the *QRS complex* (QRS complex consists of the *Q-wave*, *R-wave*, and *S-wave*) results in ventricular contraction, which produces the force to circulate blood through the pulmonary and peripheral blood vessels. The *T-wave* corresponds to ventricular repolarization, which can be thought of as the recovery from depolarization. The atria also repolarize, but this activity is masked on an EKG by the large QRS complex, which occurs simultaneously.

Vascular System: Arterial and Venous

The *arterial system* carries blood away from the heart, and blood returns to the heart via the *venous system*. Because *arteries* quickly move blood away from the heart with high pressure, they have strong, muscular walls. The arteries branch into *arterioles* that help to control the flow of blood into the *capillaries*. Arterioles have strong muscular walls that can constrict, closing completely, or become dilated, effectively controlling the flow of blood into the capillaries. Capillaries are the point of exchange for nutrients, hormones, oxygen, fluids, and electrolytes between the blood and the interstitial fluid of body tissues.

Blood from the capillaries is collected by *venules* that converge into *veins* and return the blood to the heart. Unlike arteries, veins have thin but muscular walls that can dilate or constrict. Some veins in the leg have one-way valves to help ensure the one-way flow of blood and prevent backflow. The vascular system transports oxygen needed for cellular metabolism to the body's tissues and removes the carbon dioxide waste and brings it to the lungs. *Red blood cells* transport oxygen via *hemoglobin*, an iron-protein molecule. Hemoglobin also controls the rate of chemical reactions in cells by regulating hydrogen ion concentration. Strength and conditioning professionals should be aware that *blood doping*, banned by most sport organizations, is the practice of artificially increasing the number of red blood cells to increase maximal oxygen uptake and enhance athletic performance. The practice can have serious health risks for athletes.

Respiratory System

Respiratory System Function

The respiratory system exchanges oxygen and carbon dioxide. Air first passes through the *nasal cavity* where it is purified, warmed, and humidified. Inspired air circulates to the lungs by going through the *trachea* (first-generation respiratory passage), the *right and left bronchi* (second-generation passages), and the *bronchioles* (third-generation passages). The bronchioles continue to divide for approximately twenty-three generations, down to the very small *alveoli,* where gas exchange during respiration occurs.

Exchange of Air and Respiratory Gases

The movement of air and expired gases, controlled by the expansion and recoil of the lungs, results from the movement of the *diaphragm* upward and downward (shortening and lengthening the chest cavity) and the movement of the ribs, which increases the anterior to posterior diameter of the chest cavity. During relaxed breathing, the contraction of the diaphragm during *inspiration* creates a negative pressure vacuum, drawing air into the lungs. The relaxation of the diaphragm causes an elastic recoil of the lungs, and the chest wall compresses the lungs, causing the air to be expelled.

Heavy breathing during exercise requires extra force, provided by the contraction of the intercostals and muscles of the core, which push the abdomen upward against the diaphragm. Additionally, heavy breathing requires movement of the ribs to allow for expansion of the lungs. The ribs are elevated by muscles (external intercostals, sternocleidomastoids, anterior serrati, scaleni) during inspiration, allowing for more air to be inspired. The abdominal muscles and internal intercostals depress the chest during *expiration*. Expiration during resting conditions is passive but requires muscular contraction during exercise.

The walls of the lungs are composed of several layers of membranes, called *pleura*. *Pleural pressure* refers to the slightly negative pressure in the small spaces between the chest wall and lung pleura that enhances inspiration. Pleural pressure that is equal to or higher than atmospheric pressure will cause the lungs to collapse in a dangerous condition called a *pneumothorax*. When the glottis is open, no air moves in or out of the lungs, and the pressure inside the alveoli is referred to as *alveolar pressure*. Alveolar pressure must be below atmospheric pressure for inspiration to occur, and expiration requires an alveolar pressure higher than atmospheric pressure. The exchange of respiratory gases occurs when oxygen diffuses from the alveoli into pulmonary blood and carbon dioxide diffuses from blood into the alveoli. *Diffusion* of oxygen and carbon dioxide across cell membranes works according to a concentration gradient, where gas molecules move from regions of higher gas concentrations to regions of lower concentration.

Note that the *Valsalva maneuver* results from abdominal muscle contraction with the diaphragm when the glottis is closed, causing an increase in intra-abdominal pressure during heavy weightlifting. This is thought to help stabilize the core and spine. Athletes should be aware that when the muscle contraction is too forceful, it can cause a hernia.

Cardiopulmonary Responses to Exercise and Training

Anaerobic Exercise

Cardiovascular System

Acute anaerobic exercise causes increased cardiac output, heart rate, stroke volume, oxygen uptake, and systolic BP. Blood flow to active muscles also increases when lower resistances are used; however, decreased blood flow, resulting from the contracted muscle clamping down on capillaries, is observed with heavier resistance training. Muscular contractions greater than 20 percent of maximum voluntary contraction slow peripheral blood flow during a set, but during rest, blood flow increases over that of baseline in a process called reactive hyperemia. Chronic resistance exercise can reduce the cardiovascular response to an acute bout of resistance exercise.

Respiratory System

Ventilation significantly increases during each resistance exercise set; however, ventilation is greatest during the first minute of recovery from a set. This increase in oxygen consumption via increased ventilation is termed excess post-oxygen consumption (EPOC). EPOC serves to help the body return to baseline after the work is performed and helps perfuse tissues to carry nutrients and remove waste, resynthesize hormones and metabolic intermediates, buffer lactate, etc.

Anaerobic training adaptations include increased tidal volume and breathing frequency with maximal resistance exercise, allowing for greater oxygen intake. Slower ventilation rates with increased tidal volume are seen with submaximal exercise.

Acute Aerobic Exercise

Cardiovascular System

Numerous cardiovascular responses occur in response to an acute bout of aerobic exercise including increased *cardiac output* (amount of blood pumped by the heart in liters/minute), *stroke volume* (quantity of blood ejected with each heart beat), heart rate, systolic BP, *oxygen uptake* (amount of oxygen used by the body's tissues), blood flow to working muscles, and *vasodilation* of blood vessels. Diastolic BP remains at resting levels or decreases slightly.

Respiratory System

Acute exercise results in a number of respiratory responses including increased amounts of oxygen diffusing to muscle tissue from the capillaries, increased tidal volume (amount of air inhaled and exhaled with each breath), increased movement of carbon dioxide diffusing from the blood into alveoli, as well as increased *minute ventilation (i.e., the volume of air breathed per minute)*, allowing the maintenance of appropriate alveolar concentrations of oxygen and carbon dioxide during acute aerobic activity. Excess *post-exercise oxygen consumption* may occur after an intense bout of exercise. Resting oxygen consumption is estimated to be 3.5 milliliters of oxygen per kilogram of body weight per minute; this value is defined as *1 metabolic equivalent (MET)*. An intense exercise bout can cause an increased metabolic demand that lasts for 6–12 hours after exercise.

Chronic Aerobic Exercise

Cardiovascular System

Aerobic endurance training produces several changes to cardiovascular functions that are critical for increasing maximal oxygen uptake and optimizing athletic performance. Aerobic endurance training increases cardiac output while decreasing resting heart rate. The normal discharge rate (sixty to eighty times per minute) of the SA node slows significantly (due to increased parasympathetic tone), decreasing heart rate. At the same time, the increased stroke volume allows more blood to be pumped per contraction, so the heart can beat less frequently and still maintain the same cardiac output. Aerobic training can improve the ability of the heart to pump blood at rest, resulting in bradycardia in many highly-trained endurance athletes.

An increase in maximal cardiac output is also observed, due to the increased stroke volume. Increased muscle fiber capillary density, enhancing the circulation of oxygen and nutrients and the removal of by-products, has been associated with aerobic endurance training. An athlete's genetic potential can significantly impact training adaptions. Aerobic capacity decreases with age, and men typically have greater aerobic capacity than women.

Respiratory System

Ventilation adaptations to aerobic endurance training are highly specific to the activity used in the training. If training focuses on the lower extremities (e.g., running), adaptations would not be observed during upper extremity exercise (e.g., arm ergometer exercise). Adaptations include increased tidal volume and breathing frequency during maximal exercise.

Physiological Adaptations to Exercise, Training, and the Impact of Recovery Stages

Adaptations to Metabolic Conditioning

Physiological adaptations to metabolic training are dependent upon the system stressed. High-intensity anaerobic training stresses the phosphagen system, resulting in physiological changes such as increased muscle strength, speed, rate of force production, and anaerobic power. Stressing the phosphagen system also results in increased metabolic stores of ATP, CP, and glycogen. Increases in the strength of connective tissue may be observed, while increases in various characteristics of muscle fibers (e.g., fiber cross-sectional area, myofibrillar volume, cytoplasmic density, myosin heavy chain protein) also occur.

Physiological adaptations to aerobic training include increases in cardiovascular and muscular endurance, mitochondrial and capillary density, ventricular size and strength, and metabolic stores of glycogen, adenosine triphosphate (ATP), and triglycerides. Highly-trained endurance athletes are also better equipped for glycogen sparing, wherein fat can provide fuel at higher intensities, allowing glycogen stores to be rationed to avoid "hitting the wall" as early. Increases in tendon and ligament strength and potentially in bone density also result from chronic high-impact cardiovascular activities.

Causes, Signs, Symptoms, and Effects of Unsafe Training and Detraining

Overtraining

Training overload (increased training intensity, volume, or duration) is required to stimulate the physiological adaptations that contribute to improved athletic performance; however, excessive overload combined with inadequate recovery can produce physiological maladaptation and diminished athletic performance. Training overload can lead to functional overreaching, nonfunctional overreaching, and overtraining syndrome (OTS). Training overload can lead to acute fatigue that requires at least a few days of recovery. Functional overreaching requires days to weeks of recovery. Nonfunctional overreaching can require weeks to months of recovery. OTS can require several months or longer for recovery. In some instances, OTS may end an athlete's sports career.

Overtraining Syndrome (OTS)

If training volume and/or intensity are increased and the athlete is unable to adequately recover and adapt, he or she may experience significant overload, resulting in OTS. Other variables experienced by athletes can also contribute to OTS, such as stress, lack of sleep, environmental variables (e.g., extreme heat, increasing the possibility of dehydration), and poor diet. There are two types of OTS: *sympathetic OTS* and *parasympathetic OTS*. It is believed that the sympathetic syndrome develops before parasympathetic syndrome. Sympathetic OTS is characterized by increased sympathetic activity at rest and is seen in young athletes in speed and power sports. Parasympathetic OTS is generally associated with aerobic overtraining and is characterized by increased parasympathetic activity at rest and during exercise.

Anaerobic (Sympathetic) OTS

Anaerobic (sympathetic) OTS is characterized by an unexplained decline in athletic performance that is associated with increased neural activity, mood disturbances (e.g., more tension, depression, fatigue), reduced immunity (e.g., resulting in increased sickness and infection), decreased skeletal muscle force (F_M) production, reduced glycolytic capacity and appetite loss, and blunted increases in pituitary hormones such as ACTH and growth hormone.

Aerobic (Parasympathetic) OTS

Aerobic (parasympathetic) OTS is also characterized by poor athletic performance, including reduced performance on psychomotor tests. Other changes include reduced availability of glycogen, increased skeletal muscle soreness, increased levels of cortisol, decreased total testosterone concentration, mood changes, a greater sympathetic stress response, and reduced levels of nocturnal and resting catecholamines. Metabolism is affected by increased levels of creatine kinase and decreased lactate and cardiovascular alterations, including reduced oxygen uptake, increased resting heart rate, reduced heart rate variability, and altered BP. Some athletes experience weight gain and difficulty sleeping.

Detraining

If exercise volume and intensity decrease, the athlete will begin to lose the physiological adaptations achieved from training. Aerobic adaptations are most sensitive to inactivity. VO_2 max can be reduced by 4–14 percent after 4 weeks of reduced training stimulus and 6–20 percent after more than 4 weeks. Research has found that reduced maximal oxygen uptake results from several factors including decreased blood and stroke volume, reduced maximal cardiac output, and increased submaximal heart rate at a given workload.

Sleep

Sleep is an important part of physical and mental recovery. Given the added rigors that exercise places on the body and the intense mental demands of training and competing, athletes need especially high-quality and sufficient sleep. Adequate rest and recovery are required for optimal performance. Unfortunately, it's not uncommon for athletes to suffer from sleep disturbances or disorders, and intense exercise and the pressures and stress of competing at a high level can interfere with an athlete's ability to obtain a good night's rest on a daily basis. As such, health, performance, mental acuity, motivation, and physical resilience against illness and injury can be compromised. Practicing proper sleep hygiene and employing relaxation techniques are important for athletes to achieve quality sleep and routinely obtain at least 7–9 hours of sleep per night.

Sleep Deprivation

Sleep deprivation and sleep debt, which is an accumulation of sleep loss, can significantly reduce athletic performance. The NSCA reports that sustained wakefulness for at least 17 hours produces the same cognitive performance issues that a blood alcohol level of 0.05% does. Moreover, the accumulation of inadequate sleep (sleep debt) can exponentially increase injury risk and cause decreased alertness, reduced reaction times, and impaired concentration.

Disordered Sleep

Sleep disorders are conditions resulting in one's inability to receive an optimal amount of sleep. They affect a third of the American population between the ages of twenty and sixty. While troublesome external factors are known to occasionally disturb one's sleep patterns, when difficulties with sleep start occurring frequently, it may be indicative of a sleep disorder. There are many different types of sleep disorders, ranging in both severity and category, so each set of symptoms can vary. However, some general symptoms commonly associated with sleep disorders include anxiety, irritability, inability to focus, difficulty falling or remaining asleep, fatigue, recurring naps during the day, and depression.

Some examples of the many different types of sleep disorders include insomnia, aberrant behaviors or movements during sleep (parasomnias), restless leg syndrome, narcolepsy, and sleep apnea. A lack of sleep can also negatively affect one's energy levels, physical health, relationships, and task performance. The cause of sleep disorders is multifactorial. Some factors that can serve as potential causes of a sleep disorder include allergies and respiratory problems, chronic pain, frequent urination, and stress. Once a sleep disorder is diagnosed, there are certain courses of treatment one can pursue, including medical approaches and lifestyle changes. Because there are several different causes and types of sleep disorders, treatments can vary.

Medical approaches can include allergy or cold medications, melatonin supplements, sleeping pills, treatments for any other underlying health conditions, a dental guard to wear at night to prevent bruxism (teeth grinding), or a breathing apparatus (CPAP machine) or surgery for those suffering from sleep apnea. Lifestyle changes that could be incorporated into one's daily life include undertaking a healthier diet, exercising regularly, adhering to a sleep schedule, reducing use of alcohol and tobacco, restricting caffeine intake, and consuming less water before bed.

Techniques and Strategies for Recovery

Training and competing in sports take a significant toll on the body and mind. It is imperative that recovery is built into every training program, both on a macrocycle level and microcycle level. Periodization helps ensure athletes are given ample downtime to recover and give their bodies and minds a break. Athletes should not compete and train at their highest levels throughout the entire year without at least some periods of relative downtime or rest. Similarly, in a given week, it's inadvisable to push the limits each day in each training session without either a day off or days of relative lower intensity. The physical stress that exercise imposes on the body causes microscopic damage to structures of the body such as bones, tendons, ligaments, muscles, and fascia.

Similarly, exercise stresses physiological systems such as the endocrine system, the cardiovascular system, the immune system, the neuromuscular system, and even the digestive system. These tissues and systems need to have time to repair and rebuild after exercise and athletic training so that the exercise stimulus can have the desired effect without increasing the risk of tissue breakdown, injury, illness, or overtraining and fatigue. While rest and sleep are certainly a key component of recovery, other strategies to promote recovery include hot and cold therapy to encourage circulation and tissue recovery, optimal post-workout nutrition and hydration to replace depleted energy stores and electrolytes, compression clothing to encourage the removal of metabolic waste products from muscles, and tissue health strategies such as massage, foam rolling, dynamic stretching, and yoga.

Anatomical, Physiological, and Biomechanical Differences of Athletes

Several age-related terms will be used throughout this section. *Childhood* refers to the period of time prior to the development of secondary sex characteristics, while *adolescence* is the period between childhood and adulthood. *Youth* refers to both adolescents and children, and *older/elder/senior* refers to men and women who are over 65 years of age.

Youth

Growth, Development, and Maturation

Growth is an increase in the size of a body part or the entire body that results from an increase in the number of cells. *Development* refers to the progression that occurs from fetus to adult. *Maturation* is the process of the body becoming fully functional, which occurs at *puberty* when secondary sex characteristics develop, and the child transitions to adolescence. Note that changes that occur with puberty impact the individual's physical and motor skills as well as body composition and must be considered when developing training programs.

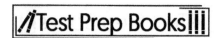

Chronological, Biological, and Training Age

There is substantial variation in the growth and development rates of children, so age can be understood from three perspectives. *Chronological age* refers to the years and months the child has been alive. Children of the same chronological age can be at different stages of development and maturation. To take pubertal development (e.g., skeletal age, somatic [body shape] sexual maturation) into consideration, *biological age* can be used. Children having the same chronological age but different biological ages have varying levels of motor skills, muscular strength, and fitness. Biological age should be used when grouping children for fitness testing and athletic competitions since it provides fairer matching of physical and athletic abilities. The gold standard method of determining biological age is to assess skeletal age via x-rays or radiographs of the wrist or iliac crest to compare bone ossification to standard reference radiographs. One additional factor that should be considered when developing a youth training program is *training age*, which is the length of time the youth has been doing a formal, supervised resistance training program.

Youth Resistance Training Program

When developing a resistance program for youth, strength and conditioning professionals must be mindful that the youth athlete is *not* a miniature adult. It is important that youth begin resistance training programs based on their previous training experience, maturity level, physical abilities, and goals; it is always better to underestimate ability level and gradually increase volume and intensity. Research has demonstrated that preadolescent girls and boys can significantly improve their muscular strength beyond the natural improvement associated with growth and maturation. Changes in muscle hypertrophy may be partially responsible for increased strength, but increased strength is primarily due to neurological factors such as motor unit recruitment, activation, synchronization, and firing.

The two most important factors in the development of a youth program are the quality of instruction, such as the demonstration of appropriate technique, and the employment of the appropriate rate of progression. In general, the program should include various single- and multi-joint resistance exercises. Sets should consist of six to fifteen repetitions using light resistance at a rate of two to three nonconsecutive sessions per week. For younger children, body weight usually provides sufficient resistance. The use of resistance bands can augment training stimulus when appropriate. It is important to focus on basic movement patterns involving large-muscle groups (squats, lunges, dead lifts, push-ups), emphasizing proper form and breathing to help develop foundational strength training patterns and to prevent injuries.

Older Adults

Many changes in body composition and neuromotor function are observed among adults over the age of sixty-five. Bones become fragile with age because of reduced bone mineral density (BMD), increasing the risk for fractures, particularly of the spine, hip, and wrist. *Osteopenia* refers to a BMD level that is between -1 and -2.5 standard deviations of the BMD of young adults, and *osteoporosis* is a BMD of 2.5 standard deviations below that of young adults. *Sarcopenia* is the loss of muscle mass, which results in the loss of strength and power. It is largely due to reduced levels of physical activity but can also be impacted by poor nutrition and hormonal and nervous system changes. Neuromotor functional changes can lead to increased risk of falling (and fractures due to reduced BMD) and can result from decreased strength and power, longer reaction time, and impairments in balance and postural stability.

Older adults use strategies such as increased muscle activity before *(preactivation)* and immediately following *(cocontraction)* contact with the ground. Increased muscle tension associated with preactivation and the joint stabilization provided by cocontraction can help to offset balance and postural problems. Multidimensional programs that consist of resistance and balance exercises result in the most improvement of neuromotor function in seniors. Aging does not decrease the body's ability to adapt to resistance exercise, so it is possible to see large improvements in muscle mass, power, strength, BMD, and motor function (e.g., walking speed). Although both aerobic and balance exercises are important and should be included in a training program, resistance training is needed to increase muscle strength, power, and mass.

Resistance training programs for older adults are similar to programs for younger adults; however, medical history, training history, nutrition, and other variables should be considered. All older adults should complete a *medical history* with a *risk factor questionnaire* prior to beginning a training program. The safety recommendations for resistance training in older adults are similar to many of those for other age groups (e.g., 5–10 minutes of warm-up, stretching after exercise, allowing 48–72 hours between training sessions).

Female Athletes

Women can gain many benefits from regular participation in resistance and aerobic exercise. It is important for strength and conditioning professionals to understand sex-related differences in body composition, strength, and physiological responses to resistance exercise to design an appropriate resistance program that will optimize athletic performance without increasing the risk of sport-related injuries. When females reach puberty, estrogen production increases fat deposition. On average, adult females weigh less than males but have a higher percentage of body fat and less lean mass. When considering absolute strength, females have about two-thirds the strength of males, with lower body strength being closer to that of males as compared to upper body strength. When strength is related to body weight, females have similar levels of lower body strength as males; however, the relative upper body strength of females is still less than that of males.

Importantly, when strength is expressed relative to the cross-sectional area of a muscle, no strength differences exist between males and females, indicating that muscle quality is not sex-specific. Women and men respond similarly to resistance training. Two important health risks specific to women are the *female athlete triad* and the increased risk (i.e., six times greater risk among females than males) of *anterior cruciate ligament (ACL) tears* of the knee. The female triad refers to the interrelationships between BMD, energy availability, and menstrual function. Females participating in heavy training volumes and/or intensities with insufficient caloric intake are at risk for osteoporosis and *amenorrhea* (i.e., the absence of a menstrual cycle for more than 3 months), and these increase the risk of stress fractures, endocrine and reproductive problems, and performance decrements. Training programs for females and males can be similar, the only difference being the amount of resistance used. Women participating in sports requiring upper body strength and those that put the knee at risk for injury can benefit from resistance exercises to strengthen these areas.

Scientific Research and Statistics in the Exercise Sciences

The Scientific Process

Human beings are, by nature, very curious. Since long before the scientific method was established, people have been making and predicting outcomes, manipulating the physical world to create extraordinary things—from the first man-made fire in 6000 B.C.E. to the satellite that orbited Pluto in 2016. Although the history of the scientific method is sporadic and attributed to many different people, it remains the most reliable way to obtain and utilize knowledge about the observable universe. Designing a science investigation is based on the scientific method, which consists of the following steps:

- Make an observation
- Create a question

- Form a hypothesis
- Conduct an experiment
- Collect and analyze data
- Form a conclusion

The first step is to identify a problem based on an observation—the who, what, when, where, why, and how. An ***observation*** is the analysis of information using basic human senses: sight, sound, touch, taste, and smell. Observations can be two different types—qualitative or quantitative. A ***qualitative observation*** describes what is being observed, such as the color of a house or the smell of a flower. ***Quantitative observations*** measure what is being observed, such as the number of windows on a house or the intensity of a flower's smell on a scale of 1–5.

Observations lead to the identification of a problem, also called an ***inference***. For example, if a fire truck is barreling down a busy street, the inferences could be:

- There's a fire.
- Someone is hurt.
- Some kid pulled the fire alarm at a local school.

Inferences are logical predictions based on experience or education that lead to the formation of a hypothesis.

Forming and Testing a Hypothesis

A hypothesis is a testable explanation of an observed scenario and is presented in the form of a statement. It's an attempt to answer a question based on an observation, and it allows a scientist to predict an outcome. A hypothesis makes assumptions on the relationship between two different variables, and answers the question: "If I do this, what happens to that?"

In order to form a hypothesis, there must be an independent variable and a dependent variable that can be measured. The ***independent variable*** is the variable that is manipulated, and the ***dependent variable*** is the result of the change.

For example, suppose a strength coach wants to see if athletes can increase their 1RM bench press more effectively by doing a training program featuring single arm chest presses with dumbbells to fatigue or by a daily regimen of the maximum number of pushups per set. Based upon what he or she already knows, the strength coach proposes (hypothesizes) that the single arm chest press plan will result in greater strength gains for the 1RM max bench press and, thus, a higher 1RM.

- Observation: Relative weakness in one arm limits 1RM bench press.
- Question: Will a program of single arm chest presses increase 1RM bench press more than a two-arm exercise?
- Hypothesis: Increasing strength in each arm individually will help increase 1RM bench press by allowing each arm to be the focus of the exercise rather than the stronger arm taking over.
- Independent variable: The type of exercise done in the training program.
- Dependent variable: 1RM bench press.

Once a hypothesis has been formed, it must be tested to determine whether it's true or false. After it has been tested and validated as true over and over, then a hypothesis can develop into a theory, model, or law.

Experimental Design

To test a hypothesis, one must conduct a carefully designed experiment. There are four basic requirements that must be present for an experiment to be valid:

- A control
- Variables
- A constant
- Repeated and collected data

The control is a standard to which the resultant findings are compared. It's the baseline measurement that allows scientists to determine whether the results are positive or negative. For the example of increasing 1RM bench press, the control may be a group of his athletes who do a standardized full-body program.

The independent variable is manipulated (a good way to remember this is: **I** manipulate the **I**ndependent variable), and the dependent variable is the result of changes to the independent variable. In the bench press example, the independent variable is the type of exercise that is the focus in the training program, and the dependent variable is the resulting increase (or lack thereof) of the 1RM bench press. In this experiment, there may be three groups—one that does the pushups every other day for 3 weeks, the control group doing a standard program, and one that does the single arm chest presses every other day for 3 weeks.

Finally, there must be constants in an experiment. A constant is an element of the experiment that remains unchanged. Constants are extremely important in minimizing inconsistencies within the experiment that may lead to results outside the parameters of the hypothesis. For example, some constants in the above case are that all athletes do the remainder of the program exactly the same, the number of days per week the training occurs is the same, the conditions to perform the 1RM test are the same, etc. If, for instance, the athletes do other exercises that differ from one another, the results will be muddled; it would be impossible to determine the actual reason for or the exercises that caused any differences that are seen.

Once the experiment begins, a disciplined scientist must always record the observations in meticulous detail, usually in a journal. A good journal includes dates, times, and exact values of both variables and constants. Upon reading this journal, a different scientist should be able to clearly understand the experiment and recreate it exactly. The journal includes all collected data, including any observed changes and other phenomena that occurred as a result of the experiment. A well-designed experiment also includes repetition in order to get the most accurate possible readings and to account for any errors, so several trials may be conducted.

Even in the presence of diligent constants, there is an infinite number of reasons—known as sources of error—that an experiment can (and will) go wrong. All experimental results are inherently accepted as imperfect, if ever so slightly, because experiments are conducted by human beings, and no instrument can measure anything perfectly. The goal of scientists is to minimize those errors to the best of their ability.

Reading, Reviewing, and Evaluating Various Sources of Information

Strength and conditioning professionals need to keep abreast of current research in the areas of exercise training and physiology, nutrition, and athletic performance because science and medicine are ever-changing fields as new research supplants older thinking. It is imperative that strength and conditioning professionals are aware of the latest thinking so that they can implement the safest, most effective training and conditioning programs as well as disseminate this information and teach their athletes. This will help keep athletes healthy and safe and optimize performance. As such, strength and conditioning professionals need to be critical readers of scientific sources.

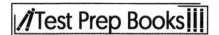

Valid scientific information must have sufficient, credible, accurate evidence that fully supports the claims and conclusions. Critical readers examine the facts and evidence used to support an author's claim. They check the facts against other sources to be sure those facts are correct. They also check the validity of the sources used to be sure those sources are credible, academic, and/or peer-reviewed. Consider that when the author of an informative scientific article uses another person's opinion to support their argument, even if it is an expert's opinion, it is still only an opinion and should not be taken as fact. A trustworthy study or science report uses valid, measurable facts to support ideas. Even then, the reader may disagree with the argument as it may go against their personal beliefs.

An authoritative argument may use the facts to sway the reader. For example, in a paper on carbohydrate loading, many experts differ in their opinions of what constitutes loading and what the benefits are (and if there are any). Because of this, a writer may choose to only use the information and expert opinion that supports their viewpoint.

Strength and conditioning professionals must be able to distinguish between reliable and unreliable sources in order to ensure the information they are gleaning is rooted in fact. When choosing print sources, published works that have been edited and that clearly identify the author or authors are typically considered credible sources. Peer-reviewed journals and research conducted by scholars are likewise considered to be credible sources of information.

When deciding on the merit of Internet sources, it is also a sound practice for researchers to look closely at each website's universal resource locator, the *URL*. Generally speaking, websites with .edu, .gov, or .org as the Top-Level Domain are considered reliable, but the researcher must still question any possible political or social bias. Personal blogs, tweets, personal websites, online forums, and any site that clearly demonstrates bias, strong opinions, or persuasive language are considered unreliable sources.

Science is often a process of checks and balances, and strength and conditioning professionals are expected to carry out this process of checks and balances as they analyze and compare information that differs between various science sources. Science demands a high degree of communication, which, in turn, demands a high degree of scientific literacy and numeracy. Strength and conditioning professionals must be prepared to analyze the different data and written conclusions of various texts. Contrary to popular belief, science is not an authoritarian field—scientific worldviews and inquiries can be wrong. It is more fruitful to think of science as a living library that is shaped by the complex activities carried out by different groups in different places. This living library is filled with ideas that are shaped by various sources and methods of research. The explanations, inferences, and discussions carried out by scientists are filled with facts that may be flawed or biased. Science, like any other field, cannot completely escape bias. Even though science is meant to be objective, its findings can still lend themselves to biases.

Thus, it is important for strength and conditioning coaches to get in the practice of not only making sense of information that differs between various science sources, but also to begin synthesizing this information into their work with athletes. The peer review process is also necessary to ensure checks and balances within the scientific field. The key to making this happen in practice is to maintain an acute awareness of when and where information or data differs. Pay close attention to the ways in which each scientist uses specific words or data to back their overall conclusions.

Below are some key reasons why data and interpretations can differ:

- Historical bias
- Cultural bias
- Interpretation or personal bias
- Lack of implementation and data collection fidelity
- Different data collection approaches
- Different data collection and data analysis tools
- Weak hypotheses

- Compounding variables
- Failure to recognize certain variables
- User error
- Changes in the environment between two studies
- Computation or statistical errors
- Interpretive blind spots
- Lack of understanding of context or environment

Reliability and Validity

Tests, tools, and methods used in science, including exercise training and testing, must be both reliable and valid. They are said to be reliable if they are free from random errors and are able to predict or measure performance or outcome consistently. For example, an aerobic capacity test is said to be reliable if an athlete takes the test on two different occasions and receives similar scores, because aerobic capacity tends to be relatively stable over time.

The following is a list of examples of known errors that can create inconsistent results when evaluating the reliability of selection tests, tools, and methods:

- A coach who doesn't follow the established testing protocol
- A test that fails to measure an important attribute
- A study that didn't use a control group

Although selection tests, tools, and methods may be deemed reliable, this does not necessarily mean they are also valid.

To be valid, a test or study involving exercise science or training should collect information on the athlete relevant to the athlete's sport and position. If, for example, a test measure does not test irrelevant qualities (like a power test for a marathoner), it can be deemed unfair or inaccurate. Information collected should be well defined, relevant, and position-related.

A strength and conditioning professional usually evaluates three elements to determine the validity of a selection tool:

- Content validity
- Construct validity
- Criterion-related validity, which is further categorized into:
  - Concurrent validity
  - Predictive validity

Content validity measures how well the test's aim covers the skills and abilities required for a specific sport or position. For example, if a measure of the anerobic power of football linemen is the intention but a VO_2 max test is used, this can be deemed an invalid test. Again, this is important to ensure there are no legal repercussions against the recruiting organization.

Construct validity determines if a test effectively assesses the characteristic it claims to measure, such as vertical reach, and that the characteristic in question is indeed important for successful performance of the position. For example, the vertical jump test to measure the vertical reach for a volleyball player would have high construct validity, but this same test would have low construct validity for a distance runner.

Tests with demonstrated ***criterion-related validity*** can predict how an athlete will perform in their position and sport based on their test scores. This is done by comparing test result data to specific metrics or criteria established in the industry. After testing is completed, a measurement comparing test scores with athletic performance is taken and expressed as a correlation coefficient ranging from -1.0 to +1.0. Because testing this validity requires a large sample size, it is often the most difficult type of validity to measure.

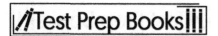

Strength and conditioning professionals can measure two types of criterion-related validity: predictive and concurrent.

Predictive validity is a measure of whether an athlete will possess the required skills, knowledge, or behavioral traits in the future. To be valid, the test results should correlate and accurately predict athletic performance in the future; in other words, the test should yield a positive correlation coefficient.

Concurrent validity determines if an athlete currently possesses the required skills or abilities. To assess this type of criterion validity, a coach administers a test to athletes to determine and compare their results to existing measures of athletic performance. The test is deemed to be valid if the athletes who receive the highest scores also perform best in their sport.

Practice Quiz

1. What is the role of acetylcholine in muscle contraction?
    a. To propagate the action potential across the neuromuscular junction
    b. To initiate the action potential so that voluntary muscle contraction can occur
    c. To bind to troponin, which alters the position of tropomyosin, causing the actin to become pulled towards the center of the sarcomere
    d. To initiate relaxation by flooding back into the sarcoplasmic reticulum and preventing actin and myosin from interacting

2. What must occur in tandem with functional overreaching to prevent overtraining?
    a. Adequate stress to induce physiological adaptations
    b. A preload period
    c. A de-load period
    d. Adequate recovery between reps and sets

3. What is the order of structures through which inspired air travels en route to the lungs?
    a. Nasal cavities, trachea, bronchioles, bronchi, alveoli
    b. Nasal cavities, trachea, bronchi, bronchioles, alveoli
    c. Nasal cavities, bronchioles, bronchi, trachea, alveoli
    d. Nasal cavities, bronchi, trachea, bronchioles, alveoli

4. Which of the following describes two variables that have an inverse relationship?
    a. As one variable increases, the other increases exponentially.
    b. As one variable increases, the other increases linearly.
    c. As one variable increases, the other decreases.
    d. As one variable increases, the other remains constant.

5. What is the primary function of the latissimus dorsi?
    a. Adduct the arm, medially rotate the arm, and extend the arm
    b. Abduct the arm, medially rotate the arm, and extend the arm
    c. Adduct the arm, laterally rotate the arm, and extend the arm
    d. Abduct the arm, laterally rotate the arm, and extend the arm

See answers on the next page.

Answer Explanations

1. A: Acetylcholine is a neurotransmitter that is released in the axon terminal after the action potential has been sent down the axon terminal. Acetylcholine then travels across the neuromuscular junction and binds to the sarcolemma. In this way, acetylcholine creates a "bridge" to propagate the action potential into the muscle cell. Depolarization initiates an action potential, so Choice *B* is incorrect. Choices *C* and *D* are functions of calcium.

2. C: Functional overreaching involves increasing stress on the body until no further stress can be placed on it without an adequate period of recovery called the de-load period. Overtraining can occur when the training load reaches a peak and is not followed by a period of de-load. Stress becomes too great and causes detrimental consequences. Choice *D* is incorrect because the de-load period is more of a macrocycle (days or weeks) factor versus the acute recovery between sets of reps.

3. B: Inspired air first enters the naval cavities, which humidify, purify, and warm the air. The air then moves to the trachea, which is the first-generation passage. The trachea splits into the left and right main bronchi. The bronchi bring the inspired air into the lungs, where it undergoes separation into advanced generations known as bronchioles. Bronchioles branch into the alveoli, which are the last generation and the location where the gases are exchanged during respiration.

4. C: When the independent and dependent variable display an inverse relationship, one variable increases while the other decreases. This can also be described as a negative correlation. Choice *A* describes an exponential relationship, Choice *B* describes a positive correlation. Choice *D* describes variables that are not correlated.

5. A: The latissimus dorsi is a large, flat muscle of the back. It acts on the arm at the glenohumeral joint, causing adduction, medial rotation, and extension.

Sport Psychology

Psychological Techniques Used to Enhance Training and Performance

Motivational Theory and Techniques

Motivation, a psychological construct, is the direction and intensity of an athlete's effort. There are several forms of motivation, including intrinsic and extrinsic motivation, achievement motivation, and motivation associated with skill development. It should be noted that athletes generally experience more than one type of motivation, and these can vary depending on the activity being performed, perceptions of competency, the level of importance the athlete places on the activity, and other factors.

- Intrinsic motivation is an athlete's internal desire for their behavior to be competent and self-determined. It originates from the athlete's love and interest in the sport and personal satisfaction (inherent reward) in performing the activity. Intrinsic motivation is generally considered the best form of motivation. It can help an athlete maintain focus on achieving short-term goals that require consistent effort to enhance the athlete's performance level.

- Extrinsic motivation, used extensively in sports, comes from external sources (e.g., coaches, teammates) in the form of individualized rewards such as praise from coaches and teammates, medals, social acceptance, avoidance of punishment, and the desire for positive reinforcement.

- Achievement motivation reflects an athlete's effort to master a specific task, achieve excellence, perform better than others, and overcome obstacles. Athletes with high levels of achievement motivation are more competitive and generally perform better than athletes with lower levels of achievement motivation. There are two types of achievement motivation. The motive to achieve success (MAS) is characterized by a desire to challenge and evaluate one's ability and be proud of accomplishments. Athletes with greater MAS like challenging situations, where the likelihood of success or failure is approximately the same. The motive to avoid failure (MAF) is characterized by the desire to avoid being perceived as a failure, preserve one's ego and self-confidence, and minimize shame. Athletes with greater MAF prefer either easy situations where they will likely succeed and avoid shame or difficult situations where success is unlikely and feelings of shame are minimized.

Imagery Techniques

Imagery techniques utilize mental visualization of specific athletic situations such as the performance of a targeted event/race. The benefits of vivid imagery include providing an athlete with exposure to the successful execution of a specific skill under a stressful competitive situation (e.g., sinking a putt on the eighteenth hole); allowing the athlete to "experience" the sights, sounds, smells, and physical exertion associated with the competitive environment on a regular basis and at a much greater frequency than actual competitions during the season; and the athlete feeling (or watching) himself or herself perform successfully and gaining confidence in the ability to perform optimally.

Reinforcement Strategies

Positive Reinforcement

The goal of positive reinforcement is to increase the occurrence of a favorable behavior (e.g., skill, movement, appropriate teamwork) or outcome (e.g., improved performance). Immediately after the positive behavior occurs, the athlete or team is given a positive incentive. This incentive is something that the athlete/team values (praise, more playing time, starting position, extra rest between sets, etc.) to encourage continued occurrence of the desired positive behavior.

Negative Reinforcement

Similar to positive reinforcement, negative reinforcement provides a "reward" after the occurrence of the desired behavior or outcome. This reward is the removal of a stimulus the athlete/team views as aversive. A strength and conditioning coach might remove the regularly performed sets of push-ups after the entire team performed an exercise using the correct technique.

Positive Punishment

Positive punishment is used to deter undesirable behavior by presenting an action, object, or event after the unwanted behavior occurs. Positive punishment might take the form of an athlete running extra sprints after practice because he or she was late or a team receiving a reprimand from the coach after incorrectly running a specific play.

Negative Punishment

Negative punishment involves the removal of a highly valued positive stimulus after an unwanted behavior or outcome occurs in order to deter future occurrences of the behavior. A team that is joking around during a resistance training session may receive negative punishment when the strength and conditioning coach turns off the music for the remainder of the training session.

Self-Confidence

Self-confidence is the belief in one's ability to perform a specific behavior such as hitting a baseball or completing a marathon. In the realm of sports, research has identified several areas of self-confidence. An athlete may have self-confidence in their ability to perform physical skills, their ability to use psychological skills (e.g., self-talk) and perceptual skills (e.g., visual scanning), their learning potential (needed to improve skills), their training, and their level of fitness.

Self-Efficacy

Self-efficacy (SE) is the athlete's perception of their ability to perform a situation-specific task successfully. The strength and conditioning professional should recognize that their actions can improve the athlete's SE by targeting the multiple sources that influence SE. The first and most significant source of SE is the athlete's past performance accomplishments. Helping the athlete set challenging but attainable short-term goals can provide performance success, which can have a positive impact on SE. The second source is vicarious experiences in which the athlete watches/models a similar athlete's successful performance (e.g., "If someone similar to me can complete that new drill, so can I."). Verbal persuasion, the third SE source, can include encouragement from coaches, teammates, oneself, and other external sources (e.g., Nike's "Just Do It" slogan). The fourth source of SE is physiological arousal and emotional/mood states. For example, helping an athlete interpret pre-competition "jitteriness" as excitement to compete because the athlete knows he or she can successfully achieve a specific performance goal can positively influence SE, as opposed to the interpretation of the "jitteriness" as a sign of being nervous or unprepared to compete.

Positive Self-Talk

Positive self-talk provides motivation ("I can get my personal best time in this race!"), encouragement ("Get ready to swim fast!"), and reinforcement ("I am prepared for this race!") and often is used to increase effort, energy, and a positive attitude. When an athlete uses *instructional self-talk*, he or she generally focuses on technical and task-related aspects of performance ("Streamline off the wall!") or strategy ("Maintain my race pace for this 800-meter run."). *Negative self-talk* typically denotes anger ("Can't believe I missed that putt. I'm such an idiot and will never win now."), doubt ("I can't do this."), negative judgment ("That was not good enough."), or discouragement ("There is no way I can win this race.").

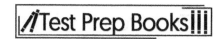

Attentional Control and Decision-Making Skills

Focus

The ability to focus or keep one's attention in the present and while in an athletic environment is critical for optimal performance. For example, a basketball player needs to stay focused on the location of the players of both teams while ignoring cheers from the crowd. This is known as *selective attention*. For success, athletes need to be able to maintain their focus on the relevant stimuli and environmental and internal physiological factors.

Arousal Management

Arousal

In sports, arousal is the intensity of motivation, anxiety, and focus experienced by an athlete and is the result of physiological and psychological activation. Arousal can be understood as a continuum of activation from deep sleep to very intense excitement. A highly-aroused athlete may experience an increased heart rate, sweating, and anxiety, while the athlete with low arousal may be lying down and feel tired and unfocused. Optimal arousal is often described as an inverse "U," wherein the ideal performance occurs with moderate levels of arousal, while either extreme can detract from performance. Arousal can be associated with both pleasant and unpleasant situations and interpreted as being positive or negative to an athlete.

Inverted-U Theory

As mentioned, the inverted-U theory posits that too little or too much arousal negatively impacts athletic performance, and there is an optimal level of arousal that facilitates optimal performance. The inverted-U graphically shows this (x-axis is level of arousal; y-axis is performance), as the shape demonstrates that low levels or high levels beyond the optimal level of arousal result in worse performance, and somewhere between low and high arousal is the range of arousal associated with optimal performance (the top of the inverted-U).

At this point, the internal and external stimuli experienced by the athlete generate the optimal amount of arousal required to enhance performance. For example, if the heart rate is not fast enough, the body might not be physiologically ready to perform, but a heart rate that is too fast can cause fatigue too early in the competition, negatively impacting performance. Depending on a variety of factors, the level of arousal needed for optimal performance varies greatly among athletes.

Individual Zones of Optimal Functioning (IZOF) Theory

This theory recognizes that there is a continuum of state anxiety that varies across athletes and that emotions can also impact an athlete's optimal zone of functioning. It is the role of the coach to help the athletes identify and reach their optimal level of state anxiety. This can be accomplished by quantifying state anxiety and mood using specific assessments. By quantifying state anxiety, it is possible to identify each athlete's ideal range of state anxiety needed to enhance performance and optimize the athlete's abilities.

Catastrophe Theory

Catastrophe theory recognizes that cognitive and somatic anxiety, along with physiological arousal, can negatively impact optimal arousal levels, leading to an abrupt decline in athletic performance. Cognitive anxiety that takes effect after the arousal threshold has been reached can quickly and detrimentally impact an athlete's thought process, causing the athlete to focus on and doubt their ability to perform, resulting in a devastating performance decline.

Reversal Theory

Reversal theory simply states that high levels of arousal and anxiety experienced by an athlete can be perceived either positively (as an indication that the athlete is excited and ready to compete) or negatively (as demonstrated by a lack confidence). For the athlete to perform optimally, arousal must be interpreted positively. This theory is novel for two reasons:

- The athlete's interpretation of the arousal—not the amount felt—is important.
- The athlete has the ability to change negative interpretations of arousal into positive interpretations, thus controlling the response to high levels of arousal.

Drive Theory

Drive theory considers the relationship between arousal and performance to be linear: the more arousal experienced by the athlete, the better he or she will perform. Clearly, this is not the case, as too much or too little arousal can negatively impact performance. Two factors that significantly impact how an athlete's level of arousal influences performance are *skill level* and *task complexity*. Athletes at lower skill levels need less arousal to perform than their highly skilled counterparts because less skilled or new athletes must concentrate on the actions being performed; too many apprehensive thoughts can interfere with the unskilled athlete's ability to concentrate.

Lower levels of arousal are also advantageous for athletes attempting difficult tasks that require a lot of conscious attention. For example, hockey goalies perform better with lower levels of arousal than athletes whose tasks do not require an extensive amount of attention. In contrast, long-distant runners can perform well at a higher level of arousal because the biomechanical task (in this case, running) is somewhat automatic and does not require a significant amount of conscious attention.

Relaxation Techniques

Diaphragmatic Breathing

Diaphragmatic breathing is a technique that can easily be taught and used by athletes to aid physical and mental relaxation. It distracts the mind from focusing on stress because it requires attention on the mechanics of breathing and the abdominal region. This technique can help reduce heart rate and muscle tension, decrease autonomic nervous system functioning, and increase parasympathetic nervous system activity, resulting in deep relaxation due to the reduced neural stimulation of the muscles and organs.

Progressive Muscular Relaxation

Progressive muscular relaxation can be used by athletes to regulate levels of physical and psychological arousal by controlling pre-competition levels of somatic and cognitive activation. It essentially consists of contracting and relaxing muscle groups until the entire body is relaxed. This form of relaxation increases the athlete's awareness of somatic tension, with the hope that relaxing the body will result in a relaxed mind.

Autogenic Training

Autogenic training is a series of exercises that are aimed at increasing the sensations of warmth and heaviness in various body parts by using a type of self-hypnosis. The athlete gets in a comfortable position and then focuses on the following five stages of relaxation in this order:

1. Heaviness of extremities
2. Warmth of the extremities
3. Regulation of cardiac activity and breathing
4. Abdominal warmth
5. Cooling of the forehead

Systematic Desensitization (Fear)

This technique utilizes a skill-based relaxation response to control cognitive arousal. In a controlled environment, the athlete visualizes the particular experience that causes fear (e.g., diver hitting his head on the board during competition) while simultaneously using breathing and muscle relaxation techniques. Progressive imagery helps the athlete to visualize the entire fear-causing experience without trying to cognitively avoid the situation. This counterconditioning replaces the fear response with relaxation.

Methods that Enhance Motor Learning and Skill Acquisition

Feedback

Feedback plays a critical role in the acquisition and refinement of new motor skills. In general, when learning a new movement skill, it is beneficial to provide more frequent feedback that decreases over time as mastery is reached. The athlete has readily accessible *intrinsic feedback* provided by their body and sensory systems. An athlete kicks a soccer ball, and sensory information from the athlete's eyes, proprioceptors, mechanoreceptors, and joint receptors in the foot provides intrinsic feedback that he or she can utilize to refine the movement. *Augmented feedback* originates from an external source, such as a coach, an observer, or technology (e.g., video, heart rate monitor, laboratory equipment). Two types of augmented feedback are *knowledge of results* and *knowledge of performance*. The difference between these two forms of feedback is whether information provided to the athlete is about the completion of a movement task (e.g., the amount of time the task took) or about the athlete's performance of the movement task (e.g., the position of the athlete's feet).

Practice Conditions

When learning a complex motor skill, there are two different strategies: whole vs. part practice. *Whole practice* is required with complex motor skills because the component movements are interrelated (such as in archery or performing a jump shot). It also works well for skills that are not particularly complex. *Part practice* is best used to teach athletes complex skills with subcomponents that are less interrelated, such as a gymnastics floor routine.

Attention and Focus

Attention refers to an athlete's awareness of internal and environmental cues. Athletes in a competitive or training environment face a continual barrage of external stimuli and internal thoughts, some of which are important for performance. *Selective attention* is one's ability to focus on relevant, task-oriented cues while ignoring other stimuli and thoughts that are irrelevant to the athletic performance at hand. The soccer player needs to stay focused on the location of the players of both teams while ignoring cheering from the crowds or announcements being made at the adjacent field. The athletes who are capable of focusing on task-relevant sensory input will experience a higher level of performance in comparison to the athletes who are incapable of blocking out non-task-related input.

Learning Styles

There are different learning styles that can vary with each athlete. The strength and conditioning professional should be aware of these learning styles because an athlete will greatly benefit from instructions during sessions that are tailored to their specific learning style. Auditory learners learn through hearing, so the strength and conditioning professional can explain exercises and give verbal cues about form. Visual learners learn through seeing, so the strength and conditioning professional can demonstrate an exercise for the athlete to observe and give printed illustrations of exercises for the athlete to take home and review. Kinesthetic learners learn through movement, involvement, and experience. The strength and conditioning professional can demonstrate and then have the athlete try an unweighted trial of the exercise or a partial range of motion to demonstrate understanding before trying the full resistance or movement.

Instructional Strategies

There are three main types of instruction that can be used with athletes: explicit instruction, guided discovery, and discovery. *Explicit instruction* facilitates the athlete's learning by providing the most information about the task in a prescriptive manner, aimed at guiding the athlete through the entire movement, often in a step-by-step fashion. *Guided discovery* gives less information to the athlete than explicit instruction but provides a more holistic description of the overall movement. By providing the goal of the task and some details about the movement, the athlete has to integrate the information provided with the movement pattern being practiced to understand how the goal is related to the movements performed. *Discovery* provides no instructions, but rather presents the overall goal of a movement. Using discovery-oriented instruction gives the athlete an opportunity to explore various methods to achieve the movement goal; however, it can be time-intensive.

Internal and External Cueing

Internal and external cueing come into play when learning new movement skills. Strength and conditioning coaches can help augment motor learning by providing verbal instruction to their athletes in the form of either internal or external cues, or a combination of both, depending on the skill being addressed. With an *internal cue,* an athlete focuses on the movements and feelings in their own limbs or body as the exercise or movement is being performed. In other words, internal cues have an internal focus. For example, a strength and conditioning professional teaching a novice athlete how to properly execute a squat may provide the verbal instruction, "Push through your heels." With an *external cue,* an athlete focuses on how the movement or the performance of the movement will affect the outcome of the exercise or the environment at large. For the athlete performing a squat, the coach could say, "Push through the ground away from you."

While both types of cues have their place and some degree of merit, most research has found that external cues are more effective at improving motor learning and movement performance. Over time, with repetition of the cues and practice on the part of the athlete, the movement or skill will become more unconscious, and less deliberate attention will be needed to perform optimally.

Mental Health Issues in Athletes

Psychological Impact of Injury in Sport

Injuries not only have the obvious physical impacts for the athlete, but they also often impose a psychological impact as well. Athletes are emotionally invested in their sport, so any injury that precludes their ability to participate in training or competition will almost inevitably be upsetting. It is common for injured athletes to feel frustrated about missing training or competitions after spending so much time, energy, and passion working toward their athletic goals. They may feel anxiety about losing fitness or other perks of participation, such as scholarship money or college recruitment potential.

Other common emotional responses include sadness, anger, and irritability. Because exercise produces endorphins, which improve mood and decrease stress and angst, if the injured athlete is unable to find an alternative way to work out, there are neurophysiological reasons why the athlete may feel moodier and anxious. Therefore, it's a good practice for strength and conditioning coaches to work with team coaches to help an injured athlete find alternative ways to exercise, if allowable and feasible.

The emotional repercussions of injuries can cause sleep disturbances, changes in appetite or eating behaviors, decreased motivation, and disengagement or social isolation. Student athletes may even have trouble in the classroom, as these symptoms can bleed into other areas of life outside of athletics. Strength and conditioning professionals should recognize that while these sorts of emotional and behavioral responses to injury are normal, they are not productive and can be really detrimental to the healing process and overall health of the athlete. As such, the strength and conditioning professional should refer injured athletes with significant or worrisome emotional reactions to appropriate mental health practitioners.

Signs, Symptoms, and Psychological Impacts of Common Mental Health Conditions

Anxiety

Anxiety is perceived as a negative emotional state, associated with the body being physiologically aroused, which is generally characterized by worry, nervousness, apprehension, and fear. The thought process responsible for the perception of anxiety as negative is a result of *cognitive anxiety*, while the physical symptoms (e.g., increased heart rate, upset stomach) of anxiety are a result of cognitive anxiety's counterpart, *somatic anxiety*. Previous negative outcomes (e.g., false start on a relay) and negative thoughts may manifest physically, negatively impacting the physical performance of the athlete. Recognizing how negative physical and psychological arousal impacts an athlete's mental state and performance can provide an opportunity to assist the athlete in understanding their reaction to anxiety in stressful situations. The athlete can begin working on perceiving the stressful situations more positively in order to control the anxiety.

Additionally, anxiety can also be categorized as trait or state anxiety. *Trait anxiety* is considered to be part of one's personality, predisposing an athlete to perceive many situations as being threatening when in fact, no physical or psychological danger exists. In general, athletes with high trait anxiety generally experience higher levels of state anxiety. *State anxiety* is a continually changing component of mood that is the subjective perception of tension and apprehension associated with increased arousal of the autonomic and endocrine systems. An athlete's level of state anxiety may change throughout a soccer game with changing situations. Depending upon the athlete's skill level, the athlete's level of trait anxiety, and the difficulty of the tasks being performed, state anxiety may have a positive, a negative, or no impact on performance.

Stress

Stress is the result of a psychological and/or physical demand placed on an athlete who does not have the ability to respond to the demand. The situation causing this imbalance of demand and response—an environmental or cognitive stressor—causes a stress response. Stress can be positive *(eustress)* or negative *(distress)* for an athlete. Training places a physiological stress on the body that is required for an athlete to improve performance.

Depression

Depression is characterized by feelings of lethargy; hopelessness; an inability to derive pleasure from once pleasurable activities; problems with sleep, eating, and substances; and/or sexual dysfunction that lasts longer than two weeks. It can be caused by genetics, an imbalance of neurochemicals, or situational contexts. Depression often presents differently in men, women, children, and older adults. Men tend to exhibit increased anger and irritability, while women tend to feel sad, worthless, and guilty. Women tend to internalize symptoms and experience depression at a higher rate and frequency than men due to unique societal issues, hormonal changes, and other factors.

Children present symptoms of depression through isolation, anxiety, or acting out. Older adults are more prone to hide symptoms of depression, attribute the feelings to another health problem, or be taken less seriously than other age demographics. It should be noted that these are generalizations and not hard rules. Athletes who are depressed may see a decline in performance, changes in sleeping habits and/or appetite, a loss of interest in training and competing, and feelings of low self-esteem, among other possible symptoms.

It is important that a strength and conditioning professional refer an athlete who they suspect is suffering from depression to an appropriate mental health professional. It is beyond the strength coach's scope of practice to diagnose or treat depression, yet they can serve as an integral cog in the support team. Depression is usually managed through psychotherapy and sometimes medication. Common medications to treat depression include SSRIs, similar to those used to treat anxiety. Depression can also be treated with serotonin and norepinephrine reuptake inhibitors, such as the brand names Cymbalta® and Effexor®.

When these options don't work, tricyclic antidepressants may be prescribed. It is uncertain how tricyclic antidepressants work, and they tend to have more intense side effects, so they are usually not prescribed unless other options have been exhausted. Even with medication, some periods of depression can become so intense and unmanageable that they place the individual in a crisis or suicidal mode. In this context, emergency services are usually needed. It is important to show the depressed athlete reassurance, comfort, and support. This can include directly asking the athlete how they would like to be comforted and supported during this time.

Signs, Symptoms, and Behaviors Associated with Eating Disorders

Disordered eating is an umbrella term used to describe abnormal eating patterns and behaviors. Disordered eating behaviors include binge eating, dieting that can be described as abnormal or obsessive, regularly skipping meals, self-induced vomiting, calorie counting to a level that is obsessive, having a self-worth tied to physique, misusing diuretics and laxatives, and unhealthy fasting or restrictive eating. The root cause of an eating disorder may vary from one individual to another, but it is believed that eating disorders can be attributed to genetics, the environment, and social and cultural factors. An eating disorder is a mental illness with a set of specific diagnostic criteria as described in the *Diagnostic and Statistical Manual of Mental Disorders* (DSM) published by the American Psychiatric Association, a professional association of psychiatric physicians. The most recent version of the DSM is the DSM-5-TR, published in 2022, and it specifies four types of eating disorders: anorexia nervosa (AN), bulimia nervosa (BN), binge eating disorder (BED), and other eating disorders.

Anorexia Nervosa

Anorexia nervosa (AN) is characterized by consistently restricting caloric intake to keep body weight at least 15 percent lower than the amount that would be healthy for age, sex, development, and health; an intense fear of becoming overweight or obese; and having a distorted self-image of body weight or shape. Historically, AN has been more prevalent in females, although more recent studies indicate that adolescent females and males suffer from the disease equally. AN can further be classified into two subtypes: restricting and binge eating. Individuals who exhibit behavior of restricting AN limit certain food groups and/or their amounts, obsessively count calories, skip meals, and are obsessive in their attempt to adhere to guidance and rules governing consumption. Individuals with AN who exhibit binge eating behavior may also restrict certain food groups and quantities, but they also display binging and purging behaviors. Binge eating involves eating a large amount of food and feeling a sense of loss of control while doing so; purging involves self-induced tactics to rid the body of food such as vomiting; using laxatives, diuretics, and enemas; or participating in excessive exercise.

Bulimia Nervosa

In bulimia nervosa (BN), similar to AN, individuals typically have a distorted self-image of body shape, weight, or size. Other behaviors characterized by BN include binge eating large amounts of food while feeling a sense of lack of control, self-induced vomiting, and misusing laxatives, diuretics, or enemas to prevent weight gain. In individuals with BN, the binge eating behavior occurs at least weekly for 3 months. Bulimia nervosa can be categorized into purging and non-purging type behavior. Purging behaviors involve tactics to remove food from the body, while non-purging behaviors involve restricting food or engaging in excessive exercise to compensate for food that has been ingested.

Binge Eating Disorder

Binge eating disorder (BED) is characterized by persistent binge eating, feeling a sense of distress when binging, or binging on average weekly for 3 months. Binge eating is closely related to BN, but individuals do not engage in purging or other compensatory behaviors that would eliminate food from their bodies.

Other Eating Disorders

Other eating disorders are now classified in the DSM-5-TR as other specified feeding or eating disorder (OSFED) or unspecified feeding or eating disorder (UFED). These two categories are intended to recognize disordered eating behaviors that do not clearly align with other diagnosed and defined eating disorders. Night eating syndrome, which entails recurrent episodes of eating at night, is one example of an OSFED.

Effects of Eating Disorders on the Body and Performance

Physiological changes can occur as a result of disordered eating, putting individuals at risk for other health issues. Physical signs and symptoms that may be associated with AN and its behaviors include rapid weight loss, mineral and electrolyte imbalances, amenorrhea in females, decreased sex drive, fainting or dizziness, hypothermia, consistently feeling cold even in warm weather, bloating, constipation, food intolerances, fatigue, low energy level, changes in the face including sunken eyes, and the development of fine hair on the face and body. Health concerns associated with AN and its behaviors include anemia, immune system compromise, gastrointestinal issues, amenorrhea in females, increased risk of infertility in men and women, renal failure, osteoporosis, cardiovascular issues, and ultimately, death.

Signs and symptoms that may be associated with BN include frequent change in weight; physical signs associated with vomiting including facial swelling, knuckle calluses, tooth decay, and bad breath; chronic sore throat; bloating, constipation, and food intolerances; amenorrhea; fainting or dizziness; and tiredness. Health concerns associated with BN include dehydration; gastrointestinal reflux; heartburn; ulcers; slowed or irregular heart beat; electrolyte imbalances; and heart failure.

BED can lead to weight gain and obesity, high blood pressure, high cholesterol, kidney failure, osteoarthritis, diabetes, stroke, gallbladder disease, irregular menstrual cycle, skin disorders, heart disease, and some cancers.

As a result of disordered eating, individuals can develop physiological issues that lead to health problems. These health problems can lead to a variety of conditions that can compromise athletic performance and even lead to death. Youth and collegiate athletes who develop disordered eating are at even greater risk of injury and physiological complications, since growth and development may be affected by disordered eating. Female athletes are also at risk for the Female Athlete Triad—a combination of energy deficiency and/or disordered eating, irregular menstrual cycles or amenorrhea, and osteoporosis or bone mineral loss.

Treatment for Eating Disorders

Disordered eating is a complex mental illness that requires early detection and treatment by qualified health care professionals. As such, coaches and trainers need to be cognizant of the signs and symptoms of disordered eating and refer individuals in need of intervention to appropriate and qualified health care professionals. The complexity of the illnesses requires a multidisciplinary approach with a team of health care professionals such as a physician, psychologist, psychiatrist, social worker, and registered dietitian who have experience and expertise in working with individuals with disordered eating.

When individuals need to change their behavior, as in disordered eating, it's important to understand that change is a process and that individuals often move through six stages referred to as the *trans theoretical model of behavior change*: precontemplation, contemplation, preparation, action, maintenance, and termination. During the precontemplation stage, individuals are not really thinking about making any changes, do not see their behavior as problematic, and are typically not ready for change. When individuals are in the contemplation stage, they recognize there is a problem, are thinking about making a change, and are usually getting ready to make change.

During the preparation stage, individuals are ready to make a change and may actually begin making small changes in their behavior. During the action phase, individuals are making consistent apparent changes in their behavior. In the maintenance stage, individuals have made changes for a sustained period, usually 6 months or longer, and are working to prevent any setbacks. During the final stage of change—termination—individuals have sustained the maintenance stage for quite some time and have no desire to return to their previous behaviors. Coaches and trainers need to be aware of these stages of change when working with individuals who need to change their behaviors as a result of disordered eating.

Signs and Symptoms of Substance Misuse

Since ergogenic aids can enhance athletic performance, there is potential for abuse. However, ergogenic aids can adversely affect major body systems including the cardiovascular, endocrine, genitourinary, dermatological, hepatic, musculoskeletal, and psychological systems. Signs and symptoms of ergogenic aid abuse include changes in blood lipids, increased blood pressure, and decreased myocardial function; gynecomastia (enlarged breasts), decreased sperm count, shrunken testicles, impotence, and infertility in men; menstrual irregularities, enlarged clitoris, deepened voice, and a more masculine appearance for women; acne and baldness; increased chance for liver tumors and damage; increased risk of tendon tears, intramuscular abscesses, and early epiphyseal plate closure; and depression, mood swings, hostility, and aggressive violent behavior.

Specific ergogenic aids banned by the Olympics and/or the NCAA include amphetamines, anabolic steroids, androstenediol, androstenedione, blood doping, dehydroepiandrosterone (DHEA), ephedrine, and human growth hormone. The Drug Enforcement Agency (DEA), the agency in the United States responsible for controlling the issues associated with controlled pharmaceuticals and chemicals, prohibits the sale or possession of anabolic steroids without the prescription of a physician. Violators may be subject to fines and/or imprisonment.

The World Anti-Doping Agency has a complete list of performance enhancement substances (PES) that are prohibited at their website (https://www.wada-ama.org/); the major categories of PES that are prohibited include anabolic agents; peptide hormones, growth factors, related substances, and mimetics; beta-2 antagonists; hormone and metabolic modulators; diuretics and masking agents; stimulants; narcotics; cannabinoids; and glucocorticoids.

Substance Abuse

Substance abuse is defined, most simply, as extreme use of a drug. Abuse occurs for many reasons, such as mental health instability, inability to cope with everyday life stressors, the loss of a loved one, or enjoyment of the euphoric state that the overindulgence in a substance causes. Abused substances create some type of intoxication that alters decision-making, awareness, attentiveness, or physical impulses.

Substance abuse results in tolerance, withdrawal, and compulsive drug-taking behavior. Tolerance occurs when increased amounts of the substance are needed to achieve the desired effects. Withdrawal manifests as physiological and substance-specific cognitive symptoms (e.g., cold sweats, shivering, nausea, vomiting, paranoia, hallucinations). Withdrawal not only happens when an individual stops abusing the substance, but also occurs when he or she attempts to reduce the amount taken in an effort to stop using altogether.

Signs and symptoms of substance abuse or misuse can include:

- Problems at work or school

- Friction with romantic partners, friends, coaches, or teachers
- Neglect of household responsibilities, self-care, or hygiene
- Reckless behavior leading to legal trouble or financial problems
- Violence
- Tolerance of the substance over time
- Inability to stop using the substance
- No longer engaging in normal activities in order to spend time/resources on the substance

Commonly Abused Substances

Tobacco

People abuse tobacco either in cigarette, cigar, pipe, or snuff form. People report many reasons for tobacco use, including a calming effect, suppression of appetite, and relief of depression. The primary addictive component in tobacco is nicotine, but tobacco smoke also contains about seven hundred carcinogens (cancer-causing agents) that may result in lung and throat cancers as well as heart disease, emphysema, peptic ulcer disease, and stroke. Withdrawal indicators include insomnia, irritability, overwhelming nicotine craving, anxiety, and depression.

Alcohol

Some individuals feel the need to have a drink to relax and calm down, as it is a central nervous system (CNS) depressant, which tends to soothe individuals and lower inhibitions. However, it also slurs speech and impairs muscle control, coordination, and reflex time. Alcohol abuse can cause cirrhosis of the liver; liver, esophagus, and stomach cancers; heart enlargement; chronic inflammation of the pancreas; vitamin deficiencies; certain anemias; and brain damage. Physical dependence is a biological need for alcohol in order to avoid physical withdrawal symptoms, which include anxiety, erratic pulse rate, tremors, seizures, and hallucinations. In its most serious form, withdrawal combined with malnourishment can lead to a potentially fatal condition known as *delirium tremens* (DTs), which is a psychotic disorder that involves tremors, disorientation, and hallucinations.

Prescriptions

Prescription medications, such as anti-anxiety, sleep, and pain medications, are commonly abused.

Marijuana

Marijuana is considered the most frequently abused illicit drug in the United States. General effects of marijuana use include pleasure, relaxation, and weakened dexterity and memory. The active addictive ingredient in marijuana is tetrahydrocannabinol (THC). It is normally smoked (but can be eaten), and its smoke has more carcinogens than that of tobacco. The individual withdrawing from marijuana will experience increased irritability and anxiety.

Cocaine

Cocaine is a stimulant that is also known as *coke, snow,* or *rock*. It can be smoked, injected, snorted, or swallowed. Reported effects include pleasure, enhanced alertness, and increased energy. Both temporary and prolonged use have been known to contribute to damage to the brain, heart, lungs, and kidneys. Withdrawal symptoms include severe depression and reduced energy.

Heroin

Heroin is also known as *smack* and *horse,* and its use continues to increase. Effects of heroin abuse include pleasure, slower respirations, and drowsiness. Overdose and/or overuse of heroin can cause respiratory depression, resulting in death. Use of heroin as an injectable substance can lead to other complications such as heart valve damage, tetanus, botulism, hepatitis B, or human immunodeficiency virus (HIV)/AIDS infection from sharing dirty needles. Withdrawal is usually intense and includes vomiting, abdominal cramps, diarrhea, confusion, body aches, and diaphoresis.

Methamphetamines

Methamphetamine is also known as *meth, crank,* and *crystal,* and its use continues to increase, especially in the West and Midwest regions of the United States. Methamphetamine is categorized as a stimulant that produces such effects as pleasure, increased alertness, and decreased appetite. Similar to cocaine, it can be snorted, smoked, or injected, and it can be eaten as well. Like cocaine, it shares many of the same detrimental effects, such as myocardial infarction, hypertension, and stroke. Other prolonged usage effects include paranoia, hallucinations, damage to and loss of dentition, and heart damage. Withdrawal symptoms involve depression, abdominal cramps, and increased appetite.

Practice Quiz

1. Which of the following is NOT an example of augmented feedback?
    a. A track coach giving an athlete a normative time for a 40-yard dash based around the athlete's sport before the athlete is timed
    b. A strength and conditioning professional showing an athlete a video of her squat form
    c. A field hockey player adjusting the spacing between her feet during a deadlift set when she realizes her weight is not evenly distributed
    d. A swimming coach giving an athlete her finish time

2. Which of the following is NOT typically a symptom of bulimia?
    a. Inflamed salivary glands of the neck and jaw
    b. Degeneration or loss of tooth enamel
    c. Electrolyte imbalances and/or dehydration
    d. Fine hair growth over the entire surface of the body

3. A gymnast repeats the phrase "I am prepared" several times before her vault. What is this an example of?
    a. Mental imagery
    b. The inverted-U theory
    c. Positive self-talk
    d. Visualization

4. What is self-efficacy?
    a. An athlete's internal belief that he or she possesses the attributes to be successful in their sport at large
    b. An athlete's internal belief that he or she is able to successfully perform a specific desired behavior
    c. An athlete's internal belief that he or she has trained to the best of their ability
    d. An athlete's internal belief that he or she is has control over anxiety, thoughts, and emotions

5. An athlete has been displaying mood swings, aggression, body acne, and testicular shrinkage. Which of the following could be a reason for these symptoms?
    a. Anorexia nervosa
    b. Excessive caffeine intake
    c. Excessive alcohol intake
    d. Ergogenic aid abuse

See answers on the next page.

Answer Explanations

1. C: Augmented feedback is given by the strength and conditioning professional to an athlete to provide further instruction, report results, reinforce adequate movement patterns, or correct faulty movement mechanics. It can be divided into two subtypes: knowledge of results and knowledge of performance. Choices *A* and *D* describe knowledge of results situations, while Choice *B* describes a knowledge of performance situation. In contrast, Choice *C* is an example of intrinsic feedback, which differs from augmented feedback in that it is derived from the athlete, not an external source.

2. D: Choice *D,* which describes lanugo, is more characteristic of anorexia nervosa. Fine hair growth over the entire surface of the body increases with anorexia as a compensatory mechanism for the body to keep warm when body fat and energy intake are insufficient. The other choices are common symptoms associated with bulimia.

3. C: The gymnast is employing positive self-talk. She is reinforcing positive thoughts, which can build confidence and self-efficacy and reduce performance anxiety.

4. B: An athlete with self-efficacy believes in their own ability to successfully carry out a desired behavior in a specific situation or environment. Choice *A* describes self-confidence, a more general feeling that, when coinciding with self-efficacy, helps an athlete believe he or she will be successful regardless of the situation. Choices *C* and *D* are characteristics that might be experienced with self-efficacy and may contribute to building self-efficacy, but they do not define the term.

5. D: His symptoms are often characteristic of ergogenic aid abuse. Additionally, he might experience mania or depression, gynecomastia, male pattern baldness, and decreased sperm count among others.

Nutrition

Nutritional Factors Affecting Health and Performance

Application of Nutrition Concepts

Food Groups

It's important that athletes, like all people, consume a wide variety of healthy foods and avoid eliminating major food groups, if possible, as this can lead to nutritional deficiencies. According to the United States Department of Agriculture (USDA), the basic food groups are vegetables, fruits, grains, protein, and dairy.

There are a number of health- and performance-related applications that can be used for meal planning. Some health- and performance-related applications that can be used for nutrition include the United States Department of Agriculture (USDA) Food Patterns, the DASH (Dietary Approaches to Stop Hypertension) Eating Plan, MyPlate, food exchanges, and the glycemic index.

USDA Food Patterns

There are three USDA Food Patterns included in the 2015–2020 Dietary Guidelines: Healthy U.S. Style Eating, Healthy Mediterranean Style Eating, and Healthy Vegetarian Style Eating. One eating pattern is not necessarily superior to another; it is more of a preference. However, a vegetarian lifestyle has been associated with a decreased risk for some chronic diseases such as heart disease and certain cancers. The USDA Food Patterns are all based on systematic review from scientific research, food pattern modeling, and analysis of intake of the U.S. population. Each USDA Food Pattern is based on the five food groups—vegetables, fruits, grains, dairy, and protein—and can be customized to meet an individual's needs based on age, sex, height, weight, and level of physical activity.

The Healthy U.S. Style Eating Pattern is based on typical foods consumed in Americans' diets with a focus on nutrient-dense foods in portions that are appropriate for the desired caloric intake. The Healthy Mediterranean Style Eating Pattern is based on the Healthy U.S. Style Eating Pattern but adjusted to align with the eating patterns of the Mediterranean diet, which have been associated with positive health outcomes. Specifically, the Healthy Mediterranean Style Eating Pattern has more fruit and seafood but less dairy than the U.S. Style Eating Pattern. The Healthy Vegetarian Style Eating Pattern is also based on the Healthy U.S. Style Eating Pattern but is adjusted to reflect the eating habits of self-reported vegetarians, as identified in the National Health and Nutrition Examination Survey (NHANES).

DASH Eating Plan

The DASH Eating Plan is based on clinical research trials that found that the plan helped individuals lower their blood pressure and low-density lipoprotein (LDL) cholesterol and improve heart health while meeting nutrient requirements. The DASH Eating Plan emphasizes whole grains, poultry, fish, and nuts along with food sources of potassium, calcium, and magnesium. Individuals are encouraged to consume as much as seven to eight servings of grains and four to five servings of fruits and vegetables per day on a 2000-calorie diet. Individuals using the DASH Eating Plan may need to gradually increase the intake of whole grains, fruits, and vegetables since the increased fiber of these foods can lead to bloating and diarrhea.

MyPlate

MyPlate is a tool developed by the USDA that is based on the five food groups and healthy eating. It is focused on variety, appropriate portion sizes, nutrient-dense foods, and low saturated fat, sodium, and added sugar intake. The MyPlate Daily Checklist and the SuperTracker are two specific online tools that allow individuals to customize nutrition planning for their specific needs.

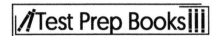

Food Exchanges

Food exchanges are used for meal planning purposes, especially for those with diabetes and/or seeking weight loss. Food exchanges divide food into six categories based on the amount of carbohydrate, fat, and protein they contain: starches/breads, fruits, milk, vegetables, meat, and fat.

- Starches and breads contain 15 grams of carbohydrate, 3 grams of protein, and 80 calories per exchange.
- Fruits contain 15 grams of carbohydrate and 60 calories per exchange.
- Milk exchanges contain 12 grams of carbohydrate; 8 grams of protein; 3–8 grams of fat depending on whether the milk exchange is a low-, medium-, or high-fat choice; and 90–150 calories depending on the fat content.
- Vegetable exchanges contain 5 grams of carbohydrate and 25 calories per serving.
- Meat exchanges contain 7 grams of protein per ounce; 0–8 grams of fat, depending on whether the source of the meat exchange is very lean, lean, medium fat, or high fat; and 35–100 calories.
- Fat exchanges provide 5 grams of fat and 45 calories.

Glycemic Index

Finally, the glycemic index and glycemic load offer insight as to how foods affect blood glucose and insulin levels. Glycemic index and load can be useful tools in meal planning to help individuals better understand the impact specific foods may have on their blood sugar. Carbohydrate counting may also be a useful tool in helping individuals monitor and understand the impact various carbohydrates have on their blood sugar.

Caloric vs. Nutrient Dense Foods

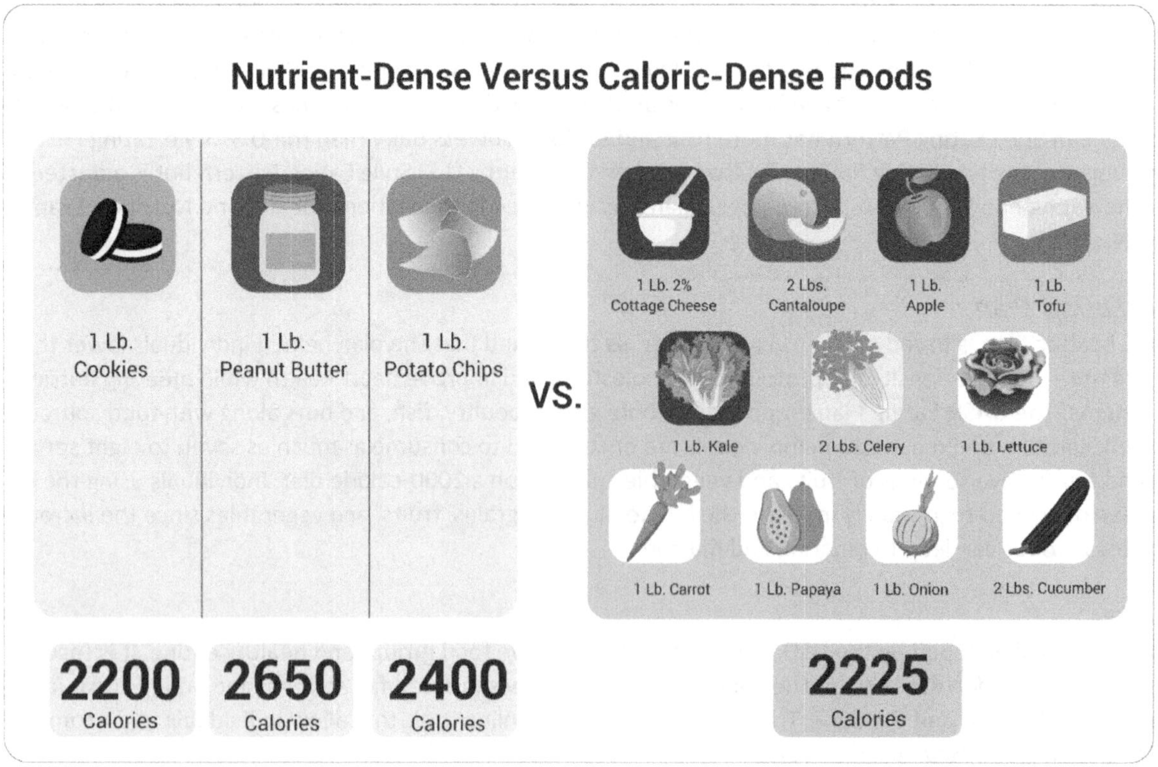

Nutrient-dense foods are rich in essential nutrients, vitamins, and minerals but low in calories, especially in comparison to calorically-dense or energy-dense foods. Calorically-dense foods provide few essential nutrients relative to the number of calories they provide. When focusing on weight loss or optimal health, it is important to focus on nutrient-dense foods. Sources of nutrient-dense foods include fresh vegetables and fruits, specifically dark green leafy vegetables like kale, spinach, and collard greens and fruits like berries, melon, mangoes, and citrus. Other nutrient-dense foods include lean sources of protein, dairy, legumes, and whole grains that have been enriched with vitamins and minerals. Calorically-dense foods include cookies, cakes, pastries, soda, chips, high-fat meats, and fast foods and other highly processed, highly caloric foods.

There are a number of systems that can be used in nutritional profiling or rating to support choosing nutrient-dense foods. Nutritional rating systems, which offer guidance on the nutritional value of food to make selection easier, differ from nutrition labeling, which provides detailed nutrient content on the specific food item according to serving size. Some nutritional rating systems include the Glycemic Index, the Guiding Star, Nutripoints, Nutrition IQ, the Naturally Nutrient Rich Score, the NuVal Nutritional Scoring System, the Aggregate Nutrient Density Index (ANDI), the ReViVer score, and the Points Food System by Weight Watchers. The Dietary Guidelines, to some extent, can also be considered a nutritional rating system.

Health Factors Associated with Dietary Choices

Dietary choices affect health risks associated with some chronic health conditions.

Saturated fats

Saturated fat is associated with an increased risk for cardiovascular disease, so the Dietary Guidelines for Americans recommends consuming no more than 10 percent of caloric intake from saturated fats. An emphasis should be made on replacing saturated fats with unsaturated fats, especially polyunsaturated fats, as this substitution is associated with improved total and LDL cholesterol.

Triglycerides

Circulating triglycerides are also affected by diet. Limiting refined, sugary foods; replacing saturated fats with unsaturated fats; and increasing fiber intake can help to keep triglycerides in the normal range of less than 150 milligrams per deciliter. High triglycerides can lead to increased risk of heart disease and diabetes.

Trans fats

Trans fats are produced through a process called *hydrogenation,* which makes packaged foods (such as coffee creamer, snack foods, store-bought baked goods, vegetable shortening, stick margarines, fast foods, and refrigerated dough products) more shelf stable. In recent years, manufacturers have begun limiting or removing trans fats per the Food and Drug Administration regulatory requirements because these fats have been shown to pose a significant risk for heart disease and should be eliminated from the diet.

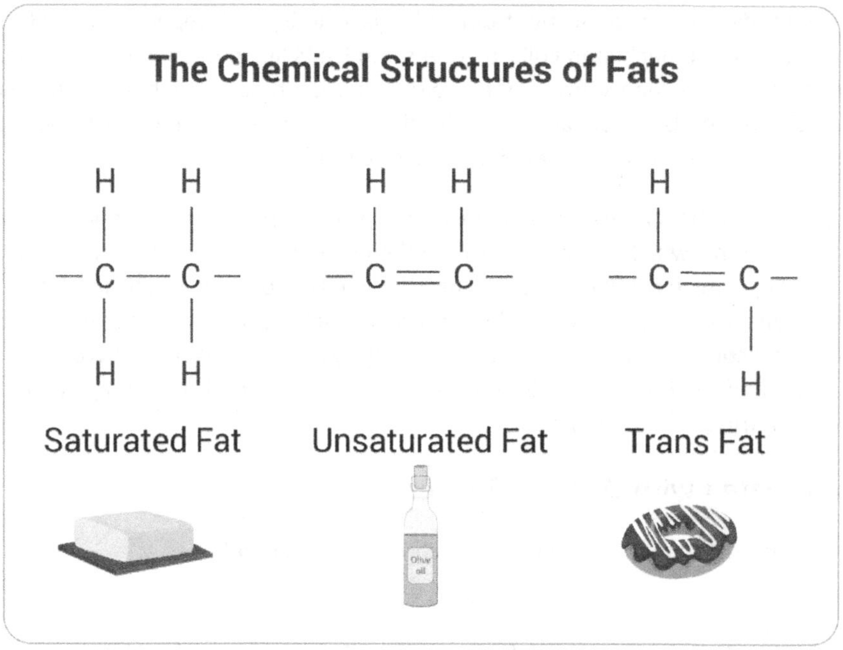

Cholesterol

Cholesterol is required for various physiological and structural functions, such as the production of cells and hormones. However, these requirements are met by the cholesterol produced in the body; little to no additional dietary cholesterol is needed. The upper limit for healthy levels of cholesterol is 200 milligrams per deciliter; high cholesterol is a risk factor for heart disease. The 2020–2025 Dietary Guidelines recommend that cholesterol intake should be minimal. The Institute of Medicine (IOM) still recommends limiting the intake of cholesterol-laden foods such as high-fat meats and dairy, which also contain high amounts of saturated fat.

Calcium

Calcium plays important physiologic roles including vascular contraction, vasodilation, muscle contraction, and nerve impulse transmission. The majority of calcium in the body is stored in bones and teeth. To support bone mineral deposition and avoid bone resorption, it is important to have adequate calcium intake. This is especially true at certain stages of the life cycle, when bones are forming or have the tendency to demineralize, as well as for athletes, who may lose additional calcium through perspiration. Postmenopausal women need to obtain adequate amounts of calcium in the diet to decrease the risk for osteoporosis. Signs and symptoms of calcium deficiency may be absent or may include muscle weakness, cramping, and increased susceptibility to fractures. Recommended intake varies by gender and throughout the lifespan, with increases for females, adolescents, lactating mothers, and postmenopausal women.

Iron

Iron in the body is primarily combined with hemoglobin, in an iron-protein compound that increases the blood's oxygen-carrying capacity sixty-five times, as well as in muscle myoglobin. Intensive workout programs put individuals at risk for developing iron-deficiency anemia, which decreases aerobic capacity since less oxygen can circulate to working tissues, leading to fatigue and reduced athletic performance. Other symptoms of iron-deficiency anemia include brittle nails, sluggishness, headaches, pale skin, and dizziness. Iron recommendations are 1.3–1.7 times higher for athletes than nonathletes and another 1.8 times higher for vegetarian athletes in comparison to those who consume animal protein, due to the lower bioavailability of nonheme iron sources in the vegetarian diet. The Recommended Dietary Allowance (RDA) for iron is as follows:

- 8 milligrams per day for men over the age of 18
- 18 milligrams per day for women ages 19–50
- 8 milligrams per day for women ages 51 and older

Females of childbearing age are at a higher risk for iron-deficiency anemia due to red blood cell loss during menstruation. Females often tend to consume less dietary iron as well. Endurance athletes may require additional iron due to foot-strike hemolysis, loss of hemoglobin in urine from strenuous training, and the small amount of iron lost in sweat. Heme sources of iron are more easily absorbed and include beef, pork, and beef liver. Nonheme sources include oatmeal, lentils, dark green leafy vegetables, and fortified cereals. Vitamin C intake can increase the absorption of iron in the small intestine; a glass of orange juice increases nonheme iron bioavailability by three times. It should be noted that excessive iron intake, especially in males, can be toxic.

Food Allergies and Sensitivities

Food allergies can be related to one or several foods for a given athlete. The allergic responses can range from mild to life threatening. The diet must be balanced and free of the allergens. Many athletes may have food sensitivities, which are issues with certain foods or food groups. Typically less severe than food allergies, food sensitivities can cause digestive issues, headaches, and discomfort. Lactose sensitivity/intolerance results from the deficiency of the enzyme lactase, which is necessary for the breakdown or digestion of lactose, a sugar found in dairy products. This deficiency can result in stomach bloating, nausea, vomiting, and diarrhea following the ingestion of dairy products. Gluten intolerance may be a symptom of celiac disease, which affects the absorption of food in the small intestine, or an allergic response to wheat gluten; however, it is most commonly due to the lack of a necessary digestive enzyme. Possible manifestations include stomach bloating, diarrhea, fatigue, and weight loss. Gluten-free diets must be free of wheat, barley, and rye in any form. This means that, in addition to bread, all processed foods must be avoided.

Effects of Hydration and Electrolyte Balance on Health

The adult male body is about 60 percent water, while the female body is about 50–55 percent water. As a result, less than optimal hydration status can affect health and performance. Dehydration can cause headaches, sluggishness, mood changes, loss of cognitive functioning, and muscle cramping. Decreased physical performance can occur with just a 2 percent loss in body weight from dehydration, and the risk of heat illness increases significantly with a fluid loss equaling 3 percent or more of body weight. During exercise, perspiration helps mitigate the increase in body temperature. During strenuous activity, individuals can lose as much as 6–10 percent of their body weight via sweating, depending on the type and duration of the activity. It is important to maintain adequate hydration before, during, and after exercise; the recommendation is 8–12 cups of water per day plus replacement of fluid loss during exercise.

Individual needs may vary, but during exercise, about 6–8 ounces of fluid are usually needed every 15–20 minutes of activity. Within the context of adequate hydration, electrolyte balance must also be preserved. The five major electrolytes that are important to health are sodium, potassium, chloride, calcium, and magnesium. Sodium, which is needed to help maintain fluid balance, nerve function, muscle contractions, and acid-base balance, is the primary electrolyte lost in sweat and must be replaced. It is important to include sodium in fluids or food as part of the rehydration process after exercise so that overhydration, or hyponatremia, does not occur as a result of drinking water alone. Adding sodium to fluids also helps to improve the absorption of water and carbohydrates. Most commercial sports drinks are formulated to provide the optimal levels of sodium and carbohydrates in solution.

Children and seniors are particularly susceptible to dehydration during exercise. Children may be unaware of the need to replace fluids during activity and may need longer to acclimate to increased temperatures. When children are exercising in hot environments, they should be well hydrated before activity and drink plenty of fluid afterward. Aging leads to decreased lean body mass and, over time, decreased body water. Seniors may also be at risk for dehydration because of decreased sensitivity to thirst and diminished ability of the kidneys to concentrate urine in the absence of adequate hydration.

Nutrition to Maximize Performance

Nutrition and Training Programs to Change Body Composition

Nutrition and training strategies can be used to guide changes in body composition. However, a calorie deficit is needed to lose body fat, which is usually best accomplished through diet and exercise. Nutrition strategies for losing body fat include altering the macronutrient composition of the diet, increasing protein and fiber intake, reducing consumption of processed and fast food, consuming five to six small meals per day, creating a reasonable calorie deficit, and drinking plenty of water.

Altering Macronutrient Composition

Studies lasting about 6 months in duration have found that moderately decreasing carbohydrates, increasing protein, and getting enough healthy fat is more successful in decreasing body fat than simply limiting caloric intake. However, results are more equivocal during 12-month and longer-term studies. It is important to remember that total caloric intake does play a role in energy balance. One pound of body fat contains about 3500 kilocalories, so caloric intake and expenditure should be modified accordingly for weight loss goals. Macronutrient composition needs to be tailored to the individual based on body composition, health status, training, and goals, but a caloric distribution of about 40–45 percent carbohydrate, 30–35 percent protein, and 25 percent fat should reduce body fat when part of a diet with appropriate caloric intake.

Increasing Protein and Fiber Intake

Increasing protein helps to support muscle tissue and is necessary to increase lean body mass and metabolism. While the minimum RDA for individuals is 0.8 grams per kilogram of body weight, this is typically not enough for individuals who are seeking to maintain lean body mass while losing body fat. Protein requirements vary based on the type, duration, intensity of training, as well as fitness and health goals; however, most athletes need at least 1.0–1.7 grams per kilogram of body weight. Depending on the individual's eating preferences, the focus should be on lean sources of nutrient-dense protein, such as beef, chicken, turkey, eggs, yogurt, fish, beans, and legumes. Since increasing fiber in the diet helps to increase satiety and fullness, plenty of fruits, vegetables, legumes, and whole grains should also be included.

Consuming Small Meals

Consuming five to six small meals per day helps prevent the metabolism from slowing, which is one of the primary reasons that excessively low-calorie diets should be avoided. To help with satiety and blood glucose control, protein should be consumed at each of the small meals. While modified fasting diets have been shown to be effective in weight loss, fasting diets should not be used long-term because of their effect on slowing the metabolism.

Drinking Water

Drinking plenty of water helps to ensure adequate hydration and plasma levels for circulating nutrients and eliminating waste more effectively. As mentioned, the body is composed of about 60 percent water, so hydration is essential for optimal health and athletic performance. The Institute of Medicine recommends about 13 cups of fluid per day for men and about 9 cups per day for women. All fluids in the diet can be counted toward daily fluid requirements. Individual requirements vary depending on health, activity, and environment, but athletes should be mindful to replace fluids that are lost through sweating. To ensure that fluid replacement is adequate after exercise, athletes should determine their sweat rate and fluid loss by weighing themselves before and after exercise.

Increasing Lean Body Mass Through Training

Strategies for increasing lean body mass through exercise include weight training and cardio interval training. Individuals require a specific program depending on their goals, but to increase lean body mass, progressive resistance training should be a part of the regimen at least three times per week. High-intensity interval training (HIIT), which involves alternating bouts of high-intensity activity with rest, is also effective for building lean body mass. Because it increases post-exercise oxygen consumption, HIIT can increase caloric expenditure and reduce body fat.

Composition and Timing of Nutrient and Fluid Intake

The body's preferred source of energy comes from muscles and liver glycogen stores; however, these stores are limited and not sufficient for sustained high-intensity athletic performance. Nutrient timing refers to effectively altering the content and timing of dietary intake—particularly carbohydrates and protein—to deliver optimal health and performance. Nutrient timing can involve the use of whole foods, isolated nutrients from food sources, and synthetic compounds, and it may vary by sport and among individuals. Research results have found that appropriate nutrient timing provides superior health and athletic performance compared to unplanned or traditional intake strategies.

Carbohydrate Loading

Carbohydrate loading is one specific nutrient timing strategy used by endurance athletes to help maximize glycogen stores. Recall that glycogen is glucose that has been converted from carbohydrates and stored in the muscles and liver. It is the body's preferred fuel source during moderate- and high-intensity activity. For optimal performance, it is important for athletes to have adequate stores of glycogen before beginning an endurance activity lasting 2 hours or more. To accomplish carbohydrate loading, athletes first deplete their carbohydrate stores by reducing carbohydrate intake while maintaining exercise volume and intensity about 5 days out from the event and then increase carbohydrate intake (to 8–10 grams per kilogram of body weight) and taper training volume for several days just before the event. Carbohydrate loading is typically recommended for activities that last longer than 120 minutes because this is roughly the threshold for depleting glycogen stores during intense exercise.

Nutrient Timing—Before, During, and After

Nutrient timing recommendations can be divided into three categories: before, during, and after exercise recommendations. The International Society of Sports Nutrition (ISSN) recommends 8–10 grams of carbohydrate per kilogram of body weight alone or with protein before resistance exercise to maximize glycogen stores. During exercise, 30–60 grams of carbohydrate per hour in 8–16 ounces of fluid should be consumed every 15 minutes or so. The addition of protein at a ratio of 3–4 grams of carbohydrate per 1 gram of protein may support endurance and the formation of glycogen after the activity.

For resistance exercise, the intake of carbohydrates alone or combined with protein improves muscle glycogen, minimizes muscle damage, and supports strength training efforts. Within 30 minutes after exercise, ingestion of carbohydrates and protein helps to rebuild glycogen stores; the ISSN recommends an intake of 8–10 grams per kilogram of body weight for carbohydrates and 0.2–0.5 grams per kilogram of body weight of protein in the post-exercise meal. The ISSN posits that the intake of essential amino acids (EAAs) stimulates muscle protein synthesis; adding carbohydrates to the amino acid intake may further help increase muscle protein synthesis. Finally, during bouts of continuous, prolonged strength training, consuming carbohydrates and protein together has been demonstrated to improve strength and body composition, typically in a 3 to 1 or 4 to 1 ratio of carbohydrates to protein.

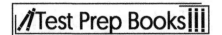

Nutritional Factors that Affect Strength and Endurance

The primary nutritional factors that affect muscular endurance, hypertrophy, strength, and aerobic endurance are carbohydrates and protein.

Carbohydrates

Carbohydrates provide fuel for neurons and red blood cells and are important for muscle contraction. They are also important because a state of positive energy balance is required in order to prevent muscle catabolism for energy. In order to support activity and meet metabolic and physiologic demands, athletes usually need about 55–65 percent of their total calorie intake to come from carbohydrates.

Protein

Once the diet contains adequate carbohydrates to promote positive energy balance, adequate protein needs to be addressed to maintain a positive nitrogen balance. Nitrogen balance is usually addressed via laboratory analysis and entails comparing nitrogen intake and output. Individual intake requirements vary based on the type, intensity, and duration of activity and training, but athletes typically need a protein intake of about 1.5–2.0 grams per kilogram of body weight to maintain a positive nitrogen balance. Endurance athletes need additional protein to help support energy needs and to facilitate repair and recovery after activity. Athletes who are focused on increasing strength and hypertrophy need more protein during the early stages of a training program; as muscles adapt to training, needs may decrease.

Protein is essential in the diet and is needed to support the building of connective tissue, cell membranes, and the development of muscle. Protein consists of amino acids, and there are twenty amino acids used in the body. There are nine essential amino acids (EAAs) that have to be acquired through the diet since they cannot be synthesized in the body. They are isoleucine, leucine, lysine, methionine, phenylalanine, threonine, tryptophan, valine, and histidine. This last one, histidine, was originally thought to only be essential for infants, but more recent studies have found that it is indeed essential for adults as well. Therefore, the discrepancy between sources that report that there are only eight EAAs and sources that report that there nine is caused by more outdated resources failing to recognize the newer research that the adult body also does not produce histidine in sufficient quantities (so it must be consumed).

There are also seven conditional amino acids that cannot be sufficiently produced in the body, so they should come from the diet: arginine, cysteine, glutamine, proline, taurine, glycine, and tyrosine. There are five non-EAAs: alanine, asparagine, aspartic acid, glutamic acid, and serine. These amino acids can be produced by the body so are not required in the diet.

Protein can be categorized as complete or incomplete. Complete proteins contain all of the EAAs, while incomplete proteins do not. Protein that comes from animal sources is usually complete and contains all of the EAAs, while incomplete proteins typically come from plant sources and do not contain all the EAAs. Proteins that have a higher amount of the EAAs are considered to have a higher amino acid profile. Good sources of animal protein include meat (beef, chicken, turkey, pork, and lamb), eggs, fish/seafood (tuna, crab, shrimp, lobster), and dairy (milk, yogurt, and cheese). Sources of plant-based protein include grains (brown rice, spelt, quinoa, amaranth, oatmeal), legumes (beans, peas, and lentils—pinto, black kidney, garbanzo, edamame, and tofu), and nuts and seeds (peanut butter, almond butter, peanuts, almonds, pistachios, walnuts, pecans, pumpkin seeds, and sunflower seeds).

Nutritional Needs of Athletes

Nutritional requirements for athletes are typically higher than for nonathletes and vary depending on the type of activity.

Carbohydrates

Carbohydrates provide 4 kilocalories per gram and are a major source of fuel for the body during moderate- and high-intensity exercise, up to 2 hours in duration. Beyond approximately this duration, stores deplete and the body relies on fatty acid metabolism for sustained energy. Carbohydrates are used for energy immediately, if needed, but excess carbohydrates are converted to glycogen and stored in skeletal muscles and the liver or converted to fat if the body's glycogen stores are full. The amount of glycogen the body can store is influenced by a variety of factors including physical training status, basal metabolic rate, body size, and eating habits, but in general, the body can store about 15 grams per kilogram of body weight. In general, athletes should consume about 6–10 grams of carbohydrates per kilogram of body weight daily, depending on the intensity, duration, and frequency of their training as well as their current health and physical goals.

Protein

Like carbohydrates, protein provides 4 kilocalories per gram. Protein, which consists of amino acids, is used to support the body in the development of tissues, enzymes, and hormones and to rebuild and repair muscles after exercise. In general, protein recommendations for athletes fall in the range of 1.5–2.0 grams per kilogram of body weight daily, depending on the type, duration, and frequency of exercise. Excessive consumption of protein does not lead to increased muscle mass because protein in excess of physiologic needs is converted and stored as fat.

Fat

Fat provides 9 kilocalories per gram and contributes significantly to resting energy requirements as well as requirements during low-intensity and long-duration exercise. Fats can be divided into two basic categories: saturated and unsaturated. Saturated fats, which are primarily found in animal sources, include butyric, lauric, myristic, palmitic, and stearic acid, while unsaturated fats typically come from plant sources such as soybeans, nuts, seeds, olives, and avocados. Fats should comprise at least 15 percent of the total caloric intake; as much as 30–40 percent can be acceptable, depending on the health, age, and needs of the individual. For athletes, an intake of 30 percent fat (10 percent saturated, 10 percent polyunsaturated, and 10 percent monounsaturated) aligns with dietary guidelines and should ensure an adequate—but not excessive—dietary intake.

The body's use of fat as an energy source during exercise depends on the length and intensity of the event and the athlete's fitness level. Generally speaking, two phenomena can describe an athlete's use of fat as an energy substrate during exercise: the crossover concept and the duration effect. The crossover concept refers to the fact that at lower intensities, the body is primarily using fat as a source of fuel, and as the intensity increases, the contribution of adenosine triphosphate (ATP) from carbohydrate metabolism increases. The duration effect is based on the principle that as the duration of the exercise bout increases, the body relies more heavily on fat, as carbohydrate stores deplete. Exactly how much of each fuel source is used also depends on the athlete's aerobic fitness; fitter athletes typically can store more glycogen but also use fat at higher intensities of exercise. Lastly, there is some evidence to suggest that women derive a greater percentage of their energy needs from fat, compared to men, at a given exercise workload.

Vitamins and Minerals

Vitamin and mineral needs of athletes may be increased but typically can be met if a balanced, varied diet is consumed with foods such as lean meats/protein, fruits, vegetables, whole grains, and dairy. B vitamins such as thiamin, riboflavin, and niacin are required to support metabolic processes; vitamin D is required for calcium absorption; and vitamins C and E are required to mitigate stress oxidation in the body. Fat-soluble vitamins (A, D, E, and K) are stored in the body, so they should not be consumed in excessive quantities. If an athlete is not meeting their vitamin and mineral requirements through diet, a multivitamin-mineral supplement is needed. Such supplements will not directly improve athletic performance, but they will help to correct a nutrition deficiency if one is present, which may prevent illness or improve performance.

Sweating can lower electrolytes and minerals such as sodium, potassium, chloride, iron, calcium, phosphorus, and magnesium. Sodium and potassium help to regulate the body's water balance and also play a significant role in muscle contraction. Chloride also helps with fluid balance and nerve conductions. Iron plays an important role in the body's ability to transport and use oxygen, and calcium is critical for bone formation, nerve conduction, and muscle contraction. Phosphorus is involved in intramuscular oxidation processes, and magnesium helps support energy metabolism. Electrolytes (sodium, potassium, and chloride) and water need to be replaced during extended exercise, particularly in hot and humid environments, because they are lost in sweat.

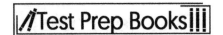

Effects, Risks, and Alternatives of Common Performance-Enhancing Substances and Methods

Ergogenic Aids and Dietary Supplements

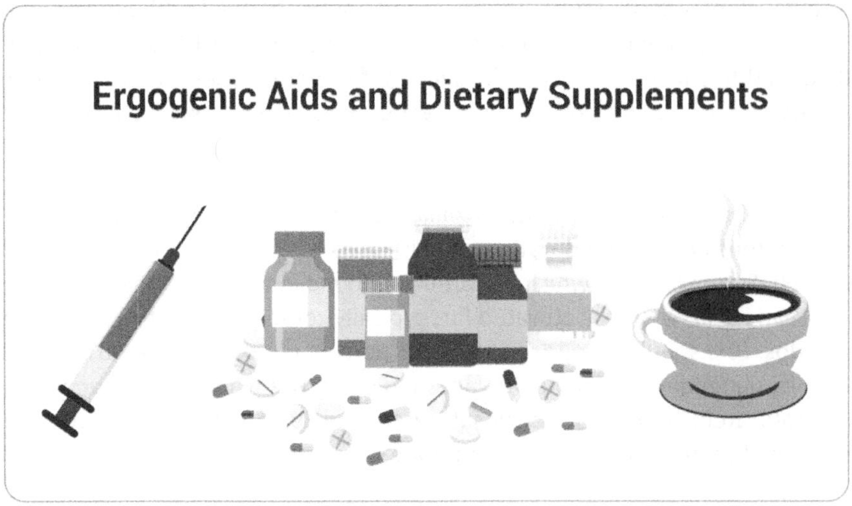

There are a variety of ergogenic aids and dietary supplements on the market available to athletes, and the options continue to grow as more supplements are created. Ergogenic aids are considered to be any substance, device, or practice that has the ability to enhance or improve an individual's performance. They can be categorized as nutritional, pharmacological, physiological, psychological, or mechanical. Availability and use of ergogenic aids have increased tremendously in the last 10 years, and research indicates that about half of the general population, 76 percent of college athletes, and nearly all athletes engaged in strength building use ergogenic aids. Some popular ergogenic aids for increasing muscle mass and strength include creatine, beta-hydroxy beta-methylbutyric acid (HMB), protein and amino acids, and beta-alanine. Popular aerobic endurance nutrition supplements include branched-chain amino acids (BCAAs), caffeine, sodium tablets, glutamine, high molecular weight carbohydrates, protein, sodium bicarbonate and citrate, and sports beverages.

Ergogenic Aids for Increasing Muscle Mass and Strength

Creatine

Creatine is a naturally occurring substance that is found in the kidneys, liver, and pancreas. It consists of the amino acids glycine, arginine, and methionine and can be found in protein sources such as meat and fish. Creatine supplementation is used to improve strength, increase lean body mass, and potentially aid in rapid muscle recovery during exercise. Creatine converts to creatine phosphate in the body, which is needed to make ATP, the energy molecule for muscle contractions. While research indicates that creatine can improve performance in high-intensity exercise, evidence does not support its use in endurance sports because it does not appear to affect aerobic metabolism.

Creatine monophosphate supplements are considered to be safe if used in recommended amounts by healthy individuals. The ISSN position on creatine monophosphate supplements concludes that creatine is an effective ergogenic nutrition supplement that athletes can use to enhance high-intensity exercise and lean body mass. The recommended regimen by the ISSN to increase muscle creatine is to take 0.3 grams per kilogram of body weight per day of creatine monohydrate for at least 3 days, then 3–5 grams per day to maintain the increased stores. Creatine at the rate of about 0.1 grams per kilogram of body weight per day added to a protein supplement may help further facilitate resistance training. The ISSN concludes that creatine monophosphate supplements may be used in youth athletes under proper guidance and supervision.

Beta-Hydroxy Beta-Methylbutyric Acid

Beta-hydroxyl beta-methylbutyric acid (HMB) comes from the amino acid leucine. HMB plays a role in the prevention of protein breakdown, or proteolysis. As a result, it is used in individuals with muscle wasting conditions and by athletes to enhance performance. HMB may be useful for individuals who are starting a strength training program and seeking to increase lean body mass. HMB can be safely used by youth and adults. Although HMB is commonly used as a supplement, it can be found in citrus fruits, catfish, and milk.

Protein and Amino Acids

Protein is needed to prevent muscle atrophy, even during strength training. The body needs to remain in positive nitrogen balance to prevent muscle atrophy and catabolism, which is the breakdown of muscle that occurs when protein is inadequate. Resistance training, along with positive nitrogen balance, is needed to build muscle. As such, protein or its building blocks (amino acids) must be present to ensure positive nitrogen balance. The RDA for protein of 0.8 grams per kilogram of body weight may be sufficient as a minimum for individuals not engaged in strength training; however, individuals engaged in strength training require at least 1.2–1.7 grams per kilogram of body weight.

When considering protein intake, it is important to consider the type of protein—complete or incomplete. Complete proteins contain all of the EAAs and usually come from animal sources. Incomplete proteins contain some of the essential nutrients and are found in foods such as beans, nuts, seeds, and grains. Incomplete proteins can be combined with other incomplete proteins or complete proteins to provide a complete amino acid profile. Athletes may also use other sources of protein isolates such as whey, casein, or soy in the form of powders, bars, drinks, etc.

Beta-alanine

Beta-alanine is used to enhance athletic performance, particularly high-intensity, anaerobic activities. Beta-alanine, a non-EAA, is a component of carnosine, along with histidine, and is produced in skeletal muscle. Carnosine is an essential buffering element in skeletal muscle. If beta-alanine is not present, carnosine production cannot occur. Beta-alanine supplementation increases muscle carnosine content, which helps to improve performance during high-intensity exercise by neutralizing acid production. Beta-alanine is usually supplemented in amounts of 3–6 grams per day for athletes engaged in anaerobic activity who are seeking performance enhancement.

Ergogenic Aids for Increasing Aerobic Endurance

Branched-Chain Amino Acids

Branched-chain amino acids (BCAAs), sometimes called the *proteinogenic amino acids,* are essential nutrients for building protein and include leucine, isoleucine, and valine. The term *branched-chain* refers to the chemical structure of the nutrients. BCAA usage is becoming increasingly popular with athletes engaged in aerobic activity, as they are believed to enhance recovery from exercise, reduce muscle damage, and decrease central fatigue.

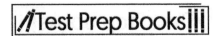

Research studies have used a range of doses for BCAAs; however, the optimal dose is not clear. Dosing for BCAAs should be based on body weight and intensity and duration of exercise.

Caffeine

Caffeine is the most widely used stimulant in the world. Research on the use and potential benefits of caffeine and athletic performance has continued to evolve, but current prevailing studies indicate that caffeine enhances endurance and alertness and reduces muscle soreness. Caffeine is known to be a mild diuretic, and as such, can potentially lead to dehydration during exercise activity if consumed in large amounts; however, this problem has not been widely cited in literature. The International Olympic Committee allows athletes to have up to 12 micrograms per milliliter of caffeine in their urine, and the National Collegiate Athletic Association (NCAA) allows 15 micrograms per milliliter in urine before any violation is cited. Optimal dosing of caffeine ranges from 3 to 6 milligrams per kilogram of body weight. Some individuals believe that caffeine should be eliminated from an athlete's diet prior to competition and that, because it is considered a gateway drug, youth should not be allowed to use caffeine.

Sodium Tablets

Sodium tablets for electrolyte replacement help prevent hyponatremia during exercise. The tablets usually contain sodium chloride, which is a dissolved salt in the body. Athletes who have hypertension or kidney disease should not take sodium supplements.

Glutamine

Glutamine is a nonessential amino acid, and it is the most abundant amino acid. It is found in the blood and muscles. Dietary sources of glutamine include beef, pork, chicken, fish, eggs, and dairy products. It has been shown to be effective in preventing illness and infection and reducing or preventing muscle soreness.

High Molecular-Weight Carbohydrates

Compared to other starches such as maltodextrin and dextrose, high molecular-weight carbohydrates are better for helping athletes replenish glycogen stores and increase gastric emptying. Waxy maize is an example of a high molecular-weight carbohydrate that does not contain sugar and is rapidly absorbed. Protein, as mentioned earlier, can be used in conjunction with carbohydrates to rebuild glycogen stores after exercise and has been shown to be more efficacious than high molecular-weight carbohydrates alone.

Sodium Bicarbonate

The use of sodium bicarbonate with caffeine 70–90 minutes before exercise has been shown to reduce fatigue. Sodium bicarbonate is essentially a buffer, which helps to prevent the acidic environment associated with fatigue during anaerobic activity. Sodium bicarbonate with citrate may lead to gastrointestinal discomfort, so it may not be the best solution for athletes.

Sports Beverages

Sports beverages support hydration, prevent hyponatremia through the maintenance and restoration of electrolytes, and help reduce fatigue during prolonged aerobic activity. Sports beverages can be divided into three categories: isotonic, hypertonic, and hypotonic. Isotonic beverages contain sodium and sugar in physiologically similar levels; hypertonic beverages contain more sodium and sugar than the body; and hypotonic beverages contain lower amounts of sodium and sugar than the body. Some believe that sports beverages with higher amounts of sodium and sugar are not needed unless athletes are engaged in activity lasting over 90 minutes. Sports beverages should ideally contain about 6–8 percent carbohydrates and be ingested at a rate of 3–8 ounces every 10–20 minutes for activities lasting around 90 minutes or longer.

Performance-Enhancing Substances and Methods

Anabolic Steroids

Anabolic steroids are synthetic derivatives of the androgenic hormone testosterone. Anabolic steroids are taken to stimulate protein synthesis, which can increase muscle size and strength, because this is one of the functions of natural testosterone. Therefore, the majority of athletes who use anabolic steroids are strength or power athletes. Testosterone is also responsible for the secondary sex characteristics, so anabolic steroid use can augment these characteristics in both males and females who take them. Additionally, like testosterone, they can cause aggression, irritability, and arousal.

When used as an ergogenic aid, anabolic steroids are usually "stacked," which means that multiple types are taken at one administration. This is done because the results of each drug are thought to be additive, such that taking a cocktail of different anabolic steroids together increases the effects or potency of each. Additionally, they are often taken in a pyramid-type dosing pattern wherein the dose taken is increased steadily over a period of weeks then dropped at the end of the cycle to minimize the side effects of excessively high doses.

Not only are anabolic steroids banned by sport governing agencies, but they also come with a variety of risks and adverse effects such as decreased heart function, hypertension, gynecomastia, impotence, acne, male pattern baldness, increased risk of tendon tears, hostility, and mood swings.

Blood Doping

Blood doping refers to artificially increasing the number of red blood cells in the body. This may be achieved by infusing red blood cells (either an autoinfusion [the athlete's own red blood cells] or a donor infusion) or by administering erythropoietin (EPO). EPO stimulates the body to produce red blood cells. Whereas red blood cell infusions rapidly increase red blood cell mass initially but results only last a few weeks, EPO allows the red blood cell count to continue to increase over time with continued use.

Since blood doping improves aerobic performance and the physical tolerance of endurance exercise, the majority of athletes who are guilty of partaking in this illegal practice are endurance athletes. Additionally, an athlete who is blood doping may have a higher tolerance for exercising at altitude and high heats because of the enhanced oxygen-carrying capacity of the blood and thermoregulatory ability afforded by more red blood cells and blood in circulation.

Impact of Alcohol and Drugs on Performance

As should be expected, the general consensus is that alcohol has a negative impact on athletic performance, although the degree to which it has an effect varies depending on the quantity and type of alcohol, the individual's body size and physiology, nutrition status, the type of exercise, and the timing of the intake relative to the bout of exercise. Research shows that acute alcohol use can impact motor skills, decision-making ability, hydration status, metabolism, and aerobic performance. Because it is a central nervous system depressant, it can also increase reaction times, reduce coordination, compromise judgment skills, and impair balance.

Most literature states that alcohol has the greatest impact on endurance exercise because the body preferentially metabolizes alcohol over carbohydrates and fats, affecting energy production. It also slows the Krebs cycle, increases lactate production, and inhibits gluconeogenesis. Any of these factors alone can increase the risk of injury, and added together, their effects elevate the risk. Alcohol use can also compromise the recovery process, which can have consequences for subsequent sessions of athletic activity. Consumed post-exercise, it can cause dehydration, sleep disturbances, and an inflammatory response in the body. It can also alter hormone activity, augmenting muscle protein breakdown and increasing cortisol production. In addition to these problems, chronic alcohol use can lead to body composition changes that are not ideal for athletes (increase in adipose tissue and decrease of lean body mass), nutritional deficiencies, and compromised immune function, all of which can increase the athlete's injury risk and are detrimental to overall health.

Practice Quiz

1. Which of the following is NOT a characteristic of a hypohydrated state?
   a. An increase in core body temperature
   b. A decrease in blood plasma levels
   c. A decrease in heart rate
   d. An increase in perceived exertion

2. When considering nutrition for hypertrophy, which amino acid is particularly beneficial and should be included in the diet every 3–4 hours throughout the day?
   a. Alanine
   b. Arginine
   c. Glutamic acid
   d. Leucine

3. A vegetarian athlete is experiencing fatigue, poor concentration, weakness, decreased exercise and work capacity, and a dry mouth. Which of the following may be the cause?
   a. She is anemic because vegetarian diets only include heme iron sources.
   b. She is anemic because vegetarian diets only include nonheme iron sources.
   c. Her body is protein deficient because vegetarian diets can only provide incomplete proteins.
   d. Her body is protein deficient because vegetarian diets provide an insufficient amount of protein to sustain training.

4. All EXCEPT which of the following are noted adverse reactions with creatine supplementation?
   a. Digestive distress and diarrhea
   b. Increase in blood pressure
   c. Stress on the kidneys
   d. Increase in body mass

5. What caloric intake level is recommended for most moderately-active females?
   a. 16 kilocalories per pound of body weight or 35 kilocalories per kilogram of body weight
   b. 17 kilocalories per pound of body weight or 37 kilocalories per kilogram of body weight
   c. 20 kilocalories per pound of body weight or 44 kilocalories per kilogram of body weight
   d. 23 kilocalories per pound of body weight or 50 kilocalories per kilogram of body weight

See answers on the next page.

Answer Explanations

1. C: A hypohydrated state occurs when hydration is inadequate to keep up the body's needs. It can lead to dehydration. It can cause an increase in core body temperature, a decrease in blood plasma levels, an increase in perceived exertion, and an increase in heart rate. Therefore, Choice *C* is the correct answer because heart rate increases rather than decreases.

2. D: Leucine is an essential amino acid, which means it must be consumed in the diet. The body cannot produce it internally. Even among the essential amino acids, leucine has been shown to be particularly critical for hypertrophy and muscle health. Athletes striving for muscle hypertrophy should consume meals that contain at least 20–30 grams of high-leucine protein every 3–4 hours throughout the day. The other amino acids listed are non-essential.

3. B: She is most likely anemic, as her symptoms are characteristic of low iron. Dietary sources of iron can be from heme sources or nonheme sources. Heme iron sources are animal-derived, such as red meat, fish, and poultry. Nonheme iron sources are those found in fruits, vegetables, grains, and iron-fortified breakfast cereals. Vegetarian athletes are susceptible to low iron levels because the bioavailability of iron in nonheme sources is quite poor, ranging from around 2–20 percent.

4. B: While creatine supplementation has many benefits for athletes, adverse effects can occur. These include an increase in body mass, gastrointestinal symptoms such as diarrhea, and stress placed on the kidneys because of the high nitrogen content. An increase in blood pressure is not typically noted as an adverse reaction to creatine supplementation.

5. B: It is generally recommended that moderately-active females consume around 17 kilocalories per pound of body weight or 37 kilocalories per kilogram of body weight. Choice *A* is more appropriate for females engaging in only light activity, while Choice *C* is for female athletes who engage in heavy activity. Choice *D* reflects the recommendation for male athletes who engage in heavy activity.

Movement Preparation

There are a variety of movement preparation techniques that strength and conditioning professionals should incorporate into training programs to help athletes warm up and prime their bodies for the workout to come. Some of the most common movement preparation techniques include soft tissue and flexibility/mobility work, such as Proprioceptive Neuromuscular Facilitation (PNF), CNS prep, and dynamic stretching.

Proprioceptive Neuromuscular Facilitation (PNF) is a technique that uses the neuromuscular responses to specific feedback from isometric and concentric contractions performed both actively and passively. These actions and responses result in changes in the muscle/joint tension relationships and enable greater ROM to be achieved. In this way, PNF uses neurological phenomena to facilitate muscular inhibition in a specific protocol designed to improve flexibility and decrease discomfort from stretching. PNF relies on autogenic inhibition whereby inhibitory signals from the Golgi tendon organs override the excitatory impulses from the muscle spindles, resulting in gradual relaxation of the muscle. PNF is typically completed with a partner.

Dynamic stretching or mobility drills emphasize the required movements of the planned activity, rather than individual muscles, by actively moving the joint through the ROM encountered in a sport prior to the sport. Dynamic stretching occurs before the activity as part of the warm-up routine to increase heart rate, temperature, and blood flow as well as CNS (central nervous system) and PNS (peripheral nervous system) activity to prepare the body. It promotes dynamic flexibility and mimics the movement patterns and ROM needed in sports activities without ballistic movements. It is less effective than static PNF stretching on increasing static ROM.

Preparatory Body and Limb Position

PNF stretching can be used for a variety of muscle groups such as the hamstrings, quadriceps, chest, and shoulder muscles. Positions vary depending on the muscle being stretched. For example, hamstrings are done with the athlete in the supine position.

For PNF, the partner or coach must not only apply appropriate resistance for the stretching athlete, but they must also be in the correct position, typically at the end range of the desired movement with the facilitator's shoulders and hips facing the direction of movement. The movements of the facilitator directly influence the movements of the athlete. The desired movement should bisect the facilitator's midline and center of gravity. The strength coach's body should be positioned in such a way that the resistance applied to the athlete should come from the trunk and hips, not the extremities.

A neutral erect spine and athletic posture should be maintained in dynamic stretching or mobility drills. Drills such as walking lunges and hip mobility drills should use proper squatting form.

Execution of Technique

There are three forms of PNF stretching: hold-relax, contract-relax, and hold-relax with agonist contraction, which all begin with 10 seconds of passive pre-stretch held at the point of mild discomfort. In the hold-relax form, after the pre-stretch, the partner applies a flexion force while the athlete holds and tries to resist the force, creating an isometric contraction for 6 seconds. The athlete then relaxes back into a passive stretch lasting 30 seconds, which is now a deeper stretch than the initial pre-stretch due to autogenic inhibition. Using the hamstrings as an example, in the contract-relax method after the pre-stretch, the athlete extends the hip while the partner resists this extension so that a concentric contraction occurs throughout the full ROM. After this, the athlete relaxes back into a passive hip flexion stretch of 30 seconds in duration, again deeper than initially performed due to autogenic inhibition (in this case, activation of the hamstrings). The hold-relax with the agonist contraction uses the idea of reciprocal inhibition, whereby the contraction of the agonist muscle causes relaxation of the antagonist so that after the regular hold-relax protocol, the second passive stretch is replaced with an active stretch to further increase the stretch.

Here are some examples:

With dynamic stretching, athletes typically complete 5–10 repetitions of each movement, either in place or over a given distance, with a progressive increase in the ROM and/or speed on each repetition or set. The movement mechanics of the sport should be reinforced in the mobility drill, along with the predominant joint positions, such as ankle dorsiflexion on a high knee drill for sprinters.

Cueing and Coaching, Monitoring for Safety

Athletes should be instructed to breathe and only push stretches to the point of mild discomfort to prevent overstretching. Because PNF relies on overriding neural regulation of the stretch reflex, it is important to exactly follow the protocols to protect the tendons and muscles. Strength coaches should pay extra attention to athletes nursing injuries or those with hypermobile joints.

With dynamic stretching, coaches should ensure that athletes move deliberately and progressively through the ROM, but in a controlled fashion that does not include bouncing. The focus should always be on proper technique and form while warming up the body and perfecting sport-specific movements.

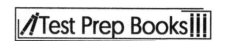

Assessment, Correction, and Modification of Exercise Technique

It is important that both the athlete and the partner or strength coach are in the proper positions and using correct techniques to effectively and safely use PNF. Coaches can get injured as well, if they attempt to provide resistance from their extremities rather than through the hips and trunk. They also must be sure to keep the hips and shoulders squarely facing the direction of movement to not induce any twisting of the spine.

Resistance Training Exercise Technique

Chronic resistance training affords strength, power, and coordination improvements as well as greater efficiency of the anaerobic systems. Nervous system adaptations occur quickly with training as motor units (an alpha motor neuron from the spinal cord and all of the skeletal muscle fibers it supplies) become conditioned to activate more efficiently, more quickly, and more often. These adaptions increase the neural stimulation for muscle fibers to contract. As more motor units activate and coordinate with each other, a higher percentage of fibers in a muscle contract simultaneously, which increases contractile strength. In fact, many of the earliest strength improvements noticed in resistance training programs are due to these neural adaptations rather than muscle hypertrophy, which takes approximately 4–8 weeks to occur. An athlete can quickly experience increases in strength and power as a result of training. Over time, muscle fibers increase in size while bone mineral density increases in load-bearing bones, helping mitigate age-related bone and muscle loss.

Free Weight Training Equipment

Dumbbells and barbells are the most commonly used free weight training equipment. While both involve "lifting weights," this equipment differs from resistance machines in that weight plates, dumbbells, and barbells in varying weights are typically held in the hands of the athlete for various exercises. Conversely, machines are prearranged setups where the athlete simply adjusts the weight and machine height. With machine equipment, an athlete can typically perform a minimal number of designated movements per machine, which are specifically designed for that exercise.

Preparatory Body and Limb Position

Proper form, including position and stance, varies depending on the free weight exercise. There are also modifications of basic exercises that alter grip position as a way to provide a different challenge to the muscles and to stress particular fibers. For example, typical dumbbell curls can occur in a standing or seated position, depending on the workout and goal of the exercise. The standing position recruits additional muscles, such as those in the core, to stabilize the body. When the exercise is done in a seated position, core muscles do not need to work as hard because the body's weight is supported by the chair, but this modification does require the targeted muscles (in this case, the biceps) to be more isolated and consequently work harder to lift the weight unassisted by any momentum that may be gathered while standing and swaying the body. Even with very skilled and disciplined athletes, the weight lifted during a seated curl may be less than the weight lifted while standing due to this muscle isolation. Therefore, trainers must consider the trade-offs of the two positions: adding a core workout component to a standing exercise versus truly isolating the primary muscle more directly by sitting.

Whether standing or sitting, athletes should be mindful to maintain proper posture with an erect spine, the shoulders back, chest out, and eyes gazing straight forward. Feet should be shoulder-width or slightly wider apart, and knees should have a slight bend when standing. During a seated curl, feet should be positioned flat on the floor under the knees, which are flexed to 90 degrees.

- *Grips*: As mentioned, grip position can also be tweaked. In a standard biceps curl, the athlete holds the dumbbell in the middle of the bar with a *supinated grip*, allowing muscle fibers to work equally and in the typical sagittal plane of motion for flexion. In a variation called *hammer curls*, the athlete holds the dumbbell in the middle of the bar but with a 90-degree internal rotation of the wrist so that palms are facing the hips, which is called a *neutral grip*.

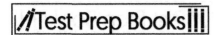

- This places slightly more of the workload on the lateral fibers of the biceps, working the lateral head more than the standard grip position. *Pronated grip* is also called *overhand grip* and occurs when the palms face the floor and the knuckles face the ceiling. In contrast, the supinated grip is also called *underhand grip,* and the palms face up while the knuckles face the floor. *Alternated grip* is when one hand is pronated and the other is supinated; *closed grip* is when the thumb is wrapped around the bar; and *false grip* is when the thumb does not wrap around the bar. Another grip pattern is the *hook grip.* It is similar to a pronated grip, but the thumb is moved under the index and middle fingers.

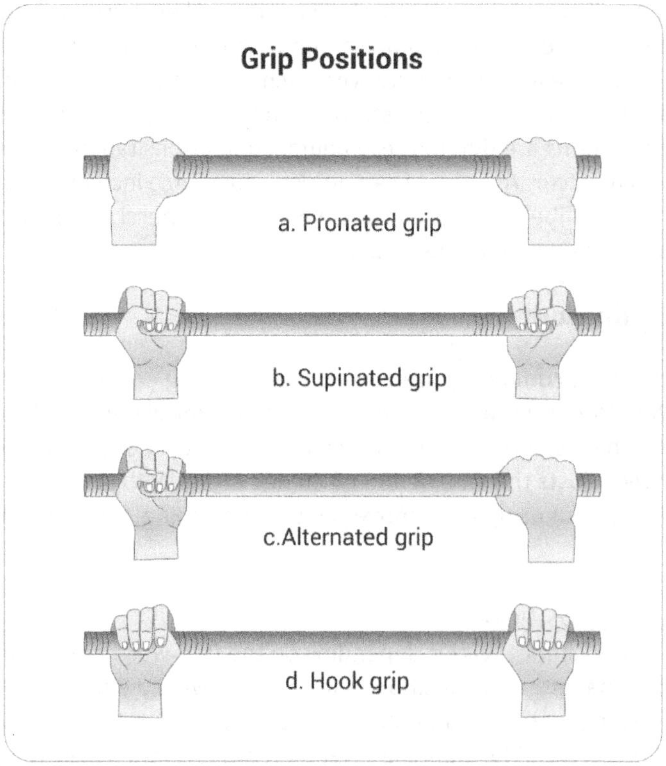

- *Squats*: Feet are typically slightly farther than shoulder-width apart, and toes should be pointing straight forward. As the athlete lowers the body into the squatted position, the hips should go backwards as if they are reaching to sit back in a chair, and the flexed knees should not come forward beyond the toes. Athletes should visualize pushing up through their heels to return to the fully upright position. Before performing squats, when facing the bar, it should be racked prior to execution at mid- to upper-chest level.

- *Free Weight Exercises*: Significantly more focus should be placed on proper form and stability of the body when performing free weight exercises than when using resistance machines, which typically support the body in the correct position and only allow movement in the desired plane. Because of this, particularly in less experienced athletes, the weight lifted in free weight exercises may be lower for any given exercise than that successfully attempted with the equivalent resistance machine. Strength coaches should pay attention to the form used while lifting in order to ensure that athletes are not swinging the weights, attempting to lift weights that are too heavy and relying on momentum for assistance, or using improper form, all which can increase injury risk.

Execution of Technique

The proper execution of lifting exercises with free weights should be demonstrated and explained thoroughly by strength coaches. Athletes often have different learning styles, so the execution and explanation of proper form and technique for exercises are imperative in order to convey this information to each athlete. Each exercise obviously has its own set of procedures for proper execution, but in general, emphasis on form and breathing technique will lead to successful execution. With exercises that are completed in a standing position, knees should be slightly relaxed and not locked, feet should be facing forward, and a strong core should be engaged to support the erect spine. Exercises in the seated and supine positions require five points of contact for optimal body support: the head is firmly on the bench or back pad, the shoulders and upper back are evenly placed and firmly on the bench or back pad, the buttocks are positioned evenly on the bench or seat, and both feet are placed flat on the floor.

In American society today, daily activities tend to focus on forward posture such as typing on a computer or holding a cell phone in front of the face and hunching over to type on it. This chronic slouched posture can lead to tightness in the anterior muscles of the chest and a stretching and weakening of posterior muscles of the shoulders, neck, and upper back. Strength coaches often need to remind athletes to pull their shoulders back and engage their rhomboids and keep their chest up and out, which opens it up for both improved breathing mechanics and a healthy posture. In all standing exercises, athletes should attempt to hold their bodies as still as possible in the upright position while refraining from swaying, rocking, or swinging the weights, which all use momentum to augment the lifting motion.

Athletes should be instructed to exhale, mostly through the mouth, during the concentric or more challenging lifting portion of the movement through the sticking point (the hardest point of the exercise). They should then inhale slowly through the nose during the eccentric or easier phase, depending on the motion. In most cases, holding the breath such as in the Valsalva maneuver is contraindicated, and it can greatly increase blood pressure and cause dizziness and disorientation. However, it can be used in certain core exercises, with care, as a way to increase torso rigidity and aid support of the vertebral column. This lessens compressive forces on the intervertebral discs and supports the normal and neutral lordotic lumbar spine. These same benefits can be achieved through the use of a weight belt, which should be used for exercises that stress the lower back, especially at near maximal loads.

With the exception of power exercises, free weight exercises should use a minimum of one or two spotters when an athlete moves the bar over the head or face, has it on the front of the shoulders, or is positioned on the back during the execution. When performing an incline bench press, the weight bar should make contact with the upper chest at the sticking point. In contrast, with a flat or decline bench press, the bar should make contact slightly lower—at or below the nipple line. There are a variety of squats, depending on the location of the bar, including front squats, back squats, and split squats (similar to a stationary lunge). With deadlifts, the conventional lift has the feet spaced about hip-width apart and hands outside of the stance. The sumo modification places the feet wider than a conventional squat, outside of shoulder-width, and the hands are inside of the stance. Romanian deadlifts are similar to conventional ones in that the feet are hip-width apart and the hands are outside of the stance.

- *Common Mistakes*: Athletes should only lift the weight that they are able to manage while safely completing the exercise with proper form through the entire range of motion, maintaining control of the weight during the lowering, eccentric phase. A common mistake is selecting a weight that is too heavy and cannot be lifted through the full range. Then the weight is dropped quickly in a hurried, uncontrolled manner due to gravity. For example, if an athlete is doing a dumbbell chest press, the weights should be pushed all the way up until the elbows are straight (but not locked), with the arms fully extended up and away from the chest. If the weight is too heavy, the athlete cannot fully extend the arms and noticeable flexion will remain in the elbows. As the weights are brought back down to either side of the chest, the coach may notice the weights plummet precipitously or even drop to the floor. This is dangerous and negates the muscular work of slowly lowering the weight. The athlete misses out on the training effect and the strength benefit of lowering the weight slowly.

- *Arousal*: For maximal benefit from any resistance exercise, athletes should dedicate their focus on form and breathing, concentrating on the workout, keeping distracting conversations to a minimum. There is an optimal point on the arousal-relaxation curve, also known as the "Inverted U" due to its shape, for best performance—somewhere in the middle of the two extremes of being too lackadaisical and too anxious about the lift. Some anticipation, anxiety, and arousal can increase levels of epinephrine, which actually primes the system for increased strength performance. On the other hand, too much stress and arousal can flood the system with epinephrine and increase heart rate and blood pressure beyond helpful levels. This can lead to a detrimental state where the exercise on top of the increased sympathetic nervous system response drives these physiologic variables too high, resulting in the body reducing its physical output during the exercise. These athletes may need coaches to calm them by working on relaxing visualizations and reducing pressure. This will help to lower their arousal state so that excess epinephrine does not negatively impact performance. Athletes who are too relaxed and unfocused do not reap the benefit of this hormonal influence on performance, and these athletes may need cheering, motivation, verbal "pumping up," and some small stimulus of external pressure to increase their arousal.

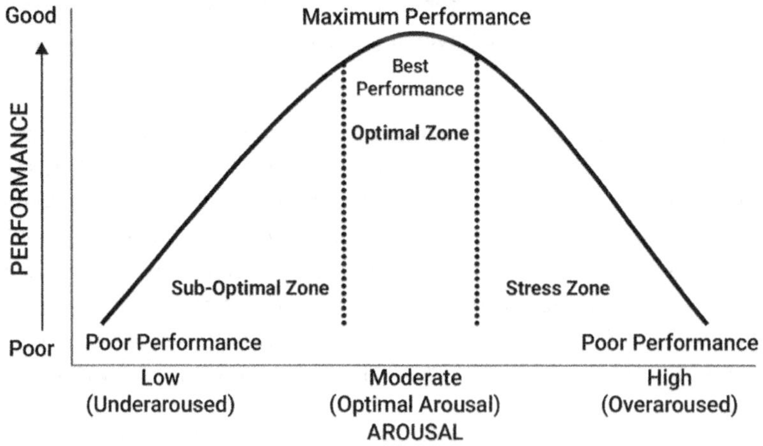

Spotting Procedures and Technique, Cueing and Coaching, and Monitoring for Safety

Spotting procedures help athletes complete exercises safely and efficiently. Not only do coaches need to know how to execute correct spotting techniques, but they must also be able to demonstrate and teach the techniques to athletes so that they can spot one another during partner activities. Spotting also helps monitor an athlete's lifting form and movement execution, allowing the spotter to give verbal cues and help correct any errors in execution. It also allows for motivation, instruction, encouragement, feedback, and certain exercise modifications that would otherwise be dangerous and physically impossible without spotters.

An example is negative resistance training, wherein athletes can handle greater weight on the eccentric or lowering portion, but need spotters to help raise the weight in the concentric phase. Spotters should be prepared to offer as much help as needed. Clear communication between the lifter and spotter is required for safety, and the pair should discuss the lift before it occurs. The spotter should ensure that the weights are evenly spaced and equally loaded on the bar and that the collars are properly used.

The required number of spotters is determined by the load being lifted, the experience and skill of the athlete and spotters, and the physical strength of the spotters. The spotters must be strong enough to handle the load that the athlete is lifting with little notice and sometimes in less than ideal angles and positions. Therefore, it is crucial that spotters are honest with themselves and lifters about their abilities. It is better to err on the side of caution and use multiple spotters when necessary, as long as they can be accommodated spatially around the lift without being overly cumbersome.

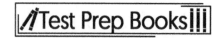

With the exception of power exercises, free weight exercises should use a minimum of one or two spotters when an athlete moves the bar over the head or face, or has it on the front of the shoulders or positioned on the back during the execution. During power exercises, athletes should be instructed to push the bar away or drop it when the bar is in front and to release it or jump forward when the bar is missed behind the head. A spotter should not be used. Two spotters are sometimes needed with heavy lifts, especially bar lifts, where one spotter should be at each end of the bar.

The location of the spotter or spotters depends on the lift being attempted. For exercises with heavy weights on a bar such as a front squat, often two spotters are needed—one at each end of the bar—to help balance the weight with the athlete and to lift from either side should an issue occur. For standing exercises such as squats and deadlifts, spotters should stand behind the lifter while the bar is still on the rack and as the lifter gets into position.

They should then move as close as possible toward the lifter without touching them, as the lifter steps away from the rack with the bar. The spotter's hands should be in the ready position near the bar while the lifter raises and lowers the weight. Once the set is complete or when failure is indicated by the lifter, the spotter should assist the lifter in returning the bar to the rack by holding on to the bar and guiding it back to the racked position. During exercises such as a dumbbell bench press, spotters should keep their hands near the lifter's forearms, close to the wrists. For a seated overhead triceps extension with a barbell, spotters should straddle the flat bench.

Once the spotter and the lifter are in the correct positions, the spotter needs to pay attention to their body and limb placement for their own safety during the lift as well as that of the athlete. When spotting over-the-face barbell exercises, the spotter should grasp the bar with an alternated grip, usually narrower than that of the athlete's grip. The spotter also should use a solid, wide base of support and a neutral spine position. Spotters should use an athletic stance, with feet slightly wider than hip-width apart, knees flexed, arms and hands up and in a ready position that is close to the bar and the athlete without touching them.

Bodyweight should be equally and soundly distributed on both feet, which should be firmly planted on the ground. Spotters must follow the movement of the athlete and the bar with their eyes as well as their hands and remain intensely focused on the task at hand until the bar is re-racked. Spotters and lifters should communicate throughout the lift if anything changes, but it is the spotter's job to verbally motivate and check in with the lifter, since the athlete is likely less physically and mentally able to talk during maximal exertion.

Assessment, Correction, and Modification of Exercise Technique

Strength coaches must correct improper technique as early as possible in the learning process in order to prevent the development of bad habits and to reduce the risk of injury. Even advanced athletes may demonstrate poor technique when fatigued, distracted, or unmotivated, so observing and giving cues on preparatory and execution forms and techniques should be a constant focus for strength coaches during workouts. For maximal effectiveness, feedback should be as specific and timely as possible, and it should be either visual, auditory, and kinesthetic, depending on each athlete's learning style. Strength coaches may position athletes in front of a mirror so they can observe and self-correct deviations in form, sometimes concurrent with a proper form demonstration alongside the athlete for comparison.

Coaches can also pair up athletes who have different skill levels to promote a learning/teaching mentorship. This can also help more experienced athletes develop leadership roles while also finding a reason to focus on their own form, which may need some fine-tuning as the athlete becomes complacent with experience. Strength coaches can use videos and handouts to supplement learning or break down exercises into smaller movement steps for kinesthetic learners. Feedback should always be positive, supportive, and instructive regardless of the method used to provide the feedback. This keeps the learning environment comfortable while motivating the athlete.

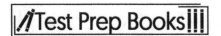

Resistance Machines

Resistance machines typically enable the proper form to be achieved more easily for exercises because they only allow movement in certain planes of motion based on the mechanical setup of the levers, hinges, pulleys, and movable pieces. However, this guidance, restriction, and stabilization make exercises completed on resistance machines less sports-specific than free weight, plyometric, or body weight exercises in which the athlete must stabilize the body while moving through the range of motion. Weight machines can be good for senior athletes and others who have poor balance and coordination. They can also be a good starting place for beginners or used for certain exercises for individuals recovering from injuries. This is because these machines are generally safer to use and usually isolate one movement, which makes them easier to use. Beginners can grasp one specific movement at a time.

Resistance machines can be helpful for rehabilitating certain body parts because they generally isolate a specific muscle group. In general, this is not advantageous for overall strength-training, especially for sports-specific work, which is important to competitive athletes. However, resistance machines have their place, particularly in injury rehab, solo sessions, rapid circuit training, and reaching higher maximal lifts. For heavy weights and maximal efforts, most machines have the advantage of not requiring a spotter, although athletes should still always exercise caution when attempting any lift. Some machines force the correct movement for the lift, which may help reduce the risk of injury and ensure that the athlete is moving through the entire range of motion for each repetition. Machine workouts can be more efficient because they are generally organized in a circuit in the layout of the gym, so the athlete can easily move from one to another. With that said, if athletes prioritize saving time and they do not properly adjust the settings to fit the machine to their body, athletes can "cheat" in the movement and increase injury risk.

As mentioned previously, most weight machines require the athlete to move the weight in a predetermined path, making it difficult to strengthen the stabilizer muscles. Similarly, usually only one exercise can be completed on each machine, making it cumbersome to keep getting up, moving to another machine, and adjusting the settings accordingly. Most machines are designed for the average-sized adult, so small youth athletes, slight women, or significantly taller and larger athletes may find the fit less than ideal. Even when the machine is adjusted as much as possible, the resulting fit may be uncomfortable and may cause difficulty performing the exercise correctly.

Preparatory Body and Limb Position

Proper form with a good neutral erect spine, chest up and out, feet flat on the floor, and shoulders back should be used on machines. The height of the bench or chair portion can usually be adjusted so that the knees are flexed to 90 degrees and the feet are flat on the floor. For machines such as the leg press, the feet should be placed on the platform slightly wider than hip-width. Knees should flex in alignment with the ankles, refraining from any tendency to deviate them laterally, which internally rotates the hips and places undo stress on the lateral compartment of the knee. Hand grip should be neutral and evenly spaced in most cases, unless a narrow or wide grip is specifically introduced as a modification. Most machines have pictures of proper alignment and positioning of pads and bars so that athletes can adjust the machine to fit their bodies. Athletes should align their joint axes with the axis of rotation of the machine to optimize joint function and prevent any incongruity in the moving axes, which can induce injury.

Execution of Technique

As with free weight exercises, proper technique on resistance machines is imperative, both to prevent injury and to maximize the benefit of the exercise. The proper execution of lifting exercises with free weights should be demonstrated and explained thoroughly by strength coaches. Each exercise obviously has its own set of procedures to carry it out properly, but in general, emphasis on form and breathing technique will lead to successful execution. Many resistance machines execute the movement in the seated position. As mentioned, exercises in the seated and supine positions require five points of contact for optimal body support: the head is firmly on the bench or back pad, the shoulders and upper back are evenly placed and firmly on the bench or back pad, the buttocks are positioned evenly on the bench or seat, and both feet are placed flat on the floor. The same general guidelines for execution that have been previously discussed should be employed with machine-based exercises as well.

Spotting Procedures and Technique, Cueing and Coaching, and Monitoring for Safety

Typically, spotters are not required with most resistance machine exercises, unlike for free weight exercises. This is because the machines will not allow the weight to fall on the athlete, even if the attempt at the lift fails. With that said, spotting can still be helpful with very heavy lifts or if the athlete is new to the exercise. In these cases, the spotter can provide verbal feedback in the way of instruction or encouragement and help correct form problems. A spotter should also be used if the athlete is uncomfortable with the lift or machine.

Assessment, Correction, and Modification of Exercise Technique

One of the benefits of resistance machines is that they make it more challenging to have improper technique compared to free weights and alternative strength-training modalities because of the constraints imposed by the design of the machines. Nevertheless, strength coaches should monitor athletes on the training floor and quickly correct any deviations from optimal form to prevent injury and to maximize the benefits of training. Athletes should be instructed to adjust settings on the machine, both in terms of sizing and resistance, to meet their individual bodies, even if working with a partner in a circuit when it would be more time-efficient to share the same setup. Mirrors work well to provide visual feedback to athletes, but their effectiveness is limited by the athlete's understanding of proper form, attention to detail, and the desire to perform exercises correctly. For this reason, strength coaches still need to monitor athletes when they are using resistance machines.

Alternative Modes of Training

Alternative modes of training include core work, stability, balance, calisthenic, and bodyweight exercises. Such exercises augment training and may help prevent injuries. Plyometric training such as pull-ups, push-ups, chin-ups, squat thrusts, lunges, yoga, jumping jacks, and planks provide resistance in the form of bodyweight. These exercises improve relative strength, core strength, and body control and they are low-cost. Many of these activities can be performed outside on the field or in an open gym with an entire team. Some coaches find that adding body work such as yoga to an athlete's regime supports athletic goals in a less intense fashion while improving flexibility, focus, breathing, and core strength. To help improve acceptance and adherence, strength coaches should educate athletes on the benefits of these practices if they are unfamiliar with them. Calisthenics can be used in conjunction with dynamic warm-ups to prepare the athletes for practice and competition.

Preparatory Body and Limb Position

For push-ups and pull-ups, arms should be roughly shoulder-width apart, although modifications affecting hand spacing are often introduced to provide variable challenges to the muscles. For example, diamond push-ups have the athlete place their hands together, directly under the chest, with the index fingers and thumbs of each hand touching to form a diamond. This modification places extra emphasis on the triceps rather than the chest muscles, such as the pectoralis major, that are emphasized during a regular push-up. With core exercises, it is important that the spine stay neutral and that athletes do not pull up on their neck while doing crunches or sit-ups. They should use their core muscles to lift the shoulder blades off of the surface, with their hands simply supporting the weight of the head rather than pulling it upward.

Yoga and Pilates incorporate many poses and positions and should be guided by a trained and certified professional. Lunges and squats require an athletic stance, feet slightly wider than hip-width apart and flat on the floor. For athletes who are limited in squat depth due to tight Achilles tendons, elevating the heels on a weight plate or other incline will help achieve a deeper squat, despite limited range of motion in the ankles. These athletes should be guided through a regular static stretching routine to help improve ankle mobility.

Execution of Technique

Bodyweight exercises improve relative, but not absolute, strength. With these exercises, athletes are often able to safely complete a higher number of repetitions than more traditional "weight lifting" exercises. This can improve muscular endurance and help prevent fatigue during long-duration activities. Athletes should inhale during the concentric or challenging phase through the sticking point and exhale on the eccentric or easier phase. The spine should stay neutral, with shoulders, hips, and ankles in alignment. While risk of injury is often lower with bodyweight-only exercises due to smaller loads than those imposed by external weights, proper form should still be followed.

Assessment, Correction, and Modification of Exercise Technique

Strength coaches should pay close attention to athletes' form and technique for common mistakes such as a swayed back on push-ups or planks or raised buttocks above the plane of the body. Other issues to note include athletes using momentum or craning and pulling the neck during core work and positioning the knees past the ankles with the hips not sitting far enough back during squats and lunges. Because of the lack of external weights used during bodyweight exercises, it is sometimes easier to perform them with improper form while not feeling any obvious physical signs of discomfort that are commonly experienced with weighted exercises. In order to prevent the development of bad habits and to reduce the risk of injury, strength coaches must correct improper technique as early as possible in the learning process. Strength coaches should always focus on observing and giving cues on preparatory and execution forms and techniques, even when working with advanced athletes, since fatigue, distractions, and lack of motivation can cause anyone to perform with poor technique.

Non-Traditional Implements

In recent years, there has been an increased interest by athletes and coaches to implement non-traditional equipment for strength and resistance training, power and speed training, and overall conditioning. Tires, logs, water-filled pipes, sandbags, kettle bells, heavy battle ropes, and a variety of medicine balls have entered the training arena, popularized by some adventure races, CrossFit, and other innovative or rogue training programs. Such implements are creative ways to essentially add tools to the tool bag of a strength coach, while accomplishing similar physiologic goals for the athletes. Still, coaches must be aware of when and how to properly use this equipment and be sure to educate and supervise athletes in their use. Much of the non-traditional equipment is best reserved for advanced athletes who have the basic foundations of movements, such as a well-mastered squat and deadlift, because programs with non-traditional equipment tend to use heavier implements in power movements that can induce injury if the exercise is not performed properly.

Nontraditional Implement-Training Methods

Strongman Training

Strongman training is a method that provides a demanding workout as well as instability by utilizing nontraditional implements in exercises. Weighted sleds, logs, tires, and stones are just a few of the implements that can be used. One of the possible benefits of strongman training is the increase in blood lactate levels due to the high-intensity training stimulus.

Log Lifting

The design of the logs used in this method generally allows for a mid-range pronated grip position. Athletes can add weight to the logs, but the amount of weight they'll be able to lift is usually less than the amount they could lift using traditional lifting equipment. During log lifting, the typical lifting movement is related to the movement in a power clean, although other movements (e.g., presses, rows, deadlifts, jerks, lunges, and squats) can be used. It has not been determined how log lifting can be used in athletic training for sports. Additionally, to date, there is not enough scientific evidence illustrating how successful log lifting is as a method of training.

Farmer's Walk

This training method utilizes resistances and loads that are unwieldy and unstable. The athlete is required to engage the core while walking straight ahead holding a load at each side, which means the load is static. Variable loads cans be used as well. Potential benefits of the farmer's walk are improved grip strength, back endurance, and total-body anaerobic endurance. However, safety can be an issue since there hasn't been enough research done to determine the best safety practices for this training method.

Tire Flipping

Before using tire flipping as a training method, a suitable tire must be chosen for the athlete. The athlete should always be taller than the tire. Shorter tires are easier to maneuver, so increasing the height of the tire will increase the challenge in flipping it. The width of the tire will also depend on the height of the athlete. Tall athletes, who typically have long arms, will need wider tires, while short athletes, who typically have shorter arms, will require more narrow tires. The tire's tread is another factor when choosing a tire. It is harder to grip and handle tread that is worn down, so it is best to choose tires with deep tread. However, for safety purposes, deep tread needs to be inspected for any rubble or metal in the crevices as well as any damage.

There are three flipping techniques that can be employed in training:

- The sumo style approach is characterized by a wide sumo deadlift stance. The athlete uses a narrow grip to bring the tire up to the level of their hips or chest. After turning their hands to face forward on the tire, they use a pressing action to complete the flip of the tire.

- In the backlift style, the athlete uses a narrow stance (feet at hip-width), flexes the knees and hips, and then grabs and pulls the tire. This is similar to the motion for a deadlift. The athlete repositions their hands when the tire is raised, allowing for completion of the flip with a forward-pressing action.

- When using the shoulders-against-the-tire technique, the athlete kneels, facing the tire, with dorsiflexed ankles and feet hip-distance apart. The chin and shoulders rest against the tire while the hands grip the tire with a supinated grip. The placement of the hands will be wide if the tire is narrow and narrow if the tire is wide, with the goal being to keep the arms as straight as possible. While lifting the knees from the ground and staying on the balls of the feet, the athlete leans into the tire, putting most of their weight into the tire. As the chest lifts, the muscles of the lower back contract. Extension of the hips and knees along with plantarflexion of the ankles produce the movement that forces the tire up and forward. The hips and shoulders rise and the athlete takes a few steps. As the tire reaches the height of the hip, one hip flexes and the quadriceps come into contact with the tire, forcing the tire to continue its upward movement. At the same time, the athlete quickly changes to a pronated position of the hands and then extends the arms while stepping toward the tire, forcing the tired to be pushed over.

Kettlebell Training

A kettlebell is a weighted implement comprised of a ball with an attached handle that can be used to perform a variety of exercises such as kettlebell swings, single leg Romanian deadlifts, and Sumo squats. Research has shown that kettlebells can be used to develop fitness. Kettlebell swings positively affect cardiovascular fitness, although to a lesser degree than treadmill running or other types of aerobic exercise. Kettlebells have been found to increase muscular strength levels. Six weeks of kettlebell training has been shown to improve vertical-jump performance and muscular strength, but these improvements are less than those achieved with traditional resistance-training exercises.

Kettlebells are best used for general preparation exercises such as squats and bent-over rows, while more traditional modes of exercise are used to develop strength and enhance athletic performance. There are different types of kettlebells. Sport kettlebells are made of steel and all weights are the same size, while cast-iron fitness kettlebells are various sizes depending on weight. When selecting the appropriate kettlebell, the handle size of cast-iron kettlebells will indicate the weight, with increasing handle size corresponding to increasing weight. Polished steel handles should be chosen over painted handles because steel handles grip chalk better and do not get as slippery from sweat as painted handles.

Unilateral Training

Unilateral or bilateral training can be used for the upper or lower body. Unilateral exercises are often used to reduce an athlete's bilateral asymmetries when asymmetries exist between unilateral and bilateral movements. They are also used as part of rehabilitation programs. Bilateral movements have been shown to increase voluntary activation of the agonist muscle(s). This is known as bilateral facilitation. It is observed in trained athletes and stronger athletes. Athletes who are untrained, weaker, or injured should use unilateral training. However, trained athletes should avoid this training style.

Examples of lower-body unilateral exercises include:

- Step-ups
- Lunges
- Single-leg squats/ Bulgarian split squats

Preparatory Body and Limb Position

Some non-traditional training implements can be used to improve grip strength. Heavy ropes require the athlete to grip very tightly while forcefully swinging the ropes. Similarly, some sandbags lack traditional handgrips, so the athlete must squeeze the material tightly while powerfully moving it. An athlete's stance and core engagement should be emphasized for all training exercises. For tire-flipping activities, athletes should use a wide base of support when squatting and keep the spine in the neutral lumbar lordosis position to protect the lower back and knees. A weight belt can help support the lumbar spine. Kettlebells offer somewhat of an exception to the rule against swinging weights and harnessing momentum, and in fact, many exercises specific to kettlebells, such as kettlebell swings, rely on swinging for proper form. In this exercise, power should come from thrusting the hips forward and not from the shoulders lifting the implement.

Execution of Technique

Many of the non-traditional exercise tools provide a challenge for anaerobic and strength-building workouts. Strength coaches should demonstrate the proper execution of each movement and should consider the use of mirrors so that athletes can monitor their own form. Weight belts can be helpful in certain cases with maximal loads. As with traditional resistance exercises, athletes should exhale through the more challenging phase of the exercise, including the "sticking point," and then inhale slowly after the "sticking point" through the completion of the movement. The Valsalva maneuver is likely inevitable when loads are greater than 80 percent of maximum, but it does help stabilize the spine and decrease intradiscal pressure. When activities require speed, force, or a combination of the two (power), athletes should be prepped, focused, and ideally aroused to bring about optimal performance.

Assessment, Correction, and Modification of Exercise Technique

Particularly when using a training implement for the first time, athletes will need extra supervision and critique of form. Strength coaches should be prudent to work with only a few athletes at a time so that athletes can get individualized attention, instruction, clarification if they have questions, and correction of improper form. While non-traditional equipment can bring fresh variety into a training program, it does have the potential for increased risk of injury if athletes are not properly trained, both in terms of their skill level as well as the particular instruction on the equipment usage.

Olympic Lifting and Plyometric Exercise Technique

Olympic lifting focuses on explosive lifting of higher weights in specific, defined motions (such as squat, deadlift, clean, and snatch). Olympic lifting challenges the cardiovascular and musculoskeletal systems by utilizing the anaerobic pathways.

Plyometric training involves jumping and power exercises such as box jumps, squat thrusts, burpees, and hurdle drills to train the muscles to achieve maximal force in the shortest time. These explosive activities help strengthen an athlete's ligaments, tendons, joints, and muscles for sports-specific movements in order to better tolerate the physiologic demands of competition. Athletes who are susceptible to injury—particularly those with poor bone density or prior ligamentous or tendon injuries (especially to the knees) or those who are post-surgery—should only do plyometric training under carefully monitored and modified conditions due to the strains and forces induced by such explosive jumping. Young athletes and senior athletes can safely do plyometric training in a more modified fashion to control the load on the body. For example, box jumps or depth jumps are likely not safe for these populations, but bounding or skipping drills and one-legged hops can be implemented into programs in healthy athletes. However, the frequency of such activities should be limited to a day or two per week, with several rest days in-between. Even at such infrequent intervals, plyometrics can play a role in improving fitness and power without posing a substantial injury risk.

Preparatory Body and Limb Position

Plyometric exercises usually involve some sort of jumping, so athletes should be taught proper landing. This involves using the arms to reduce momentum and flexing the knees to attenuate the landing forces. Athletes should engage their core muscles to help brace the torso and to provide support to the intervertebral discs. It is imperative that athletes focus their eyes on the spot they intend to jump to and maintain mental focus during each individual repetition to prevent tripping and accidental injuries. It is best not to engage in such activities late in a workout when the neuromuscular system and mental focus might be fatigued. Most plyometrics are performed with the hands either relaxed or open and flat in the neutral position, with the palms facing the body, such as in sprinting form.

Execution of Technique

Plyometrics use quick, powerful movements that involve a pre-stretch or countermovement. This serves as a stretch-shortening cycle and increases the power of subsequent movements by harnessing the stretch reflex. It also uses the natural elastic components of tendons and muscles. With the stretch-shortening cycle, rapid eccentric contractions elicit the stretch reflex and the storage of elastic energy, which increases force production of the subsequent concentric contraction. Plyometrics can be completed for the lower body, trunk, and upper body areas and can include depth jumps, medicine ball throws, catches, pushups, box jumps, and bounding drills. Adequate rest is needed between repetitions and between sets, such as 5–10 seconds between box jumps and 2–3 minutes

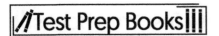

between sets. Depending on the sport and skill level, these exercises should only be completed one to three times per week in training.

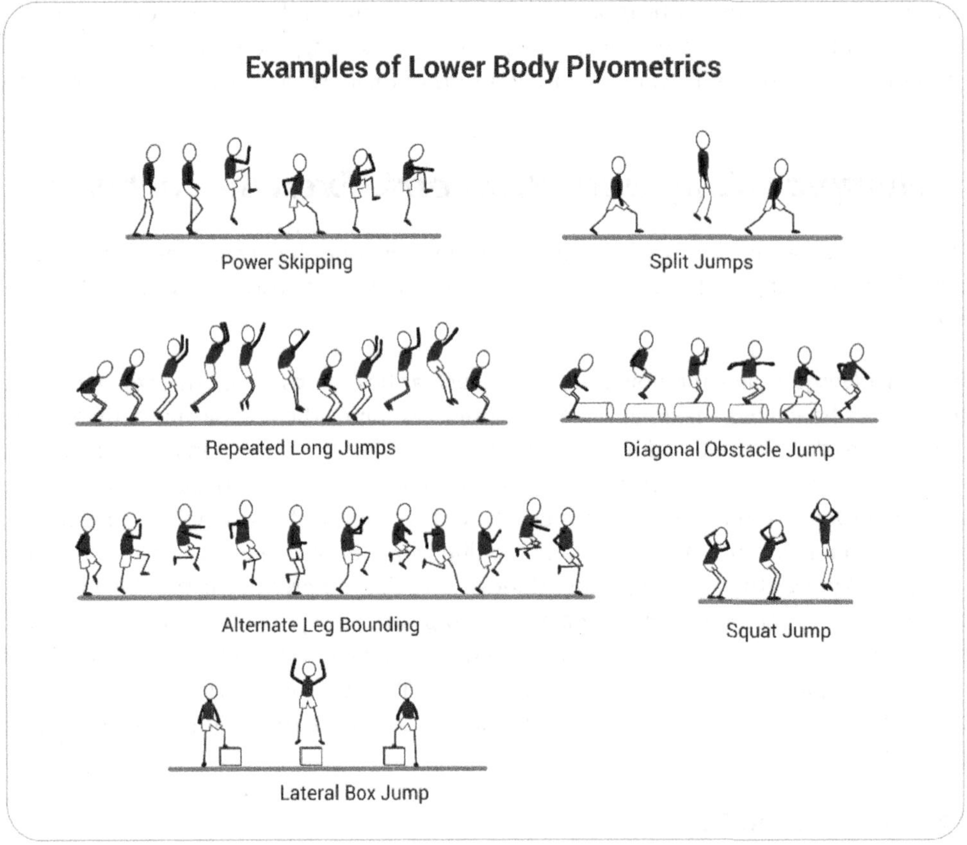

Assessment, Correction, and Modification of Exercise Technique

Because of the demand on the body during plyometric exercises, proper technique is imperative to avoid injury. Also, heavier athletes (over 220 pounds) should be constantly monitored for any joint tenderness. Special care must be considered for previously injured athletes, senior athletes, youth, and athletes with balance issues. Proper footwear and soft, rubberized flooring or grass should be used to reduce landing forces. With plyometrics, it is especially imperative to prevent the development of bad habits and to reduce the risk of injury by correcting any improper technique that is observed as early as possible in the learning process. If fatigued, distracted, or unmotivated, any athlete may demonstrate poor technique. Therefore, observing and giving cues on preparatory and execution forms and techniques should be a constant focus, even when working with advanced athletes. For maximal effectiveness, feedback should be as specific and timely as possible, and depending on the athlete's learning style, it should be either visual, auditory, or kinesthetic.

Teach and Evaluate Speed/Sprint Technique

Many athletes can benefit greatly from improving their sprint and speed techniques. The improvements can increase the maximal velocity with which the athletes can accelerate and move. Strength, in the sense of sprinting, is somewhat different than with resistance training. Force application in sprinting enables the athlete to accelerate, reach high velocities, and maintain these speeds. Force is defined as mass multiplied by acceleration. For athletic endeavors, the rate of force development (RFD) combined with impulse is important since force must be generated in a short time interval. Rate of force development is an index of explosive strength, referring to the development of maximal force in the minimal time interval, while impulse is the generated force multiplied by the time required for its production. Speed can be improved with sprint training, downhill and uphill training, and technical foot drills. Sprint training with resistance is often performed using sleds or parachutes.

Fundamental training objectives for increasing running speed center on the following:

- Minimizing ground contact braking forces: This can be accomplished by maximizing the backwards velocity of the foot and leg at touch-down and by working on creating this touch-down moment with the foot firmly under the center of gravity of the body.
- Emphasizing the brevity of ground support time: This helps bring about rapid stride rate, which takes explosive strength and can be improved through careful and specific plyometric exercise.
- Prioritizing functional training of the hamstring muscles: These muscles act simultaneously as concentric hip extensors and eccentric knee flexors: as the leg swings forward, the eccentric knee flexor strength has the greatest impact on the leg's recovery.

Preparatory Body and Limb Position

Track sprinters use blocks to help them accelerate rapidly by enabling a powerful push-off. These athletes essentially pre-load the leg like a spring by pressing backwards onto the block with their flexed leg and dorsiflexed foot, storing potential energy in the series elastic components of tendons and muscles. This enables a rapid transfer to kinetic energy when the race begins. The front knee is flexed about 90 degrees and the rear knee is flexed from 110–130 degrees. Hip angle varies with sprinting ability and experience. The front hip is flexed at 40 degrees in elite sprinters and 50 degrees in sub-elite sprinters. Additionally, the rear hip is at 80 degrees in elite sprinters and at 90 degrees in sub-elite sprinters. The athlete should place their hands just behind the starting line slightly wider than shoulder-width apart and the fingers held together. Each thumb should bridge out to the side and should be directly under each shoulder, ready to support the bodyweight. Gaze should be downward, with the back of the head and spine in alignment.

Execution of Technique

Speed is influenced by stride rate and stride length, so athletes should focus on quick turnover and powerful steps. Of these factors, stride rate has a greater impact on speed and should be the focus when designing programs for improving sprinting speed. Elite sprinters are able to perform about 5 strides per second. As running speed approaches maximal for a given athlete, stride frequency increases more than stride length to contribute to additional speed gains. Ground contact time decreases about 50 percent from the acceleration phase to maximal velocity running. Impulse production becomes more and more dependent on the athlete's ability to generate explosive ground reaction forces (GRFs). The single leg support phase of running includes the eccentric braking component and the concentric propulsion.

The flight phase of running is comprised of the recovery and ground preparation. Stride rate and stride length typically increase over the first 15–20 meters or 8–10 strides. During this time, forward lean decreases from about a 45-degree angle to fully upright by about 20 meters. Gaze should be directly forward, arms forcefully pumping at the sides with a lightly closed, relaxed fist or an open hand. Knees should drive upwards toward the chest. The core should be engaged to limit trunk rotation, support the diaphragm, and keep movement efficient.

Arms should be flexed about 90 degrees and swing toward the forehead to help overcome inertia and to increase momentum. At the start of the sprint, runners push explosively out of the blocks. The rear leg produces the greater initial force but loses ground contact earlier. However, the front leg assumes a greater influence on starting velocity and exerts force for a longer duration. In elite athletes, the peak initial forces can exceed 1500 N, and impulses can exceed 230 newton-seconds. As the front leg reaches its final amount of extension, the rear leg swings forward for the subsequent stride. During the acceleration stage, the swinging leg's thigh is perpendicular to the trunk, and the lower leg is parallel to the trunk. At maximal velocity, the flexed leg acts like a pendulum and thrusts forward at the maximal speed to assist with leg power at push-off. The lower leg swings forward passively when the thigh reaches its maximal possible knee lift.

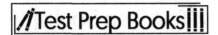

When the forward leg starts to make contact with the ground at the toe, it makes light contact with the ground slightly in front of the body's center of gravity. As weight is transferred to this leg in the forward support phase of the body, the ball of the foot fully supports the body weight, and the trunk is fully upright or assumes a 5-degree forward lean. In the rear support phase, triple extension helps the body push up and propel forward in a hip-knee-ankle angle of 50–55 degrees, with propulsion velocity dependent on push-off impulse and direction. In the maximal velocity phase, leg drive ability is facilitated by explosive arm action, somewhat like hammering, where the hands swing forward above shoulder height and the upper arm is parallel to the trunk. Then the arm swings downward and backward past the pocket area and the hips. The shoulders should be held steady, with the elbows flexed to 90 degrees and the hands lightly cupped. The mouth should be left open and relaxed to prevent any unnecessary muscular fatigue.

Assessment, Correction, and Modification of Exercise Technique

Coaches can help guide athletes in correcting form and technique with drills such as high knees, bounding, turnover drills, resisted sprints, and assisted sprints (downhill). Video analysis and playback as well as practicing with blocks can be helpful. It can be difficult to truly change running form in a radical way, but athletes can significantly improve speed and other aspects of technique through appropriate drills and a scientific approach to training. Parachutes and sled pulls provide added resistance to sprinting and strengthen the athlete's muscular and cardiovascular systems as well as their force and power. However, they should be reserved for more trained and experienced athletes, particularly sled pulls, which can cause injury if form and technique are poor or if an athlete is fatigued, weak, prone to injury, pre-pubescent, or elderly. For children, parachutes are a safer choice but should still be used with caution. Deep-water running and shallow-water sprinting drills can also be used to provide added resistance with the goal of improving strength, stamina, and ability.

Agility Technique

Agility is loosely defined as an athlete's overall coordinative abilities and technical skills used to perform the wide range of motor tasks of the sport, from fine motor control to gross, powerful, and dynamic tasks. Agility is an important component of many athletic endeavors and relies on perceptual-cognitive ability as well as the ability to decelerate and re-accelerate in the intended directions and as quickly and seamlessly as possible. Combined with speed, agility allows athletes to outperform competitors with quicker ball-handling skills, breakaways, and tactics. Agility is not simply about the change of directions: it involves changes in speed, decision-making, cognitive development, and biomechanical and metabolic efficiency.

The following factors influence agility:

- Adaptive ability: how well the athlete can respond to observed and anticipated changes in the condition or sports situation and modify their actions accordingly
- Balance: the ability to establish and maintain static and dynamic equilibrium in the body
- Combinatory ability: ability to coordinate movements of the body during a given action

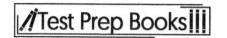

- Differentiation: the ability to accurately adjust body motions and mechanics in an efficient, economic way
- Orientation: location, control, and movements of the body within spatial and temporal parameters
- Reactiveness: the rapid, correct response to various stimuli
- Rhythm: ability to respond and implement appropriate timing and variation of dynamic motor patterns

These parameters vary in their degree of modifiability through training, depending on the athlete's age and skill level. Preadolescent athletes are generally in a time period considered to be critical and sensitive for skill development. During this time, the coordinative abilities are thought to be the most trainable. Training should center on more basic movement patterns to establish competency and build a strong baseline level of fitness. Younger athletes may not yet specialize in just one sport, which is actually advantageous for preventing injuries and developing a well-rounded athlete with the basic abilities needed for most athletic endeavors. During adolescence, athletes begin to lose some of this plasticity for skill development and should turn to specific skills and abilities for their targeted sport of focus. Agility training can include ladders, directional drills, cone drills, speed changes, line sprints, and other technique-driven footwork.

Preparatory Body and Limb Position

Preparatory body positioning for agility training depends on the exercise or drill to be performed. Nearly universal across exercises, athletes stand with their gaze forward or slightly downward to keep targets in their peripheral vision. Arms should be relaxed in the athletic position; hands should be positioned with somewhat of a slight lateral angle that is deviated in some cases for additional balance; and bodyweight should be concentrated on the forefoot rather than the heel. This allows for quicker turnover and more precise movements. There is a tendency for the athlete to slouch or drop the shoulders downward while concentrating on the ground below the foot in some situations, such as when using agility ladders. However, it is important, as with all athletic activities, to attempt to maintain as much of an upright posture as possible, with a neutral spine that is in alignment with the head and the neck. Agility training requires tremendous visual and mental focus. Athletes should be reminded to breathe in a controlled and purposeful manner. Much of the training is not particularly demanding in a cardiovascular sense, but proper breathing mechanics are always important.

Execution of Technique

Agility training requires athletes to use quick, light steps so that they are able to change directions and speeds readily. Body weight should be concentrated on the forefoot, and knees should come up toward the chest by firing hip flexors and core muscles. To strengthen the cognitive aspects of agility training, athletes should visualize the movement patterns prior to execution. For sports that require a high degree of agility, it's usually most effective to incorporate agility work into training nearly each day during the athletic training program, but only for a short amount of time due to the technique and focus required.

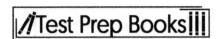

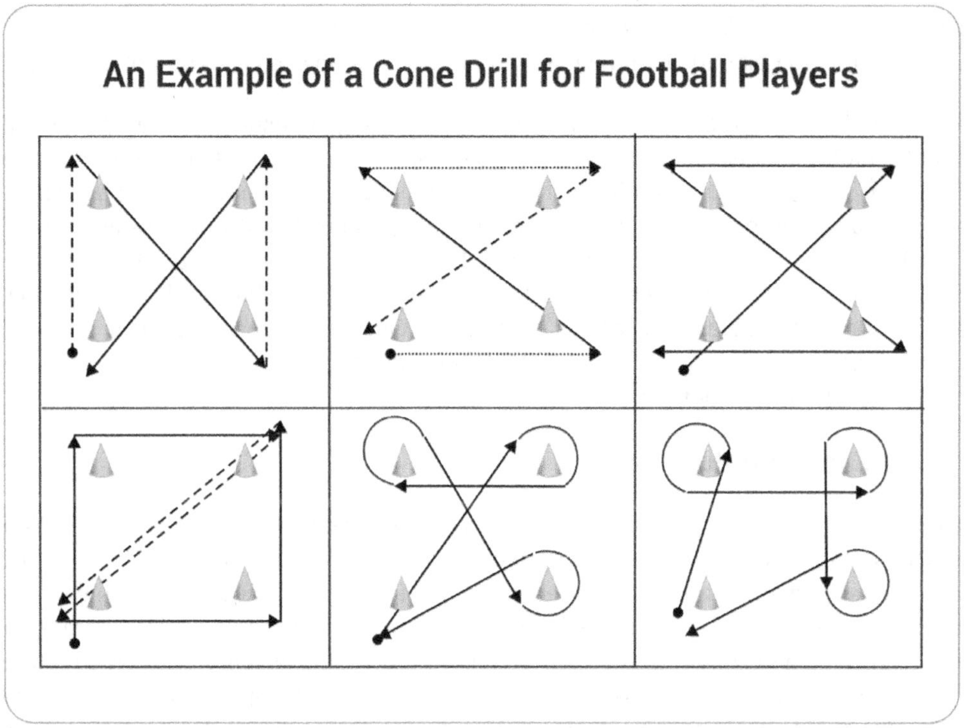

An Example of a Cone Drill for Football Players

As an athlete fatigues, the completion time for various agility exercises will increase due to slower physical performance as well as reduced mental capacity, which causes an increase in both reaction time and decision-making time. In almost all sports, agility and changes in direction or speed are not pre-planned or programmed, but must be made as instantaneous decisions. Athletes have to react to the environmental conditions, the game play, the movement and position of defending athletes, and ball position. Aspects of this on-the-fly decision-making ability are affected and improved simply with game experience over time, but some degree of rapid decision-making skills can be improved through agility drills.

Assessment, Correction, and Modification of Exercise Technique

Strength coaches can use verbal cues and video analysis to help guide technique issues. Agility practice takes time and focus, and improvements can be slow. It is important for both the athlete and coach to set reasonable goals and be patient. A lack of agility for certain skills such as cornering, backward running, and certain maneuvers such as crossovers and sidestep cutting has been implicated as a mechanism of injury in athletes. Therefore, it is important that strength coaches take the time to work with athletes to improve agility, reaction time, coordinative abilities, and rhythm. As with all fitness modalities and aspects of training, strength coaches should correct improper technique as early as possible in the learning process. In order to foster a warm learning environment and keep the athlete motivated and comfortable, all form correction feedback should be positive, supportive, and instructive.

Energy Systems Development

Aerobic energy systems need to be trained for improvements in cardiovascular fitness, metabolic conditioning, and muscular endurance. These are important for all sports; in particular, for endurance sports such as distance running, swimming, soccer, and cycling. Heart and skeletal muscle hypertrophy are the chronic adaptations that occur with regular cardiovascular and resistance training, respectively. With cardiovascular training, the heart enlarges and chamber size increases, allowing for a greater stroke volume and cardiac output. This enables the heart to be more efficient, with a resultant lowering of the resting and submaximal exercise heart rate and blood pressure. This, in turn, increases exercise time and intensity tolerance. Blood volume, both in terms of plasma and hemoglobin, increases oxygen-carrying capacity. Lactic acid metabolism also improves, allowing the aerobic system to break it down more effectively for usable energy, and muscle glycogen storage increases. Vasculature also increases, so blood perfusion of muscles improves. Other positive adaptations include increased bone mineral density, improvements in body composition, and neural adaptations.

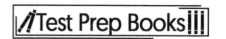

Aerobic Conditioning Activities

Strength coaches can make use of a variety of cardiovascular machines such as treadmills, bicycles, rowing machines, stair steppers, elliptical trainers, arm ergometers, and Arc trainers. The choice of the equipment may depend on the athlete's sport, training goals, availability, preference, injury, and workout plan. Coaches should teach athletes how to use the console, how to properly program the machine with the various inputs, and the proper form for each piece of equipment. For example, it is a common mistake to set an improper seat height on spin bikes and stationary bikes. This often results in a seat that is too low, a knee that is too flexed, and a less-efficient stride. Athletes should set the seat height so that they can fully extend their knee and straighten the leg downward. From there, they should lower the seat so that the knees flex about 10 degrees at the lowest point in the cycle rotation.

Machine Programming and Setup

Many cardiovascular machines have programmable workouts such as intervals, hills, and tempo sessions. They may even record heart rate to gauge intensity, or athletes may select manual or free mode. These programming options are chosen at the beginning of the workout and inputted into the console along with age, weight, and workout duration. Resistance, speed, and incline can be changed during the workout. There is often a safety button or clip that should be engaged for safety. Spin bikes use a dial that can change the relative resistance on the flywheel.

Preparatory Body and Limb Position

Athletes should use normal, healthy posture whether seated or standing and refrain from leaning on handrails. The spine should be in optimal alignment, with shoulders back and chest open. Athletes should avoid reading or watching videos since these activities can compromise form or cause slouching. On elliptical machines that have arm pedals, the elbows should be flexed to roughly 90 degrees, hands should have a neutral grip, and shoulders should remain relaxed. A recumbent bike can be used when the torso needs significant support (e.g., in cases of upper extremity injury or rib fracture). However, in terms of cardiovascular benefit, this machine typically falls significantly short of other modes. On all cycle types, athletes should keep their torso upright and refrain from oscillating from side to side with each alternating pedal stroke.

Pedal rate should typically mimic that of running at about 90 revolutions per minute, unless the athlete is specifically working on turnover, in which case the resistance can be lowered and over-speed training can occur. Some bikes display metabolic equivalents (METs), which serve as an indication of energy expenditure over that at rest and can be used as a gauge of intensity. Resistance coupled with speed factor into bicycling METs, while body weight, incline, and speed (pace) influence metabolic equivalents during treadmill running. An arm ergometer can be a good choice in cases of severe lower extremity injury or disability, or for athletes who need to work on upper body strength and muscular endurance, such as gymnasts and swimmers. This machine involves sitting upright in the provided chair and pedaling with the arms, much in the same way a normal bicycle functions with the legs.

Execution of Technique

Proper technique on cardiovascular equipment should parallel the technique used for the same activity outdoors. For example, runners on a treadmill should use arms flexed comfortably at the side, refraining from swinging them excessively across the midline. The feet should land at midfoot and not plod heavily on the heels; the body should be upright with good posture, with a slight forward lean if the treadmill is set on an incline. Athletes should use steady, constant breathing and avoid gasping and hyperventilating. If a workout is too intense and oxygen demand cannot keep up with oxygen supply, intensity may need to be reduced, unless it is designed to be an anaerobic interval. Particularly when athletes are injured and using cardiovascular equipment to cross train, they can use visualization techniques during the activity to practice mental imagery and focus.

Assessment, Correction, and Modification of Exercise Technique

Coaches should ensure that athletes are using proper form and focusing on the workout at hand. There is a tendency for athletes to "zone out" on cardiovascular equipment in an attempt to distract themselves, so coaches should stress the importance of proper form, the goal of the workout, and the role of the exercise within the training program. Strength coaches should correct improper technique as early as possible in the learning process in order to prevent the development of bad habits and reduce the risk of injury.

General Body-Only Activities

"Body-Only" exercises such as running, swimming, walking, and dance are easy modalities for athletes to implement in their training programs when they are away from the gym and its various equipment. Most sports involve some amount of running as well, so this activity is particularly important for training. Swimming provides an excellent cross training activity because it improves cardiovascular and muscular fitness while reducing stress on joints and tissues in a non-weight-bearing environment. Strength coaches may supplement training with body-only activities, especially during the off-season or breaks from school when athletes might not have easy access to a training facility.

Execution of Technique

Running and walking techniques are fairly innate and can be somewhat difficult to modify, especially in older athletes. However, strength coaches should evaluate running form for any obvious aberrations that might increase injury risk, such as heel strike, over-striding, excessive or insufficient arm swing, or hunched posture. Cadence should be roughly 90 steps per minute per leg for most healthy athletes regardless of absolute speed. Swimming requires a great deal of technique, so strength coaches may need to defer to swimming coaches for proper instruction. Swimming economy and efficiency are greatly improved with proper form, breathing technique, arm pull, and kicking pattern. In the absence of solid technique, many highly trained athletes struggle significantly with endurance swimming, so individualized critique of form and drills might need to be implemented. It is optimal for athletes to learn to breathe on both sides during freestyle swimming.

Assessment, Correction, and Modification of Exercise Technique

Video analysis of running form and swimming form might help in the coaching and correction of improper form. Specialized swimming coaches can be useful for giving pointers on improving technique. As with other aspects of training, strength coaches should correct improper technique as early as possible in the learning process in order to prevent the development of bad habits and to reduce the risk of injury. Strength coaches should focus on observing and giving cues on preparatory and execution forms and techniques during workouts. When fatigued, distracted, or unmotivated, even advanced athletes may perform with poor technique.

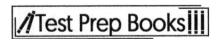

For maximal effectiveness, feedback should be as specific and timely as possible, and depending on the athlete's learning style, it should be either visual, auditory, and kinesthetic. Strength coaches may position athletes in front of the mirror so they can observe and self-correct deviations in form, sometimes concurrent with a proper form demonstration alongside the athlete for comparison. Coaches can also promote learning/teaching mentorships by pairing up athletes who have different skill levels. This can also help more experienced athletes develop leadership roles while also finding a reason to focus on their own form, which may need some fine-tuning as the athlete becomes complacent with experience. Regardless of delivery method, all form correction feedback should be positive, supportive, and instructive in order to foster a warm learning environment and keep the athlete motivated and comfortable.

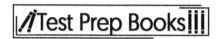

Anaerobic Conditioning Activities

There is a wide variety of anaerobic training techniques, often implementing intervals (periods of high-intensity activity interspersed with recovery rest periods), including the following:

- heavy battle rope exercise
- jumping rope
- climbing hills and stairs
- line sprints or surges
- high-intensity conditioning drills:
    - jump squats
    - burpees
    - high knees

Almost all sports have some degree of reliance on anaerobic energy systems, so this form of training needs to be prioritized in strength and conditioning programs.

Execution of Technique

Proper form is especially important during high-intensity activities when muscles, joints, tendons, and ligaments are under very high loads and speeds, subjecting them to increased force and demanding power. Strength coaches should instruct athletes to land all jumps with soft and slightly flexed knees, to pump arms powerfully and efficiently, and to breathe as much as possible. Even though these activities are not consuming a significant amount of oxygen due to their intensity and reliance on anaerobic metabolism, focusing on adequate breathing helps to maintain proper form and quickly oxygenates the muscles and removes metabolic byproducts of anaerobic metabolism, which assists in a more rapid and comfortable recovery. When running stairs or uphill sprints, athletes should lift knees as high as possible. They should maintain a slight forward lean from the ankles (not the waist) and use aggressive, powerful arm swings. When descending, steps should be light and quick. Slight knee flexion will help protect knee cartilage and ligaments. Some athletes might choose to walk down hills backwards or otherwise mix up the downhill routine.

Heavy battle ropes are a great training tool for a total body workout, upper body power, endurance, and anaerobic bouts. There is a wide variety of exercises and patterns that can be implemented. A proper athletic stance should be encouraged, with the good squatting form of knees flexed, hips staying back behind the ankles, erect spine, good posture, chest up and out, and eyes forward. Most anaerobic activities are short enough in duration that athletes should be able to maintain mental focus on sustaining intensity and using good form throughout the duration. Coaches should provide adequate recovery between bouts of heavy exertion to ensure that athletes are able to truly maximize their efforts on each attempt.

Assessment, Correction, and Modification of Exercise Technique

Coaches should monitor athletes for improper form and correct it as soon as possible, even stopping an interval early rather than letting the athlete continue with possibly injury-inducing mistakes in form. Particularly with inadequate rest or increasing fatigue, form is likely to break down, even in athletes who are skilled. In these cases, workouts might need to be shortened, or rest intervals might need to be prolonged to keep the athlete performing with proper form to reap the maximum benefits of the programmed workout.

Recovery Techniques

As mentioned, recovery is a crucial component of any sound training program. Recovery should be built into each session in one way or another, and recovery techniques can be used by athletes between sessions to reap the most out of the work done in training. By optimizing recovery, injury and illness risk are reduced. Additionally, the body is better able to rebound to perform at higher levels of intensity sooner than if the athlete did nothing to encourage recovery between sessions. Sleep, hydration, cryotherapy, hydrotherapy, tissue mobilization, and static stretching are strategies that are frequently employed to aid recovery.

Flexibility exercises can help improve range of motion, prevent injury, and prevent muscle, ligament, and tendon tightening. They also have a positive impact on elements of the nervous system, such as the Golgi tendon organs, and they prepare the body to recruit the necessary motor units for optimal athletic performance. Athletes should receive coaching on proper and improper stretching techniques, including how to hold a position in a comfortable and moderate stretch without causing pain.

Static stretches should follow the completion of the workout, especially for excessively stiff athletes or those with previous injuries. Static stretching exercises can improve the muscle tension and joint relationship over time. Static stretches done prior to exercise can reduce explosive power and increase joint laxity when stiffness is required for energy conservation, placing an athlete at greater risk of injury.

Preparatory Body and Limb Position

Static stretching should take place after the workout while the muscles are warm. There is a variety of static stretches, most targeting the major muscles of the body. Some can be completed standing, such as the standing quadriceps stretch with the foot coming up behind the buttocks, stretches for the shoulders and chest, and standing hamstring and calf stretches. Seated stretches are mostly for the hips, glutes, and hamstrings. Supine stretches can be for the quadriceps, low back, and abdominals. During all static stretches, the athlete should be instructed to maintain good posture and joint alignment, keeping joints within their normal range of motion (ROM) without hyperextension as well as keeping them within their typical planes of motion (e.g., sagittal plane for flexion) without undue twisting and contorting.

Execution of Technique

Stretches are typically held at the end range of motion for 30 seconds, followed by a brief rest, then repeated for two to three total sets. The body should be held as still as possible, refraining from any bouncing or excessive reaching and relaxing. The joints should always be in safe, anatomically-normal positions (i.e., without hyperextending or twisting out of typical planes of motion). For example, the traditional hurdler's stretch, with one leg extended in front of the body and the other knee bent with the foot back behind the buttocks, twists the knee and can damage ligaments and is therefore contraindicated. Breathing should be smooth and steady, and athletes should focus on the tension in the muscles and imagine elongating and releasing the tension.

Assessment, Correction, and Modification of Exercise Technique

To correct improper technique and prevent injuries, strength coaches should watch for ballistic, bouncing movements, joints that are twisted or hyperextended, and athletes who are grimacing or otherwise showing signs of excessive stretching.

Practice Quiz

1. Which of the following is an appropriate cardio modality for an athlete who needs weightbearing, non-impact exercise?
    a. Treadmill
    b. Stationary bike
    c. Elliptical
    d. Stair stepper

2. What does the Valsalva maneuver entail?
    a. Exhaling fully and then increasing abdominal pressure by trying to inhale while holding the glottis closed
    b. Exhaling fully and then increasing abdominal pressure by trying to inhale while trying to open the glottis for deep belly breathing
    c. Inhaling using deep belly breathing and then increasing abdominal pressure by trying to exhale while holding the glottis closed
    d. Inhaling using deep belly breathing and then increasing abdominal pressure by trying to inhale while holding the glottis closed

3. To ensure that joints are not enduring unnatural and unhealthy stress, which improper technique must the strength and conditioning professional be cognizant of when observing athletes doing agility drills?
    a. Failing to extend the hips, knees, and ankles upon acceleration
    b. Failing to flex the hips, knees, and ankles upon acceleration
    c. Failing to extend the hips, knees, and ankles upon deceleration
    d. Failing to flex the hips, knees, and ankles upon deceleration

4. Regarding adjustments for a stationary bike, which of the following is NOT true?
    a. The forefoot should stay in contact with the pedals of the bicycle throughout the pedal stroke
    b. At least five or ten degrees of knee flexion should occur at the bottom of the pedal stroke
    c. The handlebar height should ensure the athlete is in an upright position and the shoulders are prevented from rounding forward while pedaling
    d. Terminal knee extension should be avoided during the downward pedal stroke

5. What is the order of the four segments that explain each motion of the lower legs throughout the sprinting movement?
    a. Eccentric braking phase, concentric propulsive phase, recovery phase, ground preparation
    b. Ground preparation, concentric propulsive phase, eccentric braking phase, recovery phase
    c. Concentric propulsive phase, eccentric braking phase, recovery phase, ground preparation
    b. Ground preparation, concentric propulsive phase, recovery phase, eccentric braking phase

See answers on the next page.

Answer Explanations

1. C: The elliptical machine provides a non-impact form of exercise while still being a weightbearing modality because the user is standing upright against gravity. The treadmill and the stair stepper, Choices *A* and *D,* are not non-impact exercise, so they are incorrect. The stationary bike, Choice *B,* is not a weightbearing modality, so it is incorrect.

2. C: The Valsalva maneuver can help provide stability. It involves inhaling using deep belly breathing and then increasing abdominal pressure by trying to exhale while holding the glottis closed. This built-up abdominal pressure helps the athlete maintain a neutral spine, which increases the stability and safety of the movement or exercise.

3. D: Strength and conditioning professionals should ensure that as the athlete is moving through agility drills, he or she is properly flexing the hips, knees, and ankles upon deceleration to help attenuate forces. A common mistake is for athletes to change direction with a stiff, extended leg. This can be very unsafe, as it places high forces on the joints of the body.

4. A: The midfoot, rather than the forefoot, should be in contact with the pedals for optimal biomechanics and force production. The other adjustments listed coincide with the recommendations for stationary bikes.

5. A: The sprinting movement includes four main segments or phases for the lower legs. The first segment is the eccentric braking period of the lead leg. In this phase, the lead leg is extended, the ankle is pointed toward the knee, and the knee is slightly flexed so that it does not lock out terminally. The concentric propulsive phase begins once the transfer is made through the foot. During this segment, the lead leg applies a vertical force to the ground to propel the body forward, and the lead leg is pulled under the body until it releases from the ground. As the athlete propels forward, the lead leg becomes the trailing leg as it reaches the next segment, which is the recovery phase. During the recovery phase, the ankle starts dorsiflexing and the knee starts flexing as it recovers and prepares for another ground contact. The last segment is ground preparation. As the trailing leg starts to prepare to become the lead leg, the knee flexes to the same position that it acquired during the eccentric braking segment.

Program Design

Conducting a Needs Analysis

The first step in designing an appropriate program for an athlete is to create a needs analysis. The needs analysis helps the strength and conditioning professional compare the requirements of the athlete's sport to the athlete's current fitness level. An athlete's ability to complete certain movement patterns will help identify any problems with body mechanics and specific muscle groups. Physiological tests will help the coach determine the demands that the athlete's sport places on the body, which can form the basis of a conditioning and resistance-training program. The athlete's history of injuries will also help the coach anticipate potential problems the athlete may have with certain muscle movements or exercise intensities. A needs analysis is a two-step process: an evaluation of the sport and an assessment of the athlete.

Evaluation of the Sport

The portion of the needs analysis in which the sport is evaluated has three components:

- Movement analysis - In the movement analysis, the strength conditioning professional considers the limb and body movement patterns of the given sport or position.
- Physiological analysis - In the physiological analysis, the muscular strength, power, and endurance required by the sport or position are considered.
- Injury analysis - Lastly, the injury analysis involves considering the injuries commonly seen in athletes of the given sport or position.

Assessment of the Athlete

The portion of the needs analysis in which the athlete is assessed involves looking at various factors of the individual athlete that include the following:

- Training status – An athlete's training status will depend on the type of training program the athlete is undertaking; the length of time the individual has been training and competing, including the length of their entire career as well as the recent/current program; their knowledge and experience with training exercises; and the intensity level of their current and previous training.
- Physical testing and evaluation - Based on the movement analysis made during the evaluation of the sport, strength and conditioning professionals should select appropriate tests to evaluate the fitness of the athlete relative to what is required by the sport and the physical demands that the sport or the position will place on the body. Then, those results should be compared with either norms or previous benchmarks from the athlete to identify relative strengths and weaknesses.
- Primary resistance training goal - There are typically four seasons that an athlete cycles through in terms of training and competing: preseason, in season, postseason, and offseason. There should be only one training goal as the focus of each of these seasons. More than one season can have the same goal, though they often vary. Examples of resistance training goals are hypertrophy, improving muscular strength, increasing muscular endurance, and increasing power. The primary resistance training goal has a significant effect on the needs of the athlete, and thus the programming that is developed.

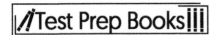

Incorporating Various Training Methods and Modes

Muscular Endurance can be improved through resistance and circuit training.

Hypertrophy can result from resistance training. Research indicates performing ≥3 exercises per muscle group will optimize increases in muscle size.

Strength gains can be achieved through resistance, bodyweight, and Strongman training.

Power improves via complex training, which combines heavy resistance training and plyometric exercises. The goal is to enhance short-term power output. Complex training uses a training stimulus that couples a heavy load (i.e., resistance exercise) with a light load (i.e., plyometric exercise) in order to optimize force and power production beyond that which can be achieved with either exercise alone. The enhanced force and power production is a result of a phenomenon call post-activation potentiation (PAP). The principle behind PAP is that heavy loading causes significant stimulation of the central nervous system, which leads to greater motor-unit recruitment and force.

The increased muscle activation resulting from the heavy load produces a faster contraction rate. By pairing a high-intensity resistance exercise set with a biomechanically similar plyometric exercise set, the resulting PAP increases force development and maximizes the production of explosive power for athletic performance. An example of complex training is a set of two to three back squats (85–90 percent) followed by three to five vertical jumps to maximal height, with a rest period of 3 minutes between the two exercises. Examples of other complex training sets are bench presses followed by plyometric push-ups and barbell lunges followed by single-leg hops.

Aerobic Endurance can be improved by combining resistance training with aerobic endurance training. Such training will provide short-term exercise performance improvements and increased strength that can help with hill climbing, the final sprint of an endurance competition, and catching up to competitors when there are breakaway groups. Resistance training can also be beneficial for faster recovery from injuries and the prevention of overuse injuries and muscle imbalances. Plyometric training can also progress aerobic endurance. Many sports, such as soccer and tennis, have both a power (anaerobic) and aerobic component. Performing plyometric exercises before aerobic endurance training can help to minimize the detrimental effect that aerobic training can have on power production. Altitude training can also be beneficial. Increased altitude causes a reduction in the partial pressure of oxygen due to drops in atmospheric pressure, which detrimentally affects gas exchange in the lungs. The body attempts to compensate for the reduced partial pressure with a number of physiological changes. It takes twelve to fourteen days for the body to acclimatize to altitude up to 2,300 meters.

Some athletes train at altitude or attempt to get the benefits of altitude training by using the "live high, train low" (LHTL) method. This requires the athlete to live at moderate altitudes (2,000–3,000 meters) and train at sea level. Living at high altitude results in metabolic and hematological adaptations that can provide ergogenic benefits by enhancing neuromuscular development during lower-altitude training. Any of the various types of aerobic training (e.g., LSD, pace/tempo, interval, HIIT, or Fartlek training) can be completed as part of altitude training.

Different Types of Training Methods and Modes

Resistance Training

Free Weights

The source of resistance for free weights is gravity. Free-weight exercises are often performed in a standing position, which places more stress on the body's muscles and bones than weight-stack machines. Free weights require muscles to support and stabilize the body. Lifting free weights is a closer replication of the movements required in sports, because it involves the coordination of multiple muscle groups (as opposed to machines, which typically isolate single muscle groups).

Weight-Stack Machines

The source of resistance for weight-stack machines is gravity; however, these machines utilize cables, pulleys, cams, and gears that allow increased control over both the pattern and direction of resistance. Weight-stack machines are safer than free weights, in part because less skill and muscle coordination are needed for control, and the design of the machines provides resistance to body movements that are difficult to duplicate with free weights (e.g., hip adduction and abduction, or leg curl). Machines also can be readied more quickly than free weights because weight selection only requires inserting a pin into the weight stack.

Circuit Training

The use of circuit training during resistance-training sessions condenses the time needed to complete a specific amount of work. The athlete goes from one exercise to the next with limited rest between the movement sets. Circuit training can be used with any type of resistance exercise movement, but the most demanding movement sets (i.e., power movements) should be completed before less demanding movement sets (i.e., core and assistance movements). There are several benefits to using circuit training, including improved time efficiency, enhanced cardiorespiratory functioning, and increased muscle endurance. Circuit training increases metabolic costs and can be beneficial for athletes interested in reducing body fat.

Plyometric Training

Explosive activities, such as plyometrics, use the stretch-shortening cycle (the fast lengthening and shortening of a muscle) to create muscle contractions. The stretch-shortening cycle involves an eccentric phase, amortization phase, and concentric phase. A muscle shortens in the concentric phase and lengthens in the eccentric phase. The amortization phase is the transition between the eccentric and concentric phases. Muscle spindles are essential to the stretch-reflex response because they are the primary proprioceptive structures in the muscle. Muscle spindles respond to eccentric muscle action. When muscles experience eccentric contractions during plyometric exercises, the muscles and surrounding tendons stretch and store energy. This musculotendinous unit where elastic energy is stored is called the series elastic component (SEC). The SEC works like a spring that returns the lengthened muscle to its shortened state during a concentric contraction. As the muscle shortens, energy is released. An athlete can use this energy to generate enough force to complete the plyometric exercises.

Lower-Body Plyometrics

Including lower-body plyometric exercises in an athlete's training program can improve sport performance by increasing the athlete's ability to produce greater force in a shorter period of time. Lower-body plyometric exercises are appropriate for almost every sport, including track and field events, sprinting, soccer, volleyball, football, baseball, basketball, cycling, distance running, and triathlons. Different sports require different movement patterns. Lateral and horizontal movements are used in baseball, football, and sprinting, while volleyball requires vertical and horizontal movements. Some sports like soccer and basketball require powerful and quick movements with changes in direction and planes.

In addition to improving the force and velocity of movement, endurance athletes also benefit because lower-body plyometric training improves muscle efficiency by training muscles to produce more force using less energy. Lower-body plyometric exercises that can be included in an athlete's training program from lowest to highest intensity include jumps in place, standing jumps, multiple hops and jumps (also called countermovement jumps), bounds, box drills, and depth jumps. Training adaptations can be obtained over relatively short periods of time (six to ten weeks), but athletes can benefit from plyometric training throughout the macrocycle.

Upper-Body Plyometrics

Upper-body plyometric exercises use the same neuromuscular mechanisms as lower-body plyometric exercises to produce sports movements. Upper-body plyometric exercises should be included in training programs for athletes participating in sports that require fast and powerful upper-body movements. These sports include tennis, softball, golf, baseball, field throwing (e.g., shot put, discus, and javelin), lacrosse, swimming, and other sprint and endurance activities. Sports that require tackling, catching, and holding off opponents can also benefit from upper-body plyometric training. Although upper-body plyometric exercises (e.g., throwing and catching a medicine ball and plyometric push-ups) are an essential training component for athletes requiring upper-body power, these exercises are not as commonly used as lower-body plyometric exercises.

Modifications for Performing Trunk Plyometrics

It is difficult to perform a true plyometric trunk exercise because the mechanical and neurophysiological mechanisms necessary for the stretch-shortening cycle may not be present. Although some elastic energy may be stored during plyometric trunk exercises, research suggests that the stretch reflex is not sufficiently involved for potentiated muscle-contraction activity to occur. The abdominal muscles are close to the spinal cord, which may result in shorter latencies for the abdominal stretch reflex. The large range of motion and time associated with the trunk movements inhibit the potentiation of the abdominal muscles. However, altering the exercise movements so that they are shorter and quicker may cause rapid eccentric muscle loading that elicits the stretch reflex and results in potentiated contraction of the muscle.

Frequency of Plyometric Training Activities

The frequency of plyometric training is primarily influenced by the athlete's sport, previous experience with plyometric training, the phase of training in a cycle or season, and the intensity and volume of daily workouts, including plyometrics, resistance training, sport practices, and aerobic training. For most sports, an athlete can perform one to three training sessions per week with 48–72 hours of recovery time between plyometric training sessions. In order to determine plyometric training frequency, the strength and conditioning professional must evaluate the intensity of the plyometric exercises performed, the number of repetitions completed for each exercise, and the total volume of all other types of training. Because there is very limited research about the frequency of plyometric training, guidelines for the frequency of training do not exist.

Plyometric Training Volumes

Plyometric exercise volumes are commonly determined as the number of repetitions and sets that are completed during a single training session. Training volumes for lower-body plyometric exercises are expressed as the number of foot contacts during a session. For example, if an athlete is doing bounding exercises, volume may be expressed as a total distance covered. Training volume for upper-body plyometrics is typically expressed as the number of catches or throws during a training session. An athlete's level of plyometrics experience is used to provide a suggested training volume:

- Beginner: 80–100 repetitions per session
- Intermediate: 100–120 repetitions per session
- Advanced: 120–140 repetitions per session

Age Considerations and Possible Limitations for Plyometric Training Activities

A wide variety of ages—not just the elite adult athlete—can safely benefit from plyometric and plyometric-like exercises if appropriate guidelines are followed. This is particularly true for prepubescent and adolescent children who gain muscular power and bone strength from participating in an appropriately designed plyometric program. Young athletes who regularly participate in plyometric training gain enhanced neuromuscular control and performance, helping to prepare them for the demands of sport competitions and practices. Plyometric programs designed for children should focus on developing correct technique to ensure quality movements while performing

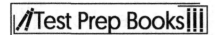

the plyometric activities and should progress from simple to more difficult plyometric exercises. Among prepubescent athletes, depth jumps and high-intensity lower-body exercises are contraindicated because they can cause the epiphyseal growth plates to close prematurely, resulting in stunted limb growth.

Adequate recovery time of two to three days should separate the plyometric training sessions for young athletes. Master athletes also benefit from plyometric training but the goals of the program and preexisting orthopedic and joint degeneration must be considered when designing the plyometric training program. With a few exceptions, the same general program development guidelines used for adult athletes can be used for developing training programs for older athletes. The program should not include more than five low- to moderate-intensity exercises, the volume should be lower, and there should be three to four recovery days between training sessions.

Speed/Sprint Training

Important Definitions

- Rate of Force Development (RFD): The change in force divided by the change in time; a sprinter wants to generate maximal force in minimal time.
- Impulse: The product of the amount of time that force is applied to the ground and the amount of force applied.
- Momentum: The relationship between the mass of an object and the velocity of movement; an increased impulse (due to greater force generation) results in either an increase in momentum (acceleration or reacceleration) or a decrease in momentum (deceleration).

Methods for Improving Sprinting

Method #1: Sprinting

The best way to improve speed (i.e., running velocity) is to do maximum-velocity sprint training. Sprinting relies on an athlete's ability to produce high forces in a short period of time. Inclusion of maximum-velocity sprinting in long-term training plans can produce neurological adaptations that can improve RFD and impulse generation. Resisted and assisted sprint training techniques are commonly used to enhance force production or specific neuromuscular adaptations in order to enhance sprinting performance.

Resisted sprint training techniques for speed development: Resisted sprint training techniques include modalities such as using harnesses for sled and parachute towing, uphill running, weighted vests, wind resistance, and sled pushing. The objectives of resisted sprint techniques are to enhance the acceleration phase biomechanics and to produce greater propulsive forces so that the athlete can cover longer distances faster. The strength and conditioning coach should be aware that loads used for training are sport-specific. Sprinters should use lighter loads (i.e., loads that do not decrease velocity by more than 10–12 percent) while field athletes who are exposed to external resistance may use loads that are 20–30 percent of the athlete's body weight.

Assisted sprint training techniques for speed development: The goal of assisted sprint training techniques is to produce an overspeed effect that causes the athlete to run at a faster pace than normal. This increased pace supports adaptation of the athlete's neuromuscular system to contract at faster rates, thus allowing athletes to increase their stride rate and maximum sprint velocity. Assisted training techniques include pulling the athlete with cords (e.g., rope towing, elastic-band/surgical-tubing pulls), high-speed treadmill sprinting with a specialized treadmill, and downhill running. Strength and conditioning professionals should recognize that running mechanics can be difficult to regulate at high speeds. The maximum speed should be no greater than 110 percent of the athlete's known maximal speed.

If speed is too great, it can lead to the following issues:

- Rushing the stance phase, which lessens the time available to produce propulsive force production
- Increasing braking forces while being towed due to the athlete's inability to handle the increased velocity
- Exposure to significant eccentric forces during downhill running due to the modified mechanics of altered foot placement

Because assisted sprint training can have detrimental effects, it is critical to consider the athlete's biomechanics and training status when deciding whether to implement assisted sprinting techniques.

Method #2: Strength

Sprint speed is dependent upon the ability to produce large forces in a minimal period of time. Weight training plays a critical role when training sprint athletes. One issue that strength and conditioning professionals need to be aware of is the importance of being able to transfer the strength qualities from the weight room to the track. Making the movement pattern, RFD, peak force, and acceleration and velocity patterns in a weight-training program specific to the demands of the sport can facilitate this transfer of the training effect.

Method #3: Mobility

Mobility Training: Mobility (the athlete's ability to move a limb through a specific range of motion) and mobility training are part of dynamic flexibility training programs. Mobility and flexibility are both important components of correct agility and sprinting mechanics because maximum range of motion is needed to perform these activities. Common sprinting mechanics issues include improper arm swinging, premature upright posture, neck hyperextension, and bouncing. A strength and conditioning professional can correct these errors to improve mobility. Helping the athlete to lengthen the push-off and stride can help vertical bouncing; keeping a steady eye level can help premature upright posture; and keeping eyes focused on the ground will improve neck hyperextension. The recovery phase is key because the sprinter's body is aligned in a way that will enhance speed.

An athlete's speed and agility may also be limited by compromised joint mobility or flexibility. Joints with poor mobility and flexibility produce improper forces, reduce sprinting speed and agility capabilities, and increase the risk for injury. Optimal mobility and flexibility allow the athlete to have fluid movements, which can help to increase turnover rates during the phases of sprinting and agility activities. Strength and conditioning professionals need to be aware of an athlete's mobility or flexibility limitations so that they can design programs that will increase mobility and flexibility and enhance sprinting and agility. Assessing the athlete's muscular balance, activity levels, and range of motion can help identify issues that can be improved and corrected through a focused training program.

Mobility Drills: Dynamic stretching is sometimes referred to as mobility drills. Mobility drills emphasize sport-specific movement requirements instead of individual muscle movements. Mobility drills increase not only range of motion, but also blood flow to muscle tissue, synovial fluid circulation to the joints, body temperature, and central nervous system activity, which are all beneficial for pre-sport activity (i.e., training or competition). These physiological changes are consistent with those that occur when an athlete goes from a resting to an active state. Mobility drills are the ideal pre-activity stretching method because static stretching does not produce the aforementioned physiological changes, and ballistic stretching is not as safe as mobility drills. Mobility drills for swimmers may include shoulder raises and arm swings, while drills for runners may include walking knee lifts, inverted hamstring stretches, and lunge walks.

Agility Training

Agility is a multicomponent skill that is used in response to a sport-specific stimulus. It includes the ability to change direction, velocity, or mode in response to a stimulus. Agility also requires perceptual-cognitive skills such as pattern recognition of players on a playing field, visual scanning, anticipation, accuracy, and reaction time.

Reaction time allows the athlete to make quick decisions based on how the nervous system and muscular system react to a stimulus. Because an athlete's ability to process a stimulus cannot be trained, improvements to reaction time will be small regardless of the training. Also, faster reaction times only result in better decision-making; they do not affect performance in explosive activities.

Agility-drill types include continuous drills, discrete drills, and serial drills. Continuous drills have no beginning or end, and they are helpful for improving running and jumping. Discrete drills help to develop movement patterns and improve an athlete's strength and power. Serial drills are sport specific and combine continuous and discrete drills. Together, these drill types can improve strength, change-of-direction (COD) ability, and perceptual-cognitive ability.

Methods for Developing Agility

Method #1: Strength

Dynamic Strength: This is the base strength that is needed for all other strength training. Dynamic strength can help provide mobility during bodyweight-only and loaded training. Examples of dynamic strength exercises for athletes include calisthenics, squats, pulls, and change-of-direction drills.

Eccentric Strength: Developing eccentric strength improves the ability to effectively absorb load during the brake phase of a COD. Examples of eccentric strength exercises for athletes include drop landings (to build the strength required during the catch phase of Olympic lifts), accentuated eccentric training, and deceleration drills (high velocity, various angles).

Multidirectional Strength: This type of strength improves the athlete's ability to hold the body position during movement demands. Examples of such exercises include lunges, Z-drills, unilateral lifts, high-velocity COD drills, and cutting-angle COD drills.

Reactive Strength: Having reactive strength enhances the athlete's ability to transfer from high eccentric load to concentric explosiveness. Examples of reactive strength exercises include plyometrics, drop jumps, and loaded jumps.

Concentric Explosive Strength: Athletes need concentric explosive strength to reaccelerate after the braking phase. This type of strength is required for the maintenance of a strong position through the transition phase of COD and agility. Example exercises include box jumps, acceleration drills, loaded squat jumps, sled pushes, and Olympic lifts.

Method #2: COD Ability

The progression of closed-skill COD drills is similar to the progression of plyometric exercises: it is based on the difficulty and intensity of each drill. The following list provides examples of progressing deceleration drills for athletes at various levels:

- Beginner Level: The athlete would start with forward deceleration drills and progress with a higher entry velocity or shorter stopping distance.
- Intermediate Level: The athlete would do lateral deceleration drills and progress with a higher entry velocity or shorter stopping distance.

- Advanced Level: The athlete would do a drill requiring deceleration to reacceleration in forward and lateral directions.

Method #3: Perceptual-Cognitive Ability
Perceptual-cognitive ability can be trained by increasing the demands of the task in order to improve performance. Within-sport skills include visual scanning and pattern recognition. Drills to improve agility focus on improving accuracy, anticipation, and decision-making time. The following list provides examples of progressing agility activities to improve perceptual-cognitive abilities for athletes at various levels:

- Beginner Level: Closed-skill COD drills with an added perceptual-cognitive element can become agility drills by including a generic stimulus such as a coach's instruction, flashing light, or whistle blow.

- Advanced Level: Drills that use sport-specific stimuli (e.g., evasive drills, small-sided games) have been shown to have a greater effect on performance.

Note: By progressively increasing the time (temporal) or spatial stress on the athlete, generic and specific stimuli within an agility skill can both be made more difficult.

Aerobic Training

Pace/Tempo Training Method

This training method is a type of aerobic endurance training that utilizes an intensity consistent with or slightly higher than race or competition intensity. The goal of pace/tempo training is to replicate the pattern of muscle fiber recruitment and physiological stress during competition in order to improve running economy, increase aerobic- and anaerobic-energy production, and increase the lactate threshold. The intensity in this type of training—sometimes called threshold training or aerobic-anaerobic interval training—corresponds to the lactate threshold and improves the aerobic- and anaerobic-energy systems, which are both active during a race. Pace/tempo training can either be steady or intermittent. Steady training consists of a twenty- to thirty-minute bout of continuous training at the athlete's lactate threshold. During exercise, muscle cells release lactate into the blood.

Resting levels of blood lactate range between 0.8 nM (nanomolar) and 1.5 nM, and lactate levels can be greater than 18 nM during intense exercise. The lactate threshold is the amount of work (i.e., percentage of VO_2 max) that causes blood lactate concentrations to increase above resting levels. In aerobic training, lactate threshold can refer to the speed of movement or exercise intensity that is associated with a specific concentration of lactate in the blood. When athletes exceed their lactate threshold during exercise, they experience substantial physical and mental fatigue. Intermittent training is similar to the steady pace/tempo approach, except that the work intervals are separated by short recovery periods. When doing pace/tempo training, it is important that the work is done at the prescribed intensity. Athletes should avoid working at a more intense pace. This type of training is generally done one to two times per week for 20–30 minutes, at the athlete's normal race pace.

Long, Slow Distance (LSD) Running

LSD training is usually done one to two times per week at an intensity of approximately 70 percent of VO_2 max and 80 percent of maximal heart rate. This type of training is slower than race pace. The distance covered should be longer than the race distance, and the training duration should be 30 minutes to 2 hours. Several physiological adaptations arise from LSD, including improved thermoregulation, cardiovascular function, mitochondrial energy production, and use of fat as energy. Lactate threshold may also increase as these adaptations make clearing lactate from the blood easier. Too much LSD can be detrimental to race performance, because neuromuscular adaptations may be made to a running intensity that is significantly lower than that required during a race.

Fartlek Training

Fartlek literally means "speed play." It combines several types of endurance training and can be used for runners, swimmers, and cyclists. Fartlek training involves low-intensity exercise (approximately 70 percent of VO_2 max) with short bursts of high-intensity (85–95 percent of VO_2 max) exercise at more irregular points, lengths, and speeds than in interval training. Fartlek training can provide an opportunity for athletes to challenge themselves on a weekly basis and help relieve the monotony of a single type of training session. It is best used during periods of heavy training leading up to an event. This type of training challenges all body systems and can improve VO_2 max, lactate threshold, energy consumption, and exercise economy. Fartlek training is generally done once per week for 20–60 minutes. The intensity varies from LSD to pace/tempo.

High-Intensity Interval Training (HIIT)

This training uses repeated high-intensity (≥90 percent of VO_2 max) exercise bouts with rest periods in between. Depending on the desired training response, short exercise bouts of 45 seconds or less or long bouts of 2–4 minutes can be used. As the duration of the high-intensity exercise gets longer, blood lactate levels will increase because energy will come from anaerobic glycolysis. The length of the rest periods between the intervals is important. Rest periods that are too short will not allow the athlete to recover enough to put forth the required effort necessary to complete the remaining high-intensity bouts. If the rest period is too long, the athlete's body may not require energy from anaerobic glycolysis and the training response will not occur. An example of appropriate work-to-rest time periods would be 2–3 minutes of high-intensity exercise followed by a rest period of 2 minutes. Running economy and speed may be improved by HIIT. This type of training is typically done once per week.

Flexibility Training

Flexibility consists of static and dynamic components and is a measure of range of motion (ROM). ROM is the degree of movement that occurs at a joint.

Static flexibility is the amount of movement around a joint during a passive movement. Static flexibility is not dependent on voluntary movement. A partner, gravity, or a machine provides the force required for the stretch.

Dynamic flexibility is the ROM during active movements that require voluntary muscle activity. In general, dynamic ROM is greater than static ROM.

For flexibility and performance, the type of sport-specific movements that athletes must perform dictates the level of flexibility they need. The strength and conditioning professional needs to base an athlete's flexibility training on the requirements of the sport, as well as the force patterns required through the ROM. Injury risk may increase if an athlete is unable to obtain the level of flexibility required by the sport. Likewise, hyperflexibility can also increase the risk for injury.

Factors affecting flexibility include:

- Joint Structure: The type and shape of the joint (e.g., ball-and-socket, ellipsoidal, hinge) and its surrounding tissue affect its ROM.
- Muscle and Connective Tissue: Many body tissues (e.g., tendons, muscle, fascial sheaths, skin, joint capsules, and ligaments) can limit ROM. Stretching takes advantage of the plasticity and elasticity of connective tissues and can affect ROM.
- Muscle Bulk: ROM can be negatively affected by substantial muscle bulk. The specific requirements of the sport (e.g., large muscles versus joint mobility) should be considered when determining a flexibility program for an athlete.

- Neural Control: ROM is controlled by the central and peripheral nervous systems, so an effective flexibility program needs to affect both systems.
- Stretch Tolerance: How well athletes can tolerate the discomfort of stretching influences their ROM. Athletes with a greater stretch tolerance generally have a greater ROM.
- Resistance Training: Heavy resistance training can decrease ROM; however, an appropriately planned resistance-training program can actually increase ROM. Increased ROM can enhance the development of force capacity.
- Activity Level: Active individuals are generally more flexible than inactive individuals, particularly if the activity includes flexibility exercises.
- Age and Sex: Young people are generally more flexible than older people, and women are generally more flexible than men.

Alternative Modes and Nontraditional Implement Training

Over the past decade or so, there has been a rising trend in the use of nontraditional implements in athletic training programs, particularly in the realms of strength and resistance training, power and speed training, and overall conditioning. Innovative and rogue training programs such as CrossFit, Strongman training, and adventure races utilize items such as tires, sandbags, heavy battle ropes, kettle bells, logs, water-filled pipes, heavy chains, weighted sleds, and a variety of medicine balls. These are tools that can be added to a strength coach's programming arsenal to give athletes creative ways to accomplish physiologic goals similar to those afforded by traditional implements.

Many of the nontraditional implements offer the advantages of variable resistance and can invoke bilateral asymmetries, which help with core activation and addressing bilateral deficiencies. Still, coaches must be aware of when and how to properly use this equipment and fully educate and supervise athletes in its use. In many cases, nontraditional implements are best reserved for advanced athletes who have mastered the foundational movement patterns (such as squats and deadlifts) because they often place a more complex demand on the neuromuscular system, which can result in injury if the requisite strength and control are yet to be obtained.

Bodyweight-Training Methods

Bodyweight training is a basic resistance-training method that utilizes an individual's bodyweight as resistance. This training helps to develop core muscles and, as a result, may decrease injury risk. Benefits of bodyweight training include the following:

- training that is specific to the athlete's anthropometrics
- incorporation of many closed chain exercises
- improvements to body control and relative strength while strengthening multiple muscle groups simultaneously
- low-cost training

The limitations of bodyweight training include the following:

- The load is limited by the athlete's weight.
- Absolute strength is not substantially improved by training.
- Changing movement patterns or repetitions are required in order to increase intensity.

As the number of repetitions increases, the outcome focus of training will change from strength to strength-endurance.

Examples of bodyweight-training exercises include:

- pull-ups
- sit-ups
- push-ups
- squat thrusts
- chin-ups
- calisthenics
- yoga
- gymnastics

Core-Stability and Balance Training Methods

The scientific definition of the anatomical core is the axial skeleton (which includes the shoulder and pelvic girdles) and all of the soft tissues (i.e., muscles, articular cartilage, tendons, fascia, ligaments, and fibrocartilage).

Isolation Exercises

These exercises usually are dynamic or isometric muscle actions that isolate the specific core musculature. The upper and lower extremities do NOT contribute to the muscle actions. These exercises can improve spinal stability because there is increased muscle activation. Performance improvements may be seen in untrained athletes as well as athletes recovering from injury; however, research suggests that these exercises generally do not improve sport performance in other athlete populations. Research indicates that ground-based free-weight exercises (e.g., snatch, deadlift, squat, push-press, and trunk-rotation exercises) produce the same or greater levels of core-musculature activation. Examples of isolation exercises include:

- side plank
- prone plank

Instability Devices

Effects of Instability-Based Exercises

Instability-based exercises utilize unstable surfaces or devices to cause imbalances that require increased stabilization functioning of the core musculature. While using these devices, the application of external forces to an individual's center of mass, called perturbations, can cause balance challenges that require core musculature to activate to make postural adjustments and maintain balance. Evidence indicates that core-musculature activation may increase with the use of instability devices. However, the agonist muscle has reduced force generation and a reduced rate of force development. Also, the overall power output and overall force-generating capacity may be 70 percent or less than that produced during exercise under stable conditions.

Effectiveness of Instability-Based Exercises Versus Ground-Based Exercises

The use of instability devices during static balance activities can help to improve balance and core stability before starting ground-based free-weight exercises done on stable surfaces. Ground-based free-weight exercises (e.g., Olympic lifts, squats) are a better exercise stimulus for developing core stability. These exercises have some inherent instability that facilitates the development of the links of the kinetic chain, which helps improve sport performance to a greater extent than instability-based exercises.

Examples of instability devices include:

- physio balls
- hemispherical physio balls (BOSU)
- inflatable disks
- balance boards
- wobble boards
- foam tubes and platforms

Variable-Resistance Training Methods

Types of variable-resistance training methods include the following:

- Constant External Resistance: Constant external resistance involves free weights and traditional resistance exercises where the external load remains constant throughout the movement. This type of movement better replicates real activities and promotes more realistic movement patterns and skeletal muscle coordination.

- Accommodating Resistance: Also known as semi-isokinetic resistance applications, accommodating resistance controls the speed of movement (i.e., isokinetic resistance) throughout a range of motion (ROM). This type of training requires specific devices that generally have poor external validity and provide an inadequate training stimulus in comparison with constant external resistance exercises.

- Variable Resistance: Variable resistance training utilizes devices that apply varied resistance as the joint angle changes in an attempt to maximize forced application across the full ROM. Strength and conditioning facilities commonly combine chains or rubber bands with traditional free-weight resistance-training methods in order to alter the loading profile, thus allowing varied resistance across the ROM.

- Chain-Supplemented Exercises: Variable resistance can be applied by the addition of chains to resistance exercise activities (e.g., back squat or bench press). The size (e.g., diameter, length, density, or number of links) of the chain controls the amount of resistance it provides. The use of chains results in a linear increase in the applied resistance. Two ways to apply chains are to let them touch the floor from the fully extended position of the movement or to hang them from lighter chains so they only touch the floor when the lowest portion of the movement pattern (e.g., bottom of the squat) is reached.

- Note: Determining the Barbell Load to Use with Chains: First, an athlete must determine what the barbell load should be without chains. Second, the athlete should take the average of the chain resistance at the top and bottom of the movement. Third, the average chain resistance should be subtracted from the desired barbell load to determine the final barbell load. For example, an athlete who wants to train at a 5-RM (repetition-maximum) load bench press must first determine the 5-RM load without the chains. If the 5-RM load without chains is 120 kg, then subtract the average chain resistance from this load. If the bottom position has a chain resistance of 0 kg and the top position has a chain resistance of 11.1 kg, the average chain resistance is 5.55 kg (11.1÷2). The athlete would need to subtract 5.55 kg from 120 kg to have appropriate barbell loading.

- Resistance-Band Exercises: There is some research supporting the efficacy of using resistance bands in combination with traditional resistance exercise. The strength and conditioning professional needs to be aware that the make-up of the resistance bands can affect their tension (resistance), and the stiffness of the band affects the amount the band can stretch (deformation). Note that the tension of a resistance band is equivalent to the product of its stiffness (k) and deformation (d), so $tension = k \times d$. Increased stretching of the band results in a linear increase in the band's tension. Note that two similar bands can be different (3.2–5.2 percent), which will increase the amount of mean tension by 8–19 percent.

A resistance band can either be attached to a barbell and then attached to a heavy dumbbell or attached with a customized attachment to a squat rack. The resistance will be greatest when the band has the highest amount of tension. At the top position and the bottom position, there will be no resistance from the band because it is no longer stretched. Thus, the stretch load increases when the athlete is ascending from the bottom position and the load decreases as the athlete descends from the top position. Once the loads at the top and bottom positions are determined, those values are averaged. If an athlete wants to use a 5-RM load of 150 kg using bands, the average of bands at the two positions is subtracted from the original load on the bar. If an athlete is doing a bench press and the load at the bottom is 0 kg and the load at the top is 26.6 kg, the average is 13.3 kg. This average would be subtracted from the total weight on the bar (without bands), so the athlete would put between 136 kg and 137 kg on the bar, attach the bands, and complete the resistance exercise.

Combinations of Various Training Methods and Modes to Reach a Certain Goal or Outcome

Training and conditioning for athletes is sometimes considered an art as much as it is a science. Once the foundational concepts of programming are understood, the strength and conditioning professional's job is to strategically combine the various modes and methods of training to optimize the chances that an athlete will attain their desired goal. This involves extensive knowledge of the litany of options available, as well as creativity, forethought, and customization. Not surprisingly, the programming for two athletes competing in different sports will likely look quite different, as the aims and requirements of the sports will be varied. However, it's also often the case that athletes participating in the same sport will need uniquely customized programs. The latter is usually seen in cases where the goals of the athletes in question are quite different, their starting fitness levels are at odds, their injury risk or health factors are not the same, or the amount of time they have available to train differs.

First, consider two athletes on a collegiate track team. If one is a miler and one throws the shot put, it's easy to understand that the methods and modes of training for each athlete will be quite disparate. However, even two milers may require dissimilar programs for optimal success. A runner who is newer to the sport or rehabbing an injury will spend a greater percentage of training time in base building, focusing on developing their cardiovascular, neuromuscular, and musculoskeletal systems. Training loads will be significantly lighter and training volume will be less than they are for a more advanced, or seasoned, runner.

Additionally, a newer or injured runner will likely need to focus on core stability, muscle activation, bodyweight training, and lower-force stability and mobility exercises, such as clam shells with a resistance band, bodyweight split squats, planks, and single-leg bridges. A healthy, advanced miler will engage in training of a higher intensity. He or she will spend a greater percentage of training time doing high-intensity intervals, such as 400-meter repeats, tempo runs at lactate threshold pace, and longer runs. Strength and resistance training will also be more intensive and advanced, incorporating external loads, variable resistance, and greater volume.

Athletes and strength and conditioning professionals should be clear on the desired goals, timetable to achieve them, and possible constraints or challenges (injuries, imbalances, low skill level, etc.) in order to properly program the best training regimen for each individual athlete.

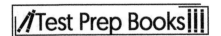

Selecting Exercises

Exercises Specific to the Movement Patterns of a Particular Sport

Ball Dribbling and Passing

Exercises and muscles used for these movements include:

- Dumbbell Bench Press: Pectoralis major, anterior deltoids, triceps brachii
- Triceps Pushdowns: Triceps brachii
- Hammer Curl: Brachialis, biceps brachii, brachioradialis
- Close-Grip Bench Press: Sternal pectoralis major, anterior deltoid, clavicular pectoralis major, triceps brachii
- Reverse Curl: Brachioradialis, brachialis, biceps brachii

Freestyle Swimming (including starts and turns)

Exercises and muscles used for these movements include:

- Pull-Up: Lower and middle trapezius, biceps brachii, pectoralis minor, teres major, brachialis, rhomboids, brachioradialis, levator scapulae, latissimus dorsi, teres minor, infraspinatus, posterior deltoid
- Forward Step Lunge: Biceps femoris, rectus femoris, gluteus maximus, iliopsoas, semimembranosus, vastus medialis, semitendinosus, vastus lateralis, vastus intermedius
- Lateral Shoulder Raise: Deltoids
- Upright Row: Deltoids, upper trapezius
- Barbell Pullover: Rhomboids, latissimus dorsi, posterior deltoid, sternal pectoralis major, teres major, pectoralis minor, levator scapulae, long head triceps
- Single-Leg Squat: Quadriceps, gluteus maximus, adductor magnus, soleus, erector spinae

Running and Sprinting

Exercises and muscles used for these movements include:

- Clean: Gluteus maximus, gastrocnemius, semimembranosus, semitendinosus, trapezius, biceps femoris, deltoids, vastus lateralis, vastus medialis, vastus intermedius, soleus, rectus femoris
- Snatch: Deltoids, semimembranosus, soleus, semitendinosus, trapezius, vastus lateralis, vastus intermedius, gastrocnemius, vastus medialis, biceps femoris, rectus femoris, gluteus maximus
- Front Squat: Biceps femoris, gluteus maximus, rectus femoris, semimembranosus, vastus lateralis, vastus intermedius, semitendinosus, vastus medialis
- Forward Step Lunge: Iliopsoas, biceps femoris, vastus lateralis, semimembranosus, gluteus maximus, semitendinosus, vastus intermedius, rectus femoris, vastus medialis
- Step-Up: Vastus medialis, gluteus maximus, vastus lateralis, semimembranosus, biceps femoris, semitendinosus, rectus femoris, vastus intermedius

- Leg (Knee) Curl: Semimembranosus, biceps femoris, semitendinosus
- Leg (Knee) Extension: Vastus medialis, rectus femoris, vastus intermedius, vastus lateralis

Exercises Based on the Type/Number of Involved Muscle Group(s)

Core Exercises

Also called multi-joint exercises, core exercises involve two or more primary joints and recruit one or more large muscle areas (e.g., shoulder, thigh, back, etc.). Multi-joint exercises stimulate muscles the most because they recruit all of the large muscle groups associated with the involved joints. As a result, they allow for the greatest amount of loading during resistance training. These exercises should be used for athletes who have a limited amount of time to train.

Examples:

- Bench Press: Sternal pectoralis major, clavicular pectoralis major, anterior deltoids, triceps brachii
- Front Squat: Biceps femoris, gluteus maximus, rectus femoris, vastus intermedius, semimembranosus, vastus lateralis, semitendinosus, vastus medialis
- Deadlift: Vastus intermedius, gluteus maximus, vastus lateralis, biceps femoris, semimembranosus, rectus femoris, semitendinosus, vastus medialis

Structural Exercises

Structural exercises are core exercises that specifically emphasize loading the spine. Loading of the spine can be direct (e.g., back squat) or indirect (e.g., power clean). A structural exercise requires the muscular stabilization of posture during the lifting movement. For example, during a back squat the athlete maintains a rigid torso and a neutral spine. These types of exercises should be the basis of training programs.

Examples:

- Power Clean (all body, power/structural): Deltoids, soleus, semimembranosus, rectus femoris, semitendinosus, vastus lateralis, biceps femoris, vastus intermedius, trapezius, vastus medialis, gluteus maximus, gastrocnemius
- Back Squat: Vastus lateralis, vastus intermedius, semimembranosus, gluteus maximus, semitendinosus, rectus femoris, vastus medialis, biceps femoris

Power Exercises

Power exercises are structural exercises that are performed very quickly or explosively. The strength and conditioning professional needs to assess the athlete's sport-specific training needs in order to determine if power exercises should be prescribed.

Examples:

- Push Press (all body, power): Deltoids, soleus, gluteus maximus, semimembranosus, vastus medialis, vastus intermedius, semitendinosus, vastus lateralis, rectus femoris, gastrocnemius, biceps femoris, trapezius

- Push Jerk (all body, power): Semitendinosus, gluteus maximus, semimembranosus, deltoids, rectus femoris, vastus lateralis, trapezius, vastus intermedius, biceps femoris, soleus, gastrocnemius, vastus medialis
- Clean: Vastus medialis, gluteus maximus, soleus, semimembranosus, gastrocnemius, vastus intermedius, biceps femoris, vastus lateralis, rectus femoris, trapezius, semitendinosus, deltoids
- Snatch (all body, power): Trapezius, soleus, gluteus maximus, vastus lateralis, semitendinosus, gastrocnemius, biceps femoris, vastus intermedius, vastus medialis, rectus femoris, semimembranosus, deltoids

Assistance Exercises

Also called single-joint exercises, assistance exercises involve one primary joint and recruit smaller muscle areas (e.g., forearm, calf, lower back, anterior lower leg, etc.).

Examples:

- Abdominal Crunch (abdomen): Rectus abdominis
- Standing Calf-Raise Machine: Gastrocnemius, soleus
- Wrist Curl (forearms): Flexor carpi ulnaris, flexor carpi radialis, palmaris longus
- Lateral Shoulder Raise (shoulders): Deltoids
- Bent-Over Row (upper back): Middle trapezius, latissimus dorsi, posterior deltoids, rhomboids, teres major
- Lying Triceps Extensions (posterior upper arm): Triceps brachii
- Stiff-Leg Deadlift (posterior hip and thigh): Semimembranosus, gluteus maximus, biceps femoris, erector spinae, semitendinosus
- Hammer Curl (biceps): Brachialis, biceps brachii, brachioradialis

Example of changing an exercise to change the muscles used (wrist) include:

- Wrist Extensions (pronated grip on the bar): Extensor carpi radialis brevis and longus, extensor carpi ulnaris
- Wrist Curl (supinated grip on the bar): Palmaris longus, flexor carpi ulnaris, flexor carpi radialis

Exercises Based on the Type of Kinetic Chain Movement

Open Kinetic Chain (OKC) Movements

OKC exercises are performed when the athlete's hands or feet are not in contact with a surface (i.e., the hands or feet are not fixed). OKC exercises for the lower extremity include knee-extension and leg-curl exercises. Examples of upper-extremity OKC exercises include triceps pushdowns, biceps curls, and wrist curls. OKC exercises allow for greater focus to be placed on specific joints or muscles.

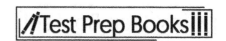

Closed Kinetic Chain (CKC) Movements

CKC exercises are performed with the extremity in continual contact with a surface (e.g., feet on the ground or hands on a machine handle). The hands or feet do not move during the exercise. Examples of lower-extremity CKC exercises are squats, lunges, and leg presses. Examples of upper-extremity CKC exercises are pull-ups and push-ups. CKC exercises allow for increased joint stability and functional movement patterns.

Exercises to Minimize Injury Potential

Muscle Balance

Resistance-training programs designed for any sport should ensure that there is a balance in exercises across opposing muscle groups. Disparities in the strength of agonist and antagonist muscles can result in an increased risk of injury. For example, if the hamstrings are weaker than the quadriceps, then it is important to add hamstring exercises to the training program in order to address the muscle imbalance. Addressing muscle imbalance involves improving the *strength ratios* in antagonist muscle groups rather than making opposing muscle groups equally strong. One example of muscle balance is a 3:4 strength ratio between hamstrings and quadriceps.

Alternation of Upper- and Lower-Body Exercises

The alternation of upper- and lower-body resistance exercises during a training session increases recovery between exercises by maximizing the length of rest periods. Alternating exercises is beneficial for untrained athletes who may find doing multiple upper- or lower-body exercises in a row too strenuous.

Order of Resistance Exercises

The order of resistance exercises during a session should be power exercises, followed by core exercises, and then assistance exercises. Power exercises require the most skill and concentration and are detrimentally affected by fatigue. Fatigue can result in poor technique, which can increase the risk of injury.

Split Routine

Intermediate and advanced athletes may use a split routine where they focus on training different muscle groups on different days. This format allows athletes to do resistance training almost every day. Although training daily goes against the recommended 1–3 days of rest between resistance-training sessions, each session in a split routine focuses on a different muscle group, so there is adequate recovery time between the sessions that train the same muscle groups. Adequate recovery time decreases the risk of overstressing the muscles and potentially increasing the risk of injury.

Flexibility

Athletes that do not have the level of flexibility required for their sport or have too much flexibility are at an increased risk of injury. Flexibility training can help to increase an athlete's ROM during sport-related movements. Hyperflexibility will require the strength and conditioning professional to take a close look at the athlete's resistance and flexibility programs to determine appropriate changes aimed at decreasing ROM. Increasing muscle bulk, participating in heavy resistance training, and reducing the number of flexibility exercises may help an athlete minimize their hyperflexibility.

Exercises to Promote Recovery

A recovery exercise is any exercise that avoids high muscular or nervous stress while, at the same time, promoting movement and restoration. Recovery exercises help with the removal of metabolic waste and byproducts while maintaining blood flow to the exercised muscles. This helps to optimize the repair of the exercised muscles by facilitating recovery and restoration. Recovery exercises are commonly done at the end of the resistance-training session or during a separate session within the microcycle. Examples of recovery exercises include low-intensity aerobic exercise or lightly loaded resistance exercises.

Principles of Exercise Order

Order of Exercises Based on the Training Goal

Exercise order is the sequence of resistance exercises that are performed during one training session. There are numerous approaches for ordering exercises. Four common approaches are as follows:

- Power, then other core, then assistance exercises
- Alternated upper- and lower-body exercises
- Alternated "push" and "pull" exercises
- Supersets and compound sets

The strength and conditioning professional needs to consider how one resistance exercise affects the effort and technical quality of the subsequent exercise. It is critical that the need for technique and effort are considered in ordering resistance exercise because fatigue can cause athletes to use poor technique, thus increasing the risk for injury.

Variations in Exercise Orders

Power, Other Core, Assistance Exercises

Training sessions typically order the exercises from the most metabolically demanding and technical (i.e., power exercises) to the least demanding exercises (i.e., core and assistance exercises). The strength and conditioning professional must consider both the technique and effort required when ordering resistance exercises because fatigue can cause athletes to use poor technique and increase their risk for injury. For example, Olympic lifts are the most demanding power exercises because they place large metabolic demands on the athlete's body, require excellent technique and concentration, and are the most affected by fatigue. Accordingly, power exercises would be completed first during a training session. Non-power core exercises (i.e., multi-joint exercises) are completed next because they require quality technique, load the spine, and place large metabolic demands on the athlete's body. Finally, assistance or single-joint exercises are performed last because they are less technical and the least demanding resistance exercises.

Alternated Upper- and Lower-Body Exercises

Alternating upper- and lower-body resistance exercises allows for greater recovery between exercises. This training order is useful when training time is limited, because it minimizes the rest needed between exercises while maximizing the rest for the upper- and lower body between sets. When minimal rest is provided between sets, the method is called circuit training. Because circuit training requires an athlete to train with minimal rest between sets, this training style helps to improve mental focus. Also, the lack of rest requires the athlete to perform more exercises in a shorter period of time, and therefore helps to reduce body fat by imposing significant metabolic demands on the athlete.

Alternating "Push" and "Pull' Exercises

This variation alternates between pushing resistance exercises, such as shoulder presses or triceps extensions, and pulling exercises, such as bent-over rows and biceps curls. Alternating push and pull exercises improves recovery and recruitment between the exercises by ensuring that the same muscle group is not used in two consecutive exercises. Examples of push-pull exercise arrangements for the lower body include back squat (push) and leg (knee) curl (pull) and leg press (push) and stiff-leg deadlift (pull). Circuit training often uses alternating push and pull exercises. This ordering method can be used with athletes starting or returning to resistance exercise training.

Supersets

A superset is the performance of two resistance exercises sequentially. The first exercise stresses an agonist muscle or muscle group and the second exercise stresses the antagonist muscle or muscle group. An example of a superset is ten repetitions of triceps pushdowns followed immediately by ten repetitions of barbell biceps curls. Supersets efficiently use training time but may not be appropriate for unconditioned athletes or those needing significant training instruction.

Compound Sets

A compound set is the performance of two different resistance exercises in a row in order to stress the same muscle or the muscle groups. For example, a set of barbell biceps curls is followed immediately by dumbbell hammer curls. Compound sets are time-efficient and demanding, causing greater stress to the muscles. This type of training is not appropriate for unconditioned athletes.

Variations in Exercise Modes

Explosive Training

Explosive training can include power exercises (structural exercises performed very fast) and various plyometric exercises (e.g., box jumps, drop jumps, loaded jumps). The goal is primarily to increase power, or the ability of muscles to generate high forces very quickly. Agility training can also help the neuromuscular system develop, which can aid in explosive power.

Strength Training

Strength training, also called resistance training, can take on a variety of forms. Weight machines, free weights (such as dumbbells, kettlebells, and weight plates), medicine balls, resistance bands, and nontraditional implements like logs and chains can all be used for strength training. Body weight exercises can also be considered strength training, depending on the move and the skill level of the athlete, as the basic definition of *strength training* is any exercise or movement that can lead to increased strength. It should be noted that strength training can be geared toward a variety of goals, including muscle hypertrophy, strength gains, and increased muscular endurance. The best equipment, load, and volume to employ will vary depending on the goal. Moreover, it's important to deliberately alter exercises and resistance training modes for the individual athlete in order to prevent the body from becoming too accustomed to the program, which can be detrimental to continual progress. Sets, reps, equipment, timing/pacing, and exercises should be rotated and steadily increased in difficultly in order to encourage physiological progress and prevent boredom.

Warmup/Workout/Cooldown

Warm-Ups are usually 10–20 minutes and consist of two specific periods, or they may be structured based on the raise, activate and mobilize, and potentiate (RAMP) protocol. The general warm-up period is 5 minutes of slow aerobic activity (e.g., jogging) followed by general stretching that focuses on ROM of the upcoming activities. This is followed by the specific warm-up period, which consists of movements that replicate those required for the upcoming activity. The RAMP Protocol consists of the following:

- Raise: Phase 1 of the protocol consists of activities that raise various physiological parameters like heart and respiration rates, body temperature, and blood flow. The activities simulate movement activities associated with the upcoming activity or develop skill patterns required for the specific sport.

- Activate and Mobilize: Phase 2 of the protocol focuses on mobility and may include dynamic stretching for muscles and mobility exercises for joints.

- Potentiation: Phase 3 of the protocol is sport specific, with a focus on progressing the intensity of the activity to the intensity required for the training or competition.

Note: This is followed by the planned workout, which may include resistance training, plyometrics, speed and agility, aerobic endurance, etc.

Workout: This is the main component of an exercise session. It may involve strength training, running, endurance exercise, sprints, power training, intervals, etc., or any combination thereof.

Cooldown: This is a period of low-intensity exercise such as stretching that allows the body's physiological parameters to return to their normal levels.

Energy System Training Prioritization

As mentioned, specific types of training can affect the phosphagen system, glycolytic system, and oxidative system in various ways. Carbohydrates, fats, and proteins can be metabolized for energy, but carbohydrates are the only macronutrient that can be metabolized without oxygen.

- Phosphagen System: The phosphagen system provides energy via anaerobic metabolism for brief, high-intensity activities (i.e., up to 6 seconds of extremely high-intensity exercise or 6–30 seconds of very high-intensity exercise). Modes of exercise that can be used to train the phosphagen system include doing resistance exercises in which each set has a low number of repetitions, sprinting less than 200 meters, and performing some types of plyometrics. To improve the phosphagen system's energy production, work-to-rest ratios for training should be between 1:12 and 1:20.

- Glycolytic System: The glycolytic system provides energy during moderate- to high-intensity and short- to medium-duration activities (i.e., 30 seconds to 2 minutes of high-intensity exercise or 2–3 minutes of moderate-intensity exercise). Glycolysis provides energy by breaking down muscle glycogen or blood glucose. Modes of exercise that can be used to train the glycolytic system include sprinting for 200 meters to 800 meters, doing high-intensity interval training, and performing some types of plyometrics. To improve the glycolytic system's energy production, work-to-rest ratios for training should be between 1:3 and 1:5.

- Oxidative (aerobic) System: This system is the primary source of energy during low-intensity and long-duration exercise (i.e., more than 3 minutes). The oxidative system uses carbohydrates (glucose and glycogen) and fats (triglycerides) to produce energy. Aerobic exercise at low to moderate intensities can be used to train the aerobic system. To improve the oxidative system's energy production, work-to-rest ratios for training should be 1:1 to 1:3.

Determining and Assigning Exercise Intensities

Methods for Assigning an Exercise Load or Exercise Heart Rate

Exercise Loads

Repetition Maximum (RM): The repetition maximum (RM) is one of the critical components in designing a resistance-training program, and it is defined as the most weight that can be lifted for a specific number or repetitions. For example, if an athlete can complete six repetitions of the leg press using 100 lb., the 6-RM is 100 lb. The RM provides the strength and conditioning professional with information about the maximum number of repetitions that can be completed at a specific percentage of the 1-RM, which is then used to prescribe loading parameters. The RM provides the number of repetitions that can be completed using a specific weight, whereas the 1-RM requires calculations to be made to determine the percentage of the load to be used. The 1-RM may provide misleading information for some athletes because they can perform a 1-RM better (i.e., the athlete has a higher percentage of fast-twitch muscle fibers) or worse (i.e., the athlete has higher percentage of slow-twitch muscle fibers) than an RM. When possible, it is best to rely on the RM to determine training loads to ensure that the athlete is using the most accurate load.

1-RM: The one-repetition maximum (1-RM) is another critical component in designing a resistance-training program and is defined as the maximum amount of weight that an athlete can lift for only one repetition while maintaining correct technique. Assessment of an athlete's 1-RM for power and structural movements provides the strength and conditioning professional with information that will be used to determine training loads. Note that load is often discussed as the weight associated with a specific percentage of a 1-RM. The 1-RM will be used to establish the load parameters for the resistance training that will be used throughout the training program (i.e., load volumes used for single-training sessions and training weeks) as well as the purpose and goals of the specific training segment. It will be necessary for the strength and conditioning professional to reassess the 1-RM at the end of the training segment in order to evaluate improvements that accrued during the segment and to plan the components (i.e., load parameters, purpose, and goals) of the next training segment.

Exercise RPE

Assessing how hard athletes are working during a training session is critical to ensure that they are putting in appropriate amounts of effort. Asking the athletes how they feel is often not sufficient because the response is subjective with no way to adequately judge the intensity of the work. Numerous methods exist to help quantify the intensity level of an athlete's work during training. Ratings of perceived exertion (RPE) can be assessed using the BORG RPE scale. The original 15-point scale ranges from 6 (no exertion at all) to 20 (maximal exertion), while the revised 10-point scale ranges from 0 (very easy) to 10 (maximum effort). Importantly, both forms of the RPE scale provide the athlete with the ability to quantify perceived exertion.

In general, the 15-point scale may be easiest for athletes to use, particularly if training sessions are based on training at a specific percentage of maximum heart rate or VO_2 max. There is a strong correlation between athletes' RPE score multiplied by 10 and their actual heart rate during exercise. For example, an RPE of 14 corresponds to an expected heart rate during exercise of 140 beats per minute. Note that RPE is the preferred method for evaluating exercise intensity among individuals who have conditions or take medications that affect their heart rate or pulse. The Borg RPE scale may be one of the easiest methods used to communicate workout intensity levels. This scale is also a cost-friendly option because it can be used without having to buy heart-rate monitors or other types of assessment systems. The table below depicts how the Borg RPE scale, the revised-RPE scale, percentage of maximum heart rate (i.e., intensity), and exercise type are related.

How Borg RPE Scales, Type of Exercise, and Percentage of Maximum Heart Rate Are Related

BORG RPE SCALE	BORG REVISED-RPE SCALE	EXERCISE TYPE	PERCENT OF MAXIMUM HEART RATE
6	0	WARM-UP	50%–60%
7			
8	1		
9			
10	2	RECOVERY	60%–70%
11			
12	3		
13		AEROBIC	70%–80%
14	4		
15	5	ANAEROBIC	80%–90%
16	6		
17	7	VO_2 max	90%–100%
18	8		
19	9		
20	10		

Exercise Heart Rate

Maximal Heart Rate (MHR): MHR refers to the highest heart rate achieved during a maximal-exercise (VO_2 max) test. This is the preferred method for determining exercise intensities that are associated with a specific percentage of MHR because it is based on the most accurate MHR data.

Age-Predicted Maximal Heart Rate (APMHR): If it is not possible to conduct a VO_2 max test to obtain an athlete's MHR, alternative methods, such as APMHR, may be used. The APMHR is calculated using a simple formula ($220 - \text{athlete's chronological age} = \text{predicted MHR}$). This is a general estimation that does not take into account actual heart-rate capacity, so the calculated predicted MHR may be higher or lower than the actual MHR. APMHR for a 20-year-old male is calculated as $220 - 20 = 200$ beats/min. If this athlete wants to exercise at 70% intensity, his target heart rate would be calculated as follows: $200 \text{ beats/min} \times .70 = 140 \text{ beats/min}$.

Karvonen Method: The Karvonen method provides a better estimate of target heart rate because it accounts for the athlete's resting heart rate (RHR), which is an indicator of fitness level. The Karvonen method uses the following formula:

$$\text{Target Heart Rate} = \big((\text{APMHR} - \text{RHR}) \times \%\ \text{intensity}\big) + \text{RHR}$$

For example, the target heart rate (also known as the percentage of MHR) is calculated for a 20-year-old athlete with a RHR of 50 beats/minute and a goal training intensity of 70% by first using the APMHR formula to calculate the estimated maximal heart rate: $220 - 20 = 200$ beats/min. Then the RHR is subtracted from this value. From here, the desired ($200 - 50 = 150$ beats/min) intensity is factored in by multiplying (($\text{APMHR} - \text{RHR}) \times \%\ \text{intensity}$), which in this case is ($150 \text{ beats/min} \times .70) = 105$ beats/min. In the last step, target heart rate is calculated by adding RHR back to this value: $105 \text{ beats/min} + 50 \text{ beats/min (RHR)} = 155 \text{ beats/min}$.

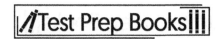

Functional Capacity (heart-rate reserve, or HRR): Prescribing aerobic-exercise intensity using heart rate is very common because of the close relationship between an athlete's heart rate and oxygen consumption. Functional capacity is also known as HRR, and it is the difference between the MHR and RHR (MHR - RHR). HRR is the most accurate method for prescribing and adjusting aerobic-training intensity because it takes advantage of the relationship between heart rate and oxygen consumption and accounts for physiological adaptation to aerobic-exercise training by taking RHR into consideration.

RHR can decrease over time in response to training. As an athlete's RHR decreases, HRR increases. The increase in HRR allows the athlete to exercise longer at a given intensity while experiencing less fatigue. The most accurate way to assess functional capacity is to do a laboratory-based VO_2 max test. This assessment is often not available to strength and conditioning professionals, so an alternative method, such as APMHR, can be used to prescribe training intensity.

Lactate

Lactate Threshold: Some research suggests that an athlete's lactate threshold may be a better indicator of aerobic capacity than VO_2 max. The strength and conditioning professional can work to increase an athlete's lactate threshold, thus allowing the athlete to work harder and longer. An increased lactate threshold can improve performance and enhance recovery from competition and training, ultimately resulting in the athlete being able to sustain higher work rates in competitions.

Maximal-Lactate Steady State: Maximal-lactate steady state is defined as the exercise intensity at which the maximal amount of lactate produced by the muscles is equivalent to the maximum amount of lactate that can be removed from the body. This state reflects the highest exercise intensity that an athlete can sustain before quickly becoming fatigued when the lactate threshold is crossed. The maximal-lactate steady state provides information about the exercise intensity level and duration that allows the athlete to maintain the balance between lactate production and clearing. This information can be used for designing endurance-training programs in which the athlete must exceed the lactate threshold in order to increase the maximal-lactate steady state and improve endurance performance.

Load or Exercise Heart Rate Based on the Training Goal

Load-Based Training for Resistance Exercise

As listed below, the recommended percentage of 1-RM load depends on training goals:

- muscular endurance: ≤ 67%
- hypertrophy: 67% to 85%
- strength: ≥ 85%
- power, single effort (e.g., long jump, discus): 80% to 90%
- power, multiple effort (e.g., volleyball, basketball): 75% to 85%

Aerobic Endurance and Heart Rate for Training Goals

Aerobic endurance-training programs are generally designed to improve maximal aerobic capacity (VO_2 max). However, other factors that influence performance also can guide training goals. These include increasing exercise economy and efficiently using fat as a fuel source, increasing lactate threshold, and increasing the size of Type I muscle fibers. There are several types of aerobic-training programs, and each of these affects one or more training goals. The heart rates associated with the training goals will be presented as a percentage of the MHR and a percentage of the HRR.

Training Goal

Training methods used to increase VO_2 max are described below:

- Interval training uses 3–5 minutes of running at intensities close to VO_2 max with rest periods (work/rest ratio of 1:1). Running at 85–95 percent of VO_2 max is equivalent to 92–98 percent of MHR or 85–95 percent of HRR.

- Fartlek training combines easy aerobic exercise (~70 percent of VO_2 max) with short bouts of fast exercise (85–95 percent of VO_2 max). Heart rate during Fartlek training should be 81 percent of MHR or 70 percent of HRR during the easy exercise and 92–98 percent of MHR or 85–95 percent of HRR during the fast exercise.

Training methods used to improve exercise/running economy are described below:

- Pace/tempo training is usually 20–30 minutes of running at or slightly above race pace. The intensity should be close to the lactate threshold. In a trained individual, lactate threshold is usually about 80 percent of VO_2 max, which is equivalent to 88 percent of MHR or 80 percent of HHR.

- High-intensity interval training consists of repeated short bouts (30–90 seconds) of high-intensity exercise (at or above 90 percent of VO_2 max) with intermittent periods of short rest. The training heart rate associated with this type of training is 96–100 percent of MHR or 90–100 percent of HRR.

- Fartlek training (aerobic exercise at ~70 percent of VO_2 max and short bouts of fast exercise at 85–95 percent of VO_2 max; heart rate at 81 percent of MHR or 70 percent of HRR for aerobic exercise and at 92–98 percent of MHR or 85–95 percent of HRR for short bouts of fast exercise)

Training methods used to increase the efficient use of fat as a fuel source are described below:

- LSD running requires a running duration of 30 minutes to 2 hours at a heart rate that is approximately 81 percent of MRR or 70 percent HRR (equivalent to 70 percent of VO_2 max)

- Fartlek training (aerobic exercise at ~70 percent of VO_2 max and short bouts of fast exercise at 85–95 percent of VO_2 max; heart rate at 81 percent of MHR or 70 percent of HRR for aerobic exercise and at 92–98 percent of MHR or 85–95 percent of HRR for short bouts of fast exercise)

Training methods used to increase lactate threshold are described below:

- LSD running to improve the clearance of lactate from the body and ultimately improve lactate threshold (30 minutes to 2 hours at approximately 81 percent of MRR or 70 percent HRR, equivalent to 70 percent of VO_2 max)

- Pace/tempo training (20–30 minutes of running at or slightly above race pace, close to the lactate threshold)

- High-intensity interval training (repeated short bouts at or above 90 percent of VO_2 max with intermittent periods of short rest; training heart rate 96–100 percent of MHR or 90–100 percent of HRR)

- Fartlek training (aerobic exercise at ~70 percent of VO_2 max and short bouts of fast exercise at 85–95 percent of VO_2 max; heart rate at 81 percent of MHR or 70 percent of HRR for aerobic exercise and at 92–98 percent of MHR or 85–95 percent of HRR for short bouts of fast exercise)

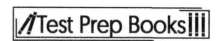

LSD running can increase the recruitment of Type I muscle fibers. Long-term LSD running affects the metabolic characteristics of muscles, causing a shift from Type IIx to Type I muscle fibers.

Determining and Assigning Training Volumes

Outcomes Associated with the Manipulation of Training Volume

Training volume is one variable that can be manipulated in order to progress an exercise-training program. The increased physical stress that can result from increases in training volume can cause physiological adaptations. General adaptation syndrome (GAS) occurs when the body is subjected to external loading. Firstly, the athlete will experience soreness, stiffness, and decreased performance (alarm phase). Secondly, the body will return to normal (resistance phase). Thirdly, the body will adapt and the athlete's muscle mass and strength will increase (supercompensation phase). If training volume is increased and the athlete is unable to adapt, the athlete may experience overload, resulting in overtraining syndrome.

Decreasing training volume and intensity—called *tapering*—is a key part of an endurance athlete's preparation for important competitions. A taper may last between 7 and 28 days, and it allows the athlete's body to completely recover from training and build muscle and liver glycogen storage. The elevation of the athlete's performance capacity that results from tapering is sometimes referred to as supercompensation. In contrast, if exercise volume and intensity decrease (resulting from illness, injury, etc., the athlete will begin to lose the physiological adaptations achieved from training, which is called *detraining.*

Volume Based on the Training Goal

Muscular Endurance: Resistance programs focused on improving muscular endurance require performing many repetitions (at least twelve) per set with lighter loads and completing two to three sets.

Hypertrophy: Resistance programs focused on hypertrophy require athletes to use heavier loads and complete fewer repetitions than they would if they were training for muscular endurance. Hypertrophy is defined as developing larger muscles. There are two forms of hypertrophy: sarcoplasmic hypertrophy and myofibrillar hypertrophy. Sarcoplasmic hypertrophy occurs when muscles adjust to high training volumes. In this form of hypertrophy, the inside of the muscle cell (the sarcoplasm) gets bigger through increasing the proteins, fluid, and mitochondria within the sarcoplasm. Myofibrillar hypertrophy occurs when the contractile proteins of the muscle (myosin and actin) are produced more rapidly after strength exercises.

As myosin and actin link to form filaments and the number of filaments increase, the muscle is able to generate more force. Greater force production results in increased muscle strength. Sarcoplasmic and myofibrillar hypertrophy occur together, although the proportion of each type of hypertrophy depends on the type of training. Bodybuilders tend to have more sarcoplasmic hypertrophy while weightlifters tend to have more myofibrillar hypertrophy. Since sarcoplasmic hypertrophy cannot occur without myofibrillar hypertrophy, athletes who want to increase muscle size will generally experience an increase in strength. In general, the guidelines for a resistance-training program aimed at increasing hypertrophy include a goal of six to twelve repetitions of each exercise done for three to six sets.

Strength: An athlete may choose to pursue a resistance program that focuses on increasing strength without increasing muscle size. For example, a powerlifter may be stronger than a bodybuilder even though the bodybuilder has larger amounts of muscle mass. Research suggests that optimal strength improvements can be achieved by doing two to five sets of six or fewer repetitions (at the corresponding RM load) for core exercises. Assistance exercises may require only one to three sets.

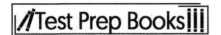

Power: Lower volumes than required for strength are typically used to maximize the performance quality of the resistance exercise to increase power. Fewer repetitions (one to five repetitions over three to five sets) and lighter loads are used to decrease volume.

Aerobic Endurance: In running or other modes of endurance exercise (e.g., cycling, swimming), volume is based on distance. When the intensity of the endurance exercise is known, it is possible to calculate the total metabolic cost, which is equivalent to volume load for resistance exercise. The most efficient way to substantially increase running volume is to do LSD training. Volume can be increased by either increasing the duration of the run over time (i.e., start at 30 minutes and build to 2 hours) or increasing the number of days per week that LSD running is completed. Generally, it is better to increase the duration of the LSD training than to increase the number of training sessions per week. LSD training that is done too often can be detrimental to competitive performance and can alter the muscle fiber recruitment patterns that are required during a race. Increasing the number of intervals completed during high-intensity interval training or increasing the duration of Fartlek training runs can also increase training volume.

Determining and Assigning Work/Rest Periods, Recovery and Unloading, and Training

Work/Rest Periods and Recovery

The length of rest periods between sets and different resistance exercises depends on three variables: the goal of training, the relative load lifted, and the athlete's training condition. Athletes in poor condition need longer rest periods when starting a resistance-training program. Generally, the amount of rest between sets is positively associated with the load (i.e., heavier loads require more rest, lighter loads require less rest).

Different rest period lengths can lead to a variety of physiological changes and should be considered in the context of the athlete's goals. Longer rest periods promote nervous system and muscular system recovery, while shorter rest periods promote cardiovascular conditioning.

Recommended Rest Period Length Per Training Goal

Muscular Endurance: It is recommended that rest periods between workloads are less than 30 seconds. Because muscular endurance training uses light loads and many repetitions, only a short amount of rest is used. Circuit training typically uses rest periods of 30 seconds or less between resistance exercises.

Hypertrophy: It is recommended that rest periods between workloads are between 30 and 90 seconds. To increase muscle size, research suggests that it is best to use a limited rest period that does not allow the athlete to fully recover before starting the next set. Strength and conditioning professionals should recognize that resistance exercises using large muscle groups might require extra recovery time because of the metabolic demands of the exercises.

Strength: It is recommended that rest periods between workloads are 2–5 minutes. Maximal or near-maximal repetitions require longer rest periods, particularly for lower-body and all-body structural exercises.

Power: It is recommended that rest periods between workloads are 2–5 minutes, which is similar to the rest periods for developing strength. Maximal or near-maximal repetitions (i.e., heavy load) require longer rest periods, particularly for lower-body and all-body structural exercises.

Metabolic Conditioning: The work-to-rest ratios should be based on the specific energy system stressed. For the phosphagen system, ratios of 1:12 to 1:20 are best. Fast glycolysis should use 1:3 to 1:5 work-to-rest ratios. The glycolytic (fast glycolysis) and oxidative systems together use ratios of 1:3 to 1:4. The oxidative only is optimized with a ratio of 1:1 to 1:3.

Plyometric Exercises: Plyometric exercises involving maximal effort can improve *anaerobic power*, but adequate recovery time is needed for full recovery. The time between sets is based on a work-to-rest ratio that depends on the volume and type of drill. Work-to-rest ratios are often 1:5 to 1:10. Rest periods between repetitions of certain exercises (e.g., depth jumps) may be five to ten seconds.

Recommended Recovery for Various Types of Training

Resistance Exercise: Typically, one to three days of rest is recommended between resistance-training sessions that focus on the same muscle groups.

Plyometrics: Generally, two to four days of recovery is needed between plyometric-training sessions. This specific number of days will depend on the athlete's sport and the sport season. A specific body area should not be trained on consecutive days.

Aerobic Endurance Exercise: At least one rest day, or active rest day, per week is recommended with endurance-training programs.

Training Frequency

Resistance-training frequency is primarily based on the sport season and the athlete's training status. The training goal(s) associated with each sport season and the athlete's training status will influence the number of weekly resistance-training sessions. For example, if hypertrophy is the training goal for the off-season, the athlete will complete between four and six sessions per week. During preseason, the training goal might be strength. Because there is an increase in sport-specific training in preseason, the athlete will have less time for resistance training and the number of sessions per week will be reduced to three to four sessions per week.

During the in-season, one to three sessions per week are recommended, and in the postseason period (active rest), the athlete should participate in zero to three sessions per week, depending on the goal and training status of the athlete. The strength and conditioning professional needs to determine the resistance-training goal for each sport season as well as the number of weekly training sessions that will be possible based on the athlete's entire training program. More advanced athletes may be able to handle four to seven sessions per week, while novices may only be able to safely handle two to three sessions per week.

Determining and Assigning Exercise Progression

Determining and assigning exercise progression for an aerobic-exercise program requires the manipulation of the following variables:

- Exercise Mode: The specific type of activity the athlete is doing (examples include swimming, running, cycling, resistance exercise, and plyometrics)
- Training Frequency: The number of exercise sessions completed daily or weekly
- Exercise Duration: The length or amount of time of the training session or bout of aerobic exercise

- Training Intensity: The amount of effort expended during a training session

Aerobic-Exercise Progression

Progression starts with increases in the frequency, intensity, and/or duration of aerobic endurance exercise; however, these increases should not be greater than 10 percent per week. Elite athletes reach a point where it may not be feasible to increase the frequency or duration of exercise, so progression will involve the manipulation of the intensity of the exercise. Exercise intensity should be monitored using RPE, heart rate, or METS (if machines provide this information) depending on which method was originally used to determine the original exercise intensity prescription. At least one recovery day, or active recovery day, should be included each week.

Plyometric-Training Program Length and Progression

Most plyometric-training programs are six to ten weeks in length; however, a four-week plyometric program has been shown to improve vertical-jump height. Similar to many of the other plyometric-training variables, there is limited research examining the effectiveness of programs having varying lengths, so the optimal program length has not been determined. It should be noted that doing plyometric training throughout the season can be beneficial for athletes in sports that require quick and powerful movements. Because plyometrics are a type of resistance training, program progression should follow the principles of progressive overload, which systematically increase training intensity, volume, and frequency in varying combinations. The strength and conditioning professional develops the training schedule and progressive overload based on the sport, training phase, and design of the strength and conditioning program. Athlete experience, sport requirements, and sport season are used to determine the length and progression of the plyometric-training program. Remember that plyometric training is added to an athlete's strength and conditioning program in order to develop more power.

Resistance-Training Progression

Timing of Load Increases

Two-for-Two Rule: The two-for-two rule provides a conservative guideline of structure and consistency for determining when an athlete's training load should be increased across training sessions. Using the rule allows athletes to understand how their training load progresses for each exercise and that sustained performance is needed in order for progression to occur. The rule indicates that when an athlete is able to do two additional repetitions during the last set of the exercise and the athlete does this in two consecutive sessions, the weight should be increased at the next training session.

Quantity of Load Increases

Making the decision to increase load can be difficult. The strength and conditioning professional must consider the athlete's physical condition as well as the body area where the load increase will occur. An athlete who is sleep deprived or who has a poor diet will not be able to increase the training load as readily as an athlete who is well-rested or who has a balanced diet. Also, an athlete who trains too frequently will not be able to progress as quickly as an athlete who gets an appropriate amount of rest between training sessions.

There are general guidelines for increasing load; however, the amount of variation in the exercises and volume loads will significantly affect what load-value increases are appropriate for a specific athlete. Guidelines for specific load increases, as well as relative load increases, can be used to determine load progression. The general recommendations for absolute load increases for weaker, smaller, or less-trained athletes are 2.5–5.0 lb (1–2 kg) per week for upper body exercises and 5–10+ lb (2–4+ kg) per week for lower body exercises. Stronger, larger, or more-trained athletes may increase upper body loads by 5–10+ lb (2–4+ kg) per week and lower body loads by 10–15+ lb (4–7+ kg) per week. Relative load increases of 2.5–10.0 percent, rather than absolute load-increase values, can be used for all athletes.

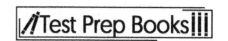

Periodization Models

Periodization

Periodization is a training plan that uses logical phases of training, during which training variables are manipulated to produce physiological adaptations, manage fatigue, minimize overtraining, and promote maximum athletic performance. The periodization plan includes all aspects of training that are planned over a specific period of time (typically one year or, in some cases, two to four years). The preplanned training loads, load volumes, and training intensities are designed to apply the training stress necessary to cause adaptive responses in the athlete. Periodized training consists of segments that are organized around the athlete's sport season and sport activities in a way that will allow training adaptations to occur at appropriate times, thereby improving the athlete's competitive performance.

Macrocycle

The macrocycle is the primary periodization component consisting of the entire annual training program. A macrocycle is typically a year but can be several months or, in rare cases, up to a four-year developmental plan (e.g., Olympic training cycle). The macrocycle consists of smaller segments that are used to focus on specific aspects of training in order to develop the specific athletic qualities required for the athlete to peak and perform optimally during competition. A common macrocycle divides the athlete's training year into off-season, preseason, in-season (i.e., competition), and postseason periods.

Mesocycle

A mesocycle is a segment of the macrocycle that is generally a block of two to six weeks (four weeks is the most common length). This time frame has been shown to optimize adaptations to training.

Microcycle

A microcycle is the shortest training segment, lasting from several days to weeks. Variables like intensity and volume can be manipulated to alter the athlete's training within the microcycle segment. The manipulation of the microcycle training is an important part of tapering athletes for competition. An athlete's training progress can be consistently monitored and altered across the microcycle.

Preparatory Period

The preparatory period is usually the starting point of the periodization training plan. It is usually the longest period and most often corresponds to the off-season when there are no competitions. This period establishes a base level of conditioning that will provide the athlete with the ability to tolerate increased training intensity. The preparatory period is divided into the general preparatory phase and the specific preparatory phase.

General Preparatory Phase

The general preparatory phase takes place during the early part of the preparatory period and focuses on developing the general physical conditioning that will be required for the athlete to handle more intense training. The conditioning during this phase consists of high-volume and low-intensity training and includes activities like slow distance swims, resistance training using high repetitions and light to moderate loads, and low-intensity plyometrics.

Hypertrophy/Strength-Endurance Phase

The hypertrophy phase, also known as the strength-endurance phase, takes place during the general preparatory phase. The two primary goals of the hypertrophy phase are to develop the athlete's physical endurance base and increase lean body mass. This phase uses low to moderate intensity and high volume. For example, exercises might consist of three to six sets of eight to twenty repetitions at 50–75 percent of 1-RM.

Specific Preparatory Phase

The specific preparatory phase builds on the general conditioning base and begins to focus on more sport-specific training.

Basic Strength Phase

The basic strength phase occurs during the specific preparatory phase and focuses on increasing the strength of primary sport-specific muscle groups. This is achieved by using higher-intensity and moderate-volume training. For example, exercises might consist of two to six sets of two to six repetitions at 80–95 percent of 1-RM.

First Transition Period

The first transition period is the training segment between the preparatory phase and the competitive period. This "precompetitive" period focuses on converting strength into power. The last week of the first transition period focuses on recovery with reduced work volume and intensity, thus allowing the athlete to recover from training in preparation for the competitive period.

Strength/Power Phase

Definitions:

- Strength: The ability to produce force
- Power/Explosive Strength: The time rate of doing work (power = work x time)
- Work: The product of the force exerted on an object, and the distance the object moves in the direction in which the force is exerted (also called displacement; work = force x displacement)

The strength/power phase is the primary phase of the first transition period (the second segment of the preparatory period). The focus during the strength/power phase is on increasing the intensity of training to pre-competition levels. Resistance-training exercises consist of low to very high loads and low volumes. For example, exercises might consist of two to five sets of two to five repetitions at 30–95 percent of 1-RM.

Competitive Period

The focus of the competitive period (also called the competition period) is preparing the athlete for competition. This is achieved by increasing strength and power. Training intensity increases and volume decreases. Resistance-training exercises consist of moderate and high intensities and moderate volumes. Individual sports with a competition period of several weeks (e.g., fencing or judo) will use a peaking program, while team sports with competition periods of several months will use a maintenance program.

Peaking Programs: The objective of a peaking program is to get the athlete in peak performance condition for one to two weeks. To reduce fatigue, the training progressively shifts from higher-intensity to lower-intensity training as the athlete goes through the taper prior to competition. Resistance-training exercises consist of very high to low intensities and low volumes. For example, exercises might consist of one to three sets of one to two repetitions at 50–93 percent of 1-RM. Trying to extend a peak beyond one to two weeks will decrease fitness and reduce performance capacity.

Maintenance Programs: The extended duration of the competitive period requires training to be manipulated across microcycles. Alterations in training intensity and volume effectively maintain strength and power while simultaneously controlling the fatigue that results from frequent competitions. Resistance-training exercises will be modulated between moderate to high intensities and moderate volumes. For example, resistance exercises would consist of approximately two to five sets of three to six repetitions at 85–93 percent of 1-RM. It should be noted that the two-to-five-set recommendation does not include warm-up sets and is the target number of sets for core exercises only.

Second Transition Period

The second transition period (also called active rest or restoration period) is between the competitive period and preparatory period of the next macrocycle and is typically one to four weeks in duration. During this period, intense training is avoided in order to allow athletes to recover from injury and get both physical and mental rest. If this period lasts longer than four weeks, the preparatory phase will need to be longer to allow enough time for the athlete to regain a conditioning base. During this period, athletes can participate in other recreational sports and resistance training, if desired, using very low volumes and loads.

Unloading/Deloading Week

The second transition period can be designed to have one-week rests between three-week training phases. The week of rest allows the body to "unload" in preparation for the upcoming training.

Periodization Models

Linear Periodization Model: This is the "traditional" resistance-training periodization model. It is called linear because of the gradually progressive increases in mesocycle intensity, but this is actually a misnomer because the linear model has substantial amounts of variation in intensities and volumes at the microcycle level and across the mesocycle. Resistance-training exercises will consist of the same number of sets and repetitions daily over a certain span of time, but the load will vary. This type of training results in volume-load changes.

Undulating Periodization Model: Also called the nonlinear periodization model by individuals in the strength and conditioning industry, the undulating periodization model has daily fluctuations in training intensities and volumes for core resistance-training exercises. During a training week, one day may be focused on strength (four sets with a 6-RM load), the second day might focus on power (five sets with a 3-RM load), and the third set might focus on hypertrophy (three sets with a 10-RM load).

Training Variations Based on a Sport Season

Professional and collegiate sports usually have an annual schedule broken into four sport seasons: off-season, preseason, in-season, and postseason. In periodization, the macrocycle is typically an annual training plan, so the four sport seasons easily relate to the training periods in the periodization model.

Off-Season

Off-season lasts from the end of postseason to the beginning of preseason with the actual duration of the off-season varying greatly depending upon the sport. An athlete in the off-season must build up cardiorespiratory strength gradually with low-intensity and long-duration training before progressing to a shorter and more intense program in the preseason and preparing for competition. The off-season occurs during the preparatory period. The general and specific preparatory phases (subdivisions of the preparatory period) are broken into mesocycles. The mesocycles focus on hypertrophy/strength endurance and basic strength and are planned based on an athlete's needs and preparation for the competition period. For example, if basketball players need to increase muscle mass, they would complete a greater number of mesocycles that focus on the hypertrophy/strength-endurance phase.

Preseason

Preseason follows the completion of the off-season and leads into the first competition. Preseason often coincides with the first transition period and focuses on the strength/power phase with an increase in the intensity of training. Preseason training builds on the physical capacity developed during off-season training with the goal of increasing performance capacity for the competitive period.

In-Season

Also known as the competition period, the in-season consists of all the competitions and tournament games for the year.

Postseason

Postseason corresponds to the second transition period and begins after the final competition. Postseason provides athletes with an active rest period during which intense training is avoided. Because detraining can occur during postseason, longer postseasons require longer preparatory periods during the next year's off-season.

A Periodized Program Specific to the Athlete's Demands of a Sport, Position, and Training Level

As previously discussed, periodized training programs use deliberate, scientifically-supported phases of training, during which training variables are manipulated to produce specific physiological adaptations, manage fatigue, minimize overtraining, and promote maximum athletic performance. Periodized training plans are usually split into large macrocycles (usually one or two per year, depending on the sport and athlete's skill level and goals) that are then further broken down into meso- and microcycles. Strength and conditioning professionals must tailor the length of these cycles as well as the training variables (mode, duration, intensity, and volume of exercise) for a given athlete's sport, position, training level, and competition schedule. The goal is to help each athlete reach their peak physical performance level at the most crucial competitions of their season and/or year. For example, when working with a collegiate basketball team, the strength coach would want to build the program in such a way that the players would peak during the March madness tournament. The specific volume, workouts, and workloads needed to achieve this will vary for each athlete based on their starting fitness, position, and experience.

Designing Programs for Injured Athletes During the Reconditioning Period

Common Injuries

- Dislocation: A joint is completely displaced from its articulating surfaces.
- Subluxation: A joint is partially displaced from its articulating surfaces.
- Strain: A macrotrauma to muscles causes the muscle tissues to partially or completely tear.
- Sprain: A macrotrauma injures joint ligaments.
- Macrotrauma: A tissue (i.e., bone, muscle, ligaments, etc.) is overburdened, which results in poorer tissue health and quality.
- Microtrauma: A tissue becomes overstressed from overtraining.
- Tendinitis: A tendon becomes inflamed from stress on the joint due to overuse or surface resistance.
- Fibrosis: Scar tissue forms near joints. This age-related disorder affects the health and quality of muscle tissue and can limit joint movement, thus increasing the risk of injury.

Tissue Healing and Reconditioning

Inflammatory Response Phase

This phase is characterized by pain, swelling, redness, increases in inflammatory cells, and reduced collagen production; it typically lasts two to six days. Inflammation starts immediately after injury and can occur both locally at the site of injury and systemically.

Treatment Goals: The suggested treatment to minimize inflammation and decrease pain is PRICE (protection, rest, ice, compression, and elevation). Electrical stimulation may also be used as a treatment. Maintenance of the function of the cardiovascular system and the strength, endurance, and power of the musculoskeletal tissues are important.

Exercise Strategies: The injured area should get rest. Exercises that do not directly involve the injured area can be performed after the strength and conditioning professional discusses the exercises that are indicated and contraindicated for the injury with the athletic trainer.

Fibroblastic Repair Phase

This phase is characterized by decreased inflammatory cell activity, collagen-fiber production, and organization. It starts after inflammation materials have been removed and may last up to two months. The breakdown of nonviable tissue (catabolism) due to injury occurs and nonviable tissues are replaced. To increase the integrity of the tissue, scar tissue and capillaries form in the injured area with Type III collagen being produced and put down transversely along the injured structure.

Treatment Goals: The suggested treatment for this phase is to continue reducing inflammation, minimize muscle atrophy, maintain ROM (minimize contractures and adhesion formation), and improve strength and function. Minimizing joint deterioration and muscle atrophy in the injured area is the primary treatment goal.

Exercise Strategies: Under the consultation of a team doctor or athletic trainer, submaximal isometric exercises can be performed if the athlete is free of pain. Isokinetic exercise with equipment can be used; however, this method is limited because few sport motions occur at a constant speed. Isotonic exercises can be performed with concentric and eccentric muscle movements to increase the strength of the healing tissue. Proprioceptive exercises can be used to improve neuromuscular control. These include completing common exercises such as push-ups on uneven surfaces and using equipment (e.g., mini trampolines, balance boards, or stability balls) that create uneven surfaces for training. Removing visual input by closing the eyes during these exercises can further develop balance. To further challenge the body, the final exercise strategy is to increase the speed of the exercises being performed. In order to protect the fragile new tissue, active-resistance exercises that focus on the injured tissue should NOT be performed.

Maturation-Remodeling Phase

The final phase of tissue repair is characterized by stronger Type I collagen getting laid down longitudinally to increase the strength of the new tissue. Tissue remodeling can continue for more than one year after injury. The realignment and remodeling of the collagen fibers due to increased loading and hypertrophy cause the stressed collagen fibers to realign along the maximally efficient lines of stress, thus allowing the tissue to become more organized and have increased strength.

Treatment Goals: The treatment goals for this phase are to return to the prior level of function, regain full ROM, and go back to the sport activity. Sport-specific exercises can be added in order to apply progressive stress to the injured area.

Exercise Strategies: Functional sport-specific rehabilitation and reconditioning exercises that mimic the demands of the sport should be introduced along with functionally specific strengthening exercises that are consistent with the speed requirements of the sport. Examples of such exercises include closed kinetic chain exercises, joint-angle-specific exercises, more challenging neuromuscular control exercises, and exercises that require velocity-specific muscle activity.

Progression of Rehabilitation and Reconditioning Exercises

Strength and conditioning professionals should use their experience designing programs for uninjured athletes and apply it to the development of reconditioning and rehabilitation programs for injured athletes. The goals of rehabilitation and reconditioning training need to be determined so that a program can be developed that will help the athlete return to the sport as soon as possible.

Resistance-Training Program Design for Rehabilitation and Reconditioning

- DeLorme Program: This program uses a pyramid-style design that consists of three sets of ten repetitions that progress from light to heavy loads. For example:
  - Set #1: Ten reps at 50 percent of ten-repetition max (10-RM)
  - Set #2: Ten reps at 75 percent of 10-RM
  - Set #3: Ten reps at 100 percent of 10-RM
- Oxford Program: This program is very similar to DeLorme's program except the progression of the three sets goes from heavy to light loads. For example:
  - Set #1: Ten reps at 100 percent of 10-RM
  - Set #2: Ten reps at 75 percent of 10-RM
  - Set #3: Ten reps at 50 percent of 10-RM
- Daily Adjustable Progressive Resistive Exercise (DARPE): More manipulation of the intensity and volume of exercises is allowed by the DARPE training system as compared with the DeLorme and Oxford programs. DARPE consists of four sets with a variable number of repetitions. The number of repetitions can range from ten during the first set to one during the fourth set. For example:
  - Set #1: Ten reps at 50 percent of estimated 1-RM
  - Set #2: Six reps at 75 percent of estimated 1-RM
  - Set #3: The maximum number of reps that can be completed at 100 percent or 1-RM
  - Set #4: Performance during the third set determines the adjustment that should be made to the resistance for the final set.
- Individualized Resistance Exercise Programs for Injured Athletes: The resistance programs discussed above have been shown to increase muscle strength and might be appropriate to use for some rehabilitation resistance-training programs. The lack of flexibility within these programs makes it difficult to individualize the program to be sport-specific for the injured athletes. Similar to programs for uninjured athletes, programs for injured athletes should follow the specific adaptation to imposed demands (SAID) principle, which says the specific demands placed on a system will cause that system to adapt. Applying the SAID principle to the resistance-training goal requires the design of the resistance program to be based on those exercises that will achieve the training goal.

Instability-Based Exercises for Injury Rehabilitation

Note that instability-based exercises are used in rehabilitation. They have been shown to effectively reduce lower back pain and enhance the stabilization of knee and ankle joints as a result of more efficient soft-tissue stabilization of the joints. Research studies have shown that *anterior cruciate ligament* (ACL) injury risk may be reduced with the use of instability devices, particularly after an ACL injury has been rehabilitated.

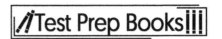

Aerobic and Anaerobic Training Program Design for Rehabilitation and Reconditioning

There is no research evidence to support the use of a specific aerobic-training program for rehabilitation. The strength and conditioning professional should develop an aerobic-training program that is sport specific and replicates the metabolic demands required during sport performance. The rehabilitation/reconditioning program design should account for contraindicated exercises based on the injury, but it can be developed based on the prescription guidelines used for healthy athletes.

A sport such as wrestling has both aerobic and anaerobic metabolic demands, so interval training is appropriate. Sports with anaerobic metabolic demands, such as powerlifting, need to focus on maintaining anaerobic fitness. Aerobic and anaerobic training can be modified in order to allow injured athletes who require these types of training to maintain their aerobic and anaerobic capacities. During the inflammatory phase, the injured area should not be stressed. There are many strategies for modifying aerobic and anaerobic training during this phase in order to allow maintenance of aerobic capacities. Alternative forms of aerobic exercise can be utilized. Athletes with injuries to the upper body can use lower-extremity exercises such as cycling and deep-water running, while athletes with lower-body injuries can use upper-body ergometers.

Consider a field-hockey athlete who has an acute injury to the left ankle. Initially during the inflammatory phase, there will be numerous contraindicated exercises for lower-extremity strengthening. However, upper-body resistance and aerobic exercises can be done in order to maintain muscular strength, endurance, and cardiorespiratory fitness. Exercises to strengthen the uninjured lower extremity can also be performed, such as single right-leg squats with weights. The strength and conditioning professional needs to ensure that the injured area is protected, so modifications may need to be made to single-leg exercises.

In another example, the goals of a marathon runner with a patellofemoral injury in the inflammatory response phase will be to maintain cardiorespiratory fitness, muscular strength and endurance in the adjacent joints and muscles, and avoid exercise that requires muscular activity from the quadriceps, as this area must be rested to reduce inflammation. During this phase, cardiovascular exercise that does not exacerbate the pain or increase knee movement is allowable, such as upper body ergometer work. In the fibroblastic repair phase, the athlete may begin using a step machine or stationary bike depending on the decisions of the sports-medicine team, again, as long as it does not exacerbate the knee. Water-based exercises may also be considered.

The athlete can perform isometric quadriceps strengthening at full knee extension (progressing to multiple angles) and progress to pain-free isotonic quadriceps strengthening, based on the recommendation of the sports-medicine team. With continued progress, the runner should be able to perform two to three sets of fifteen to twenty repetitions of resistance exercises using submaximal intensity (≤50% 1-RM). Finally, in the maturation-remodeling phase, the athlete can start running again, gradually increasing distance and speed. He or she can increase knee ROM as tolerable and add lunges and squats. The intensity of resistance exercises can increase to 50–75 percent of 1-RM (maximal intensity).

Practice Quiz

1. Which of the following is a benefit of plyometric exercises?
    a. They are most effective at improving balance and coordination in older athletes.
    b. They can provide the same benefits as weight training without the equipment.
    c. They are safe for all populations.
    d. They are the easiest exercises to master with proper form.

2. Which of the following regarding pain is true?
    a. Type I pain is experienced during exercise, but subsides once exercise ceases.
    b. Type II pain is painful but not detrimental and can be recovered from within the normal recovery time periods.
    c. Type I pain is pain experienced 1½ hours following exercise and can last for hours or days.
    d. Type II pain is less likely to indicate a new injury and is more indicative of strain from appropriately progressed exercise loads.

3. Which of the following occurs when tissue damage includes ruptures to the capillaries, allowing blood to pool under the skin?
    a. Tendinitis
    b. A macrotrauma
    c. A first-degree burn
    d. A contusion

4. A strength and conditioning professional has an athlete completing high repetitions using low weight with short rest periods of 0–90 seconds between sets. The weight for work is increased gradually as the program progresses and the athlete reaches points of adaptation. Which of the following is likely the primary goal of the athlete's program?
    a. Hypertrophy
    b. Increased power
    c. Increased strength
    d. Increased muscular endurance

5. How are intermediate athletes defined?
    a. Athletes who have been training at least two times per week for two months or more
    b. Athletes who have been training at least three times per week for two months or more
    c. Athletes who have been training at least three times per week for one year or more
    d. Athletes who have been training at least two times per week for one year or more

See answers on the next page.

Answer Explanations

1. B: Plyometrics can provide many health and fitness benefits without the need for equipment, facility space, or machines. Although they just require the athlete's own body weight, the athlete can achieve the same benefits afforded by more traditional "weight training," but in any environment and at any time that the athlete finds suitable. With that said, plyometrics are not necessarily safe for all athletes and the strength and conditioning professional must consider the athlete's age, experience, physical restrictions, capabilities, injury risk factors, and training goals, as each of these factors will allow or prohibit certain exercises. Therefore, Choice *C* is incorrect. Additionally, while they can be safe for some older athletes, Choice *A* is incorrect because plyometrics are better at improving strength and power rather than balance and coordination. Plyometrics are not necessarily that easy to learn and master, and proper form can be difficult, so Choice *D* is incorrect.

2. A: There are two primary types of pain to consider during the injury recovery process. Type I pain is experienced during exercise, but once exercise stops, the pain subsides. Even though Type I pain is uncomfortable, it is not detrimental and can be recovered from within the normal recovery time periods. Type II pain is pain experienced 1½ hours following exercise and can last for hours or days. Type II is concerning because it can indicate either an exacerbation of a previous injury or a new injury caused by pushing too hard.

3. D: A contusion, or bruise, can occur anywhere throughout the body, but most people associate these injuries with the aesthetic blue, black, purple, or green areas that appear on the skin following an injury. It indicates that the specific afflicted area of tissue has been damaged extensively, resulting in ruptures to capillaries, which allows blood to pool under the skin and form a bruise. Tendinitis is inflammation of the tendons. Macrotraumas are normally seen in acute injuries and include things like broken bones, joint dislocations, and sprains. First-degree burns occur when the superficial layers of the epidermis are exposed to heat or a caustic substance.

4. D: The work/rest periods and program progression best align with the goal of increasing muscular endurance. For hypertrophy, the load, volume, and intensity may vary widely (depending upon the athlete's fitness level and experience), but repetitions and sets are separated by shorter rest periods that range between 0 and 60 seconds. Power training should involve relatively few repetitions with increasingly high weight, requiring 3–5 minutes between sets. Higher weights or loads are needed to induce improvements in muscular strength.

5. B: Generally speaking, athletes who have been training at least three times per week for two months or more are considered intermediate athletes. They are between the novice and mastering stages of exercise performance. Therefore, they require consistent evaluation and programming that allows for improvement in mastered exercises. Intermediate athletes can usually safely perform three days of total-body workouts or four days of upper/lower body splits that train each major muscle group twice weekly. Novice athletes are those that have been training less than two or three months, with two or fewer sessions per week. Advanced athletes have been training consistently for at least one year and completing around four sessions per week.

Organization and Administration

Organizational Environment

Policies and Procedures for Facility Operation

During the pre-operation phase, policies and procedures regarding facility and equipment cleaning and maintenance, rules, scheduling, and emergency procedures should be planned, assigned to various personnel in certain cases, and written for distribution to employees. To prevent the spread of microbes, mats and exercise surfaces should be wiped down with germicidal agents after every use, particularly those that combat the spread of HIV and hepatitis. Floors also require regular cleaning. Non-absorbent surfaces should be mopped and wooden platforms should be monitored for cracks. Regular dusting should remove and prevent grime buildup. These actions will help keep the floor free of obstacles and prevent slips and falls. Regular maintenance should be performed on all equipment in accordance to the manufacturer's recommendations. Cables, pulleys, and bands should be checked for fraying. Facility rules in regard to appropriate attire and footwear, hours, scheduling and canceling policies, payment methods and prices, locker use, etc. should also be formalized. Staff should be trained and rehearsed in all emergency procedures at least quarterly, and procedures should be posted under telephones.

Primary Duties and Responsibilities of Staff

It is important that all strength and conditioning staff members uphold the facility's goals, mission, and mindset, bringing a high level of professionalism, honesty, trustworthiness, work ethic, and knowledge to their roles. The NSCA requires that strength and conditioning specialists obtain certification. Duties for each position should be detailed in the business and operation plans, as well as required experience and education, expected salary, and schedule. All staff members should maintain CPR/AED certification, and fully understand and rehearse all emergency procedures to reduce the risk of liability issues.

Effective Communication and Collaboration with Other Professionals

Strength and conditioning coaches will need to communicate and collaborate with many other professionals, such as team coaches, physicians, school administrators, and the media. It is the responsibility for the strength and conditioning professional to be respectful, informed, and collaborative when working with others. An athlete's best interest should always be the driving force and at the forefront of decisions and plans.

Strength and conditioning coaches are allied health professionals, and as such, are part of the medical community. They need to be able to communicate effectively with physicians and other health professionals on an ongoing basis to follow up on client referrals and progress using adherence to HIPAA and confidentiality guidelines. To be credible and effective communicators, strength and conditioning coaches should be mindful to use proper medical and anatomical terminology.

Strength and conditioning coaches should have a network of various types of healthcare providers such as physicians, physical therapists, mental health professionals, chiropractors, and nutritionists that they can utilize to provide athletes with comprehensive, reputable care. Appropriate referrals minimize liability by ensuring the strength and conditioning professional acts only within their scope of practice. It also maximizes program effectiveness by addressing the many concerns and challenges faced by athletes, which may otherwise prevent full sport participation and goal achievement.

Athletes with injuries may need to see an athletic trainer, sports medicine staff, an orthopedist, or a physical therapist. Athletes with weight issues or dietary concerns may benefit from consulting a sports dietician or, in a school setting, the school's nutritionist. Psychological services may be necessary for other athletes, and guidance counselors may be useful for athletes who are in school. Strength and conditioning professionals should not only identify the appropriate professional, but also help facilitate the introduction in a respectful and positive manner.

Design, Layout, and Organization of the Strength and Conditioning Facility

Designing a feasible strength and conditioning facility from the ground up requires careful forethought and planning, often involving a committee of trained professionals to achieve the necessary physical goals of the facility in an affordable, realistic manner. The four phases in the design of a new facility are discussed below:

1. *Pre-design phase*: Determining needs, feasibility, and the master plan.

- *Needs assessment:* Determines what space, equipment, and layout are needed
- *Feasibility study (SWOT analysis):* Identifies the strengths, weaknesses, opportunities, and threats, to ensure the business will be financially viable and profitable
- *Master plan:* Includes the building and construction plan and design, and the budget and operational plan

2. *Design phase*: Finalizing the design and blueprint according to city building codes, while focusing on the flow of the facility in terms of equipment, traffic, personnel, etc.

3. *Construction phase*: This phase involves meeting deadlines and avoiding budget overruns, and is based on the master plan. It is often the longest phase. Efforts should be made to meet project deadlines to avoid increases in cost and litigation concerns.

4. *Pre-operation phase*: Finishing the interior design, hiring staff, and planning daily procedures for smooth operation

Modifying an existing facility can be simpler and less expensive in many cases, but still must include many of the same pre-design and planning elements; this can be more challenging because equipment or building construction may already be set in a certain manner that would be difficult or impossible to modify. In either case, strength and conditioning coaches must bring to the committee thoughts and needs regarding flooring; ceiling height (taking into account the platforms of cardio equipment and weight decks, box jumps, and mirror placement so that athletes and coaches can observe form, which in turn can affect window placement); good ventilation and lighting; and ample margins around each piece of equipment. Most manufacturers publish the footprint of equipment for design planning purposes, and planners should bear in mind the need for close proximity to outlets.

Professional Practice

Working Within the Scope of Practice for the Strength and Conditioning Staff

The NSCA divides the legal responsibilities and professional scope of practice for certified strength and conditioning professionals into two domains. The first, "Scientific Foundations," includes Exercise Science, Sport Psychology, and Nutrition. The second, "Practical/Applied," includes Exercise Technique, Program Design, Organization and Administration, and Testing and Evaluation. Under these domains, there are defined legal duties and responsibilities and standards of practice. It is imperative that strength and conditioning professionals familiarize themselves with these defined terms and always operate within their scope of practice. For example, strength and conditioning professionals are not permitted to diagnose health conditions. Performing duties outside of the scope of practice can harm athletes and will result in disciplinary action, including legal implications.

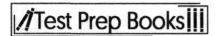

Abiding By the NSCA Codes, Policies, and Procedures

Strength and conditioning professionals should keep abreast of all NSCA codes, policies, and procedures as it is their responsibility to act in accordance with these policies at all times. NSCA develops these policies and procedures to maintain a high degree of professionalism in the strength and conditioning profession, and failure to abide by them is grounds for discipline. The Professional Code of Ethics details the need to always act with integrity, honesty, and ethical behavior and to report any and all unethical behavior. The NSCA website contains the full Professional Code of Ethics and the related policies and procedures, including disciplinary actions, for those who fail to abide by the requirements. The Conflict of Interest Policy is the primary policy strength and conditioning professionals should be concerned with. This policy is spelled out on the NSCA website.

Abiding By Standards and Practices of Relevant Governing Bodies

Just as the NSCA develops their codes, policies, and procedures to ensure a certain level of professionalism in the industry and to manage risk, other governing bodies related to strength and conditioning programming usually have their own similar sets of expectations. NSCA-certified strength and conditioning professionals are to abide by these as well. For example, the National Collegiate Athletic Association (NCAA) has defined rules and regulations and a scope of practice for strength and conditioning coaches, so if an NSCA-certified CSCS is working with NCAA athletes, these rules must be followed as well.

Recognizing and Responding to Symptoms of Unsafe Training Practices

Coaches should be mindful to pace athletes at an appropriate rate and refrain from giving athletes too much too soon, especially regarding competitions and practices outside of the strength training program, which can lead to overtraining and overuse issues. *Overtraining* is a condition that occurs when an individual trains with too much frequency and/or intensity, causing fatigue, greater injury risk, sleep issues, changes in appetite or body weight, lack of motivation, depression or moodiness, and performance decline. Signs of overtraining also include elevated resting heart rate, soreness that does not resolve within a day or two after exercise (as is normal with resistance training), and increased susceptibility to illness. Similarly, *overuse* injuries, such as stress fractures and tendinitis, can occur when the workload is too high and insufficient rest and recovery leads to tissue damage.

Strength coaches should also be aware of temperature-induced illness – particularly heat exhaustion and heat stroke – when training athletes outdoors. Signs can include dizziness, nausea, vomiting, clammy skin, confusion, visual disturbances, headache, weakness, and even heart arrhythmias. To prevent such illness, athletes should be encouraged to drink plenty of fluids; wear light, breathable layers of clothing; take frequent breaks in the shade; reduce intensity in hot, humid environments; or modify the workout to indoor settings.

Referring an Athlete to Seek Input from Allied Health Professionals

While athletes may rely heavily on the advice and expertise of strength coaches, strength and conditioning coaches can only educate on topics within their scope and must refer athletes to appropriate sources for all else. Strength coaches should maintain a list of physicians and allied health professionals, such as physical therapists, nutritionists, and mental health professionals, whom they respect and trust, to provide competent referrals to athletes outside of their scope of practice. When networking with such professionals, strength coaches should be aware that referrals can work both ways, and that through professional, positive relationships with other local clinicians, they may get referrals back for conditioning programs.

Identifying Common Litigation Issues and Reducing or Minimizing the Risk of Liability

Training facilities should create policies and procedures to reduce possible areas of liability, such as handling injury prevention/risk management during training sessions, reviewing emergency procedures, maintaining confidential records, and retaining comprehensive facility and staff liability insurance. Because many aspects of strength training present inherently high injury risk, training staff should make all attempts to keep the training area safe and up to code, keep the floor clear of tripping hazards, closely monitor every session, make certain first aid supplies and AED machines are in close proximity, ensure equipment is routinely serviced and checked, and insist that staff carry liability insurance.

Personal injury liability insurance protects against libel, slander, and invasion of privacy. *Professional liability insurance* protects against injuries caused by services or negligence. *Commercial liability insurance* covers individuals and the business against incidents and accidents that occur at the facility and must be purchased by trainers who own their own studios. *Negligence* is a failure to perform at the accepted standard (due care), while *gross negligence* is to do so consciously. In addition to carrying the necessary liability insurance, trainers can defend against negligence claims by documenting all services daily and performing at the highest industry standards.

Strength coaches are responsible for creating and maintaining a safe training environment within the facility, including safeguarding athletes from risk of injury, illness, and undue emotional distress. By creating safety protocols, keeping the facility clean and organized, and fostering a supportive environment, these risks can be reduced.

Practice Quiz

1. A policies and procedures manual for a strength and conditioning facility should include all EXCEPT which of the following?
   a. Staff duties and responsibilities
   b. A statement of program goals and objectives
   c. Daily financials in the form of a profit and loss statement
   d. A code of ethics and professionalism

2. Which of the following is recommended to ensure that the facility and the equipment within the facility are maintained and cleaned frequently enough?
   a. Creating and using a checklist with all duties related to facility and equipment upkeep
   b. Creating and maintaining an appropriate code of ethics and professionalism
   c. Creating and posting a missions statement and values statement for the facility
   d. Creating and maintaining a policies and procedures manual

3. Which of the following correctly shows the ratios for the number of recommended strength and conditioning professionals to athletes for the different age groups?
   a. 1:20 for junior high school, 1:15 for high school, 1:10 for collegiate athletes
   b. 1:10 for junior high school, 1:15 for high school, 1:20 for collegiate athletes
   c. 1:15 for junior high school, 1:20 for high school, 1:15 for collegiate athletes
   d. 1:15 for junior high school, 1:20 for high school, 1:10 for collegiate athletes

4. In addition to posting a facility rules document for athletes to see in a prominent location, how should a strength and conditioning facility help ensure athletes are aware of the rules?
   a. Ensure team coaches explain the rules to their athletes
   b. Foster an atmosphere where specific rules are not necessary
   c. Have athletes attend a facility orientation in which the rules are stated
   d. Keep the rules the same without ever updating or amending them

5. Strength and conditioning professionals should take which of the following groups into consideration first when planning the schedules for use of the facility?
   a. Novice athletes
   b. Advanced athletes
   c. In-season athletes
   d. Off-season athletes

See answers on the next page.

Answer Explanations

1. C: It is essential that all strength and conditioning facilities create and adhere to a policies and procedures manual. This manual helps ensure things run safely, smoothly, and effectively. A policies and procedures manual should include a mission statement, statement of program goals, program objectives, staff duties and responsibilities, operational procedures, equipment manuals, equipment cleaning duties and records, statement of return-to-participation guidelines, legal documents, and code of ethics and professionalism. Daily financials are not included in this document and should comprise separate accounting documentation.

2. A: To ensure that the facility and the equipment within the facility are maintained and cleaned routinely as necessary, a checklist should be created. A cleaning and maintenance checklist should include all the duties related to facility and equipment upkeep, such as a schedule of when the cleaning and maintenance will be performed, floor and wall cleaning procedures, ceiling cleaning operation, and exercise equipment cleaning and maintenance requirements. The other options are good policies and practices for a facility to adopt, but they do not specifically target cleaning and upkeep.

3. B: Although not always feasible, it is recommended that the supervisor to athlete ratios in the strength and conditioning facility are 1:10 for junior high school, 1:15 for high school, and 1:20 for collegiate athletes.

4. C: To help ensure that all training sessions are performed in a safe and effective manner, a strength and conditioning facility should compile, post, and enforce a list of rules and guidelines. In addition to posting this document in a prominent location, athletes and any other personnel using the facility should attend a facility orientation in which the rules are explained. This will help ensure that athletes are aware of the rules and understand them. Facility rules should include proper attire for training sessions, the preparticipation screening process, workout sheet guidelines, rules for using the equipment, the people with access to the use of the facility, and procedures involved in disciplinary actions for violations of the stated rules.

5. C: In-season teams should have priority in scheduling time at the facility in an ideal scenario because in-season teams are typically busier and have less flexible schedules because of their competitions. With this in mind, the strength and conditioning professional should first schedule all in-season teams based around their practice schedules, competitions, athletes' class schedules, and team meetings. After this, off-season athletes should be scheduled. Generally speaking, the experience level of the athlete is a less important factor when planning schedules. Teams will often include athletes with different levels of experience. With that said, advanced athletes may require longer or more frequent sessions per week.

Testing, Ongoing Monitoring, and Data Evaluation

Selecting Appropriate Evidence-Based Tests to Maximize Test Reliability and Validity

Test selection, proper administration that adheres to the set protocol, and trained raters influence the reliability and validity of any given test for an athlete. Some tests are only valid for certain populations, such as the 8 Foot Up and Go test of agility in the elderly. All tests are valid only if they are conducted according to the specified protocol, and tests are significantly less reliable if the rater is unfamiliar with test administration, such as a coach performing skinfold measurements without practice at selecting the correct sites and pinching the tissue appropriately.

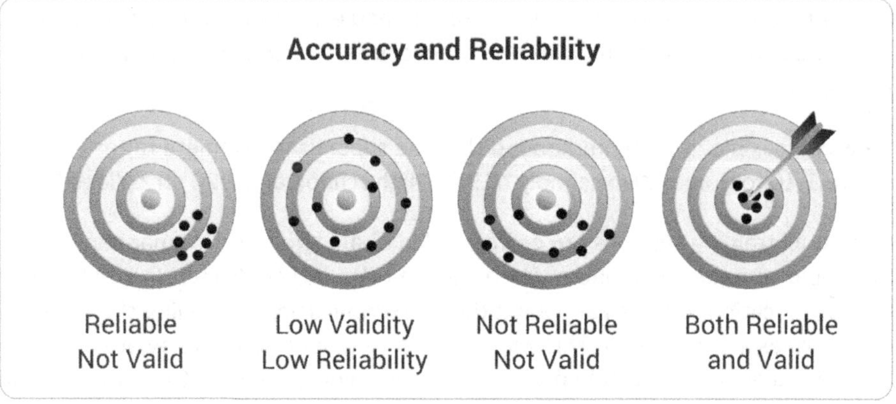

Tests Based Upon Sport, Sport Position, and Training Status

Selecting the appropriate tests involves considering the physiological energy systems required by the sport compared to the test, movement specificity, and the athlete's experience with training and testing. To choose the most appropriate tests, strength coaches should perform a needs analysis of the sport and position to determine what aspects of fitness are most important (speed, power, strength, agility, etc.) and therefore should be tested. From there, tests should be selected based on their validity for such fitness components as well as the athlete's training status. For example, a VO_2 max running assessment should be selected rather than a cycle protocol for a distance runner. This choice will prevent local muscle fatigue that could occur after performing an unaccustomed activity, which would reduce overall performance and achievement of a true maximal result. By the same reasoning, a Wingate test of anaerobic power is probably not a good choice for a basketball player who never cycles; the vertical jump test is preferable.

Using Equipment, Personnel, and Time Efficiently

When testing individual athletes, strength coaches have flexibility in test selection because equipment usage, personnel to score or observe tests, and time efficiency are not much of a concern. Many coaches, however, will need to test entire teams or multiple athletes at one time, so these become factors to consider. Field tests such as the Rockport walk test, 1-mile run, or step test typically require minimal equipment and occur outside "in the field," while laboratory tests such as the Wingate test of anaerobic power require equipment. When testing teams or multiple athletes, field tests may be more appropriate because they do not usually require much equipment. In addition, these tests can be conducted more efficiently by having athletes complete them at the same time.

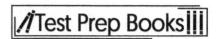

Administering Testing and Implementing Monitoring Protocols and Procedures to Ensure Reliable Data Collection

To ensure reliable data collection and scoring, tests should be conducted according to their established protocols and procedures, and in a logical order so that fatigue and testing error do not confound results.

Testing and Monitoring Equipment and Proper Use

To avoid errors in scores based on equipment malfunction or influence, all testing equipment should be assessed for proper function and calibrated prior to use in testing. For example, prior to using a metabolic cart to measure expired gases, the cart should be calibrated by entering the environmental data (humidity, barometric pressure, temperature) as well as volume of expired air with the 3L calibration syringe. The use of some equipment also requires that certain preparation steps are followed to produce a valid response. For example, bioelectrical impedance machines to measure body fat are very sensitive to body water levels, so athletes should urinate before the test. In addition, prior to the test, they cannot eat or drink for at least 30 minutes, exercise for at least 12 hours, drink alcohol for at least 48 hours, or consume caffeine.

Testing and Monitoring Procedures

Many tests have procedures for a warm-up and require proper rest between trials, but for those that do not have a warm-up built into the test, coaches should make sure that athletes have performed a thorough warm-up of the metabolic and physiologic systems that will be used in the test. For example, if performing a 1RM bench press test, athletes should warm up with light cardiovascular exercise to increase blood flow, heart rate, and muscle perfusion. Next, they should complete a few sets with increasing weight, below max, to prepare the muscles for the test. Tests should also be recorded in a logical order with the most fatiguing assessments last. Studies have found that strength scores are lower after cardiovascular endurance assessments, but not vice versa, so strength tests should be conducted prior to strenuous distance runs or 300-yard shuttle runs. If tests need to be repeated due to some sort of error, it is usually preferable to revisit them on another day so that any accumulated fatigue from the first attempt does not confound the subsequent re-take.

Testing to Assess Physical Characteristics and Workloads

Some common physical characteristics can be measured as follows:

Body fat:

- Skinfold measurements: Caliper measurements of subcutaneous fat from pinches of skin tissue at specific body sites are plugged into equations to estimate body fat percentage.

- Plethysmography (BOD POD®): A laboratory tool uses air displacement to calculate volume of the body along with weight to determine body fat.

- Bioelectrical impedance: Bioelectrical impedance analysis uses the principle that fat mass and fat free mass have different resistances to electrical current. When the resistances are measured, body fat percentage can be calculated.

- Infrared: Fat mass and fat free mass are assessed via a specialized infrared-light-emitting probe placed against an area of the body.

- Dual-Energy X-ray Absorptiometry (DEXA): This is a machine that measures bone mineral density.

- Circumference measurements: Circumference measurements with measuring tape at specific body sites are plugged into equations to estimate body fat percentage.

Performance parameters:

- Muscular strength: 1RM bench press for upper body and 1RM leg press for lower body
- Anaerobic capacity or power: Wingate cycle ergometer test, vertical jump test, Margaria-Kalamen stair sprint test, medicine ball throw
- Muscular endurance: Push-up test, curl-up test
- Aerobic endurance: Cooper 12-minute run test, 1.5 mile run test
- Agility: 25-yard shuttle test, zig-zag test, quadrant jump test, hexagon test, box drill

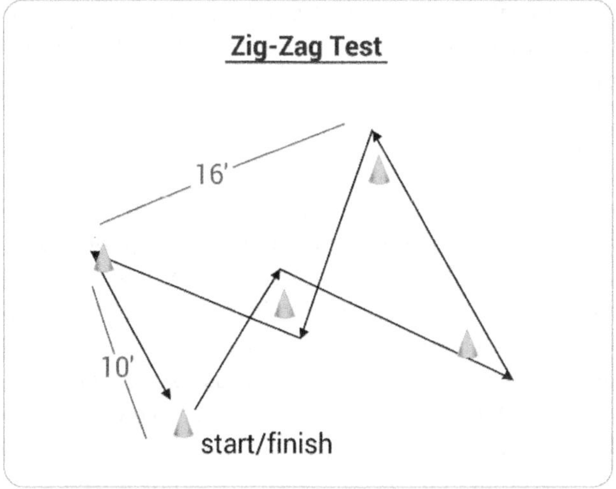

- Speed: Line drills, 300-yard shuttle test, sprint tests like 50m sprint, plate tapping test for upper body speed
- Flexibility: sit-and-reach test

Evaluating and Interpreting Results

Once tests are completed, the scores are evaluated and the results are translated into usable information to help plan training programs.

Validity of Test Results

Validity refers to the extent to which a test measures what it is intended to measure, such as a strength test actually measuring force production. *Reliability* of a test refers to a test's ability to produce consistent measures. Selecting the appropriate test for an athlete affects the validity and reliability of the test; some tests are valid only for certain populations, and subjective tests become less reliable if they have multiple raters for different administrations of the test.

Typical vs. Atypical Test Results Based on a Sport or Sport Position

Typical assessment scores are somewhat dependent upon sport and position within that sport. For example, highly trained football players tend to have high scores for 1RM bench press and leg press, but score less favorably on cardiorespiratory endurance assessments such as the 1.5-mile run. Most athletes are in sports and positions that suit their physiologic strengths, both through self-selection based on genetic influence as well as years of training to hone certain aspects of fitness. Power athletes tend to have favorable scores for strength and speed assessments compared with endurance athletes, who tend to fair better in muscular and cardiovascular endurance. Dancers, gymnasts, and figure skaters tend to score well in flexibility assessments. Atypical results occur when something other than what should be expected, based on the athlete's training background and genetics, occurs. Atypical results can sometimes indicate that the testing was not conducted correctly or that the athlete failed to perform up to potential for one reason or another in that assessment.

Designing or Modifying a Training Program Based on Test Results

Each of the recommended fitness assessments has standards that the strength coach can compare an athlete's results to. *Norm-referenced standards,* such as VO_2 max score, compare the athlete's performance against that of similar individuals, and scores are presented in percentiles. The 50th percentile indicates the athlete performed better than half of the comparative population and worse than half. It is important that the coach not only reports the percentile score, but also educates athletes on their scores' relative value. *Criterion-referenced standards* are based on research- and normative-based achievement levels of health and fitness that, if reached, predict lower disease risk for the athlete. These may be lower standards than those likely achieved by athletic populations.

Test results can be used by coaches to help plan training programs. Taken together with an understanding of the most important fitness components for a given athlete based on sport and position, norm-referenced standards for each test score for an athlete can be used by coaches to identify the greatest areas of deficit. These areas, along with those that are most important for the position, can be emphasized in training programs. For example, if a baseball pitcher scores in the 90th percentile for upper body 1RM strength and in the 70th percentile for muscular endurance based on the push-up test, coaches would want to focus on increasing muscular endurance because the athlete is less proficient with endurance (according to percentile rank) and pitching an entire game requires a high level of upper body muscular endurance.

Practice Quiz

1. Regarding the use of test results, which of the following is NOT true?
    a. In most cases, program modifications will be the result of a submaximal performance within the testing battery.
    b. The strength and conditioning professional should verify the validity of the results prior to incorporating changes to a program.
    c. Lower-body strength, upper-body strength, and total body power are often key indicators for modifications that will be required for optimal performance.
    d. At least one aspect of a training program should be modified based on test results.

2. What does the Margaria-Kalaman test measure?
    a. Maximum muscular strength
    b. Maximum muscular power
    c. Aerobic capacity
    d. Speed

3. Generally, which of the following is NOT considered when determining the convergent validity over the gold standard test?
    a. The need for using less equipment
    b. The need for more valid and effective testing
    c. The need for fewer testing professionals
    d. The need for more efficient testing

4. Which of the following is NOT a body composition test?
    a. Hydrostatic weighing
    b. Skinfold measurements
    c. BMI
    d. Bioelectrical impedance

5. An athlete is anxious to participate in testing. Which of the following can the strength and conditioning professional do to best help assuage the athlete's anxiety?
    a. Perform the tests first thing in the morning before the athlete has eaten breakfast
    b. Perform the tests after practice where teammates can watch and cheer the athlete on
    c. Explain the purpose of testing and help the athlete engage in some relaxation techniques
    d. Provide external rewards for the athlete, such as a trophy or free t-shirt

See answers on the next page.

Answer Explanations

1. D: Although it's often true that test results can point to areas of weakness or areas that should receive greater focus in an athlete's program, and thus will require program modification, this is not always the case. Modifications and changes to an athlete's training program should only be performed when a significant capability is not being met with optimal results. Sometimes, test results indicate that the program is working and the athlete is progressing appropriately. It is important to not make unnecessary changes prematurely and to give the athlete's body time to adapt to the prescribed program. The other choices are indeed true. The first step is to ensure the test results are properly analyzed and appear valid. Usually, program modifications will be the result of a submaximal performance within the testing battery. Lower-body strength, upper-body strength, and total body power often indicate where modifications will be required for optimal performance.

2. B: The Margaria-Kalaman test falls in the battery of tests designed to measure maximum muscular power, or high-strength speed, along with tests such as the 1RM power clean, standing long jump, and vertical jump. The Margaria-Kalaman test measures the anaerobic power of the lower extremities and involves running up flights of stairs.

3. B: Convergent validity refers to the extent to which the intended test correlates with the testing data of the accepted "gold standard" test used for the given athletic ability. The use of more efficient testing, the need for fewer testing personnel, and the need for using less equipment are often reasons why a strength and conditioning professional opts to use an alternative test over the "gold standard." Choice *B,* the validity and effectiveness of the alternative test, is not a correct reason because by definition, the "gold standard" test is taken to be the most effective and valid measure for the given athletic trait or skill. Convergent validity is, in fact, concerned with the validity of the alternative compared to the "gold standard," not the other way around.

4. C: Body mass index, BMI, is not a measure of body fat. It is a measure of body density because it is looking at total mass (including lean body mass) versus height. The other choices are body fat assessments.

5. C: Explaining the purpose and benefits of testing can help an athlete understand what he or she has to gain from the testing and why it is an important part of the training program and process. For example, program design and modifications should be based on appropriate test results. Verbally confirming how test results can help an athlete reach their personal goals can be a powerful motivator. Additionally, relaxation techniques, such as progressive muscle relaxation or mindfulness meditation, can help lower anxiety. The other options are likely not as effective. It is important to be properly fueled before testing, so Choice *A* is incorrect. Having the whole team there might increase anxiety, so Choice *B* is not the best option. Lastly, external rewards can help, but this is not always feasible. It would be more beneficial to the athlete's future in athletics for the athlete to learn about the benefits of testing and appropriate coping mechanisms. Therefore, Choice *D* is incorrect.

CSCS Practice Test #1

Exercise Sciences

1. Which of the following is NOT a component of a sarcomere?
    a. Actin
    b. D-line
    c. A-band
    d. I-band

2. Which of the following best describes the likely ratio of Type I and Type II muscle fibers in a competitive tennis player?
    a. High Type I, low Type II
    b. High Type I, high Type II
    c. Low Type I, high Type II
    d. Low Type I, low Type II

3. Which of the following correctly lists the structures of a muscle from largest to smallest?
    a. Fasciculus, muscle fiber, actin, myofibril
    b. Muscle fiber, fasciculus, myofibril, actin
    c. Sarcomere, fasciculus, myofibril, myosin
    d. Muscle fiber, myofibril, sarcomere, actin

4. What area of the heart is responsible for initiating rhythmic electrical impulses?
    a. Purkinje fibers
    b. Atrioventricular (AV) bundle
    c. Sinoatrial (SA) node
    d. Atrioventricular (AV) node

5. When reading an electrocardiogram, ventricular repolarization is associated with which graphical component?
    a. QRS complex
    b. P-wave
    c. T-wave
    d. PR segment

6. Which of the following are responsible for the exchange of nutrients, hormones, oxygen, fluids, and electrolytes between blood and the interstitial fluid of body tissues?
    a. Arterioles
    b. Venules
    c. Capillaries
    d. Hemoglobin

7. Myosin cross-bridges attach to the actin filament when the sarcoplasmic reticulum is stimulated to release which one of the following?
    a. Calcium ions
    b. Acetylcholine
    c. Troponin
    d. Adenosine triphosphate (ATP)

8. During heavy breathing, which of the following muscles do NOT help to elevate the ribs during inspiration?
   a. Sternocleidomastoids
   b. External intercostals
   c. Rectus abdominis
   d. Anterior serrati

9. Which of the following sport-related movements occurs primarily in the transverse plane?
   a. Dribbling a soccer ball
   b. Hitting a tennis backhand
   c. Punting a football
   d. Throwing a shot put

10. Which of the following muscles does NOT rotate the arm?
   a. Teres minor
   b. Subscapularis
   c. Infraspinatus
   d. Supinator

11. A biceps curl is an example of which type of lever?
   a. First-class lever
   b. Second-class lever
   c. Third-class lever
   d. Fourth-class lever

12. Which of the following upper body movements take place in the sagittal plane?

I. Elbow extension
II. Wrist flexion
III. Shoulder abduction
IV. Neck left tilt

   a. I, IV
   b. I, III, IV
   c. I, II
   d. II, III

13. Soccer dribbling requires a specific type of joint movement at the ankle and in a certain movement plane. Which of the following answers gives the correct joint movement and movement plane?
   a. Eversion/transverse
   b. Inversion/frontal
   c. Eversion/frontal
   d. Inversion/transverse

14. Which one of the following answers provides the correct name and fascicular arrangement description associated with the biceps brachii muscle?
   a. Fusiform; spindle-shaped muscles
   b. Multipennate; tendon branches within the muscle
   c. Longitudinal (AKA: parallel); long axis of fascicles is parallel to long axis of muscle
   d. Radiate (AKA: convergent); muscle has broad origin (fan or triangular shape)

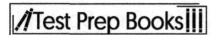

15. Which of the following refers to when a muscle contracts but does not shorten or lengthen?
   a. Eccentric
   b. Isotonic
   c. Concentric
   d. Isometric

16. Which of the following is the equation for power?
   a. Force × distance
   b. Work/time
   c. Work/distance
   d. Force × time

17. A collegiate track sprinter is doing interval training at a 1:12 work-to-rest ratio. This type of training is working what energy system?
   a. Fast glycolytic and oxidative
   b. Oxidative
   c. Fast glycolytic
   d. Phosphagen

18. Which substrate is capable of producing the most ATP?
   a. Carbohydrates
   b. Fat
   c. Protein
   d. Glycogen

19. The electron transport chain resynthesizes ATP by the process of oxidative phosphorylation. Which of the following is NOT used during this process?
   a. Hydrogen ions
   b. Lactate
   c. Nicotinamide adenine dinucleotide (NADH)
   d. Flavin adenine dinucleotide ($FADH_2$)

20. The phosphagen system uses creatine phosphate stored in muscles to produce ATP. Which of the following is NOT true about the reaction?
   a. The reaction produces energy at a fast rate.
   b. The reaction uses the process of substrate-level phosphorylation to resynthesize ATP.
   c. The reaction uses the process of oxidative phosphorylation to resynthesize ATP.
   d. The reaction is not capable of providing energy for continuous, long-duration activity.

21. Which of the energy systems is the primary system working when the body is at rest?
   a. Glycolytic
   b. Oxidative
   c. Anaerobic
   d. Phosphagen

22. What is the net production of ATP from the complete metabolism of one molecule of glucose?
   a. 4
   b. 24
   c. 38
   d. 40

23. The process of breaking large molecules into smaller molecules to provide energy is known as which of the following?
    a. Metabolism
    b. Bioenergetics
    c. Anabolism
    d. Catabolism

24. If oxygen is available during glycolysis, what happens to pyruvate?
    a. It is converted to lactate.
    b. It is transported to the sarcoplasm for the Krebs cycle.
    c. It is transported to the mitochondria for the Krebs cycle.
    d. It is converted to lactic acid.

25. Cortisol is secreted by which of the following?
    a. Adrenal cortex
    b. Anterior pituitary
    c. Posterior pituitary
    d. Testes and ovaries

26. Which of the following is NOT an anabolic hormone?
    a. Testosterone
    b. Growth hormone
    c. Insulin-like growth factor
    d. Epinephrine

27. Which of the following is NOT a physiological function of testosterone?
    a. Increases protein synthesis
    b. Increases the rate of cellular metabolism
    c. Increases cardiac output
    d. Increases the production of red blood cells

28. What type of resistance exercise training promotes increased concentrations of growth hormone?

	Number of Sets	Intensity	Rest Interval
a.	3	High	1 minute
b.	3	Low	3 minutes
c.	1	High	1 minute
d.	1	Low	3 minutes

29. Which of the following is not a function of catecholamines?
    a. Decreases blood pressure
    b. Increases available energy
    c. Increases rate of muscle contraction
    d. Increases muscle blood flow

30. Which of the following resistance exercise variables would best enhance serum testosterone concentrations?
    a. Long rest intervals (greater than 2 minutes)
    b. Small-muscle exercises such as biceps curls
    c. Heavy resistance loads (85–95 percent of 1RM)
    d. One set of each resistance exercise

31. Which of the following is NOT an endocrine sign or symptom associated with overtraining syndrome?
   a. Altered cortisol concentrations
   b. Increased growth hormone
   c. Decreased total testosterone concentration
   d. Decreased ratios of total and free testosterone to cortisol

32. The physiological functions of decreasing glucose utilization, increasing protein synthesis, increasing renal plasma flow and filtration, and enhancing immune cell function are associated with which hormone?
   a. Insulin-like growth factor
   b. Testosterone
   c. Growth hormone
   d. Epinephrine

33. Which of the following characteristics of the mechanical load associated with resistance exercises are important for the stimulation of bone growth?

I. Speed of loading
II. Intensity of the load
III. Direction of the force
IV. Type of load

   a. I, III, IV
   b. II, III, IV
   c. I, II, III
   d. I, II, III, IV

34. High-intensity resistance training causes all muscle fibers to hypertrophy because of the order of motor unit recruitment. What is the name of this phenomenon where smaller motor units are recruited first, followed by the recruitment of larger units when more force is needed?
   a. Selective recruitment
   b. The size principle
   c. Maximal recruitment
   d. Synchronization of motor unit activation

35. High-intensity anaerobic training causes changes to connective tissue growth and structure. Which of the following is NOT a change that occurs in tendons in response to this training?
   a. Increased collagen fibril diameter and number
   b. Increased tendon flexibility
   c. Increased formation of long filaments
   d. Increased collagen fibril packing density

36. An acute bout of anaerobic resistance exercise significantly impacts the cardiovascular system. During resistance exercise, which cardiovascular responses occur?

I. Increased heart rate and systolic blood pressure
II. Increased cardiac output
III. Increased peripheral blood flow
IV. Increased stroke volume

a. I, II
b. I, II, III
c. I, II, IV
d. I, II, III, IV

37. At what point during acute resistance exercise sets is ventilation the greatest?
a. Immediately before starting the resistance exercise set
b. During the resistance exercise set
c. During the first minute of recovery from the exercise set
d. After the resistance exercise training session is completed

38. Increased tendon stiffness is associated with which of the following?
a. Greater muscular recoil and power production
b. Decreased ability of the tendon to withstand tensional forces
c. Enhanced muscular flexibility
d. Increased risk of injury

39. Which of the following collegiate athletes is most likely to have low bone mineral density?
a. A swimmer who runs during preseason and has two resistance training sessions per week during the season
b. A lacrosse player who plays midfielder
c. A gymnast whose primary events are the floor exercise and the vault
d. A distance cyclist with one resistance training session per week

40. Which of the following is NOT true about the impact of aerobic training on bone growth?
a. High-intensity activities such as running or aerobics are required to stimulate bone growth.
b. The intensity of the activity must continue to increase systematically to ensure that the bones experience continual overload.
c. Any type of high-intensity aerobic activity can stimulate bone growth.
d. If the intensity of the activity cannot be increased, increasing the rate of the limb movement can continue to stimulate bone growth.

41. Which of the following is a common adaptation to aerobic endurance training that athletes can easily measure?
a. Resting heart rate
b. Stroke volume
c. Systolic blood pressure
d. Diastolic blood pressure

42. An aerobic endurance athlete experiencing detraining will first experience a decline in which of the following?
a. Maximal oxygen consumption
b. Resting heart rate
c. Stroke volume
d. Muscular strength

43. Which of the following is NOT an adaptation to aerobic endurance training?
a. Increased blood lactate concentrations
b. Increased stroke volume
c. Increased blood flow to working muscles
d. Increased cardiac output

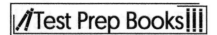

44. Which of the following individual characteristics that influence adaptations to aerobic endurance training can be controlled by the athlete?

a. Age
b. Sex
c. Negative health behaviors (e.g., smoking)
d. Genetic potential

45. Which of the following is NOT a sign or symptom of aerobic overtraining syndrome?

a. Increased resting heart rate
b. Reduced oxygen uptake
c. Increased muscle glycogen
d. Increased cortisol concentration

46. A strength and conditioning professional is developing a resistance training program for a youth athlete who has 3 years of resistance training experience. Which age (based on the information that the age provides) would be the most important to consider while developing the training program?

a. Biological age
b. Training age
c. Chronological age
d. Skeletal age

47. Many factors go into the development of a resistance training program for youth athletes. Which of the following components are necessary to create the best program possible for a young athlete?

I. Quality of instruction by the strength and conditioning professional
II. An appropriate rate of progression
III. Treatment of the athlete as a miniature adult
IV. Training sessions scheduled as nonconsecutive sessions to allow appropriate recovery

a. I, II
b. II, III
c. I, II, IV
d. I, III, IV

48. Youth experience improvements in strength, agility, and power primarily because of the development of which system?

a. The musculoskeletal system
b. The nervous system
c. The respiratory system
d. The cardiovascular system

49. Which of the following is true about muscle strength in women?

a. Women have about 1/2 the absolute body strength as compared to men.
b. The absolute upper body strength of women is similar to men.
c. When strength is related to body weight, females and males have similar lower body strength levels.
d. When strength is expressed as cross-sectional area of a muscle, females have about 2/3 the strength of men.

50. Which of the following is NOT an aspect of the female athlete triad?
   a. Anterior cruciate ligament (ACL) tears
   b. Amenorrhea
   c. Energy availability
   d. Bone mineral density

51. A 69-year-old woman would like to begin a resistance training program and knows that her physical inactivity has resulted in strength loss but does not know if it has impacted her bone mineral density. A bone density scan showed that her bone mineral density level was 1.5 standard deviations below the bone mineral density of young adults. Based on these results, what condition is the women experiencing?
   a. Reduced neuromotor functioning
   b. Osteopenia
   c. Sarcopenia
   d. Osteoporosis

52. Which of the following does NOT need to be considered when developing an optimal training program for an older adult?
   a. Medical history
   b. Risk factor questionnaire
   c. Resistance and aerobic training history
   d. The older adult's request for the program to contain only resistance exercises

Sport Psychology

1. Although Robert is not the best basketball player on the team, he loves participating in the game and having the opportunity to work on new skills. He also is good at maintaining his focus on achieving his short-term goals. What type of motivation is driving Robert's behavior?
   a. Extrinsic motivation
   b. Achievement motivation
   c. Outcome motivation
   d. Intrinsic motivation

2. Which of the following in NOT a characteristic of the ideal performance state?
   a. The absence of fear
   b. A high level of arousal
   c. A sense of personal control
   d. A narrow focus of attention on the activity

3. During training, removal of an element of the workout that the athlete considers negative represents which of the following reinforcement techniques?
   a. Negative reinforcement
   b. Positive reinforcement
   c. Negative punishment
   d. Positive punishment

4. Beth has elevated levels of psychological arousal prior to competing that have been detrimental to her performance. She recently learned a new relaxation technique that involves alternating between tensing the muscles and relaxing the muscles in succession over the entire body. What specific technique is Beth using to reduce arousal?

a. Diaphragmatic breathing
b. Imagery
c. Progressive muscular relaxation
d. Systematic desensitization

5. A basketball player getting ready to shoot a free throw blocks out the opposing players and noisy crowd in order to focus on making the shot. This behavior is an example of which of the following?

a. Internal attention
b. Selective attention
c. Focus
d. Optimal functioning

6. A swimmer obtained her best time in the 100-yard butterfly during a split squad meet at the beginning of the training season. This is an example of what type of self-efficacy source?

a. Vicarious experience
b. Performance accomplishment
c. Verbal persuasion
d. Physiological states

7. Sarah is learning how to do the long jump, an event that she never participated in during high school. Which type of motor skill learning may be best for her coach to implement for this event?

a. Part practice
b. Guided discovery
c. Whole practice
d. Discovery

8. John met with his coach to outline his goals for performing the 5000-meter race. One goal is to maintain his running form during the final 400 meters of the race. What type of goal is this?

a. Short-term goal
b. Outcome goal
c. Long-term goal
d. Process goal

9. Which of the following is correct regarding eating disorders?

a. Eating disorders are not attributed to genetics.
b. Eating disorders can be resolved in a matter of months.
c. Eating disorders align with a set of specific criteria.
d. Eating disorders are usually attributed to stress.

10. A coach notices that an athlete seems to have a distorted body image, and the athlete reports using laxatives to cleanse the body. This behavior aligns with what eating disorder?

a. Anorexia nervosa
b. Bulimia nervosa
c. Binge eating disorder
d. An unspecified eating disorder

11. A visual learner would probably prefer which of the following?
    a. Reading about proper squatting technique
    b. Trying to squat back into a chair before a full body squat
    c. Watching video tutorials of squatting form
    d. Listening to you explain the major tips for the perfect squat form

12. An elevated heart rate and upset stomach are examples of which of the following?
    a. Trait anxiety
    b. State anxiety
    c. Cognitive anxiety
    d. Somatic anxiety

13. Which of the following accurately describes an operant?
    a. A behavior reinforced by a stimulus
    b. The avoidance of a specific behavior
    c. The motivation to avoid a punishment
    d. The motivation to earn a reward

14. A swimmer lies on his couch and then tenses and relaxes his muscles starting from his neck, working down his arms, his torso, and then his legs. What is the purpose of this activity?
    a. To replace an anxiety-increasing fear response with feelings of relaxation
    b. To increase his arousal levels to a more optimal level according to the inverted-U theory
    c. To increase his awareness of somatic tension, with the hope that relaxing the body will result in a relaxed mind
    d. To reduce heart rate and muscle tension, decrease autonomic nervous system functioning, and increase parasympathetic nervous system activity, resulting in deep relaxation due to the reduced neural stimulation of the muscles and organs

15. Which of the following correctly describes the five stages of relaxation in autogenic training?
    a. A focus on the warmth of the extremities, then heaviness of the extremities, then regulation of cardiac activity and breathing, then abdominal warmth, and then cooling of the forehead.
    b. A focus on the heaviness of the extremities, then warmth of the extremities, then regulation of cardiac activity and breathing, then abdominal warmth, and then cooling of the forehead.
    c. A focus on the heaviness of the extremities, then warmth of the extremities, then abdominal warmth, then regulation of cardiac activity and breathing, and then cooling of the forehead.
    d. A focus on the warmth of the extremities, then regulation of cardiac activity and breathing, then heaviness of the extremities, then abdominal warmth, and then cooling of the forehead.

16. A strength and conditioning coach is taking a video of a long jumper competing at a track meet. She shows it to the athlete and they look at the positioning of the athlete's hips right before he takes off after the run portion to jump into the pit. What type of feedback does this provide?
    a. Knowledge of results
    b. Knowledge of performance
    c. Knowledge of augmented feedback
    d. Intrinsic feedback

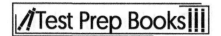

17. A strength and conditioning coach explains the goal of a squat to a novice athlete and the coach says to push through the heels and to keep the chest up. What type of instruction has the strength and conditioning coach provided?

a. Discovery
b. Explicit instruction
c. Implicit instruction
d. Guided discovery

18. Which of the following is NOT true about withdrawal when considering substance abuse?

a. It manifests as physiological and substance-specific cognitive symptoms.
b. Examples of symptoms can include paranoia, hallucinations, cold sweats, shivering, nausea, vomiting.
c. It happens when an individual stops abusing the substance and when he or she attempts to reduce the amount taken.
d. It results in needing greater amounts of the substance to achieve the desired effects.

19. Which of the following is NOT true regarding internal and external cueing?

a. Most research has found that internal cues are more effective at improving motor learning and movement performance.
b. With an external cue, an athlete focuses on how the movement or performing it will affect the outcome of the exercise or the environment at large.
c. With an internal cue, an athlete focuses on the movements and feelings in their own limbs or body as the exercise or movement is being performed.
d. An internal cue for an athlete doing a plank could be, "Pull your belly button toward your spine."

20. What is the word used to describe the direction and intensity of an athlete's effort?

a. Self-confidence
b. Reinforcement
c. Motivation
d. Focus

21. Which of the following is NOT a type of motivation in sport psychology?

a. Competitive motivation
b. Extrinsic motivation
c. Achievement motivation
d. Intrinsic motivation

22. What kinds of games would an athlete with high MAF prefer?

a. Difficult but fair challenges with an equal likelihood of success or failure
b. Difficult challenges with very high stakes
c. Easier challenges where success is more likely
d. Athletes with high MAF have no preference on challenge difficulty

23. What is the source of an athlete's intrinsic motivation?

a. Their love or interest in the sport
b. The personal satisfaction in doing well in the sport
c. The inherent reward of success
d. All of the above

Nutrition

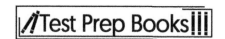

1. Which meal planning approach may be best suited for an individual seeking to lower blood pressure through weight loss?
    a. Healthy U.S. Eating Style
    b. Food exchanges
    c. DASH Eating Plan
    d. Glycemic index

2. What is the typical recommended carbohydrate intake for athletes?
    a. 3–7 grams of carbohydrates per kilogram of body weight
    b. 4–8 grams of carbohydrates per kilogram of body weight
    c. 5–9 grams of carbohydrates per kilogram of body weight
    d. 6–10 grams of carbohydrates per kilogram of body weight

3. An athlete would like to gain muscle mass. With regard to diet, what should the athlete be instructed to do?
    a. Supplement the diet with branched-chain amino acids.
    b. Consume protein in the diet in excess of normal requirements to help build lean tissue.
    c. Eat a diet that consists of 1.5–2.0 grams of protein per kilogram of body weight.
    d. Add protein powder to meals and snacks as needed.

4. Which of the following statements is most accurate about vitamin and mineral supplementation for athletes?
    a. Athletes cannot meet their nutrition needs with food alone.
    b. Most athletes require vitamin and mineral supplementation.
    c. Vitamin and mineral supplements help to improve athletic performance.
    d. Vitamin and mineral supplements can help to correct a deficiency.

5. Which statement best describes current advice about dietary and blood cholesterol?
    a. Cholesterol is produced in the body, but additional amounts are required through the diet.
    b. Dietary cholesterol has little impact on blood cholesterol.
    c. Foods high in saturated fats do not typically contain cholesterol.
    d. A normal range for cholesterol is below 220 milligrams per deciliter.

6. Which athlete is at the highest risk for iron-deficiency anemia?
    a. Male athlete who strength trains regularly
    b. Female endurance athlete
    c. Adolescent athlete
    d. Female vegan athlete who strength trains

7. Dehydration at which level can negatively affect athletic performance?
    a. 1 percent of body weight
    b. 2 percent of body weight
    c. 3 percent of body weight
    d. 5 percent of body weight

8. Nutritional rating systems designed to help with selecting nutrient-dense foods include all of the following EXCEPT _______.
   a. glycemic index
   b. Nutripoints
   c. food exchanges
   d. Points Food System

9. Which macronutrient composition is best suited for short-term weight loss?
   a. 70 percent carbohydrates, 20 percent protein, and 10 percent fat
   b. 60 percent carbohydrates, 20 percent protein, and 20 percent fat
   c. 55 percent carbohydrates, 30 percent protein, and 25 percent fat
   d. 45 percent carbohydrates, 30 percent protein, and 25 percent fat

10. Which statement best describes nutrient timing?
   a. Nutrient timing is altering the content of the total diet.
   b. Nutrient timing is altering the total content and timing of the total diet.
   c. Nutrient timing is altering the carbohydrate and protein content and timing of the diet.
   d. Nutrient timing is altering the carbohydrate and fat content and timing of the diet.

11. Carbohydrate loading is recommended for activities lasting longer than 120 minutes and can be accomplished by consuming which of the following?
   a. 8–10 grams of carbohydrates per kilogram of body weight
   b. 7–9 grams of carbohydrates per kilogram of body weight
   c. 6–8 grams of carbohydrates per kilogram of body weight
   d. 5–7 grams of carbohydrates per kilogram of body weight

12. Essential amino acids are required by the body and include which of the following?
   a. Arginine and cysteine
   b. Isoleucine and lysine
   c. Alanine and glycine
   d. Glutamine and histidine

13. Beta-hydroxy beta-methylbutyric acid (HMB) plays a role in the prevention of what?
   a. Cytolysis
   b. Hydrolysis
   c. Proteolysis
   d. Hydrogenolysis

14. Which amino acid must be present for the development of carnosine, an essential muscle buffering element?
   a. Histidine
   b. Beta-alanine
   c. Carnosine
   d. Leucine

15. An athlete would like to use an ergogenic aid for delaying fatigue. Which of the following is a good option?
   a. Sodium tablets and/or sports beverages
   b. Glutamine and/or sodium tablets
   c. Branched-chain amino acids and/or caffeine
   d. Sports beverages and/or caffeine

16. Which of the following is an example of a high molecular weight carbohydrate?
   a. Sodium bicarbonate
   b. Maltodextrin
   c. Dextrose
   d. Waxy maize

17. Which of the following is a banned ergogenic aid?
   a. Amphetamines
   b. Insulin
   c. Glucose tablets
   d. Hydroxycut

18. Which of the following statements is accurate about ergogenic aids?
   a. About 30 percent of the general population use ergogenic aids.
   b. The use of ergogenic aids is decreasing.
   c. About 76 percent of college athletes use ergogenic aids.
   d. Ergogenic aids are substances that enhance an individual's performance.

19. An athlete would like to start using creatine as an ergogenic aid. The athlete should receive which of the following advice?
   a. Creatine can be made in the body and supplementation is not safe for athletes.
   b. Research indicates that creatine is best suited for endurance sports.
   c. The ISSN has concluded that athletes should consider other ergogenic aids.
   d. Creatine can be started at 0.3 grams per kilogram of body weight.

20. Who arbitrates the five major recognized food groups in the United States?
   a. The International Food Information Council
   b. The Food and Drug Administration
   c. The United States Department of Agriculture
   d. The American Nutrition Association

Exercise Technique

1. Which of the following is NOT a benefit of resistance machines?
   a. They can be used easily without a spotter.
   b. They can help newer athletes learn proper form and maintain control of the motion within the desired plane of movement.
   c. They can improve sports-specific movements and strength, incorporating core stability.
   d. Athletes can often lift higher maximal weights and isolate specific muscles, improving absolute strength.

2. When using starting blocks for sprinting, which of the following best describes optimal hand position?
   a. Hands should be slightly less than shoulder-width apart with the fingers held together and thumbs under the shoulders.
   b. Hands should be slightly wider than shoulder-width apart with the fingers held together and thumbs under the shoulders.
   c. Hands should be slightly less than shoulder-width apart with the fingers spread apart and thumbs under the armpits.
   d. Hands should be slightly wider than shoulder-width apart with the fingers spread apart and thumbs under the armpits.

3. Box jumps, depth jumps, and medicine ball throws are examples of what type of training?
   a. Plyometrics
   b. Agility exercises
   c. Non-traditional modalities
   d. Speed training

4. During agility exercises, weight should be concentrated on what part of the foot?
   a. Forefoot
   b. Midfoot
   c. Hind foot
   d. Heel

5. Which of the following is NOT true regarding the incorporation of yoga training into an athlete's regimen?
   a. It improves core strength.
   b. It improves flexibility.
   c. It improves mental focus and relaxation.
   d. It improves absolute strength.

6. Free weight exercises have all of the following benefits over resistance machines EXCEPT which of the following?
   a. They may be completed without a spotter.
   b. They can improve core stability.
   c. They can provide a more sports-specific strength training method.
   d. Each exercise can be performed in a variety of ways, rather than strictly dictated in one certain way.

7. What is the most challenging part of a strength exercise called?
   a. Eccentric phase
   b. Concentric phase
   c. Sticking point
   d. Maximal point

8. For most strength exercises, which of the following breathing patterns is optimal?
   a. Inhaling through the mouth during the concentric phase and exhaling through the nose during the eccentric phase
   b. Exhaling through the mouth during the concentric phase and inhaling through the nose during the eccentric phase
   c. Inhaling through the nose during the concentric phase and exhaling through the mouth during the eccentric phase
   d. Exhaling through the nose in the concentric phase and inhaling through the mouth during the eccentric phase

9. Mirrors and video analysis can be helpful in which of the following ways?
   a. Correcting improper form
   b. Allowing a strength coach to focus less on monitoring athletes
   c. Correcting improper technique
   d. Providing visual feedback regarding form and technique

10. Which of the following is NOT an adaptation to chronic cardiovascular conditioning?
    a. Increased heart chamber size
    b. Increased stroke volume
    c. Increased cardiac output
    d. Increased submaximal heart rate

11. Depth achieved during a squat is often limited by which of the following?
    a. Knee injuries
    b. Hamstring tightness
    c. Achilles tendon tightness
    d. Gastrocnemius (calf) weakness

12. When using free weights, how many points of contact should be made for supine and seated exercises?
    a. 2
    b. 3
    c. 4
    d. 5

13. Which direction should the palms face when using a supinated grip?
    a. Upward toward the face
    b. Downwards toward the feet
    c. Inward toward the hips
    d. Out laterally away from the body

14. Which athlete would benefit most from agility work on most days of the week?
    a. A soccer midfielder
    b. A baseball pitcher
    c. A shot putter
    d. A swimmer

15. Which athlete would benefit most from plyometrics at least three days per week?
    a. A cross country runner
    b. A hockey player
    c. A figure skater
    d. A swimmer

16. What is the name for the grip pattern where palms face the floor and the knuckles face the ceiling?
    a. Pronated grip
    b. Supinated grip
    c. Hook grip
    d. False grip

17. Golgi tendon organs are stimulated in PNF stretching and cause relaxation of which of the following?
    a. The antagonist muscle by its own contraction
    b. The stretched muscle by its own contraction
    c. The antagonist muscle by contracting the stretched muscle
    d. The stretched muscle by contracting the antagonist muscle

18. Activation of muscle spindles is decreased in which of the following stretching methods?
    a. Dynamic
    b. Passive
    c. Static
    d. PNF

19. In order of decreasing percentage of total training volume, for a distance runner's program, which of the following would you suggest for the given activities?
    a. Cardiovascular/metabolic conditioning, muscular endurance, agility training, plyometrics
    b. Cardiovascular/metabolic conditioning, muscular endurance, plyometrics, agility training
    c. Cardiovascular/metabolic conditioning, agility training, muscular endurance, plyometrics
    d. Cardiovascular/metabolic conditioning, plyometrics, muscular endurance, agility training

20. In order of decreasing frequency for a tennis player's training program, which of the following should be suggested for the given activities?
    a. Speed training, cardiovascular conditioning, plyometrics, agility training
    b. Cardiovascular conditioning, speed training, agility training, plyometrics
    c. Cardiovascular conditioning, agility training, speed training, plyometrics
    d. Agility training, speed training, plyometrics, cardiovascular conditioning

21. Which of the following is NOT a form of PNF technique?
    a. Contract-relax
    b. Contract-relax with agonist contraction
    c. Hold-relax with agonist contraction
    d. Hold-relax

22. Which of the following is the correct protocol for the hold-relax PNF technique?
    a. 10-second passive pre-stretch, isometric contraction for 6 seconds, passive stretch for 30 seconds
    b. 10-second passive pre-stretch, isometric contraction for 6 seconds, passive stretch for 10 seconds
    c. 6-second passive pre-stretch, isometric contraction for 10 seconds, passive stretch for 30 seconds
    d. 6-second passive pre-stretch, isometric contraction for 10 seconds, passive stretch for 10 seconds

23. Benefits of static stretching include all EXCEPT which of the following?
    a. It improves muscle-joint tension relationship
    b. It can warm up muscles prior to workout
    c. It can increase joint laxity
    d. It can reduce risk of injury

24. With which of the following athletes should you use extra precaution when programming plyometric exercises?
    a. A distance runner
    b. A 250-pound lineman
    c. A female athlete
    d. A figure skater

25. Which of the following anatomic structures detects rapid movement and initiates the stretch reflex?
    a. Extrafusal muscle fibers
    b. Mechanoreceptors
    c. Golgi tendon organs
    d. Muscle spindles

26. Static stretches should be held for about how many seconds and performed for how many sets?
    a. Thirty seconds, two to three sets
    b. Thirty seconds, three to five sets
    c. Ten seconds, two to three sets
    d. Ten seconds, three to five sets

27. Tire flipping, kettlebells, sandbags, and battle ropes are implements best reserved for which of the following?
    a. Highly trained athletes
    b. Younger athletes
    c. Athletes rehabbing injuries
    d. Newer athletes

28. Which type of stretching should be done prior to workouts, and which type of stretching should follow the workout?
    a. Static (prior to workouts), dynamic (following workouts)
    b. Dynamic (prior to workouts), static (following workouts)
    c. Flexibility (prior to workouts), dynamic (following workouts)
    d. Dynamic (prior to workouts), flexibility (following workouts)

29. Which of the following factors is most influential in improving sprinting speed?
    a. Leg length
    b. Stride length
    c. Stride rate
    d. Impulse time

30. If an athlete has medial tibial stress syndrome, which type of cardiovascular equipment would NOT be a wise choice?
    a. Arm ergometer
    b. Elliptical
    c. Spin bike
    d. Treadmill

31. Which of the following exercises should spotters NOT be used for?
    a. Dumbbell chest press
    b. Incline barbell bench press
    c. Front squat
    d. Power jerk

32. Benefits of the Valsalva maneuver include all EXCEPT which of the following?
    a. It increases blood pressure.
    b. It increases torso rigidity.
    c. It decreases compressive forces on the intervertebral disks.
    d. It supports the normal lordotic lumbar spine.

33. During a heavy front-loaded squat, there should be how many spotter(s) positioned in what location(s)?
    a. One spotter should be in the middle of the bar in front of the lifter.
    b. One spotter should be in the middle of the bar behind the lifter.
    c. One spotter should be on either end of the bar, for a total of two spotters.
    d. One spotter should be in front of and one spotter should be behind the lifter, for a total of two spotters.

34. The number of required spotters is dependent upon all EXCEPT which of the following?
    a. The load being lifted
    b. The number of strength coaches available
    c. The experience and skill of the athlete and spotters
    d. The physical strength of the spotters

35. When spotting over-the-face barbell exercises, the spotter should use what type of grip on the bar?
    a. Hook grip
    b. Pronated grip
    c. Alternated grip
    d. Supinated grip

36. Correct spotting position includes all BUT which of the following?
    a. Knees locked
    b. Feet flat on the floor
    c. Hands up in ready position
    d. Erect, neutral spine

37. Negative resistance training is best described as which of the following?
    a. Reducing training volume prior to competition to taper and improve performance
    b. A detraining effect that occurs when athletes fail to train with high enough frequency
    c. Lifting heavier weights on the lowering, eccentric portion and getting assistance during the lifting, concentric phase
    d. Lifting heavier weights on the lifting, concentric portion and getting assistance during the lowering, eccentric phase

38. Benefits of bodyweight exercises include all BUT which of the following?
    a. They increase relative strength
    b. They increase absolute strength
    c. They can be performed on the field or away from the gym
    d. Athletes can often complete many repetitions, improving muscular endurance

39. Which of the following is NOT one of the most common types of movement preparation techniques for athletes prior to workouts or competitions?
    a. PNF
    b. CNS prep
    c. Intensive weight training
    d. Dynamic stretching

40. What does the acronym PNF mean?
    a. Parietal Neurovascular Facility
    b. Proprioceptive Neuromuscular Facilitation
    c. Proprioceptive Neurovascular Facilitation
    d. Proprietary Neuromuscular Facility

41. Why is dynamic stretching an effective pre-workout warmup routine for athletes?
    a. Dynamic stretching moves the joints through the sport-specific range of motion.
    b. Dynamic stretching works the individual muscles throughout the body.
    c. Dynamic stretching uses specific ballistic movements.
    d. Dynamic stretching is more effective than static PNF stretching.

42. What position should the athlete be in when using PNF stretching of the hamstring muscles?
    a. Prone
    b. Supine
    c. Right lateral recumbent
    d. Left lateral recumbent

43. Where should the strength coach be positioned when applying PNF stretching to an athlete?
    a. At the athlete's head with the athlete lying supine, facing towards the athlete
    b. At the athlete's feet with the athlete lying prone, facing towards the athlete
    c. At the end range of desired movement, with hips and shoulders facing opposite of the direction of movement
    d. At the end range of desired movement, with hips and shoulders facing in the direction of movement

44. How many forms of PNF are there?
    a. Two
    b. Three
    c. Four
    d. Five

45. PNF should begin with a ten-second passive pre-stretch that is held at what point?
    a. The point of preliminary relaxation
    b. The point of maximum flexibility
    c. The point of moderate discomfort
    d. The point of mild discomfort

Program Design

1. Before designing a strength and conditioning program for an athlete, what step should the strength and conditioning professional take to get useful information about the athlete and their sport?
    a. Create a long-term plan
    b. Begin selecting exercises
    c. Perform a needs analysis
    d. Determine the athlete's rate of perceived exertion

2. Which of the following shows the correct dynamic correspondence and training volume?
    a. 120 to 140 repetitions of lower-body plyometrics for a beginner basketball player
    b. 80 to 100 repetitions of upper-body plyometrics for a beginner baseball player
    c. 100 to 120 repetitions of lower-body plyometrics for an advanced volleyball player
    d. 80 to 100 repetitions of upper-body plyometrics for an intermediate soccer player

3. After completing a needs analysis, a strength and conditioning professional determines that an athlete needs improved range of motion for sprinting. Which training method would be best for reaching this goal?
    a. Mobility training
    b. Tactical metabolic training
    c. Pace/tempo training
    d. Repetition training

4. An athlete is performing three sets of chest presses with six repetitions per set. Using the two-for-two rule, how should the athlete increase their training load?
    a. By performing eight repetitions on the third set for the next two training sessions
    b. By performing five sets of six repetitions for the next two sessions
    c. By adding two additional training sessions every two weeks
    d. By performing the eccentric and concentric phases of the chest press for two seconds each

5. Which of the following factors would NOT affect an athlete's ability to increase their training load?
    a. Lack of sleep
    b. Poor diet
    c. Training too often
    d. Focusing on core exercises

6. Which physiological adaptation is expected after an athlete has participated in an aerobic-training program?
    a. Heart rate reserve decreases and resting-heart rate increases
    b. Heart rate reserve increases and resting-heart rate decreases
    c. Heart rate reserve increases and resting-heart rate increases
    d. Heart rate reserve decreases and resting-heart rate decreases

7. Which of the following statements about rest periods is FALSE?
    a. Longer rest periods promote nervous-system recovery
    b. Longer rest periods promote muscular-system recovery
    c. Longer rest periods promote cardiovascular conditioning
    d. Shorter rest periods promote cardiovascular conditioning

8. Which of the following is the method for organizing the strength and conditioning program and preplanning an athlete's training load and volume to improve their physical ability over a certain amount of time?
    a. Training macrocycle
    b. Mesocycle
    c. Preparatory phase
    d. Periodization

9. Which of the following statements about kinetic chain movements is true?
    a. Pull-ups are a closed kinetic chain movement.
    b. Hamstring curls are a closed kinetic chain movement.
    c. Lunges are an open kinetic chain movement.
    d. Leg extensions are a closed kinetic chain movement.

10. What is an example of an appropriate modification for an injured athlete?
    a. A volleyball player with a rotator-cuff injury does shoulder presses.
    b. A basketball player with a sprained knee does leg extensions.
    c. A tennis player with an elbow injury does squats.
    d. A golfer with lower-back pain does back extensions.

11. Which of the following injury-analysis definitions is correct?
   a. A dislocation occurs when a joint is partially displaced from its articulation surface, while a subluxation occurs when a joint is completely displaced from its articulation surface.
   b. Macrotrauma to joint ligaments is called a strain, while macrotrauma to muscle tissue is a sprain.
   c. When tissues are overburdened and their health is negatively affected, a macrotrauma occurs, and when tissues have been overtrained or have not had time to recover, a microtrauma occurs.
   d. Tendinosis occurs when a tendon becomes acutely inflamed after a joint is overused, experiences excess force, or is overtrained.

12. Arrange the following three steps to reflect to process by which tissue healing occurs:

I. Tissue repair
II. Inflammation
III. Tissue remodeling

   a. I, II, III
   b. II, I, III
   c. II, III, I
   d. III, II, I

13. An athlete wants to increase muscular hypertrophy for a bodybuilding competition. How many repetitions and exercises should be assigned to optimize success in the stated goal?
   a. Six to twelve repetitions per set; three exercises per muscle group
   b. Two to four repetitions per set; three exercises per muscle group
   c. Fifteen repetitions per set; three exercises per muscle group
   d. Six to twelve repetitions per set; one exercise per muscle group

14. Which of the following is true regarding muscle balance?
   a. The strength in opposing muscle groups must be equalized.
   b. The strength ratios in antagonist muscle groups must be improved.
   c. Muscle balance is not an integral part of a strength-training program.
   d. Even if an athlete has improper muscle balance, the body will maintain its normal movement patterns during exercises.

15. Which type of exercises give muscle tissue the most stimulation and are beneficial for limited training time, and which type of exercises involve the core muscles and should be the basis of training programs?
   a. Multi-joint; Assistance
   b. Structural; Primary
   c. Primary; Assistance
   d. Multi-joint; Structural

16. An athlete has limited time to train. She wants to improve mental focus and lose body fat. Which type of training would benefit her most?
   a. Split-routine training
   b. 1-RM
   c. Circuit training
   d. Percentage-based training

17. What type of training will help a soccer player to improve his speed and endurance?
   a. Running up hills
   b. Dragging sleds
   c. Wearing a weighted vest
   d. All of the above

18. An athlete would like to improve strength and power for a weightlifting competition. In which order should she complete the following exercises?

I. Olympic lifts
II. Back extensions
III. Biceps curls

   a. I, II, III
   b. II, I, III
   c. III, II, I
   d. II, III, I

19. Which of the following agility-drill classifications is correctly matched with its description?
   a. Serial drills combine continuous and discrete drills and are sport-specific.
   b. Discrete drills are continuous in nature and are useful for developing running and jumping skills.
   c. Continuous drills are helpful for developing specific movement patterns.
   d. Continuous drills can make athletes stronger and more powerful.

20. How can a coach correct a sprinter who "bounces" when she runs?
   a. The coach should help her to practice swinging her arms correctly during short runs.
   b. The coach should her increase her stride rate.
   c. The coach should advise her to keep her head stable with her eyes focused on a specific target.
   d. The coach should advise her to keep her eyes focused on the ground.

21. How many repetitions and sets should be used when training an athlete for muscular endurance?
   a. Six to twelve repetitions for three sets
   b. Six to twelve repetitions for five sets
   c. Twelve to fifteen repetitions for three sets
   d. Two to six repetitions for five sets

22. Which of the following intensity and duration combinations is appropriate for off-season athletes?
   a. Low intensity and short duration
   b. Low intensity and long duration
   c. Moderate intensity and short duration
   d. High intensity and short duration

23. What information should be given to a football player who wants to improve his reaction time?
   a. Reaction time depends on the muscular system, not the nervous system.
   b. Improving reaction time will also improve performance in explosive activities.
   c. He can improve reaction time significantly by being trained to process information at a faster rate.
   d. He can only make small improvements in his reaction time.

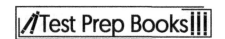

24. After doing chest presses, an athlete complains of soreness, stiffness, and lower performance. What advice could a strength and conditioning professional give him?

a. "You have trained too hard and will not be able to increase your performance beyond this point."
b. "Keep training as hard as possible and eliminate your recovery time so that your body will experience super-compensation more rapidly."
c. "You are experiencing the first phase of GAS. If you give your body time to recover, your symptoms will improve and you will eventually become stronger and have more muscle mass."
d. "You're in the alarm phase of GAS. You should stop your training immediately and see a physician."

25. Which of the following is NOT an appropriate progression method for promoting physiological adaptations in an athlete during the training phase?

a. Increasing training-load intensities to improve speed
b. Increasing training density
c. Increasing training volume
d. Changing the duration of rest between sets

26. Which of the following approaches should be used to help an athlete recover from previous training sessions and improve neural patterns while promoting supercompensation?

a. Linear periodization
b. Unloading/deloading week
c. Undulating/nonlinear periodization
d. Rehabilitation

27. Which of the following exercises would help an athlete restore neuromuscular control after an injury?

a. Doing bodyweight squats on a flat surface
b. Jumping on a flat surface
c. Doing push-ups on a flat surface
d. Jumping on a trampoline

28. Which of the following movement combinations would be most appropriate for a complex-training model?

a. Bench press at 80% to 90% for two to three reps; plyometric push-ups for three to five reps
b. Chest press at 50% to 60% for fifteen to twenty reps; bodyweight sit-ups for twenty-five reps
c. Back squats at 70% for twelve to fifteen reps; maximum-height box jumps for six to eight reps
d. Leg press at 70% for twelve to fifteen reps; bodyweight calf raises for twenty-five reps

29. Which of the following statements is true about recovery time and training frequency for endurance athletes?

a. Athletes training at a low intensity need the same number of training sessions but more recovery time than those training at a high intensity.
b. Athletes training at a high intensity need the same number of training sessions but more recovery time than those training at a low intensity.
c. Both athletes participating in high-intensity training and those doing low-intensity training need the same amount of recovery time.
d. Athletes who are doing high-intensity training sessions should get more time to recover and should train less frequently than low-intensity athletes.

30. Interval training for aerobic athletes and anaerobic athletes is similar in which way?

a. Intervals last the same amount of time for aerobic and anaerobic athletes.
b. Rest periods last the same amount of time for aerobic and anaerobic athletes.
c. Both types of athletes are training at higher levels of intensity compared with their VO_2 max.
d. Both types of athletes use a 2:1 work-to-rest ratio.

31. Which group of athletes would derive the LEAST benefit from Fartlek training?
   a. Powerlifters
   b. Runners
   c. Swimmers
   d. Cyclists

32. What is the most important part of the stretch-shortening cycle response?
   a. Eccentric phase
   b. Concentric phase
   c. Amortization phase
   d. Series elastic component

33. When an athlete performs biceps curls, which of the following is true regarding the phases of the stretch-shortening cycle?
   a. When the athlete raises the weight, the biceps are in the eccentric phase.
   b. The amortization phase is between the eccentric phase and the concentric phase.
   c. When the athlete lowers the weight, the biceps are in the concentric phase.
   d. The athlete is in the amortization phase after he or she begins the biceps curl.

34. What is true about muscle spindles?
   a. They are the most important feature in the stretch-reflex response.
   b. They are the primary baroreceptive structures in the muscle.
   c. They are sensitive to concentric muscle action.
   d. They are the secondary proprioceptive structures in the muscle.

35. In which phase of a sprint is it most important to have excellent mechanics while moving at the highest possible velocity in the shortest time?
   a. Flight phase
   b. Propulsion phase
   c. Recovery phase
   d. Support phase

36. What is the Karvonen method?
   a. The prediction of maximum heart rate based on age
   b. The calculation of target heart rate based on age
   c. The prediction of maximum heart rate based on resting heart rate
   d. The calculation of target heart rate based on resting heart rate

37. An athlete does one set of five repetitions of shoulder presses with 50 lb. dumbbells. How can a coach calculate how much work he does during the set?
   a. Work equals the amount of weight he lifted.
   b. The coach can divide the weight he lifted by the number of repetitions.
   c. The coach can multiply the weight he lifted by the number of repetitions.
   d. The coach cannot calculate his work with this information.

38. Which of the following statements is true about fibrosis?
   a. Fibrosis may cause some discomfort but will not affect an athlete's mobility.
   b. There is no link between fibrosis and aging.
   c. Since fibrosis is associated with tissue regeneration, this condition has no effect on the overall health of muscle tissue.
   d. Fibrosis can affect an athlete's movement patterns and lead to acute and chronic injuries.

39. What is the difference between the repetition maximum test and the 1-RM test?
   a. They are the same test.
   b. The repetition maximum test can help identify an athlete's weaknesses when doing multiple repetitions that may not be identified during a single repetition.
   c. The repetition maximum test requires calculating loading parameters for an athlete when he or she is doing multiple repetitions, while the 1-RM test does not have this requirement.
   d. The 1-RM test can be used to establish loading parameters for an athlete, while the repetition maximum test cannot be used to establish these parameters.

40. 1. Which of the following is true about a needs analysis?
   a. It includes a movement analysis of the athlete.
   b. It considers injuries that are common to the sport.
   c. It results in multiple goals for each competition season.
   d. It utilizes a standard battery of strength tests.

41. You are conducting a needs analysis on a collegiate swimmer. Which of the following should you do?
   a. Compare the physical evaluation results with those of other athletes on the team.
   b. Evaluate the physiological demands of cycling, which the swimmer uses to cross-train.
   c. Review the athlete's current understanding of and experience with training exercises.
   d. Skip the injury analysis because the athlete has never had an injury.

42. Which of the following statements are true?

   I. Resistance training improves strength.
   II. Complex training improves hypertrophy.
   III. Strongman training improves aerobic endurance.

   a. I only
   b. II only
   c. III only
   d. I and III

43. What is one benefit of free weights over weight-stack machines?
   a. Free weights are safer because they require less skill and coordination in use.
   b. Free weights coordinate more muscle groups to better replicate athletic movement.
   c. Free weights place less stress on the body's muscles and bones.
   d. Free weights' source of resistance is gravity, which is most effective for training.

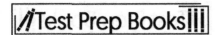

Organization and Administration

1. When a certified strength and conditioning coach fails to perform what is typically considered to be a standard practice of care, it may be deemed to be which of the following?
    a. Negligence
    b. Malpractice
    c. Liability
    d. Scope of practice

2. Which is NOT a symptom of overtraining?
    a. Lowered resting heart rate
    b. Depression or moodiness
    c. Sleep disturbances
    d. Changes in appetite or body weight

3. Which of the following is NOT recommended for an athlete suffering from a heat-related illness?
    a. Move to the shade
    b. Drink fluids
    c. Remove excess clothing
    d. Continue the workout indoors

4. Which of the following is NOT an overuse injury?
    a. Shin splints
    b. Tennis elbow (lateral epicondylitis)
    c. Metatarsal stress fracture
    d. Groin strain

5. What must all strength and conditioning coaches do?
    a. Obtain first aid certification
    b. Be certified strength coaches
    c. Be former competitive athletes
    d. Establish the mission and values for the facility

6. What pieces of equipment should be evaluated prior to every single use?

    I. Medicine balls
    II. Exercise bands
    III. Cables on weight machines
    IV. Emergency stop buttons on cardio equipment

    a. All of the above
    b. I, III, IV
    c. II, III, IV
    d. III, IV

7. In designing the interior layout of a training facility, which of the following need to be considered?

I. Outlet placement
II. Footprint of machines and equipment
III. Ceiling height
IV. Mirror placement

a. All of the above
b. I, II, III
c. I, II, IV
d. II, III, IV

8. Which of the following defines individually identifiable health information such as demographics, prior and current health history, social security number, etc.?

a. Health Insurance Portability and Accountability Act (HIPAA)
b. Health Insurance Portability and Privacy Act (HIPPA)
c. Family Exercise Rights and Privacy Act (FERPA)
d. Family Educational Rights and Privacy Act (FERPA)

9. To reduce liability risk, certified strength and conditioning specialists should do all EXCEPT which of the following?

a. Adhere to NSCA Professional Code of Ethics
b. Rehearse emergency action plans and maintain CPR certification
c. Abide by the NSCA scope of practice for certified strength and conditioning professionals
d. Model healthy lifestyle and behavior choices for athletes

10. Which of the following is within the scope of practice of a CSCS?

a. Diagnosing a meniscal tear
b. Making a customized nutrition plan for an athlete
c. Giving a cross-friction massage for scar tissue to a baseball player
d. Teaching an athlete exercises to do at home on the weekends

11. The need for strength and conditioning professionals to always act with integrity, honesty, and ethical behavior and to report any and all unethical behavior is detailed in which of the following?

a. NSCA's Conflict of Interest policy
b. NSCA's professional liability insurance for certified strength and conditioning specialists
c. NSCA's Professional Code of Ethics
d. NSCA's Disciplinary Policies and Procedures manual

12. What is the purpose of a feasibility study when designing a strength and conditioning facility?

a. To develop the building and construction plan and design
b. To determine what space, equipment, and layout are needed
c. To conduct a SWOT analysis to ensure the business will be financially viable and profitable
d. To develop the budget and operational plan

13. Which of the following is the correct order of the four phases of designing a new facility?

a. SWOT Analysis, Construction, Pre-operation, Operation
b. Construction, Pre-operation, Predesign, Design
c. Pre-operation, Predesign, Design, Construction
d. Predesign, Design, Construction, Pre-operation

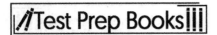

14. Regarding phases of new facility design, which of the four phases is likely to take up the most time?
   a. Predesign
   b. Design
   c. Construction
   d. Pre-operation

15. Which phase of new facility design is most likely to include a SWOT analysis?
   a. Pre-operation
   b. Predesign
   c. Design
   d. Construction

Testing, Ongoing Monitoring, and Data Evaluation

1. A marathon runner scores in the 40th percentile for 1RM bench press and the 70th percentile for VO_2 max, based on a 1.5-mile run. Which of the following should a coach emphasize in a training program?
   a. Upper body strength
   b. Cardiovascular endurance
   c. Lower body strength
   d. Upper body endurance

2. Which of the following anaerobic power tests is likely the LEAST optimal choice for a volleyball player?
   a. Vertical jump test
   b. Wingate test
   c. Margaria-Kalamen stair sprint test
   d. Medicine ball throw

3. A tennis player scores in the 60th percentile for 1RM leg press and the 70th percentile on the push-up test. Which of the following should a coach focus more on in a training program?
   a. Lower body strength
   b. Upper body strength
   c. Cardiovascular endurance
   d. Upper body endurance

4. When selecting the most appropriate assessments for an athlete, the strength and conditioning coach should consider which of the following?

   I. The athlete's strengths and weaknesses
   II. The athlete's sport
   III. The athlete's position
   IV. The athlete's training level

   a. All of the above
   b. II, III, IV
   c. I, II, III
   d. II, III

5. Which of the following is true of testing equipment?
    a. It is needed for field-based tests.
    b. It needs to be calibrated prior to use.
    c. It produces more accurate results than tests with minimal equipment.
    d. It makes it easier to test multiple athletes at one time.

6. Which of the following does NOT typically affect the validity of an assessment?
    a. Population tested
    b. Order of tests conducted
    c. Test selection
    d. The rater's skill level

7. Prior to a 1RM bench press, an athlete should do which of the following?

    I. A 5- to 10-minute jog
    II. One minute of push-ups
    III. A few sets of submaximal bench presses
    IV. A 300-yard shuttle test

    a. All of the above
    b. I, III, IV
    c. I, II, III
    d. I, III

8. Which of the following does NOT take place in the pre-design phase of building?
    a. SWOT analysis
    b. Feasibility study
    c. Needs assessment
    d. Finalizing the blueprint

9. How often should emergency procedures be reviewed and rehearsed?
    a. At least every month
    b. At least every week
    c. At least every three months
    d. At least twice per year

10. Which type of insurance protects against claims of libel, slander, and invasion of privacy?
    a. Personal injury liability
    b. Professional liability
    c. Commercial liability
    d. Negligence liability

11. To control the spread of germs in the facility, what should athletes be taught and instructed to do?
    a. Supplement with Vitamin C and zinc
    b. Wear appropriately supportive sneakers
    c. Wipe down all used equipment with antibacterial agents after use
    d. Engage the emergency stop buttons on cardio equipment

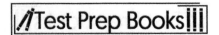

12. Which of the following is the correct order of phases for designing a new fitness facility?
    a. Pre-design, design, construction, pre-operation
    b. Design, pre-construction, construction, pre-operation
    c. Pre-design, design, pre-construction, pre-operation
    d. Pre-planning, design, pre-construction, construction

13. What type of score is VO_2 max?
    a. Norm-referenced score
    b. Criterion-referenced score
    c. Reliability-referenced score
    d. Validity-referenced score

14. An elite cross country skier gets a VO_2 max score that indicates she is in the 30th percentile for her age. Which of the following may be true of this performance?
    a. This indicates she has good cardiovascular endurance, which makes sense because of her sport.
    b. This is an atypical result, and there may have been an error in the protocol, equipment, or scoring.
    c. This is an atypical result, and the test should be conducted again after a 5- to 10-minute break.
    d. This makes sense because she is a cross country skier, so her cardiovascular endurance would be low.

15. Which of the following agility tests would NOT be appropriate for a collegiate hockey player?
    a. Hexagon test
    b. 8 Foot Up and Go test
    c. Zig-zag test
    d. Box drills

16. What should strength coaches conduct prior to selecting tests for athletes?
    a. Feasibility study
    b. Needs analysis
    c. SWOT analysis
    d. Body composition assessments

17. In which of the following situations is it necessary to refer to an allied health professional?
    a. An athlete who has questions about pre-workout hydration
    b. An athlete who has performance anxiety but is not ready to address it
    c. An athlete who wants a nutritional plan to add muscle mass
    d. An athlete who has tight hamstrings after increasing training volume

18. Which of the following would best improve time efficiency when testing a large group of athletes?
    a. Conducting field tests
    b. Conducting laboratory tests
    c. Tests that use one piece of equipment, such as a treadmill
    d. Testing athletes one at a time in a particular order

19. Which of the following tests' results would be LEAST important for a shot-putter?
    a. 1RM bench press
    b. Push-up test
    c. Box drill
    d. Vertical jump test

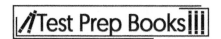

20. Which of the following answer choices gives the correct order in which the listed assessments should be administered.

a. Skinfold, push-up test, step test, 1RM bench press, sit-and-reach
b. Skinfold, step test, push-up test, 1RM bench press, sit-and-reach
c. Skinfold, sit-and-reach, step test, 1RM bench press, push-up test
d. Skinfold, 1RM bench press, push-up test, step test, sit-and-reach

21. Which of the following tests' results is LEAST important for a soccer midfielder?

a. 1RM bench press
b. Cooper 12-minute run test
c. Box drill
d. Vertical jump test

22. Which of the following tests' results is LEAST important for a baseball pitcher?

a. 1RM bench press
b. Push-up test
c. Quadrant jump test
d. Vertical jump test

Answer Explanations #1

Exercise Sciences

1. B: A D-line in not a component of a sarcomere. Sarcomeres are the smallest functional unit of a muscle and contain the actin and myosin proteins responsible for the mechanical process of muscle contractions. Sarcomeres are divided into sections or regions based on the presence of the contractile proteins. The A-band, H-zone, I-band, and Z-line are defined regions within a sarcomere.

2. B: Tennis requires significant involvement of both Type I (slow-twitch) and Type II (fast-twitch) muscle fibers. Type I muscle fibers have a high capacity for aerobic energy supply and are fatigue-resistant—two traits that allow the player to maintain performance levels over multiple sets. Type II muscle fibers are easily fatigable but are capable of high force development, which is beneficial for short sprints to the ball, etc. Large locomotor muscles, such as the quadriceps, have a mixture of Type I and Type II fibers.

3. D: Muscle fibers (myocytes) are long, striated, cylindrical cells that are approximately the diameter of a human hair (50–100 micrometers), are multinucleated, and are covered by a fibrous membrane called the sarcolemma, which is similar in function to the cell membrane of other animal cells. Myofibrils, one of the smaller functional units within a myocyte, consist of long, thin (approximately 1 micrometer) chain proteins. The smallest functional unit of a muscle fiber, a sarcomere, contains the actin and myosin protein filaments that are responsible for the mechanical process of muscle contractions.

4. C: The sinoatrial (SA) node is the initiator of the rhythmic electrical impulses of the cardiac cycle. The SA node is located in the upper wall of the right atrium and contains a small locus of specialized muscle fibers that naturally generate action potentials.

5. C: On an EKG, the T-wave corresponds to the recovery of the ventricles from depolarization, which is also known as repolarization. On the reading, this occurs after the QRS complex—the graphical representation of ventricular depolarization and contraction.

6. C: Capillaries are responsible for the exchange of nutrients, hormones, oxygen, fluids, and electrolytes between the blood and interstitial fluid in tissues. Hemoglobin helps carry oxygen and iron in circulating red blood cells. Arterioles and venules are intermediately-sized blood vessels, but their walls are too thick for cellular-level exchange.

7. A: During the excitation-contraction coupling phase, an electrical discharge at the muscle starts a series of chemical events on the surface of muscle cells. This causes the release of calcium ions (CA^{2+}) from the sarcoplasmic reticulum, resulting in the increase in intracellular calcium, which helps the myosin globular heads attach to the thin actin filaments.

8. C: Heavy breathing requires the movement of the ribs to accommodate lung expansion. The muscles that help to elevate the ribs during inspiration are the external intercostals, sternocleidomastoids, anterior serrati, and scalenes. The rectus abdominis consists of two superficial abdominal muscles that do not affect rib movement.

9. B: The transverse plane is a horizontal plane that divides the body into upper and lower regions. A backhand or forehand tennis swing occurs in the horizontal plane at approximately the midsection of the body. Punting a football and throwing a shot put are movements that occur in the sagittal plane, and dribbling a soccer ball takes place mostly in the frontal plane.

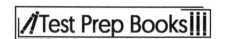

10. D: The supinator is responsible for rotation of the forearm, helping to pivot the radius on the ulna; the other three muscles are responsible for the rotation of the arm.

11. C: A third-class lever has resistive force (F_r) at one end of the lever and the fulcrum at the opposite end. Muscle force (F_M) is applied in the middle of the lever. During a biceps curl, the F_r is the barbell (in the hand), the F_M is the contraction of the biceps, and the elbow joint is the fulcrum in the middle. There are few physiological examples of first- and second-class levers, although the head on the neck is a first-class lever, and the metatarsophalangeal joint serves as the fulcrum of a second-class lever when one stands on their toes.

12. C: Elbow extension and wrist flexion are two upper body movements that take place in the sagittal plane, which cuts through the anterior and posterior of the body, dividing the body into right and left sides. Shoulder abduction and neck left tilt movements both occur in the frontal plane.

13. B: Ankle inversion helps expose the inside of the foot for an adequate kicking surface, which is required for soccer dribbling. Inversion takes place in the frontal plane, which runs through the center of the body from side to side, dividing the body into front and back halves.

14. A:

Name of Fascicular Arrangement	Structure of Fascicular Arrangement	Muscle Example
Circular	Fascicles are arranged in a concentric ring	Orbicularis oris (muscles surrounding mouth)
Convergent (sometimes called radiate)	Muscle has a broad origin and is fan- or triangular-shaped	Pectoralis major; gluteus medius
Parallel/longitudinal	Long axis of fascicles is parallel to long axis of muscle	Rectus abdominis
Unipennate	Short fascicles insert obliquely into only one side of tendon	Extensor digitorum longus; tibialis posterior
Bipennate	Fascicles insert into opposite sides of one central tendon	Rectus femoris
Multipennate	Tendon branches within the muscle	Deltoid
Fusiform	Spindle-shaped muscles	Biceps brachii

15. D: Isometric contractions occur when a muscle generates a force but is unable to shorten because the resistance force is greater than the generated force. In this situation, force is still generated, but the action does not cause movement or external work. Shortening occurs with concentric contractions, lengthening occurs with eccentric contractions, and no change in tension occurs with isotonic contractions, although length may change.

16. B: Power (measured in watts [W]) is the rate that work is performed and, accordingly, is calculated as work divided by time. Power can also be calculated as the force applied to an object multiplied by velocity. Choice *A*, force × distance, is the equation for work.

17. D: The phosphagen system is the primary energy system stressed when using a work-to-rest ratio of 1:12 to 1:20. Additionally, an exercise duration of 5–10 seconds that uses 90–100 percent of maximum effort is used to stress this system. Energy is rapidly generated with this system because there are very few steps in the process, but only a small amount of energy is released, which is why exercise duration fueled with this pathway is so brief.

18. B: Fats have a greatest capacity for ATP production compared to carbohydrates and protein.

19. B: The electron transport chain (ETC) uses two pyruvate molecules, six nicotinamide adenine dinucleotide (NADH) molecules, two flavin adenine dinucleotide ($FADH_2$) molecules, and hydrogen atoms to produce ATP. Hydrogen atoms form a proton concentration gradient down the ETC and provide the energy required to produce ATP. NADH and $FADH_2$ molecules rephosphorylate ADP to ATP via the ETC, with each NADH producing three ATP molecules and each $FADH_2$ producing two ATP molecules.

20. C: Oxidative phosphorylation is the process of ATP being resynthesized via the actions of the ETC. The ETC is not part of the phosphagen system.

21. B: The primary source of ATP during low-intensity activity and while the body is at rest is the oxidative system. This system utilizes carbohydrates and fats as substrates. The glycolytic and the phosphagen systems are both anaerobic systems that supply energy during high-intensity exercise.

22. C: One molecule of glucose results in the net production of thirty-eight ATP materials. Complete glycolysis with oxidation accounts for ten ATP molecules, and the Krebs cycle and ETC produce thirty ATP molecules for a total ATP production of forty molecules. Two molecules of ATP are invested in glycolysis, so the net production is thirty-eight ATP molecules.

23. D: Catabolism is the process of breaking large molecules into smaller molecules to release energy for work. Carbohydrates and fats are catabolized to provide energy for exercise and daily activities. Anabolism synthesizes larger molecules from smaller constituent building blocks. Bioenergetics and metabolism are more general terms involving overall energy production and usage.

24. C: When sufficient oxygen is available, pyruvate is transported to the mitochondrial matrix to take part in the Krebs cycle. Pyruvate is converted to acetyl-coenzyme A (acetyl-CoA) by pyruvate dehydrogenase, resulting in the loss of CO_2, and the acetyl-CoA enters the Krebs cycle to resynthesize ATP. Under anaerobic conditions, fermentation occurs, pyruvate is converted to lactate, and NADH is reduced to NAD+.

25. A: Cortisol is a glucocorticoid secreted by the adrenal cortex. The other structures listed also secrete hormones, but not cortisol.

26. D: Epinephrine is a catecholamine secreted by the adrenal medulla and is involved in the fight-or-flight response to stress. Testosterone, growth hormone, and insulin-like growth factor are the primary anabolic hormones. Anabolic hormones help the body with anabolic functions like synthesizing larger compounds from smaller constituent parts.

27. C: Cardiac output is not impacted by testosterone. Testosterone increases protein synthesis, muscle and bone growth, the rate of cellular metabolism, and the production of red blood cells.

28. A: Growth hormone concentration levels can be increased acutely by performing three high-intensity sets of each resistance exercise with short rest periods between sets.

29. A: Epinephrine and norepinephrine are catecholamines that increase the blood flow to muscles due to vasodilation. They also elevate blood pressure, increase the rate of muscle contraction, increase energy availability, enhance metabolic enzymatic activity, and increase the rate of testosterone secretion.

30. C: Acute increases in serum testosterone concentrations can be achieved by using heavy resistance loads of 85–95 percent of 1RM. Additionally, performing exercises that involve large muscle groups (such as squats, dead lift, and power clean), completing moderate to high exercise volumes by performing multiple exercises or multiple sets, and utilizing short rest intervals of 30–60 seconds can also result in higher serum testosterone concentrations.

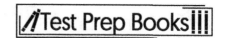

31. B: Overtraining syndrome is associated with blunted increases in pituitary hormones including growth hormone, so an increased level of growth hormone is not a symptom of overtraining syndrome.

32. C: The anterior pituitary gland secretes growth hormone and has a significant influence on the metabolic system and energy availability. Growth hormone has numerous other physiological functions including decreasing glucose utilization and glycogen synthesis, enhancing the function of immune cells, increasing availability of glucose and amino acids, increasing renal plasma flow and filtration, and increasing collagen synthesis and cartilage growth.

33. C: The characteristics of mechanical load that stimulate bone growth are the speed of loading, the intensity of the load, and the direction of the force. In accordance to Wolff's Law, bone adapts to the stresses (or lack thereof) placed upon it. The load type is not identified as a specific component of the mechanical load that is needed to stimulate bone growth.

34. B: As part of the neural response to high-intensity resistance training, the recruitment of motor units in an orderly manner is controlled by the size principle. The size principle is a method used by motor units to modulate force production, and it is dependent upon how many motor units are activated. If more force is needed for an activity, a greater number of motor units will be recruited. The smallest motor units are recruited first, and as more force is needed, larger motor units are sequentially activated. These strategies are designed to help the body be as efficient as possible.

35. B: Tendon stiffness increases in response to anaerobic training, and therefore, tendons become less flexible. While this may sound negative, stiffer tendons have a better mechanical advantage and are more efficient at transferring muscular work to the connected joints to produce powerful movements. High-intensity anaerobic training causes connective tissue growth and structural changes. Specific changes within a tendon include an increase in collagen fibril diameter, number, and packing density.

36. C: Choice *C* is the only answer containing the three correct functions while excluding option III (increased peripheral blood flow). Muscular contractions greater than 20 percent of maximum voluntary contraction slow peripheral blood flow during a set, but during rest, blood flow increases to levels above baseline. Acute anaerobic exercise increases cardiac output, heart rate, stroke volume, and systolic blood pressure.

37. C: Ventilation significantly increases during each resistance exercise set; however, ventilation is greatest during the first minute of recovery from the set. This is termed excess post-oxygen consumption (EPOC) and serves to help the body return to homeostasis after the work is performed. By increasing ventilation rate, more oxygen enters the body to help perfuse tissues and resynthesize hormones and metabolic intermediates such as creatine phosphate, buffer lactate, etc.

38. A: Anaerobic training increases tendon stiffness, which is directly associated with greater muscular recoil and power production because a stiffer tendon is better able to transfer forces from muscular contractions to the joints the muscles control, resulting in better efficiency and, thus, higher power. Flexibility is not improved. Decreased ability to withstand tensile forces and increased risk of injury do not necessarily occur due to increases in tendon stiffness; many other factors, such as biomechanics, proper load selection, fatigue, training status, and hydration, are involved.

39. D: To avoid developing low bone mineral density, athletes should participate in weight-bearing exercise, regular resistance exercise training sessions, and other dry-land exercises. The cyclist and swimmer both participate in non-weight-bearing sport activities. The swimmer runs during off-season and has a regular resistance training program; both activities can help to build and maintain bone mineral density. The distance cyclist has only one resistance training session per week. The cyclist is the athlete most likely to have the lowest level of bone mineral density.

40. C: Aerobic programs that stimulate bone growth must be high-intensity weight-bearing activities such as running and aerobics. Bone growth is not stimulated by non-weight-bearing activities, so although aerobic exercises such as swimming and cycling provide many health benefits, they do not promote bone growth.

41. A: Resting heart rate is an adaptation that athletes can easily assess by measuring their pulse upon waking in the morning. Aerobic training can improve the ability of the heart to pump blood at rest by increasing chamber size, cardiac muscle strength (particularly in the ventricles), and the afterload, which is the amount of blood returned to the chamber during diastole (relaxation or filling), resulting in a greater stroke volume of blood ejected per beat. These factors together account for the bradycardia of highly-trained endurance athletes.

42. A: VO_2 max or maximal oxygen consumption can be reduced by 4–14 percent over 4 weeks of reduced training stimulus or rest and 6–20 percent over a down period of more than 4 weeks.

43. A: Increased blood lactate concentrations is not an adaptation to aerobic endurance training. There are numerous cardiovascular responses that occur in response to an acute bout of aerobic exercise. These physiological changes include increases in the following: stroke volume and heart rate and resultant cardiac output, systolic blood pressure, oxygen uptake into tissues, blood flow to working muscles, and vasodilation of blood vessels.

44. C: The athlete can control various health behaviors that can impact adaptations to aerobic endurance training. While genetic potential can significantly impact training adaptions, maximal aerobic power decreases with age, and men typically have greater aerobic power than women, athletes cannot control these factors.

45. C: Decreased muscle glycogen, not increased muscle glycogen, has been identified as a sign of aerobic overtraining syndrome.

46. B: Training age refers to the length of time that the youth athlete has participated in a formal, supervised resistance training program. Both biological and chronological age should be considered in the development of the program; however, these factors do not provide information about potential adaptations to resistance training achieved from past training programs.

47. C: While strength and conditioning professionals should never treat youth athletes as miniature adults, they should provide easily understandable, quality instruction and progress athletes at a conservative but appropriate rate. Youth athletes are typically new to formal training programs and their sport, so they should receive thorough verbal and then visual demonstrations of appropriate resistance exercise techniques, utilizing kinesthetic learning and part practice as well. The program should start with low resistance and use sets of six to fifteen repetitions for a variety of single- and multi-joint exercises. This training should involve two to three training sessions occurring on nonconsecutive days each week and focus on proper form and technique, fun, and positive feedback.

48. B: Changes in muscle hypertrophy may be partially responsible for increased strength, but strength gains are primarily due to neurological factors resulting from nervous system development. Factors include increased motor unit recruitment, activation, synchronization, and firing.

49. C: When considering absolute strength, females have about two-thirds that of males, with lower body strength being closer to that of males as compared to upper body strength. When strength is considered relative to body weight, lower body strength is similar in the sexes; however, the relative upper body strength of females is still less than males. Importantly, when strength is expressed relative to the cross-sectional area of a muscle, no strength differences exist between males and females, indicating that muscle quality is not sex specific.

50. A: Although females are six times more likely than males to experience an ACL tear, this injury is not part of the female athlete triad. The triad stems from disordered eating, which leads to insufficient caloric intake for expenditure. This causes a cessation in menstruation (amenorrhea), and over time, this reduces bone mineral density due to the lack of estrogen needed for adequate calcification of bones.

51. B: A bone mineral density level between 1 and 2.5 standard deviations below the young adult comparator group indicates that the woman has osteopenia. Osteoporosis is defined as a bone mineral density of 2.5 or more standard deviations below the normal range for young adults. Sarcopenia refers to the loss of muscle mass, causing decreases in strength and power.

52. D: Any training program developed for an older adult should be multidimensional with aerobic and resistance exercise and balance training to maximize improvement of neuromuscular function. Developing a resistance training program for older adults is similar to developing a program for younger adults. Additionally, the strength and conditioning professional should take a detailed medical history, ask about previous aerobic and resistance training programs, and have the older adult complete a risk assessment questionnaire. In most circumstances, it may be appropriate for the older adult to have a medical examination from their primary physician and get a signed form stating the older adult can participate in the program.

Sport Psychology

1. D: Robert's behavior is driven by intrinsic motivation. He loves the game, gets personal satisfaction out of participating, and is continually working on new skills and improving. With achievement motivation, athletes are looking to master a specific task, outperform competitors or otherwise achieve excellence, and overcome obstacles. Extrinsic motivation typically comes in the form of individualized rewards such as praise from coaches and teammates, medals, social acceptance, avoidance of punishment, the drive for positive reinforcement, and other sources outside of the athlete. The construct of outcome motivation does not exist.

2. B: The ideal performance state is referred to as "the zone" in many sporting applications. It is characterized by a sense of personal strength and effortless performance and control, increased attentiveness and focus on the activity at hand, confidence and feelings of capability, and mental clarity. Arousal that is too high leads to anxiety and can impair performance.

3. A: Negative reinforcement involves the removal of a certain element that the athlete views negatively. An example of using this technique is if an athlete completes the workout with a great attitude and demonstrates leadership, then he or she wouldn't have to perform the resisted runs at the end. By removing the negative element (difficult resisted runs), the probability of the operant occurring again might increase.

4. C: Progressive muscular relaxation is used by athletes to control anxiety. It is particularly useful for controlling pre-competition levels of somatic and cognitive anxiety and regulating levels of physical and psychological arousal. This relaxation technique consists of tightening and relaxing muscle groups throughout the body in succession until the entire body is relaxed.

5. B: Selective attention is the ability to focus on relevant, task-oriented cues while ignoring other stimuli and thoughts unrelated to the athletic performance. The basketball player blocking out external distractions while focusing on the free throw shot is utilizing selective attention.

6. B: Self-efficacy (SE) is the athlete's perception of their ability to perform a situation-specific task successfully. There are numerous sources that influence SE, especially an athlete's past performance accomplishments and experiences. The swimmer's successful performance in preseason is an example of a past performance accomplishment. *Vicarious experience* refers to the athlete watching someone similar achieve a successful performance and then deciding that he or she, too, can have a successful performance. *Verbal persuasion* refers to encouragement from coaches, athletes, teammates, oneself, and other external sources. *Physiological states* refers to whether an athlete interprets their arousal as facilitative or detrimental.

7. A: This question requires understanding the characteristics of long jump and applying the concepts for motor skill practice. Given that the long jump has a low degree of interdependence of parts but is highly complex, it is best to use part practice. Sarah's coach can break down the event into several sections (e.g., the run, the take-off, body position after take-off). The whole practice method teaches the skill in its entirety and is better reserved for skills that are not very complex but are highly organized or for skills that have a high degree of interdependence, in that they can't be easily broken into steps because all parts or movements go together. Discovery and guided discovery are two types of instruction. Guided discovery gives less information to the athlete than explicit instruction but provides a generalized description of the overall movement. Discovery provides no instructions. Instead, it simply gives the overall goal of a movement.

8. D: John's goal is a process goal because it focuses on a specific action (maintenance of running technique in the final 400 meters of race) and is under his control. Successful achievement of the goal is dependent upon the amount of effort he puts in. An athlete has little control over an outcome goal, which typically is an event outcome, because he or she is unable to control the efforts and abilities of the competitors.

9. C: This option is correct since the other statements about eating disorders are not accurate. An eating disorder is a diagnosed mental illness with a specific set of eating patterns and behaviors as described in the *Diagnostic and Statistical Manual of Mental Disorders* (DSM) published by the American Psychiatric Association. Eating disorders are attributed to genetics, cannot be resolved in a matter of months, and are not attributed to stress.

10. B: In bulimia nervosa (BN), similar to anorexia nervosa (AN), individuals typically have a distorted body image. Individuals with AN have a distorted body image but do not engage in purging behaviors. Binge eating disorder is closely related to BN, but individuals do not engage in purging or other compensatory behaviors to eliminate consumed foods. An unspecified eating disorder is one that does not align specifically with the criteria for AN, BN, or binge eating disorder.

11. C: Visual learners ideally learn through observing, so Choice *C* would be best for these individuals. Kinesthetic learners learn best through movement, physical involvement, and experience. Strength and conditioning professionals working with kinesthetic learners should demonstrate an exercise and then have the client try a simplified version of the movement such as completing an unweighted repetition of the exercise or moving through a partial range of motion. Before trying the full resistance or movement, these intermediate steps can demonstrate understanding while reducing injury risk. Auditory learners grasp information best through listening.

12. D: An elevated heart rate and upset stomach are physical manifestations of anxiety, which are considered somatic anxiety. Trait anxiety, Choice *A,* is considered to be part of one's personality, predisposing an athlete to perceive many situations as being threatening when, in fact, no physical or psychological danger exists. State anxiety, Choice *B,* is a continually changing component of mood that is the subjective perception of tension and apprehension associated with increased arousal of the autonomic and endocrine systems. Cognitive anxiety, Choice *C,* is the thought process responsible for the perception of anxiety as negative.

13. A: An *operant* is a specific outcome that is targeted through stimulus conditioning, though it is not initially the result of a specific stimulus; instead, at first, it is a behavior that occurs spontaneously. It is through the different reinforcing or deterring techniques (or consequences from the operant) that the operant becomes the targeted outcome of a stimulus. Four different reinforcement techniques can be used to reinforce the operant and increase the probability of its occurrence. These techniques are positive reinforcement, negative reinforcement, positive punishment, and negative punishment.

14. C: The swimmer is engaging in progressive relaxation, which aims to increase an athlete's awareness of somatic tension, so that the athlete can try to relax the muscles and bring about both a relaxed body and mind. Choice *A* describes the goal of somatic desensitization for fear responses. Choice *B* is incorrect because progressive muscle relaxation does not aim to increase arousal; it should decrease arousal. Choice *D* is incorrect because it describes the goals of diaphragmatic breathing.

15. B: Autogenic training is a series of self-hypnotic exercises aimed at increasing the sensations of warmth and heaviness in various body parts. The athlete finds a comfortable position and then focuses on five stages of relaxation. These stages start with a focus on the heaviness of the extremities. The focus then moves to the warmth of the extremities. The third stage is a focus on regulation of cardiac activity and breathing. The fourth stage focuses on abdominal warmth. The last stage is the cooling of the forehead.

16. B: This scenario constitutes knowledge of performance, which is a type of augmented feedback. It deals with the performance of a movement task. In this case, it is the position of the hips before the jump. Knowledge of results, Choice *B*, deals with how successful the completion of the movement task was. In this case, it might involve giving details about how far the athletes jumped. Intrinsic feedback, Choice *D*, is provided by the athlete's body and sensory systems. Choice *C* is incorrect because "knowledge of augmented feedback" isn't a term used; rather, it is simply augmented feedback, which is feedback that originates from an external source. This scenario is a type of augmented feedback, with the external source being the video. Thus, Choice *C* would be correct if it only said augmented feedback, but the terminology used is incorrect.

17. D: This is an example of guided discovery because the coach provided the goal of the movement and some details about the movement itself but did not give complete, explicit instruction on how to perform the squat. The athlete will have to integrate the information provided with the movement pattern being practiced to understand how the goal is related to the movement performed. Discovery, Choice *A*, provides no instructions, but rather presents the overall goal of a movement. Therefore, the coach would not have given the instructions to push through the heels or keep the chest up. Explicit instruction, Choice *B*, gives all the details of the task in a prescriptive manner, which was not done in this case. Implicit instruction, Choice *C*, is fictitious, but would probably be most like guided discovery.

18. D: Choice *D* describes building tolerance to a drug. The other choices listed are indeed true about withdrawal from a substance.

19. A: While both types of cues have their place and some degree of merit, most research has found that external cues—not internal cues—are more effective at improving motor learning and movement performance. The other answer choices are true.

20. C: Choice *C* is correct because in sport psychology, motivation is determined by where and how intensely an athlete's effort manifests. Choices *A, B,* and *D* all contribute in some way to motivation, but are not themselves motivation.

21. A: Choice *A* is correct because a competitive nature is a product of achievement motivation, which is Choice *C*. Choices *B* and *D* are also recognized types of motivation.

22. C: Choice *C* is correct because MAF stands for motive to avoid failure, which is mostly fueled by ego preservation. High-MAF athletes will most often prefer easy situations that avoid potential shame. Choice *A* is the preference for high-MAS athletes, Choice *B* is just called an unfair game, and Choice *C* being correct disproves Choice *D*.

23. D: Choice *D* is correct because intrinsic motivation is defined as the athlete's internal desire to improve themselves and succeed in the given activity. Choices *A* and *B* are the two halves of intrinsic motivation, and Choice *C* is just a rewording of Choice *B*.

Nutrition

1. C: The DASH Eating Plan is based on clinical research trials, which helped individuals lower their blood pressure and low-density lipoprotein (LDL) cholesterol and improve heart health. The Healthy U.S. Eating Style, food exchanges, and glycemic index are not specifically designed to help individuals lower their blood pressure.

2. D: Carbohydrate needs for athletes vary depending on the intensity, duration, and frequency of exercise, but typically range from 6–10 grams of carbohydrates per kilogram of body weight. The amounts given in the other answer choices might supply nonathletic individuals with sufficient carbohydrate intake, but research indicates that athletes need 6–10 grams per kilogram of body weight.

3. C: Protein requirements vary depending on the type, duration, and frequency of exercise, but recommendations usually range from 1.5–2.0 grams per kilogram of body weight per day for athletes. Supplementing the diet with branched-chain amino acids can supply additional protein, but the focus should be on dietary sources through whole foods. Excessive protein is converted and stored as fat and does not contribute to increased lean body mass.

4. D: Vitamin and mineral supplementation does not improve athletic performance but can help to correct a deficiency if one is present. Athletes can usually meet their nutritional requirements with food, and therefore, supplementation is not typically necessary.

5. B: High cholesterol is a risk factor for heart disease, but research indicates that dietary cholesterol does not significantly impact blood cholesterol. Cholesterol is required by the body for various physiological and structural functions. However, these requirements are met by the cholesterol produced in the body; little to no additional cholesterol is needed from the diet. Foods high in saturated fat also typically contain cholesterol. A normal range for cholesterol is 200 milligrams per deciliter or lower, not 220 milligrams per deciliter.

6. D: Of the given choices, a female vegan athlete would be at the highest risk for iron-deficiency anemia. Iron recommendations are 1.3–1.7 times higher for athletes than nonathletes in general and another 1.8 times higher for vegetarian athletes in comparison to those who eat animal protein. While females and adolescents are at high risk for iron-deficiency anemia, a female vegan athlete would be at a higher risk.

7. B: Decreased physical performance can occur when dehydration levels cause a reduction in just 2 percent of body weight.

8. C: The food exchange system is designed to support meal planning but not necessarily the selection of nutrient-dense foods. The other options are all systems designed to be used in nutritional profiling or rating to support selecting nutrient-dense foods.

9. D: Macronutrient composition needs to be tailored to the individual based on body composition, training, and goals, but a caloric distribution of about 40–45 percent carbohydrates, 30–35 percent protein, and 25 percent fat should lead to body fat loss in the short term. The other options all provide a higher amount of carbohydrates than would be optimal for short-term weight loss.

10. C: Nutrient timing refers to effectively altering the content of the diet, particularly carbohydrate and protein, combined with the right timing to deliver optimal health and performance. Nutrient timing does not refer to altering the total content of the diet, the total content of the diet and timing, or the carbohydrate, fat, and timing of the diet.

11. A: Carbohydrate loading is typically recommended for activities lasting longer than 120 minutes by consuming a high-carbohydrate diet of about 8–10 grams of carbohydrates per kilogram of body weight. The ranges listed for carbohydrate loading in the other options are not supported by research.

12. B: This option has the correct combination of essential amino acids, while the other options include conditional and/or nonessential amino acids. Arginine and cysteine are conditional amino acids; alanine and glycine are nonessential amino acids; and glutamine and histidine are conditional amino acids.

13. C: Beta-hydroxy beta-methylbutyric acid (HMB) plays a role in the prevention of protein breakdown, or proteolysis. HMB does not play a role in cytolysis, hydrolysis, or hydrogenolysis.

14. B: Beta-alanine is the specific nonessential amino acid that must be present for the development of carnosine. Histidine is a component of carnosine; carnosine and leucine are not required for the development of carnosine.

15. C: Branched-chain amino acids and caffeine is the best answer choice, since the other options do not represent combinations of ergogenic aids that are used to delay fatigue. Sodium tablets help to prevent hyponatremia during exercise. Glutamine is used typically to help prevent illness and infection and reduce or prevent muscle soreness. Sports beverages are used for hydration and the prevention of hyponatremia and fatigue; however, caffeine is used as a stimulant to enhance endurance, increase alertness, and reduce muscle soreness.

16. D: Waxy maize is the correct choice, since the other options are not considered to be high molecular weight carbohydrates. Sodium bicarbonate is used in combination with caffeine to help reduce fatigue. Maltodextrin and dextrose are starches but not considered to be high molecular weight.

17. A: Amphetamines are correct because the other options are permitted in sports. Insulin, glucose tablets, and Hydroxycut are not substances that are classified as ergogenic aids and, thus, are not banned.

18. C: About 76% of college athletes and nearly all athletes engaged in strength building exercise use ergogenic aids. Ergogenic aids are used by about half of the general population, and research indicates their use has increased in the last 10 years. Ergogenic aids not only enhance athletic performance, but also include nutritional, pharmacological, physiological, or psychological substances.

19. D: A recommended regimen by the ISSN to increase muscle creatine is to start taking 0.3 grams per kilogram of body weight per day of creatine monohydrate for at least 3 days. Creatine is a naturally occurring substance that is found in the kidneys, liver, and pancreas, and the ISSN states that it can be safely and effectively used to enhance high-intensity exercise and lean body mass. Evidence does not support the use of creatine in endurance sports because it does not appear to have an effect on aerobic metabolism.

20. C: Choice *C* is correct because the idea of the five food groups being vegetables, fruits, grains, protein, and dairy was asserted and is maintained by the USDA. Choices *A, B,* and *D* are all real nutrition-related organizations in the United States, but they are not responsible for the categorization of the main food groups.

Exercise Technique

1. C: Because resistance machines are often used in the seated position and they only allow movement in one given plane, the core does not need to work to stabilize the body and they do not improve sports-specific skills as well as free weights do. Benefits of resistance machines include the fact that they can be used more easily without a spotter, they can help newer athletes learn proper form and maintain control of the motion within the desired plane of movement, and they can provide support that often allows athletes to lift higher maximal weights and isolate specific muscles, thus improving absolute strength.

2. B: When using starting blocks for sprinting, the athlete should place their hands just behind the starting line slightly wider than shoulder-width apart with the fingers held together. The thumbs should bridge out to the side and should be directly under the shoulders, ready to support bodyweight.

3. A: Box jumps, depth jumps, and medicine ball throws are examples of plyometrics. Agility exercises include things such as ladder drills and cones; non-traditional modalities might include kettlebells, heavy ropes, and tires; and speed training involves sprint training and foot drills.

4. A: During agility exercises, weight should be concentrated on the forefoot to allow for quick movements and changes in direction.

5. D: Incorporating yoga training into an athletic regimen can be beneficial for improving core strength, flexibility, and mental focus and relaxation. Because it involves bodyweight only, it improves relative strength but not absolute strength.

6. A: Exercises with free weights should use a minimum of one or two spotters when an athlete moves the bar over the head or face, has it on the front of the shoulders, or has it on the back during the execution. Resistance machines frequently do not need a spotter because they have safety features designed into them, but for certain maximal lifts, a spotter is recommended. Free weight training can improve core stability and can provide a more sports-specific strength training method. Each exercise can be performed in a variety of ways, rather than strictly dictated in one specific way.

7. C: The most challenging part of a strength exercise is called the sticking point. In a bench press, this is where the direction of the bar changes from coming down toward the chest to being pushed back up.

8. B: For most strength exercises, the athlete should exhale through the mouth during the concentric phase through the sticking point and then inhale through the nose during the eccentric phase. Breathing should be slow and controlled.

9. D: Mirrors and video analysis can be used to provide visual feedback regarding form and technique to guide corrections. They do not correct form or technique in and of themselves, but are useful tools to help identify such issues and begin the process of correcting improper technique. For safety and to reduce liability, strength coaches should always focus on monitoring athletes.

10. D: Increased submaximal heart rate is not a chronic adaptation to cardiovascular exercise. In fact, heart rate decreases at a given submaximal workload due to improvements in cardiorespiratory economy. Heart chamber size increases, as does preload (the amount of blood that fills a chamber before it contracts to eject it), resulting in a higher stroke volume per heartbeat. This means that more blood, oxygen, and nutrients get moved per pump of the heart. Blood volume and hemoglobin content of the blood also increase.

11. C: Depth of squats is often limited by Achilles tendon tightness. For athletes who are limited in squat depth due to tight Achilles tendons, elevating the heels on a weight plate or other incline will help achieve a deeper squat, despite limited range of motion in the ankles.

12. D: Exercises in the seated and supine positions require five points of contact for optimal body support: the head is firmly situated on the bench or back pad, the shoulders and upper back are evenly placed firmly on the bench or back pad, the buttocks are positioned evenly on the bench or seat, and both feet are placed flat on the floor.

13. A: In a supinated grip, palms face upward toward the face and knuckles face the floor. In a pronated grip, knuckles are up and palms face the floor.

14. A: Soccer requires a great deal of agility, so these athletes benefit from agility work on most days in each training cycle. Because agility technique takes a high degree of focus and cognition, it is best to complete it in high-frequency, short-duration sessions in a training program. This is usually accomplished by short agility drill sessions most days of the week.

15. B: Hockey players need to have significant explosive power, strength, and speed, so they benefit greatly from plyometrics, which develop explosive power. Three days per week is about the maximum frequency that is recommended for plyometrics, given their intensity and the demand they place on the anatomic structures of the body and physiologic systems. Beyond this, there is increased risk of injury, even in experienced athletes. Most athletes can benefit from some plyometric training, but such a frequency is not needed for the endurance athletes listed.

16. A: The grip pattern where palms face the floor and the knuckles face the ceiling is called a pronated grip.

17. B: Golgi tendon organs are stimulated in PNF stretching and cause relaxation of the stretched muscle by its own contraction.

18. D: Activation of muscle spindles is decreased in PNF stretching, which capitalizes autogenic inhibition to send inhibitory signals from the Golgi tendon organs to the brain. These inhibitory signals override the excitatory impulses from the muscle spindles, which causes the muscle to gradually relax. Normally, stimulation of muscle spindles induces a contraction of the stretched muscle.

19. B: In order of decreasing percentage of total training volume, for a distance runner's program, cardiovascular/metabolic conditioning should be prioritized because this forms the foundation of the runner's fitness, followed by muscular endurance, which is also needed for endurance running. Plyometrics will help build some power, strength, and speed, and may help strengthen the anatomy to prevent injuries. Agility is least necessary as a focus for endurance runners, since they are mostly trying not to change speed or direction, and especially because the question is asking about percentage of volume and not frequency.

20. C: This question is tricky because it is asking about the frequency of various components of training, so the focus is not only on the specifics of tennis, but also on general guidelines for frequency of types of training in a program. Tennis requires strong cardiovascular fitness, so this should form the foundation of the training program. Since some amount of aerobic conditioning should occur on essentially all training days in a program, cardiovascular conditioning activities should be performed the most, both in volume and frequency. Speed and agility are incredibly important for successful tennis playing as well; it is here that planning safe programming in terms of frequency comes into play.

Speed training likely should take on a larger percentage of training volume (a greater number of total minutes dedicated to speed training during the week compared to agility), but speed training should be limited to just a few days per week to allow the body to fully recover from the demands and damage it causes. Agility is best completed in short, frequent bouts due to its high cognitive demand. Therefore, agility should occur more frequently than speed training. Plyometrics develop explosive power, which is important for tennis players, but should be limited to two days per week to prevent injury from overtraining and overstressing the anatomy.

21. B: There are three forms of PNF stretching: hold-relax, contract-relax, and hold-relax with agonist contraction, which all begin with 10 seconds of passive pre-stretch held at the point of mild discomfort. In the hold-relax form, after the pre-stretch, the partner applies a flexion force while the athlete holds and tries to resist the force, creating an isometric contraction for 6 seconds, then the athlete relaxes back into a passive stretch lasting 30 seconds, which is now a deeper stretch than the initial pre-stretch due to autogenic inhibition. The hold-relax with the agonist contraction uses the idea of reciprocal inhibition whereby the contraction of the agonist muscle causes relaxation of the antagonist. Therefore, after the regular hold-relax protocol, the second passive stretch is replaced with an active stretch to further increase stretch.

22. A: The hold-relax PNF protocol begins with a 10-second passive pre-stretch held at the point of mild discomfort. Then the partner applies a flexion force while the athlete holds and tries to resist the force, creating an isometric contraction for 6 seconds. After this, the athlete relaxes back into a passive stretch lasting 30 seconds. This is now a deeper stretch than the initial pre-stretch due to autogenic inhibition.

23. B: Static stretches should follow the workout, especially for excessively stiff athletes or those with past injuries. It can improve the muscle tension and joint relationship over time. Static stretches performed prior to exercise can reduce explosive power and increase joint laxity when stiffness is required for energy conservation, placing an athlete at greater risk of injury.

24. B: While care and caution should be employed for all athletes doing plyometrics, the football player poses the greatest risk of injury due to his weight. Because of the demand on the body, proper technique is imperative to avoid injury. Heavier athletes (over 220 pounds) should also be monitored for any joint tenderness because the forces on their joints coupled with the weight of the body can place excessive stress on the tissues. Special care must be considered for previously injured athletes, senior athletes, prepubescents, and those with balance issues. Proper footwear and soft, rubberized flooring or grass should be used to reduce landing forces.

25. D: Muscle spindles detect rapid movement and initiate the stretch reflex. Golgi tendon organs are mechanoreceptors that control the flexibility and extensibility of the muscles and joints when they are stretched or during reactive forces or muscular contractions. Extrafusal fibers are the main skeletal muscle fibers in a muscle.

26. A: Static stretches should be held for about 30 seconds and performed for two to three sets for maximal efficacy. They should follow a workout for athletes with chronic tightness, and not precede it.

27. A: Tire flipping, kettlebells, sandbags, and battle ropes are implements best reserved for highly trained athletes. Such implements are creative ways to add variety to workouts while accomplishing similar physiologic goals. Coaches must still be aware of when and how to properly use this equipment and be sure to educate and supervise athletes in their use. Much of the non-traditional equipment is best reserved for advanced athletes who have the basic foundations of movement, such as a well-mastered squat and deadlift, because programs with non-traditional equipment tend to use heavier implements in power movements, which can induce injury if not carried out safely.

28. B: Dynamic stretching should be done prior to workouts and static stretching should follow the workout. Dynamic stretching occurs before the activity as part of the warm-up routine to increase heart rate, temperature, and blood flow as well as CNS and PNS activity to prepare the body. Static stretches should follow the workout, especially for excessively stiff athletes or those with past injuries. Static stretching can improve the muscle tension and joint relationship over time. Static stretches performed prior to exercise can reduce explosive power and increase joint laxity, placing an athlete at greater risk of injury.

29. C: Speed is influenced by stride rate and stride length, so athletes should focus on quick turnover and powerful steps. Of these factors, stride rate has a greater impact on speed and should be the focus when designing a program for improving sprinting speed. Leg length cannot be readily modified, especially after growth has ceased.

30. D: Medial tibial stress syndrome, or shin splints, is an overuse injury made worse by pounding or impact, so treadmill running should be avoided. Non-weight-bearing cardiovascular equipment such as an arm ergometer or bike is ideal. The elliptical can be a workable option as long as it does not cause pain. It is weight-bearing, but non-impact.

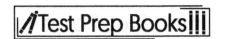

31. D: Spotters are not used in power exercises such as the power jerk. With the exception of power exercises, free weight exercises should use a minimum of one or two spotters when an athlete moves the bar over the head or face, has the bar on the front of the shoulders, or has the bar on the back during the execution. During power exercises, athletes should be instructed to push the bar away or drop it when the bar is in front and to release it or jump forward when the bar is missed behind the head; a spotter should not be used.

32. A: The Valsalva maneuver can be used in certain core exercises, with care, as a way to increase torso rigidity to aid in support of the vertebral column, which lessens compressive forces on the intervertebral discs and supports the normal and neutral lordotic lumbar spine. Blood pressure can increase with the Valsalva maneuver, but this is not a benefit, and in fact, can cause undesirable dizziness and disorientation.

33. C: During a heavy front-loaded squat, there should be two spotters—one positioned on either end of the bar—to help balance the bar and to remain in constant communication with each other and the lifter.

34. B: The required number of spotters is determined by the load being lifted, the experience and skill of the athlete and spotters, and the physical strength of the spotters. The spotters must be strong enough to handle the load that the athlete is lifting with little notice and sometimes in less than ideal angles and positions, so it is crucial that spotters are honest with themselves and the lifter about their abilities. It is safer to err on the side of caution and use multiple spotters when necessary, as long as they can be accommodated spatially around the lift without being overly cumbersome.

35. C: When spotting over-the-face barbell exercises, the spotter should use the alternated grip pattern, usually narrower than the athlete's grip. In this position, one hand is supinated and one is pronated.

36. A: Spotters should use a solid, wide base of support and a neutral spine position. Spotters should use an athletic stance, with feet slightly wider than hip-width apart, knees flexed, arms and hands up and in the ready position and as close to the bar and athlete without touching them as possible. Bodyweight should be equally and soundly distributed on both feet, which should be firmly planted on the ground. Knees should not be locked but should maintain a degree of flexion, ready to support the weight and go into a squat if necessary, to accept the weight of the bar. Locking the knees can be dangerous, since it places excessive stress on the knee ligaments and cartilage as well as the lower leg muscles and bones and the low back.

37. C: Negative resistance training is best described as lifting heavier weights on the lowering, eccentric portion and getting assistance from spotters during the lifting, concentric phase. It is a specific resistance training protocol based on the concept that most athletes can handle heavier loads on the eccentric portions of exercises, but are not able to lift the load concentrically, so they need assistance. However, if they are only to use the load they can handle concentrically, they are never fully challenging the stronger eccentrically working muscles, so negative resistance training addresses this discrepancy. It is an advanced lifting technique.

38. B: Bodyweight training, such as pull-ups, push-ups, chin-ups, squat thrusts, lunges, yoga, jumping jacks, and planks, provides resistance in the form of bodyweight, so it improves relative strength and core strength, is low-cost, and improves body control. Because external weights are not used, it does not improve absolute strength.

39. C: Intensive weight training is a type of workout that would occur after the movement preparation techniques. Movement preparation techniques most often involve flexibility and mobility work, such as that provided by Choices *A, B*, and *D*.

40. B: PNF refers to Proprioceptive Neuromuscular Facilitation, which is a technique that uses neuromuscular responses to isometric and concentric contractions. Choices *A, C*, and *D* are made-up answers.

41. A: Dynamic stretching involves actively moving the joints through the ranges of motion that an athlete will use in their particular sport. This is in opposition to stretching techniques that focus on individual muscles, Choice *B*. Dynamic stretching does not involve ballistic movements, Choice *C*, and is less effective than PNF with regards to increasing static ROM, Choice *D*.

42. B: The athlete should be in the supine, or upward-facing, position when using PNF to stretch the hamstring muscles. Choice *A*, prone, is a downward-facing position. The lateral recumbent positions in Choices *C* and *D* involve lying on one's side, which would not be an appropriate position for stretching the hamstrings.

43. D: The strength coach should be positioned at the end range of the desired movement, with their hips and shoulders facing in the direction of movement. Choice *C* is the correct placement but facing the incorrect direction. Choices *A* and *B* are made-up answers.

44. B: There are three forms of PNF: hold-relax, contract-relax, and hold-relax with agonist contraction. Choices *A, C,* and *D* are made-up answers.

45. D: The ten-second passive pre-stretch should be held at the point of mild discomfort. Holding a pre-stretch at the point of moderate discomfort or maximum flexibility, Choices *C* and *B* respectively, could cause injury to the athlete, as they are not property warmed up during the pre-stretch. Choice *A* is not actually a stretch at all.

Program Design

1. C: The needs analysis will help to determine the types of movements and physical requirements of an athlete's sport, how much time he or she has to train for the sport, and whether the athlete is a beginner or advanced athlete. Appropriate exercises for developing the specific skills that the athlete needs (i.e., dynamic correspondence) can be selected based on this information. The appropriate progression can be planned based on how much time he or she can dedicate to training.

2. B: Dynamic correspondence involves choosing an appropriate exercise for an athlete based on their sport. For this question, it is important to note that the number of repetitions for plyometric exercises is related to the skill level of the athlete. Beginner athletes should perform 80 to 100 repetitions, while intermediate and master athletes should perform 100 to 120 repetitions and 120 to 140 repetitions, respectively. Lower-body plyometric exercises are beneficial for athletes who need to sprint, jump, and make other forceful lower-body movements. Upper-body plyometrics are important for sports that require throwing, catching, tackling, and blocking.

3. A: Mobility training improves flexibility for athletes who have limited range of motion. Tactical metabolic training uses the athlete's sport to create metabolic conditioning drills that mimic the sport's speed and endurance requirements. Pace/tempo training involves training the athlete at the lactate threshold to improve their aerobic- and anaerobic-energy systems for the competition. Repetition training requires the athlete to perform several high-intensity sprints for thirty to ninety seconds back-to-back with long rest periods in between.

4. A: The two-for-two rule provides a method for gradually increasing an athlete's strength-training load. Using this method, the athlete should add two repetitions to the last set for two training sessions in a row. Then, the training load can be increased during the following session. In this question, the athlete should add two repetitions to the third set. Therefore, he or she will do eight repetitions instead of six. The athlete should continue this pattern for two training sessions in a row before increasing the load.

5. D: Core exercises can improve an athlete's strength across their whole body in addition to specific muscle groups. However, sleep deprivation, lack of nutrition, and overtraining can all reduce an athlete's ability to increase training load. Rest is an important part of strength training and can help an athlete prevent overtraining. Proper nutrition is essential for fueling the workout and providing the building blocks for developing more muscle mass.

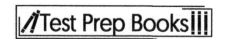

6. B: The heart rate reserve increases and the resting heart rate decreases. Heart rate reserve is defined as the difference between the maximal heart rate and the resting heart rate. Even though heart rate initially increases during exercise, resting heart rate decreases as a person adapts to aerobic activity. As resting heart rate decreases, the heart rate reserve will increase because the difference between maximal and resting heart rate will increase.

7. C: Longer resting periods improve cardiovascular conditioning. When an athlete needs to improve cardiovascular conditioning, he or she may decrease resting time to bolster aerobic endurance.

8. D: Periodization involves planning and organizing an athlete's entire training program (strength training, range of motion, conditioning, sports drills, etc.) and planning the training loads and volumes to generate physiological changes in a certain amount of time. The training macrocycle represents the developmental goals for the athlete over the entire training program. The mesocycle breaks the macrocycle into two- to six-week segments to reach specific training goals. The preparatory phase is the athlete's offseason or preseason period.

9. A: Open kinetic chain exercises allow the loaded limbs to move freely while closed kinetic chain exercises limit this movement. Pull-ups and lunges are closed kinetic chain exercises because the athlete cannot freely move their hands or feet when they are planted on the ground. Hamstring curls and leg extensions allow the limbs to swing freely, so these are open kinetic chain exercises.

10. C: When modifying exercises to accommodate injuries, exercises that involve the injured area should not be assigned. A tennis player doing squats can build lower-body strength while allowing the elbow to heal.

11. C: Overburdening a tissue results in a macrotrauma while overtraining a muscle leads to a microtrauma. The definitions in answer Choices *A* and *B* have been switched. In answer Choice *D*, a definition for tendin*osis* is given as acute inflammation, which is tendin*itis*. Tendinosis is chronic inflammation of the tendon.

12. B: The tissue-healing process begins with inflammation or swelling and is followed by tissue repair. During tissue repair, damaged tissues are removed while blood vessels and collagen fibers are formed. In the final remodeling phase, new tissues become stronger and more functional.

13. A: Training for muscular hypertrophy requires six to twelve repetitions. Completing more than twelve repetitions improves muscle endurance, while doing fewer than six repetitions improves strength as long as the resistance lifted poses the appropriate challenge at the given repetition level. Using three different exercises per muscle group can significantly increase muscle growth.

14. B: Muscle balance is crucial for any strength-training program because a lack of balance causes the body to have abnormal movement patterns and increases the risk of injury. Creating muscle balance means to improve strength ratios between opposing muscle groups. An example of muscle balance is a 3:4 strength ratio between hamstrings and quadriceps.

15. D: Multi-joint exercises stimulate muscles the most and allow for the greatest amount of loading during resistance training. Primary exercises are core exercises that are sport-specific and involve large muscle groups and multiple joints. Structural exercises are core exercises that load the spine. Assistance exercises engage small muscle groups and single joints.

16. C: Circuit training improves mental focus and requires an athlete to do a variety of exercises (from most intense to least intense) with little rest in between sets. This training program improves cardiorespiratory function and has a high metabolic cost, which leads to increased body-fat loss.

17. D: Running up hills, dragging sleds, and wearing weighted vests will help the athlete to improve speed by increasing the resistance during aerobic training.

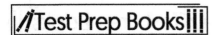

18. A: Exercises should be ordered from most to least technical, with power movements first, core exercises second, and single-joint exercises last. Olympic lifts are power movements and require extensive technique, whereas biceps curls require little technique and involve a single joint.

19. A: Serial drills are sport-specific and combine continuous and discrete drills. Continuous drills have no beginning or end, and they are helpful for improving running and jumping. Discrete drills help to develop movement patterns and improve an athlete's strength and power.

20. B: Lengthening the sprinter's push-off and stride will reduce vertical bouncing. Answer Choices *A*, *C*, and *D* are corrections for improper arm swinging, premature upright posture, and neck hyperextension, respectively.

21. C: Performing an exercise for at least twelve repetitions will improve muscular endurance, whereas six to twelve repetitions will enhance muscular hypertrophy and fewer than six repetitions will improve muscular strength.

22. B: An athlete in the off-season must build up cardiorespiratory strength gradually with low-intensity and long-duration training before progressing to a shorter and more intense program in the preseason and preparing for the competition.

23. D: Only small improvements can be made to an athlete's reaction time, because reaction time depends on the nervous system and information-processing rates cannot be trained. Reaction time is not related to improvements in explosive activities.

24. C: This athlete's symptoms and history are consistent with GAS. GAS occurs when the body is subjected to external loading. Firstly, the athlete will experience soreness, stiffness, and decreased performance (alarm phase). Secondly, his body will return to normal (resistance phase). Thirdly, his body will adapt and his muscle mass and strength will increase (supercompensation phase).

25. A: Training intensity must be decreased to improve speed. Increasing training volume and changing the duration of rest periods between sets will also promote physical adaptations in the athlete.

26. B: The unloading/deloading week uses lower training volumes and decreases intensity so that the athlete can recover and be prepared for future training sessions. This training week allows the athlete to continue improving neural patterns and promotes supercompensation.

27. D: Doing exercises on an unstable or uneven surface (e.g., doing bodyweight squats or push-ups on a BOSU) helps to improve neuromuscular control by stimulating and challenging the nervous system in new ways, which necessitates adaptation.

28. A: The complex-training model combines heavy resistance training with intense plyometrics to challenge the nervous and musculoskeletal systems. Only answer Choice *A* combines a heavy resistance exercise (80% to 90%) with intense plyometrics.

29. D: The greater the intensity of training, the more recovery time the athlete needs before the next training session. Therefore, athletes training at high intensity should have fewer training sessions per week than athletes training at low intensities.

30. C: Interval training involves working at higher levels of intensity compared with one's VO_2 max. Interval lengths and rest periods are very different. Aerobic athletes use a 1:1 work/rest ratio during interval training.

31. A: Fartlek training is an aerobic endurance-training method that combines lower-intensity exercise with brief sprints or other intervals and is most appropriate for runners, swimmers, and cyclists.

32. D: The series elastic components are the hub of activity for eccentric muscle contractions and involves the muscles and tendons. When muscles and tendons stretch, the series elastic components store elastic energy until there is a concentric contraction. The other answer choices are phases of the stretch-shortening cycle.

33. B: The amortization phase is the transition between the eccentric and concentric phases. A muscle shortens in the concentric phase and lengthens in the eccentric phase. When an athlete begins a biceps curl, this is the concentric phase. When he/she lowers the weight, this is the eccentric phase.

34. A: Muscle spindles are essential to the stretch-reflex response because they are the primary proprioceptive structures in the muscle. Muscle spindles respond to eccentric muscle action.

35. C: The recovery phase is key because the sprinter's body is aligned in a way that will enhance speed.

36. D: The Karvonen method allows for the calculation of target heart rate by using resting heart rate.

37. C: Work can be calculated by multiplying the weight by the number of repetitions. For this athlete, the calculation is $work = 50\ lb. x\ 5\ repetitions$.

38. D: Fibrosis is an age-related disorder that causes scar tissue to form near joints. As a result, fibrosis affects muscle health and quality and can restrict joint movement. Restricted joint movement can affect movement patterns and increase the risk of injury.

39. B: Both tests establish loading parameters; however, the repetition maximum test will determine how well an athlete can perform multiple repetitions of an exercise at a certain load while the 1-RM test only determines how well he or she can complete one repetition. In order to apply the 1-RM test to an athlete's training load at different intensities, the number of repetitions that should be done at a certain load must be calculated. Both tests are important because an injured athlete may perform one repetition easily but struggle to perform the number of repetitions calculated using the 1-RM.

40. B: A needs analysis includes an injury analysis of the sport and/or position, which informs the training program to reduce the likelihood of such injuries. Choice *A* is incorrect because the movement analysis is conducted by examining the movement patterns of the sport or position, not the athlete. Choice *C* is incorrect because each training and competition season should have only one goal. Choice *D* is incorrect because the strength and conditioning tests conducted during physical testing and evaluation are selected by professionals to reflect the physical demands of the specific sport or position.

41. C: As part of the needs analysis, you should consider the athlete's history with training, their knowledge and experience with training exercises, and the intensity of their current and previous training. Choice *A* is incorrect because the results of the physical evaluation should be compared with that specific athlete's previous data or statistical norms. Choice *B* is incorrect because the physiological analysis focuses on the primary sport; appropriate cross-training exercises would be part of the program developed through the needs analysis. Choice *D* is incorrect because the injury analysis focuses on injuries common to the sport, not the athlete's previous injuries.

42. A: Resistance, bodyweight, and Strongman training improve strength. Choice *B* is incorrect because complex training, the combination of heavy resistance training and plyometrics, improves power; hypertrophy, or increase in muscle size, results from resistance training. Choice *C* is incorrect because Strongman training improves strength, while resistance training and aerobic endurance training improve aerobic endurance. Therefore, Choice *D* is also incorrect.

43. B: Lifting free weights coordinates multiple muscle groups; this more closely mimics movements in sports than do machines, which tend to isolate single muscle groups. Choice *A* is incorrect because weight stack machines require less skill and muscle coordination, which makes them safer. Choice *C* is incorrect because free weights, often used in the standing position, place more stress on the body's muscles and bones. Choice *D* is incorrect because gravity is the source of resistance for both free weights and weight-stack machines.

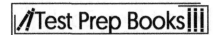

Organization and Administration

1. A: When a certified strength and conditioning coach fails to perform what is typically considered to be a standard practice of care, it may be deemed to be negligence.

2. A: Overtraining is a condition that occurs when an individual trains with too much frequency and/or intensity, causing fatigue, greater injury risk, sleep issues, changes in appetite or body weight, lack of motivation, depression or moodiness, and performance decline. Signs of overtraining also include elevated resting heart rate, soreness that does not resolve within a day or two after exercise (as is normal with resistance training), and increased susceptibility to illness.

3. D: To resolve heat-related illness, athletes should drink plenty of fluids, remove excess layers of clothing, and move to the shade. Once symptoms have set in, it is too late to continue the workout inside. Exercise will need to stop. To prevent heat-illness in the first place, the workout can take place inside.

4. D: A groin strain is typically an acute injury. Overuse injuries such as stress fractures, shin splints, and tendinitis can occur when the workload is too high and insufficient rest and recovery leads to tissue damage.

5. B: All strength and conditioning coaches must be certified strength and conditioning coaches and have CPR/AED certification. First aid certification is recommended, although not required. The mission and values for a facility may be created by the strength coach, with or without others in the business, but are often created by the owner or manager of the business, prior to hiring a strength coach.

6. C: While medicine balls should be checked weekly or so for cracks, which can cause sand to leak out, unless they are old or get substantial use, they likely are not something that needs to be checked prior to every use. Even if they do have sand leaks, they should not injure an athlete when they are starting to fall apart. Exercise bands routinely become thin, which can cause them to snap, and cables become frayed. Emergency stop buttons on cardio equipment should also be checked prior to usage.

7. A: The outlet position, equipment footprint, ceiling height, and mirror placement must all be taken into consideration in order to provide athletes and coaches with a safe environment conducive to training of all formats.

8. A: Health Insurance Portability and Accountability Act (HIPAA) defines individually identifiable health information such as demographics, prior and current health history, social security number, etc. FERPA is the Family Educational Rights and Privacy Act, and it relates mainly to protected information about education, particularly in school settings.

9. D: While modeling a healthy lifestyle is important, it does not reduce liability risk for certified strength and conditioning professionals. Strength and conditioning professionals should be mindful to adhere to NSCA Professional Code of Ethics, rehearse emergency action plans, maintain CPR certification, and abide by the NSCA Scope of Practice for certified strength and conditioning specialists.

10. D: Teaching the athlete exercises to do at home helps develop self-efficacy and augments the athlete's training. Customized nutrition plans should be from registered dieticians or nutritionists; licensed massage therapists should provide therapeutic massage; and diagnosing meniscal tears is the role of a physician.

11. C: NSCA's Professional Code of Ethics details the need to always act with integrity, honesty, and ethical behavior and to report any and all unethical behavior. It is designed to help maintain a high degree of professionalism in the strength and conditioning profession. NCAA does not offer their own branded professional liability insurance.

12. C: The feasibility study should involve a SWOT analysis, which identifies the strengths, weaknesses, opportunities, and threats to ensure the business will be financially viable and profitable. Choices *A* and *D* are part of the master plan, and Choice *B* describes a needs assessment.

13. D: The correct order of the four phases of new facility design is predesign, design, construction, and finally, pre-operation. Predesign is when most of the planning takes place. The design phase is when those plans are finalized with architects and other experts, followed by construction, when the site is built according to those plans. The final phase, pre-operation, is also referred to as the start-up phase, when the focus is mainly on staffing and anything else that needs to be considered before opening the facility.

14. C: Construction is often the longest of the four phases of designing a new facility, concerned chiefly with ensuring that deadlines are met, and the project stays within budget. Predesign is the initial phase when needs are assessed, and a master plan is developed. Once a plan is in place, the design phase can be completed by finalizing blueprints that enhance the flow of the facility and meet city building code regulations. The final phase, pre-operation, is when interior designing, staffing, and daily planning needs occur, usually encompassing approximately 15% of the total project time.

15. B: A SWOT analysis is conducted to reveal strengths, weaknesses, opportunities, and threats, also commonly referred to as a feasibility analysis. These are the essence of the initial phase, predesign, when a general layout of what should be done and what to avoid is developed

Testing, Ongoing Monitoring, and Data Evaluation

1. B: A marathon runner requires a great deal of cardiovascular endurance. Even though this runner's score was relatively low for 1RM bench press (40th percentile vs. 70th), it is still more important to increase the runner's cardiovascular endurance, given the demands of the sport, compared to upper body strength. The 70th percentile leaves a large margin for improvement. Even though VO_2 max does have a large genetic component, it is likely that this runner can significantly improve marathon times by targeted endurance training. The need for upper body strength is much less important in distance running, although muscular endurance is important.

2. B: The Wingate test is conducted on a cycle ergometer, and so it is least applicable to a volleyball player because that sport does not involve biking. Vertical jump, Margaria-Kalamen stair sprint, and medicine ball throws would all be good assessments for this athlete.

3. D: A tennis player relies heavily on upper body endurance (which is measured by the push-up test), so this should be prioritized. Lower body strength is important, but significantly less so, and as this athlete's percentile scores are fairly close and both are within acceptable range, upper body endurance should be more of the focus in training.

4. A: There are many factors that the strength and conditioning coach must consider when selecting the most appropriate assessments for an athlete. There are a wide variety of assessments available for coaches to choose from, and the most appropriate choice should be made by taking into account the athlete's strengths and weaknesses as well as the athlete's sport, position, and training level. Coaches may need to make compromises on some of these variables if the entire team needs to be tested at one time, if tests are only conducted in the field so limited equipment is available, and if there is a tight testing schedule, all of which would not allow for certain test protocols.

5. B: All testing equipment should be assessed for proper function and calibrated prior to use in testing to avoid errors in scores based on equipment malfunction or influence. For example, prior to using a metabolic cart to measure expired gases, the cart should be calibrated by entering the environmental data (humidity, barometric pressure, temperature) as well as volume of expired air with the 3L calibration syringe. Testing equipment is used in a laboratory, not field-based tests, and it is harder to test multiple athletes at one time because of the need to use the equipment (for instance, a handful of athletes should not be on one treadmill all at once).

6. D: The rater's skill level typically affects the reliability or consistency of a test score. Validity refers to a test measuring what it is intended to measure, such as a strength test actually measuring force production. Reliability of a test refers to its ability to produce consistent measures. Selecting the appropriate test for an athlete affects the validity of a test; some tests are valid only for certain populations. Other tests are valid only for certain measures (for instance, a 1RM bench press measures upper body strength but should not be used as a measure of upper body endurance). The test order matters in that fatiguing tests should not be conducted prior to less fatiguing tests, or they can confound the results.

7. D: Prior to a 1RM bench press, an athlete should perform a thorough warm-up of the metabolic and physiologic systems that will be used in the test. In this instance, athletes should warm up with light cardiovascular exercise to increase blood flow, heart rate, and muscle perfusion, then complete a few sets with increasing weight below max, to prepare the muscles for the test. The one minute of push-ups is a muscular endurance test and uses the same muscles as the 1RM bench press, which can lead to fatigue before the test. The 300-yard shuttle runs are also fatiguing and have been shown to reduce strength performance, so push-ups for endurance and the 300-yard shuttle should be avoided prior to a 1RM bench press.

8. D: The pre-design phase includes a needs assessment, determining what space, equipment, and layout are needed; a feasibility study or SWOT analysis, identifying the strengths, weaknesses, opportunities, and threats to ensure the business will be financially viable and profitable; and a master plan, including the building and construction plan and design and the budget and operational plans. Finalizing the blueprint takes place in the design stage.

9. C: Emergency procedures should be reviewed and rehearsed at least quarterly.

10. A: Personal injury liability insurance protects against libel, slander, and invasion of privacy. Professional liability insurance protects against injuries caused by services or negligence. Commercial liability insurance covers individuals and the business against incidents and accidents that occur at the facility and must be purchased by trainers who own their own studios.

11. C: To control the spread of germs in the facility, athletes should be taught and instructed to wipe down all used equipment with antibacterial agents after use. The other options are practices that athletes should be taught as well, but do not help prevent the spread of germs.

12. A: The order of phases for designing a new fitness facility are: pre-design, design, construction, pre-operation.

13. A: VO_2 max is a norm-referenced score. Norm-referenced standards compare the athlete's performance against that of other similar athletes and scores are presented in percentiles. The 50th percentile indicates the athlete performed better than half of the comparative population and worse than half. It is important that the coach reports not just the percentile score, but educates an athlete on their score's relative value. Criterion-referenced standards are derived from research- and normative-based achievement levels of health and fitness that, if reached, predict lower disease risk for the athlete. These may be lower standards than those likely achieved by athletic populations.

14. B: Cross country skiing requires a high degree of cardiovascular endurance, so the 30th percentile is an atypical score for an elite athlete. There was likely an error in the protocol, equipment, or scoring. The test should not be conducted again after just a 5- to 10-minute break because the athlete will not have recovered from using maximal effort; a re-test should occur on another day.

15. B: The 8 Foot Up and Go test is an agility test for senior citizens, while the others are for healthy, athletic populations.

16. B: To choose the most appropriate tests, strength coaches should perform a needs analysis of the sport and position to determine what aspects of fitness are most important (speed, power, strength, agility, etc.) and should be tested. Body composition assessments are part of the battery of test options, so it would not make sense to perform them prior to testing, as they are part of testing. Feasibility studies and SWOT analysis are part of business planning.

17. C: While coaches are able to provide information and advice pertaining to fitness and training, the scope of practice is limited to these areas and nutrition planning cannot be provided legally by a strength and conditioning professional. Referring the athlete to a registered dietician or nutritionist would be the proper course of action for nutrition planning.

18. A: Field tests typically require minimal equipment and occur outside "in the field," such as the Rockport walk test, 1-mile run, or step test, while laboratory tests such as the Wingate test of anaerobic power require equipment. When testing teams or multiple athletes, field tests may be more appropriate because they do not usually require much equipment. In addition, the tests can be conducted more efficiently by having many athletes complete them simultaneously.

19. C: Since agility is less important for shot-putters, the box drill test's results would be the least important for a shot-putter. Shot-putters do need good upper body muscular strength and endurance as well as some amount of leg power to give momentum to throws, so the 1RM bench press, push-up test, and vertical jump test are appropriate.

20. D: Guidelines suggest this order:

1. Skinfold
2. 1RM bench press
3. Push-up test
4. Step test
5. Sit-and-reach

The reason there are guidelines for the order of assessments is to ensure that one assessment does not affect another. Measurements of physical attributes should be first since they don't cause fatigue. Agility tests come next, though there were none listed in this practice question's answer choices. Muscular strength tests should follow to optimize peak strength before prematurely fatiguing muscles through drawn out muscular endurance tests like the push-up test. In this case, the muscular test is the 1RM bench press. While there should be a rest period following this assessment, note that since it's just "One Rep Max", it won't be too tiring nor will it be aerobic. Next comes sprint tests (none here), and then local muscular endurance tests. Push-ups are a principal example of this. After muscular endurance tests, anaerobic tests and then aerobic capacity tests should be conducted. Step tests are one of the latter. Finally, once the muscles have been given sufficient warm-up to prevent injury, flexibility tests should be performed.

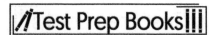

21. A: Soccer midfielders need cardiovascular endurance, agility, and lower body power and speed, so the Cooper 12-minute run test, box drill, and vertical jump test are good choices. Upper body strength is less important in this position, so a 1RM bench press is less important.

22. C: Agility is less important for baseball pitchers, so the quadrant jump test is not the best choice. Pitchers do need good upper body muscular strength and endurance, as well as some amount of leg power to give momentum to pitches, so the 1RM bench press, push-up test, and vertical jump test are more appropriate.

CSCS Practice Test #2

Exercise Sciences

1. What is the term used for stress that is applied to the body until performance begins to decline before a period of rest?
    a. Functional overreaching
    b. Non-functional overreaching
    c. Overtraining
    d. Detraining

2. Implementation of specific tasks during athletic movements or specific exercises is known as which of the following?
    a. Discovery
    b. Explicit instruction
    c. Specific instruction
    d. Guided discovery

3. Which of the following muscle actions is occurring in the pectoralis major as the weight is lowered to the chest in a barbell bench press exercise?
    a. Isometric muscle action
    b. Isokinetic muscle action
    c. Eccentric muscle action
    d. Concentric muscle action

4. Which of the following is NOT a component of an electrocardiogram?
    a. P-wave
    b. T-wave
    c. QRS complex
    d. U-wave

5. Which of the following is NOT a mechanism for expansion and retraction of the lungs?
    a. Upward movement of the diaphragm
    b. Downward movement of the diaphragm
    c. Elevation of the ribs
    d. Relaxation of the abdominal muscles

6. Which of the following encompasses the components of the axial skeleton?
    a. Bones of the hips, knees, and ankles
    b. Bones of the pelvic girdle, shoulder girdle, arms, and legs
    c. Bones of the ribs, sternum, vertebral column, and skull
    d. Bones of the hands, feet, wrists, and ankles

7. During training, children and adolescents often see an increase in performance primarily due to which of the following adaptations?
    a. Neural adaptations
    b. Muscular strength adaptations
    c. Reactive adaptations
    d. Aerobic adaptations

8. Which of the following allows relaxation from a muscle contraction?
   a. Lack of sodium available for contraction
   b. Lack of contractile fibers and relaxation of the neuron
   c. Lack of available calcium and cessation of signal from the motor neuron
   d. External resistance overload and Golgi tendon organ activation

9. What is the primary location of hemoglobin?
   a. Lymphocytes
   b. White blood cells
   c. Adrenal glands
   d. Red blood cells

10. Which of the following accurately describes bone periosteum?
   a. Spongy tissue located within the bone matrix
   b. Cells within the bone that bring nutrients to the bone tissue
   c. Specialized bone tissue that connects the bones to tendons
   d. Central location of bone where growth occurs during development

11. Which of the following accurately describes detraining?
   a. Loss of physical attributes attained from training after a period of inactivity
   b. Performance increases from training at reduced intensities from the initial ones
   c. Adaptation from periods of rest that allow the body to attain performance improvements
   d. Performance increases from normal development rather than from physical training

12. Why will cardiac output increase as the intensity and workload increase within a given submaximal bout of exercise in a trained athlete compared to an untrained athlete?
   a. Heart rate is slower than it would have been previously
   b. The heart is beating faster than it used to at the same workload
   c. Vital organs require more oxygenated blood
   d. Stroke volume increases

13. The joints between the vertebrae of the human body are of which type?
   a. Fibrous joints
   b. Synovial joints
   c. Cartilaginous joints
   d. Ball and socket joints

14. Which of the following is NOT a recommended guideline when training children and adolescents?
   a. 1RM testing
   b. One to three sets of six to fifteen repetitions for exercises
   c. Performing an appropriate warm-up
   d. Direct supervision from a qualified strength and conditioning professional

15. As actin and myosin filaments interact, what occurs to the Z-lines?
   a. Z-lines start to separate
   b. Z-lines begin to move towards each other
   c. Z-lines disappear
   d. Z-lines are unchanged

16. What is the term used for the motor neuron and the muscle fibers it innervates?
    a. Neuromuscular junction
    b. Axon terminal
    c. Motor unit
    d. Myofibril excitation

17. Which of the following is the term used for when the ability of a receptor site to respond to a specific hormone decreases?
    a. Non-responsiveness
    b. Decreased receptor function
    c. Autoregulation
    d. Downregulation

18. Injuries that occur with advanced-aged athletes are due to which of the following?
    a. Loss in neuromotor function
    b. Balance issues
    c. Sarcopenia
    d. Vestibular changes

19. Muscle mass loss that often occurs with older athletes is known as which of the following?
    a. Sarcopenia
    b. Aging muscle loss
    c. Geriatric muscle loss
    d. Atrophy

20. Which of the following is an adaptation of the cardiopulmonary system in response to training?
    a. Decreased oxygen uptake
    b. Vasoconstriction
    c. Decreased maximal heart rate
    d. Increased maximal oxygen uptake

21. Which connective tissue surrounds the individual muscle fibers of the human body?
    a. Epimysium
    b. Fascicles
    c. Endomysium
    d. Perimysium

22. What muscle fiber type is associated with marathon running?
    a. Type IIx
    b. Type IIa
    c. Type I
    d. Type III

23. What is the term used when a hormone can partially interact with a receptor site?
    a. Hormone partial interaction
    b. Hormone blocking interaction
    c. Partial-reactivity
    d. Cross-reactivity

24. Which of the following is a disadvantage of using high intensity interval training?
    a. Excessively high heart rates are often experienced
    b. Inappropriate metabolic adaptations can occur
    c. Non-specific movement patterns are reinforced
    d. Stress can rise to counterproductive levels

25. Which of the following is a way that force can be controlled during a muscular contraction?
    a. Activation of actin and myosin
    b. Activation of the motor end plate
    c. Activation of motor units
    d. Activation of an action potential

26. The exchange of inspired air and internal gases is the primary role of which of the following systems?
    a. Lymphatic system
    b. Vascular system
    c. Neuroendocrine system
    d. Respiratory system

27. Within which plane is the body moving during forward lunges?
    a. Transverse plane
    b. Frontal plane
    c. Sagittal Plane
    d. Lateral Plane

28. What is the length that residual effects remain in maximal strength after periods of inactivity?
    a. 5 ± 5 days
    b. 30 ± 5 days
    c. 15 ± 5 days
    d. 18 ± 4 days

29. During the contraction phase of a dumbbell bent-over row, the latissimus dorsi acts as which of the following?
    a. Synergist
    b. Neutralizer
    c. Agonist
    d. Antagonist

30. Where does the electrical impulse for the heart's conduction originate?
    a. AV bundle
    b. Aortic valve
    c. Purkinje fibers
    d. SA node

31. Which of the following is NOT a strategy used for optimizing hormone levels with training?
    a. Use of multi-joint movements
    b. Use of compound movements
    c. Implementing exercises that use large muscle groups
    d. Focusing on stabilizing muscles

32. Which of the following energy systems is the primary source of ATP generation for the 100-meter dash?
    a. Oxidative
    b. Anaerobic glycolytic (fast glycolysis)
    c. Phosphagen
    d. Aerobic glycolytic (slow glycolysis)

33. Which of the following is a specific guideline for older-adult resistance training?
    a. Static stretching should occur before and after training sessions.
    b. Dynamic stretching should occur before and after training sessions.
    c. Static stretching should occur before exercise and dynamic stretching should follow after the workout.
    d. Dynamic stretching should occur before exercise and static stretching should follow after the workout.

34. Which of the following is a common fault when training children and adolescents?
    a. Prescribing individualized programming
    b. Believing the anatomy and physiology are the same as in adults
    c. Prescribing aerobic workloads that are programmed around the specific sport
    d. Spending too much time on instruction and not enough on training

35. Which of the following is NOT a component of bone?
    a. Calcium carbonate
    b. Calcium phosphate
    c. Sodium bicarbonate
    d. Protein

36. What is the ideal work to rest ratio when trying to train the glycolytic energy system?
    a. 1:12–1:20
    b. 1:15–1:30
    c. 1:1–1:3
    d. 1:3–1:5

37. Which of the following is NOT a primary function of the cardiovascular system?
    a. Exchange of oxygen
    b. Transportation of nutrients
    c. Removal of waste products
    d. Breakdown of nutrients for energy

38. After puberty, which of the following is a common characteristic observed in both males and females?
    a. Equal muscle quality
    b. Equal muscle mass
    c. Equal body fat
    d. Equal flexibility

39. What are the upper limits of "normal" for systolic and diastolic blood pressure?
    a. 120/40 mmHg
    b. 120/80 mmHg
    c. 150/80 mmHg
    d. 150/40 mmHg

40. Which of the following is NOT an adaptation of tendons to exercise training?
 a. Increased fibril diameter
 b. Increased number of cross-links
 c. Increased flexibility
 d. Increased number of connective fibers

41. What is the term used when the body remains in a higher state of oxygen consumption after the cessation of exercise?
 a. Post-exercise oxygen syndrome
 b. Post-exercise increased cardiac output
 c. Excess post-exercise oxygen consumption
 d. Excess post-exercise aerobic capacity

42. Which of the following is NOT considered an anabolic hormone?
 a. Insulin
 b. Growth hormone
 c. Insulin-like growth factor
 d. Cortisol

43. What is a common hormonal response in males undergoing puberty?
 a. Increase in circulating testosterone
 b. Increase in cortisol at rest
 c. Increase in circulating estrogen
 d. Decrease in growth hormone

44. Which type of muscle is used for maintaining posture?
 a. Smooth muscle
 b. Skeletal muscle
 c. Cardiac muscle
 d. Dorsal muscle

45. If an athlete has an abundance of type I muscle fibers, what type of sport would he or she be best suited for?
 a. Powerlifting
 b. Boxing
 c. Marathon running
 d. Golf

46. Which activity would make the most use of the triceps muscles?
 a. Sprinting
 b. Squats
 c. Pull-ups
 d. Throwing

47. Which muscle is responsible for rotating the forearm?
 a. Pronator teres
 b. Brachialis
 c. Flexor carpi ulnaris
 d. Anconeus

48. If an athlete has a torn biceps femoris, which movement would be difficult or painful to do?
    a. Bending the arm
    b. Rotating the foot
    c. Extending the arm
    d. Bending the knee

49. A football player suffers an injury that is inferior to the right femur. What could his injury be?
    a. Fractured right tibia
    b. Fractured left femur
    c. Torn triceps
    d. Fractured coccyx

50. Which of the following terms means "on or affecting the same side of the body?"
    a. Lateral
    b. Ipsilateral
    c. Bilateral
    d. Contralateral

51. An athlete has an injury that is inferior to the clavicle. It is superior to the ilium and anterior to the spine. In addition, the injury is lateral to the sternum and medial to the right humerus. Where might the injury be located?
    a. The right ulna
    b. The right ankle
    c. The right rib cage
    d. The right scapula

52. If an athlete suffers a muscular injury and has difficulty shrugging her shoulders as a result, which muscle is likely in need of rehabilitation?
    a. Erector spinae
    b. Trapezius
    c. Pectoralis major
    d. Biceps brachii

Sport Psychology

1. The operation of processing environmental, external, and internal cues that come to one's awareness is known as which of the following?
    a. Conscious thinking
    b. Attention
    c. Subconscious thinking
    d. Mindful engrossment

2. Which of the following is defined as the use of recreating successful athletic events or endeavors within the athlete's mind?
    a. Mental arousal
    b. Mental imagery
    c. Mental stimulation
    d. Mental practice

3. A gymnast getting ready to perform her last routine in the all-around competition is worried about the routine and is experiencing an increased heart rate, sweating, and "butterflies." The physical symptoms experienced by the gymnast are associated with which type of anxiety?
   a. Environmental anxiety
   b. Physical anxiety
   c. Cognitive anxiety
   d. Somatic anxiety

4. Adaptation that occurs from stress placed on the body is the definition of which of the following?
   a. Specific adaptation syndrome
   b. Acute adaptation syndrome
   c. Exercise resistance syndrome
   d. General adaptation syndrome

5. Which of the following is NOT considered a form of feedback during instruction?
   a. Augmented feedback
   b. Segmented feedback
   c. Knowledge of results
   d. Knowledge of performance

6. Which of the following is defined as administering tasks, objects, or events that would likely decrease the occurrence of a negative operant?
   a. Negative punishment
   b. Positive punishment
   c. Negative reinforcement
   d. Positive reinforcement

7. Which of the following is usually best suited for whole practice instruction?
   a. Skills of high complexity but low organization
   b. Skills of low complexity but high organization
   c. Skills of low complexity and organization
   d. Skills of high complexity and organization

8. Which of the following accurately describes instructional guided discovery?
   a. Only instructing the athlete on the goal of the task
   b. Giving specific instructions but limiting information to allow athletes to process the movement
   c. Showing an athlete a video of the movement then requiring them to perform the exercise
   d. Instructing the athlete on each specific aspect of the movement and providing feedback along the way

9. Which of the following is a sign of overtraining?
   a. Increases in illness frequency
   b. Increases in muscular flexibility
   c. Decreases in delayed onset muscle soreness
   d. Decreases in resting heart rate

10. Social acceptance, trophies, awards, and induction into a hall of fame are all examples of which of the following?
   a. Extrinsic motivation
   b. Self-motivation
   c. Intrinsic motivation
   d. Positive self-talk

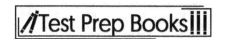

11. For exercises that use multiple joints and muscles, such as the Olympic clean and jerk, which of the following instruction modalities have been shown to be the most successful?
    a. Whole practice instruction
    b. Part practice instruction
    c. Sub-part instruction
    d. Comprehensive instruction

12. Generally speaking, what's the most significant source of an athlete's self-efficacy?
    a. The athlete's past performances
    b. The coach's feedback or support
    c. Vicarious experiences
    d. Physiological arousal and emotional/mood states

13. Which of the following accurately describes the inverted-U theory?
    a. As the arousal levels rise, performance levels will increase proportionally
    b. Arousal levels increase performance up to an optimal level, but further increases are associated with reduced performance
    c. Arousal levels have no effect on performance and therefore should not be focused on throughout training sessions
    d. As arousal levels decrease, performance increases as the athlete becomes more comfortable and less anxious

14. Which of the following relates to the intensity and focus of one's effort?
    a. Motivation
    b. Motive to achieve success
    c. Motive to avoid failure
    d. Reinforcement

15. Which of the following is NOT associated with optimal arousal levels for athletes?
    a. Increased mental activation
    b. Increased performance anxiety
    c. Increased positive thoughts
    d. Increased control in decision-making tasks

16. A common motive observed in athletes to protect their ego, self-worth, and self-esteem is known as which of the following?
    a. Motive to avoid failure
    b. Motive to achieve success
    c. Motive to protect oneself
    d. Motive to avoid judgement

17. Which of the following is a challenge when attempting to identify an athlete with bulimia nervosa?
    a. They are consistently hydrating.
    b. Their weight loss could be from an increase in energy expenditure and not an eating disorder.
    c. The athlete is often at a healthy weight.
    d. The athlete never consumes food in front of the strength and conditioning professional.

18. Which of the following is NOT a symptom of disordered eating?
   a. Dehydration
   b. High body fat
   c. Hypertrophy
   d. Muscle wasting

19. Which of the following is a symptom of anorexia nervosa?
   a. Smooth, radiant skin
   b. Elevated body temperature
   c. Bradycardia
   d. Hypertension

20. What are imagery techniques?
   a. Practices to help an athlete react to obstacles of varying sizes and speeds
   b. The internal visualizations of athletic moments before they occur
   c. Plans made for playstyles on a board, marking athletes with "X's" and "O's"
   d. Practices that hone an athlete's kinesthetic sense

21. A coach rewards their athletes for winning a game by cancelling the mile run that was scheduled for the next day. What reinforcement strategy are they applying?
   a. Negative reinforcement
   b. Positive reinforcement
   c. Positive punishment
   d. Negative punishment

22. Which of the following is an example of positive punishment?
   a. Supplementing your diet with a food you do not like
   b. Running an extra mile after practice
   c. Adding another two repetitions to every exercise for a training session after you lose
   d. An additional training session after you win to prepare for the next challenge

23. What is the most significant source of an athlete's self-efficacy?
   a. Their current physical state
   b. Their past performances
   c. Their relationships with other team members
   d. Verbal persuasion

Nutrition

1. In which of the following ways is the cardiovascular system affected by anabolic steroid abuse?
   a. Increased myocardial function
   b. Increased risk in development of liver tumors
   c. Decreased testicular size
   d. Elevated blood pressure

2. Which of the following is the daily protein recommendation for athletes competing in a strength sport?
   a. 1.4 to 1.7 grams of protein per kilogram of body weight
   b. 1.4 to 1.7 grams of protein per pound of body weight
   c. 1.7 to 2.0 grams of protein per kilogram of body weight
   d. 1.7 to 2.0 grams of protein per pound of body weight

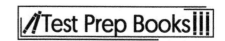

3. How many grams of protein should a male American football player consume after a competition?
    a. 10 to 15 grams of protein
    b. 20 to 25 grams of protein
    c. 30 to 35 grams of protein
    d. At least 40 grams of protein

4. Which of the following is a nitrogenous compound that helps supply energy to the cells?
    a. Branched-chain amino acids
    b. Leucine
    c. Creatine
    d. Nitric oxide

5. What caloric deficit is recommended for the goal of fat loss?
    a. Approximately 250 calories a day
    b. Approximately 500 calories a day
    c. Approximately 750 calories a day
    d. Approximately 1000 calories a day

6. The glycemic index tracks and monitors which of the following physiological responses?
    a. Blood glucose levels 2 hours after consumption
    b. Blood glucose levels 1 hour after consumption
    c. Muscle glycogen stores immediately post-exercise
    d. Muscle glycogen stores immediately after consumption

7. Which of the following is a nutritional recommendation for improving muscular endurance?
    a. Low-carbohydrate intake throughout the day
    b. Low-fat intake throughout the day
    c. Protein consumption post-exercise
    d. Protein consumption pre-exercise

8. Which of the following stimulates red blood cell production?
    a. Calcium
    b. Leucine
    c. Sodium chloride
    d. Erythropoietin

9. Who issued the MyPlate food guidance tool that is commonly used for nutrition information for both athletes and the general population?
    a. United States Department of Agriculture
    b. United States Food and Drug Administration
    c. National Strength and Conditioning Association
    d. National Food and Nutrition Service

10. An athlete with a goal of muscle hypertrophy should consume which of the following?
    a. 30 to 100 grams of lower-glycemic carbohydrates post-activity
    b. 30 to 100 grams of higher-glycemic carbohydrates post-activity
    c. 10 to 15 grams of low-leucine protein every 2–3 hours throughout the day
    d. 10 to 15 grams of high-leucine protein every 2–3 hours throughout the day

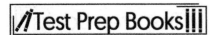

11. Which of the following is NOT considered a psychological effect of anabolic steroid abuse?
   a. Increased aggression
   b. Increased arousal
   c. Increased irritability
   d. Increased relaxation

12. How many grams of carbohydrates should be consumed in a pre-competition meal that is consumed at least 4 hours prior to the athletic event?
   a. 1–2 grams per kilogram of body weight
   b. 1–4 grams per kilogram of body weight
   c. 4–6 grams per kilogram of body weight
   d. 8–10 grams per kilogram of body weight

13. Which of the following is NOT a main category of MyPlate recommendations?
   a. Legumes
   b. Fruits
   c. Vegetables
   d. Protein

14. In terms of carbohydrate-loading techniques, which of the following protocols is more popular?
   a. Daily loading period
   b. Pre-event loading period
   c. Week-long loading period
   d. Three-day loading period

15. Which of the following is NOT considered a nutrient-dense food?
   a. Fruits
   b. Banana bread
   c. Vegetables
   d. Lean meat

16. Which of the following are the main electrolytes lost in sweat?
   a. Sodium, chloride, potassium, magnesium, calcium
   b. Sodium, chloride, potassium, calcium
   c. Sodium, chloride, potassium, iodine, calcium
   d. Sodium, chloride, potassium, magnesium, iodine

17. Which of the following is considered the limit of creatine storage in the human body?
   a. 40–60 millimoles per kilogram
   b. 60–80 millimoles per kilogram
   c. 100–120 millimoles per kilogram
   d. 150–180 millimoles per kilogram

18. Which of the following is NOT a symptom of low iron levels in athletes?
   a. Increased concentration
   b. Increased fatigue
   c. Weakness
   d. Decreased work capacity

19. Which of the following is NOT a real meal-planning health application?
   a. Food exchange lists
   b. The USDA EatRight Health Aide
   c. The DASH
   d. The glycemic index

20. How many USDA food patterns are in the 2015–2020 Dietary Guidelines?
   a. 5
   b. 2
   c. 6
   d. 3

Exercise Technique

1. During multiple hops or jumps in plyometric training, what should the athlete focus on during the time spent in contact with the ground?
   a. Increasing ground contact time to ensure full force is applied on every jump
   b. Allowing the body to naturally absorb the pressure of the body upon landing
   c. Keeping the legs extended to increase the braking technique
   d. Reducing ground contact time to ensure a fast rate of force development

2. Which of the following is NOT a correct body position when using a stair stepper machine?
   a. Knees aligned over the toes
   b. Toes pointed forward
   c. Head looking upward
   d. Spine in a neutral position

3. Which of the following is a technique used to increase resistance during the portion of the exercise where typically there is less resistance?
   a. Accommodating resistance
   b. Force-velocity technique
   c. Manual resistance
   d. Intensity increase technique

4. During speed and sprint training, which of the following techniques can be used to improve the athlete's movement patterns?
   a. Having the athlete perform each movement as quickly as possible to improve technique at high speeds
   b. Slowing down the movement of the drill to attain proper mechanics before increasing intensity
   c. Providing verbal training cues while the athlete moves through the full intensity speed drill
   d. Performing technique work while using upper and lower limbs consecutively

5. During the front squat, where should the spotters be located?
   a. In front of the athlete
   b. Laterally, to each side of the barbell
   c. Behind the athlete with their hands placed on the barbell
   d. Spotter are not needed for the front squat

6. What is the muscle action of the hip during the midflight phase of a sprint?
    a. Concentric flexion
    b. Eccentric flexion
    c. Concentric extension
    d. Eccentric extension

7. Where are the hands located while utilizing a narrow grip width on an Olympic barbell?
    a. Near the center of the barbell, where there is no knurling
    b. On the knurling, outside the first power rings
    c. Near the center of the barbell while still in full contact with the knurling
    d. A thumbs-distance away from the smooth part of the barbell

8. When utilizing resistance machines for training, which of the following will NOT increase the effectiveness of the exercise?
    a. Making sure the athlete's body stays in contact with the pads
    b. Making the tempo of the movement as explosive and powerful as possible
    c. Achieving full range of motion on every repetition
    d. Making sure the athlete utilizes the Valsalva maneuver while executing the exercise

9. What is the purpose of the slight countermovement that occurs when doing plyometric exercises?
    a. To use more momentum when executing the exercise
    b. To apply more force by actively engaging the stretch-shortening cycle
    c. To engage the entire musculature of the body
    d. To increase pressure placed on the joints

10. When fatigued, which of the following is a common fault observed during conditioning exercises?
    a. Shoulders rounding forward
    b. Spine hyperextending
    c. Relaxed breathing patterns
    d. Head leaning back

11. During agility drills, which of the following describes the position of the hips upon deceleration?
    a. The hips stay extended and the center of gravity is high
    b. The hips rotate in the direction of the movement
    c. The hips stay static and do not move
    d. The hips will flex as the center of gravity becomes lower

12. During free-weight resistance training, which of the following positions should be maintained to ensure a safe and effective exercise?
    a. Back flat, chest rounded, and head looking upward
    b. Back in hyperextension, chest up, and head looking downward
    c. Back flat, chest up, and head in a neutral position
    d. Back flat, chest up, and head looking upward

13. The five-point position for the bench press includes which of the following?
    a. Left foot on floor, right foot on floor, glutes on bench, upper back on bench, back of head on bench
    b. Left hand on barbell, right hand on barbell, head on bench, upper back on bench, glutes on bench
    c. Left foot on bench, right foot on bench, left hand on barbell, right hand on barbell, back on bench
    d. Left foot on floor, right foot on floor, glutes on bench, upper back on bench, back of head tucked and off the bench

14. For lower-body plyometric exercises, which of the following ensures the athlete's body is in proper alignment?
    a. The chest is rounded, knees are located over the ankles, and the athlete's weight is shifted to the heels
    b. The head is anterior to the knees, the hips are located back, and the athlete's weight is shifted towards the toes
    c. The spine is hyperextended, knees pointed slightly towards each other, head is looking straight ahead
    d. The shoulders, knees, and mid-feet are in line with each other when looking at the athlete from the side

15. On a treadmill, what must occur before the machine will turn on?
    a. The safety switch must be inserted, and the attachment must be placed on the athlete's body
    b. The machine must be wiped clean
    c. The treadmill must be set at a slight incline
    d. The athlete needs to start with a warmup

16. Which of the following accurately describes agility?
    a. Acceleration through changes in direction
    b. The ability to accelerate, decelerate, and rapidly change direction
    c. The ability to decelerate and hold the body stable in a static position
    d. The ability to maintain balance in unstable environments

17. While training at 85 percent intensity for a set of 5 repetitions, the athlete's focus and arousal should be at which of the following levels?
    a. Focus high, arousal low
    b. Focus high, arousal high
    c. Focus low, arousal low
    d. Focus low, arousal high

18. When should the strength and conditioning professional make corrections to faulty movement mechanics that occur during the training process?
    a. The next training session when the athlete is fully rested
    b. After the set of repetitions is performed
    c. Promptly, even if it interrupts the training set or repetitions
    d. It is not needed, as the athlete will feel the faulty movement and correct it themselves.

19. When would the use of a weightlifting belt be warranted?
    a. While the athlete is performing warmup sets
    b. During exercises that place a low load on the spine
    c. While attempting percentages that require maximal effort
    d. While using upper-body resistance machines

20. When flipping a tire, where should the chest be placed to increase the athlete's stability?
    a. Away from the tire, using the Valsalva maneuver
    b. Against the tire, using the Valsalva maneuver
    c. Rounded away from the tire
    d. The chest is not a main concern when flipping a tire

21. Where should the knees be placed upon landing during lower-body plyometric exercises?
    a. In a staggered stance to actively dissipate the load of the body
    b. Together, to increase joint stability at the ankle
    c. Outward, to maintain a constant angle relative to each other
    d. Fully extended, to prevent the body from absorbing too much pressure

22. When administering exercises that require the athlete to run, jog, or walk, where should the pressure on the foot be located in order to maintain the natural curvature at the arch of the foot?
   a. Towards the heel
   b. Towards the ball of the foot
   c. Towards the medial portion of the foot
   d. Towards the outside of the foot

23. Which of the following does NOT require the use of a spotter?
   a. Bench press
   b. Back squat
   c. Lying barbell triceps extension
   d. Power clean

24. Which of the following is NOT a technique used for proprioceptive neuromuscular facilitation?
   a. Hold-relax technique
   b. Relax-release technique
   c. Contract-relax technique
   d. Hold-relax technique with agonist contraction

25. Where should the athlete's hands be located when using a lower-body resistance machine?
   a. Clasped together on the back of the head
   b. Grasped firmly on the handles of the machine
   c. Crossed across the athlete's chest
   d. On the lower body to feel the lower-body muscles contracting

26. Which of the following accurately describes the pronated grip used for the barbell Romanian deadlift?
   a. While looking down, one hand will be facing palm up while the other is palm down
   b. While looking down, both hands will be facing down, with knuckles up, in an overhand grip
   c. While looking down, both hands will be facing upright, with knuckles down, in an underhand grip
   d. While looking down, the palms will be facing one another, and the knuckles will be outward

27. When high force is placed on the athlete during upper-body plyometric exercises, what is a common mistake made by the athlete during the execution of the exercise?
   a. The head lifts off the ground when pushing forward
   b. The feet move away from the body as the power is generated for the exercise
   c. The elbows flare out and more pressure is added to the shoulder girdle
   d. The hips move forward as the athlete attempts to produce maximal power for the movement

28. When performing cardiovascular exercise on a rowing machine, how does the athlete or strength and conditioning professional increase or decrease the resistance of the machine?
   a. Adjust resistance on the seat of the machine
   b. Adjust the air vents to allow or restrict air flow
   c. Adjust resistance on the rowing handle of the machine
   d. Adjust the console of the machine

29. Which of the following occurs during a general warmup?
   a. Core temperature increases
   b. Muscles tighten
   c. Central nervous system fatigues
   d. Range of motion decreases

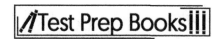

30. What is the term used for the portion of the movement where the force of the external resistance will peak due to joint angles?
    a. Peak point
    b. Maximal force zone
    c. Full-intensity position
    d. Sticking point

31. Which of the following accurately describes the amortization phase during plyometric training?
    a. The eccentric, lowering action of the body before the concentric muscle action
    b. The concentric, upward movement of the body
    c. The counteraction of the body to increase the stretch reflex
    d. The phase between eccentric and concentric muscle action of the body

32. When adjusting a stationary bicycle to the needs of the athlete, what position should the knee be in at the full downward stroke of the pedal?
    a. The knee should be terminally extended
    b. The knee should be in flexion around 90 degrees
    c. The knee should be flexed 5–10 degrees
    d. The knee should be slightly extended

33. What can be done to ensure proper breathing patterns are maintained during anaerobic conditioning?
    a. Intensities can be increased
    b. Rest periods can be decreased
    c. Water can be given to the athlete
    d. Rest periods can be increased

34. All EXCEPT which of the following are benefits of static stretching?
    a. Increased range of motion
    b. Enhanced recovery
    c. General body warmup
    d. Useful as a corrective exercise

35. If the athlete is continuously showing signs of the knees caving in during hip, knee, and ankle free-weight exercises, which of the following would NOT be a good verbal command for the technical flaw that needs correcting?
    a. "Keep outside pressure on the way up."
    b. "Keep your hips engaged throughout the movement."
    c. "Keep your chest up during the entire movement."
    d. "Your knees should track over, but not beyond, the toes."

36. Which of the following is NOT a segment of the lower-limb breakdown of sprinting mechanics?
    a. Eccentric braking period
    b. Concentric propulsive phase
    c. Ground preparation phase
    d. Acceleration phase

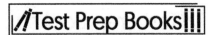

37. What is the placement of the hands relative to the body when utilizing proper arm action during running, walking, and jogging?
   a. During the upward movement, the hand should reach as high as the chest, and during the downward movement, the hand should reach as low as the lateral hip.
   b. During the upward movement, the hand should reach as high as eye level, and during the downward movement, the hand should reach as low as the naval.
   c. During the upward movement, the hand should reach as high as the jaw, and during the downward movement, the hand should reach as far back as the glutes.
   d. During the upward movement, the hand should reach as high as the chest, and during the downward movement, the hand should reach as low as the anterior hip.

38. During the first couple strides of a sprint, how does the force displacement shift?
   a. From horizontal displacement to vertical displacement
   b. From vertical displacement to horizontal displacement
   c. From transverse displacement to vertical displacement
   d. From transverse displacement to horizontal displacement

39. When should strength coaches push stretches to the point of maximum flexibility?
   a. Never
   b. When the athlete is sufficiently warmed up and prepared for extra stretching techniques
   c. When the athlete is fully relaxed, and the coach is performing passive stretching techniques
   d. During dynamic stretching when the athlete is in full control of their movements

40. Coaches can avoid injury to themselves through what techniques?
   a. Providing resistance using their hips and trunk
   b. Providing resistance using their extremities
   c. Facing hips and shoulders perpendicular to the direction of movement
   d. Turning the hips to one side while providing resistance

41. How long does it typically take for muscle hypertrophy to occur?
   a. Four to eight workout sessions
   b. Four to eight days
   c. Four to eight weeks
   d. Four to eight months

42. What is the primary difference between dumbbells/barbells and weight training equipment?
   a. Dumbbells and barbells are only used for one type of weight training exercise.
   b. Dumbbells and barbells are handheld free weights, while machines are pre-arranged setups.
   c. Weights cannot be added to free weight training equipment.
   d. Weight training equipment cannot be adjusted for the athlete's height or weight.

43. While using dumbbells for curls, which position engages the body's core muscles as a means of stabilizing the body?
   a. Standing position
   b. Seated position
   c. Lying supine
   d. Lying prone

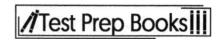

44. Which body position provides the most targeted workout during curls through isolating the muscles?
    a. Inverse
    b. Standing
    c. Seated
    d. Reverse

45. When working with free weights, athletes should stand with their feet how far apart?
    a. Feet together, heels touching
    b. Approximately six inches apart
    c. Shoulder width
    d. As far apart as they can comfortably stand

Program Design

1. Which of the following is a general guideline when prescribing free-weight exercises for beginners?
    a. Utilize three sets of eight to twelve repetitions
    b. Utilize five sets of three to five repetitions
    c. Begin the training program by testing the athlete's 1RM
    d. Use new training modalities to manipulate the athlete's adaptation

2. A loading period, usually lasting 3–4 weeks of training, is termed which of the following?
    a. Macrocycle
    b. Microcycle
    c. Mesocycle
    d. Ramping cycle

3. Which of the following is a recommended intensity range for an athlete looking to increase anaerobic capacity?
    a. 67–75 percent of maximal heart rate
    b. 85–90 percent of maximal heart rate
    c. 75–85 percent of maximal heart rate
    d. 90+ percent of maximal heart rate

4. What is the proper term used for muscles that oppose or support the prime mover of a movement?
    a. Agonist
    b. Synergist
    c. Secondary mover
    d. Antagonist

5. To determine the total load of a single training bout, which of the following equations should be used?
    a. Sets × repetitions
    b. Sets × repetitions × load
    c. Load × repetitions
    d. Sets × repetitions × duration

6. Which of the following is NOT considered a lower-body free-weight exercise for a beginner's program?
    a. Barbell thruster
    b. Back squat
    c. Power clean
    d. Dumbbell lunge

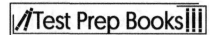

7. When training for power, how much rest should be given between sets?
   a. 30 seconds to 1 minute
   b. 1 to 2 minutes
   c. 3 to 5 minutes
   d. 5+ minutes

8. Which of the following terms is the principle of consistently adding resistance to an athlete's exercise in an effort to improve muscle adaptation and avoid plateaus?
   a. Progression
   b. Specificity
   c. Adaptation
   d. Overload

9. Which of the following is the cycle that is commonly used to prepare an athlete for more intense activity and lasts around 7 days?
   a. Macrocycle
   b. Mesocycle
   c. Microcycle
   d. Preparatory cycle

10. What is the main goal for programming flexibility exercises into a training program?
   a. Warming up
   b. Cooling down
   c. Strengthening
   d. Increasing range of motion of the joints

11. Which of the following is NOT a consideration of individualized program design?
   a. Specific movement patterns of a particular sport
   b. Fatiguing exercises performed first within a training session
   c. Power movements performed first within a training session
   d. Exercise selection based around the predominant muscle fiber type used for a particular sport

12. The capability of the aerobic pathway to be activated and engaged throughout a bout of long-duration exercise is known as which of the following?
   a. Aerobic endurance
   b. Aerobic capacity
   c. Aerobic performance
   d. Anaerobic capacity

13. Proper training stance for most bilateral exercises will include which of the following body positions?
   a. Chest up, back flat, knees fully extended
   b. Back straight, heels together, knees fully extended
   c. Back rounded, knees soft, and feet shoulder-width apart
   d. Back straight, knees soft, and feet shoulder-width apart

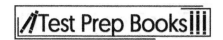

14. Which of the following should be considered when incorporating plyometric exercises into an athlete's resistance training program?
    a. Athlete's age
    b. 1RM back squat
    c. Sex
    d. 1RM power clean

15. Which of the following training adaptations will occur when high repetitions and short rest periods are prescribed?
    a. Strength
    b. Muscular endurance
    c. Cardiovascular endurance
    d. Power

16. Why does tissue in the repair phase of injury healing lack some strength?
    a. Collagen synthesis decreases during the repair phase
    b. There are too many inflammatory cells in the area
    c. The new collagen fibers are aligned haphazardly
    d. Cellular mediators like histamine cause edema, which inhibits the function of contractile tissue

17. An exercise that is used to exhaust a single muscle group prior to performing a multi-joint exercise is known as which of the following?
    a. Pre-fatigue exercise
    b. Pre-exhaustion exercise
    c. Pre-loaded exercise
    d. Pre-failure exercise

18. Which of the following is known to promote recovery from intense bouts of exercise?
    a. Commercial energy drinks
    b. Protein supplementation
    c. Coffee
    d. Fast-paced breathing

19. Which of the following is NOT considered a basic fundamental principle for program design?
    a. Working large to small muscle groups in a workout
    b. Alternating pushing exercises with pulling exercises
    c. Alternating upper-body exercises with lower-body exercises
    d. Performing two pushes for every pull

20. Which of the following is NOT a process that occurs after an athlete sustains an injury?
    a. Inflammation phase
    b. Repair phase
    c. Rehabilitation phase
    d. Remodeling phase

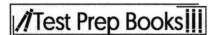

21. Which of the following is the type of training session that includes high-intensity outputs followed by short rest periods?
    a. Maximum effort training
    b. Agility training
    c. Metabolic conditioning
    d. Interval training

22. Which of the following terms refers to the body returning to its pre-training status after the cessation of a training program?
    a. Recovery
    b. Reversibility
    c. Atrophy
    d. Deload

23. Which of the following is NOT a mode for varying the intensity of an exercise?
    a. Utilizing slow concentric muscle actions
    b. Increasing lever length
    c. Varying balance demands
    d. Maintaining focus

24. Which of the following is considered the first proposed model of periodization, termed by Hans Selye?
    a. Linear Periodization
    b. Undulating Periodization
    c. General Adaptation Syndrome
    d. General Accumulation Syndrome

25. Which of the following rest periods should be utilized when intending to develop muscular endurance?
    a. 0 to 45 seconds
    b. 45 to 90 seconds
    c. 90 seconds to 2 minutes
    d. 2 to 5 minutes

26. The principle of the body's natural ability to grow accustomed to certain routines is known as which of the following?
    a. Accommodation
    b. Adaptation
    c. Resilience
    d. Alarm state

27. Which of the following describes a syndrome of overuse injury that occurs from irresponsible loading of intensity within a training program?
    a. Sprain
    b. Strain
    c. Microtrauma
    d. Overtraining

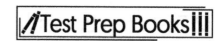

28. Which of the following is considered a "return to play" principle that must be taken into account when an athlete is rehabbing from an injury?
    a. The athlete should return when he or she feels able to fully participate.
    b. The athlete should return when the head sport coach feels the athlete is able to participate.
    c. The athlete should return when the healing tissues can be stressed without pain.
    d. The athlete should return to play after completing a proper, evidence-based rehabilitation program.

29. Which of the following describes minor ruptures or tears within the muscles, ligaments, and tendons that result in inhibited and limited function?
    a. Sprain
    b. Dislocation
    c. Strain
    d. Microtrauma

30. Which of the following is the correct set of terms that make up the *FITT Principle*?
    a. Fitness, Intensity, Training, Timing
    b. Frequency, Intensity, Time, Type
    c. Frequency, Intensity, Training, Type
    d. Fitness, Intensity, Time, Type

31. To develop power, exercises should be performed in which of the following repetition ranges?
    a. 1–5 repetitions
    b. 5–8 repetitions
    c. 8–12 repetitions
    d. 12–15 repetitions

32. Which of the following is categorized as a free-weight exercise implement?
    a. Lat pull-down machine
    b. Leg press machine
    c. Treadmill
    d. Kettlebell

33. Which of the following is considered a multi-joint exercise for the upper body?
    a. Barbell curls
    b. Triceps extensions
    c. Wrist curls
    d. Bench press

34. For the novice and intermediate athlete, which of the following training percentage ranges should be prescribed for the goal of muscular endurance?
    a. 30–60 percent of 1RM
    b. 60–70 percent of 1RM
    c. 70–85 percent of 1RM
    d. 85–100 percent of 1RM

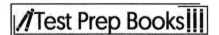

35. The greatest resistance or weight that can be moved through the full range of motion with proper posture and in a controlled manner is known as which of the following?
   a. Maximal effort load
   b. One-repetition maximum
   c. One-repetition load
   d. Submaximal load

36. What does each number represent during each muscle action for an exercise with a $4 \times 1 \times 0$ tempo?
   a. 4-second eccentric, 1-second isometric, 0-second concentric
   b. 4-second concentric, 1-second isometric, 0-second eccentric
   c. 4-second eccentric, 1-second concentric, 0-second isometric
   d. 4-second isometric, 1-second concentric, 0-second eccentric

37. When training with the main goal of hypertrophy, what is the correct repetition range that should be prescribed?
   a. 6 to 12 repetitions
   b. 1 to 5 repetitions
   c. 12 to 20 repetitions
   d. 5 to 8 repetitions

38. The negative portion of an exercise that, when slowed down, can cause a lot of muscle damage in a minimal number of sets and repetitions is known as which of the following?
   a. Eccentric muscle action
   b. Concentric muscle action
   c. Isometric muscle action
   d. Isokinetic muscle action

39. Which of the following is the term used for the general approach to improving fitness benefits and reducing the incidence of injury by systematically staggering cycles or periods of intense training?
   a. Programming
   b. Systematic intensity
   c. Periodization
   d. Long-term athletic development

40. Which sequence correctly describes the order of the cycle that muscles undergo during plyometric activities?
   a. Concentric, amortization, eccentric
   b. Energy release, recovery, energy storage
   c. Lengthening, transition, contraction
   d. Stretching, shortening, rest

41. A trainer has developed a program for a 65-year-old seasoned recreational runner with no plyometric experience. It includes thirty repetitions each of four low-to-moderate intensity lower-body plyometric exercises performed once weekly. Which portion of the program is ill-advised?
   a. The athlete is outside of the recommended age range for plyometric training.
   b. The program should also include lower-body plyometric exercises.
   c. The training frequency is inadequate for the athlete to benefit from the program.
   d. The training volume is not appropriate for the athlete's level of experience.

42. What is the goal of maximum velocity sprinting in sprint training?
    a. To facilitate improvements of no more than 110% of the athlete's maximal speed
    b. To improve the athlete's range of motion and flexibility
    c. To increase the amount of force generated in the least amount of time
    d. To produce neurological adaptations that reduce impulse generation

43. Which of the following is appropriate when developing a resisted sprint training plan for a field athlete?
    a. Be alert to the potential for an athlete to exhibit increased braking forces.
    b. Calculate the total sled weight to equal 20% to 30% of the athlete's body weight.
    c. Limit the towing rope's tension so that it doesn't decrease velocity by more than 10-12%.
    d. Use weighted vests and harnesses only when downhill running.

Organization and Administration

1. What happens to the performance of athletes who become overtrained?
    a. It improves
    b. It declines
    c. It stays the same
    d. It improves slightly before declining

2. A legal responsibility toward the athletes to ensure a safe and effective training environment describes which legal term?
    a. Liability
    b. Tort
    c. Informed consent
    d. Negligence

3. When designing a facility, why is ceiling height important for areas designated for medicine ball exercises, plyometric training, and Olympic exercises?
    a. It improves the aesthetics of the facility.
    b. It allows larger pieces of training equipment to be placed in the same area as the exercises being performed.
    c. It ensures the exercises being performed will not be obstructed by the ceilings.
    d. It allows the facility to be designed with more lighting options.

4. Which of the following can safeguard against legal issues in terms of equipment liability?
    a. Modifying equipment to meet the needs of the athlete
    b. Purchasing equipment from reliable companies that stand behind their products
    c. Purchasing equipment based solely on the budget given for the project
    d. Performing maintenance on the equipment only when needed

5. Any time a facility is NOT located on the ground floor, what capacity should the floor have to withstand?
    a. 100 pounds per square foot
    b. 50 pounds per square foot
    c. 100 pounds per square meter
    d. 50 pounds per square meter

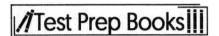

6. To ensure training sessions are performed in a safe and effective manner, how should equipment be placed within the facility?

a. Equipment should be organized into groups that coincide with the goals of the training equipment.
b. Equipment should be placed in a circuit so that each different machine can be used in a high-intensity training session.
c. Equipment should be placed around the perimeter so there is open space in the middle of the facility.
d. Equipment should be organized depending on the amount of space each piece takes up.

7. Which of the following is NOT a sign of a heat-related illness?

a. Cramping
b. Inability to speak clearly
c. Lack of perspiration
d. Reduced heart rate

8. Why should mirrors be placed at least 20 inches from the floor?

a. So athletes will be able to clearly see themselves in the mirror
b. To prevent contact with any rolling or bouncing piece of free-weight equipment
c. To give enough room for a vacuum to reach the wall without contacting the mirror
d. To ensure athletes are in a proper position when using the mirror as a coaching tool

9. How long is the duration of nonfunctioning overreaching?

a. Couple of hours to couple of weeks
b. Couple of days to weeks
c. Weeks to months
d. Months to years

10. Which of the following choices gives the recommended and optimal ranges for the temperature of the facility?

a. 70–80 degrees recommended and 72–78 degrees optimal
b. 65–75 degrees recommended and 65–72 degrees optimal
c. 68–78 degrees recommended and 68–74 degrees optimal
d. 68–78 degrees recommended and 72–78 degrees optimal

11. Why is it important to set the eligibility criteria of facility use?

a. To ensure certain criteria are met in terms of the standards of the facility and those who use it
b. To ensure the equipment does not become worn down from overuse
c. To ensure participants will always have a strength and conditioning coach when training
d. To ensure a certified medical professional is on duty at all times

12. Which of the following is NOT a main role of a strength and conditioning professional?

a. Training athletes in physical performance
b. Creating individual nutrition plans for the athletes
c. Motivating athletes to push themselves to be their best
d. Designing training programs that adhere to scientific foundations in strength and conditioning

13. Which of the following should NOT be included in the facility rules document?

a. Proper attire for training
b. Rules of using the equipment
c. Workout sheet guidelines
d. Emergency action plan

14. When designing for environmental factors within the facility, a plan should be in place to keep the relative humidity below ___, with air being exchanged at least ___ times per hour to prevent stagnant air odors.

a. 60%; 8
b. 80%; 6
c. 40%; 8
d. 60%; 4

15. When designing a new facility, athletes must be comfortable and safe during training. Which of the following is the minimum square footage per athlete that should be adhered to in the designs?

a. 200
b. 100
c. 50
d. 10

Testing, Ongoing Monitoring, and Data Evaluation

1. Which of the following is NOT a subcategory of criterion-referenced validity?

a. Concurrent validity
b. Convergent validity
c. Predictive validity
d. Construct validity

2. To measure endurance parameters for a specific individual athlete or sport, which of the following can ensure validity and reliability?

a. Using testing protocols that are specific to the energy demands of the athlete
b. Ensuring athletes are using maximal effort
c. Requiring minimal rest between bouts
d. Using an aerobic-based test regardless of individual or sport

3. To begin 1RM testing, which of the following should occur first?

a. Athletes should start with a load of 70 percent of the goal 1RM.
b. Athletes should begin with a light resistance for 5–10 repetitions.
c. Athletes should start with a load of 80 percent of the goal 1RM.
d. Athletes should begin with a light resistance for 1–3 repetitions.

4. Which athletic capability is tested by the Yo-Yo Intermittent Recovery Test?

a. Local muscular endurance
b. Agility
c. Aerobic capacity
d. Anaerobic capacity

5. Which of the following is NOT used during body composition and anthropometry testing?

a. Skinfold calipers
b. Stopwatch
c. Bodyweight scale
d. Height measurement tools

6. Which of the following could lessen the validity and reliability of a given test?
   a. Using exercises for which technical proficiency has yet to be met
   b. Using exercises that the athletes are accustomed to
   c. Using exercises that are specific to the biomechanical movement patterns of the sport
   d. Using exercises that are specific to the sex of the athlete

7. Which of the following reflects the proper work-to-rest ratio for oxidative-based testing protocols?
   a. 1:12–1:20
   b. 1:5–1:10
   c. 1:1–1:3
   d. 1:3–1:5

8. Why is it important to compare the final testing data with the typical testing data associated with the specific sport or individual athlete?
   a. To show that the current program is effective
   b. To show the sport coaches that the strength and conditioning coach is competent
   c. To prove content validity
   d. To determine specific athletic capabilities that need to be improved upon

9. Which of the following will help to ensure the health and safety of the athlete during a testing session?
   a. Athletes should be allowed water and breaks as often as needed.
   b. Athletes should be encouraged to push themselves to maximal intensity at all times.
   c. Rest periods should push the limits within the work-to-rest ratios.
   d. Only the testing administrator should be present during testing sessions.

10. Which of the following is considered a maximum muscle power testing protocol at high speeds?
   a. 1RM back squat
   b. 1RM deadlift
   c. 1RM power clean
   d. Maximum push-up

11. Which of the following describes a common flaw that occurs after analyzing test data?
   a. Not making any modification to the current training program
   b. Completely changing the entire periodization of the program
   c. Punishing athletes based on the test results
   d. Changing the program without giving ample time for proper adaptation to occur

12. For valid and reliable test results, which of the following should be FIRST within the sequence of testing protocols?
   a. Maximum lower body tests
   b. Maximum power tests
   c. Maximum upper body tests
   d. Local muscular endurance tests

13. Which of the following is NOT an acceptable test for maximum muscular strength with low speeds?
   a. 1RM bench press
   b. 1RM back squat
   c. 1RM partial curl-up
   d. 1RM bench pull

14. Skinfold calipers are commonly used for which of the following measurements?
    a. Body mass index (BMI)
    b. Girth measurements
    c. Anthropometry
    d. Body composition

15. To optimally prepare athletes for testing, which of the following should occur?
    a. Testing sessions should not be known to the athletes prior to testing
    b. Athletes should be made aware of what tests they are to perform
    c. The test day should be known but the specific tests should not
    d. The tests should be explained but the testing day should not be known

16. Which of the following is NOT a consideration of environmental factors within testing sessions?
    a. Athlete's clothing
    b. Humidity
    c. Temperature
    d. Running surface

17. How many testing personnel are encouraged for optimal, valid data during testing sessions?
    a. One tester to enhance the validity of the testing data
    b. Two testers per athlete
    c. Multiple testers for optimal testing efficiency
    d. Athletes can be used for testing personnel to enhance the availability of personnel used for testing sessions

18. To ensure optimal preparation, which of the following should occur prior to testing within the testing session?
    a. Athletes should perform maximal power testing upon arrival to the testing location.
    b. A proper warmup should occur to increase core temperature and joint elasticity.
    c. Athletes should undergo endurance testing upon arrival to the testing location.
    d. A proper warmup should occur to decrease core temperature and joint elasticity.

19. Ideally, how many testing sets should be performed to measure the 1RM data?
    a. One to two testing sets
    b. One to three testing sets
    c. Three to five testing sets
    d. Five to eight testing sets

20. Which of the following types of validity is best described as the athlete's or casual observer's perception of whether the selected test is accurate?
    a. Construct validity
    b. Content validity
    c. Criterion-referenced validity
    d. Face validity

21. Body fat assessments include all EXCEPT which of the following?
    a. Skinfold measurements
    b. DEXA scans
    c. BMI
    d. Bioelectrical impedance

22. Practices that strength coaches can implement to foster a safe training environment include all EXCEPT which of the following?

a. Clearing loose equipment from the floor
b. Encouraging teamwork and positive, supportive attitudes
c. Mopping wooden floors and checking wooden platforms for cracks
d. Keeping weight benches and lifting platforms as close together as possible

Answer Explanations #2

Exercise Sciences

1. A: When performance begins to decline from stress that is applied to the body throughout training, it is known as functional overreaching. Often, functional overreaching is a planned method of increasing stress prior to a period of rest or of reduced intensity. It is important for the strength and conditioning professional to understand a difference between overreaching and overtraining.

2. B: Throughout training, the strength and conditioning professional may instruct the athlete on specific tasks to perform during the movement. This is known as explicit instruction. Explicit instruction can be very beneficial with simple, single-joint exercises but may be less effective with more advanced, multi-joint, compound movements. Therefore, the strength and conditioning professional should assess the movement category and administer instruction techniques that best suit the exercise, as well as the individual.

3. C: The pectoralis major contracts eccentrically when the barbell is lowered to the chest in a barbell bench press exercise. Almost exclusively, any lowering phase of the external resistance or body will be categorized as an eccentric muscle action of the agonist muscle due to the need to control the downward phase of the movement. Because gravity will cause the load to drop, the muscles must contract eccentrically to control the load. It is important to understand the difference between concentric, eccentric, and isometric muscle actions when designing training protocols for athletes.

4. D: The heart's conduction system can be observed through a graph known as an electrocardiogram. The graph that is displayed during an electrocardiogram is comprised of a P-wave, a QRS complex (Q-wave, R-wave, S-wave), and a T-wave. The P-wave and QRS complex represent the depolarization phase of the atria and ventricles, respectively. The T-wave represents the repolarization phase of contraction.

5. D: During respiration, the lungs expand and retract to control volume of air within the system. The expansion and retraction are controlled by two different mechanisms: the upward and downward movement of the diaphragm and the depression and elevation of the ribs. Although the abdominals can have a role in the expansion and retraction of the lungs, their involvement entails activation and contraction, not active relaxation.

6. C: For the strength and conditioning professional, it is important to understand the differences between the appendicular and axial skeletons. The axial skeleton consists of the ribs, sternum, vertebral column, and the skull, and the appendicular skeleton consists of the bones of the hips, knees, ankles, feet, pelvic girdle, shoulder girdle, arms, wrists, and hands. Acquiring a basic understanding of bone anatomy can be beneficial when speaking with other medical personnel, such as athletic strength and conditioning professionals and team doctors.

7. A: The hormonal response to exercise will not be the same for children and young adolescents as that of the general athletic population. In prepubescent children, circulating hormones such as testosterone, growth hormone, and insulin-like growth factor are limited. Therefore, many of the strength gains afforded from training programs are increased hypertrophy of the musculature and neural adaptations. The neural adaptations, including enhanced recruitment of motor units, primarily drive improvements.

8. C: During a muscle contraction, the motor neuron sends an electrical impulse, in the form of an action potential, for the muscle to contract. Furthermore, calcium plays a major role in the interaction. As long as calcium is available, the myosin and actin will continue to interact. When calcium is insufficient or when the action potential ceases, the interaction of the myofibrils will stop and the muscle will relax.

9. D: Hemoglobin is the main vehicle within blood for oxygen transport to the rest of the body. Hemoglobin is located within the red blood cells. As the red blood cells travel through the body via the cardiovascular system, the oxygen can reach the cells of the body.

10. C: Almost all bones are surrounded by a specialized tissue called periosteum, which serves as a site for tendon attachment. As muscles contract, tendons, which are connected to bones by the periosteum, pull on the bones, causing movement. Choice *B* is incorrect because although periosteum contains vasculature and nerves, it is not "cells within the bone," but rather an outer coating on the bone made of fibrous tissue.

11. A: The decline in fitness gains attained through training after a period of inactivity is called detraining. When the physical stress is removed for an extended period of time, the body responds by regressing back towards an untrained status. The result of this regression is a partial or complete loss of the positive adaptations that resulted from a proper and specific training program.

12. D: Cardiac output is the total volume of blood pumped by the heart over time. It is a product of the heart rate (how fast the heart is beating) and stroke volume (the volume of blood ejected with each beat). Aerobic training can increase both cardiac output and stroke volume. As muscles are performing work, the need for oxygenated blood increases. Therefore, the increase in cardiac output is correlated to the increased intensity and workload of the exercise.

13. C: The intervertebral disks of the human body are cartilaginous joints that allow limited movement in particular planes. Choice *A* is incorrect because fibrous joints are nearly-immobile connections between bones, such as in the skull. Choices *B* and *D* are incorrect because synovial joints are highly mobile joints in the body, while ball and socket joints are one type of synovial joint.

14. A: When administering training to children and adolescents, guidelines for youth resistance training must be followed. First, the youth athlete must understand the benefits and risks associated with the training program. Throughout training, when performing each exercise, the child should be closely monitored by a strength and conditioning professional at all times and should never be left alone. Prior to training, an appropriate and thorough warm-up should be performed. Children and adolescents do not respond to training as adults do; therefore, the exercise response should be closely monitored. Guidelines for exercise volume is approximately one to three sets of six to fifteen repetitions at an appropriate weight that can be sustained without compromising form. Although 1RM testing is often utilized in adult training, children and adolescents need a thorough learning period to learn technique and movement patterns. Therefore, 1RM testing would not be suitable for the youth athlete as it can be highly unsafe.

15. B: The z-line of a sarcomere is where actin filaments are anchored, and each sarcomere is defined by the bounds of adjacent z-lines. The sliding-filament theory states that as the actin and myosin bind and pull towards one another, the z-lines at the ends move towards each other as the muscle fiber shortens.

16. C: The motor unit is the term used for the motor neuron and all of the muscle fibers it innervates. When an action potential travels down the motor neuron, as long as it is of sufficient intensity to exceed the minimum threshold, all of the fibers in the motor unit will contract together.

17. D: When a receptor site decreases its ability to respond to a specific hormone or negates the response process altogether, it is known as downregulation of receptor function. Downregulation can greatly alter the sensitivity of the receptor, thereby changing the hormonal response of the human body.

18. A: Neuromotor function begins to decline with age and can be related to many of the injuries sustained in older adults. Injuries such as falls, dislocations, and skeletal fractures become common in the elderly. With these factors in mind, strength and conditioning professionals can safely administer neuromotor facilitating exercises into the training of the aging athlete. Furthermore, the strength and conditioning professional must also follow all guidelines for working with this population.

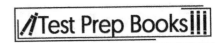

19. A: The loss in muscle mass that occurs with the aging process is called sarcopenia. While this is a natural process for all aging adults, the process can be slowed in adults who remain active since it is thought to mainly occur because of inactivity. Resistance exercise can help preserve muscle mass and slow the decline in strength. Therefore, it is important for older adults to remain physically active. When muscle mass is lost, muscular strength and power also begins to decline. A muscle's cross-sectional area typically starts reducing after the age of 30 and will continue to decline if the athlete does not engage in regular, challenging resistance training.

20. D: The cardiovascular system is afforded many benefits from aerobic training. One of these adaptations is the increase in maximal oxygen uptake to meet the increased demand of the heart and muscles for oxygen. Maximum oxygen uptake is a product of cardiac output and the arteriovenous difference, which is a measure of how well the tissues extract oxygen from the circulating blood.

21. C: The endomysium surrounds each individual muscle fiber. Fibers are bundled into fascicles, which have a connective tissue covering called the perimysium. Multiple fascicles are grouped together to form the entire muscle, which is covered by the epimysium.

22. C: Type I fibers are classified as slow-twitch muscle fibers and are most suitable for a marathon runner. Type IIa and Type IIx are both fast-twitch muscle fibers and are more conducive to explosive sporting activities. Type I fibers are efficient muscle fibers that are relatively fatigue-resistant and primarily rely on oxidative pathways for energy production, making them the ideal muscle fiber for a marathon runner.

23. D: When a hormone has the ability to partially interact with a receptor site, it blocks any other interaction from occurring at that site in a process termed cross-reactivity.

24. D: High Intensity Interval Training (HIIT) is a variation of interval training that incorporates intermittent rest periods and repeated bouts of intense work. This can be a very useful workout when time is limited in a session but a strong metabolic conditioning stimulus is desired. Running, cycling, and jump roping are common modes of exercise used in HIIT training. When used properly, HIIT has the ability to produce advantageous adaptations to metabolic, neuromuscular, and cardiopulmonary systems simultaneously. Although there are many advantages to HIIT, one must be cautious when using HIIT concurrently with other means of athletic development. HIIT can be very stressful on the body and can result in a higher incidence of injury or overtraining. Therefore, one of the major drawbacks of high intensity interval training is that stress can rise to counterproductive levels.

25. C: During training and daily life, the body can moderate the force of muscular contractions in two primary ways. The first is through the frequency of activation of the motor units. If a motor unit is only activated once, then a twitch will result and the force will be low. As more action potentials are fired, twitches begin to overlap and summate, and the force of the contraction will increase. The second way the body can control the force of a contraction is through recruitment, which involves altering the number of motor units stimulated. Through the recruitment strategy, the body and brain can detect the amount of motor units that are required for a given activity as well as what type of fibers are needed for the activity and then send action potentials to those motor neurons accordingly.

26. D: The respiratory system allows for the cells and tissues of the body to receive oxygen and remove carbon dioxide through the process of breathing. The lymphatic system is the part of the immune and vascular systems that transports lymph fluid in the body, so Choice *A* is incorrect. The vascular system is responsible for the circulation of blood and lymph, so Choice *B* is incorrect. The neuroendocrine system involves both the nervous system and the endocrine system where they pertain to endocrine signals, or hormones, making Choice *C* incorrect.

27. C: Understanding the planes in which the body moves can be very beneficial when communicating with other medical personnel such as athletic strength and conditioning professionals and team doctors. Therefore, the strength and conditioning professional must acquire knowledge of the movement planes of the human body. When performing a forward lunge, the movement is occurring within the sagittal plane because there is forward flexion and extension of the hips, knees, and ankles and the body is moving forward when visualized from the side.

28. B: When considering detraining effects, it is important to understand the length of time that residual effect gained during programming will last for each athletic attribute. For maximal strength, residual effects tend to remain 30 days, plus or minus 5 days, until regression occurs.

29. C: The prime mover in any exercise is known as the agonist. Therefore, the agonist during the dumbbell bent-over row, is the latissimus dorsi, since it is one of the prime movers for the exercise.

30. D: The heart's electrical impulse originates in the SA node, which is considered the intrinsic pacemaker of the heart. It then travels to the AV node and then onward. This conduction system is what stimulates the heart to contract and maintain its rhythm.

31. D: When trying to achieve the optimal hormonal response to training, the strength and conditioning professional should be knowledgeable about the exercises that elicit such responses. Using both multi-joint movements that are ground-based and movements that use large muscle groups can increase blood concentrations of the anabolic hormones such as testosterone and growth hormone. Therefore, the strength and conditioning professional should incorporate exercises such as deadlifts, squats, power cleans, front squats, and Romanian deadlifts into all training programs that are geared toward increasing muscle strength and size.

32. C: The phosphagen system is the primary energy system used in the beginning of movement and when ATP must be generated extremely quickly during short-duration exercises of very high intensity. This system has a small amount of ATP readily available, which is why it is exhausted first during exercise. It also can generate a small amount of ATP very quickly since the energy-generation pathway is so short, so it is the system of choice for high-intensity activities lasting about ten seconds or less.

33. D: There are many guidelines to follow when administering resistance training to older adults. One of these guidelines involves stretching to increase flexibility. It is always advisable to do a thorough warm-up with dynamic stretching prior to a workout and follow the session with static stretching for all of the major muscle groups.

34. B: A lack of understanding of safe youth resistance training is unfortunately common in the strength and conditioning profession. Too often, children and adolescents are treated as adults in terms of programming and exercise selection. Responses to resistance training are different between adults and children because of the differences in anatomy and physiology, particularly the immature skeleton and prepubescent hormonal profile of the child. These differences need to be considered when designing programs for youth athletes.

35. C: Basic bone anatomy consists of non-living minerals as well as living bone cells. Bone is primarily made of calcium carbonate, calcium phosphate, and the protein called collagen. Sodium bicarbonate is not a foundational element of bone.

36. D: When designing activities specific to the energy system of the sporting activity, work-to-rest ratios become vitally important. The work-to-rest ratio is the amount of predetermined time for the exercise to occur (work period) to the length of time exercise should cease (rest). Work-to-rest ratios for the glycolytic energy system are approximately 1:3–1:5.

37. D: The strength and conditioning professional must understand the structure and function of the cardiovascular system and how it responds to the training process. Primarily, the cardiovascular system is responsible for transporting oxygen and nutrients throughout the body and delivering them to the cells and tissues for use as well as removing waste such as carbon dioxide, from the cells. The breakdown of nutrients for energy is a function of the digestive system, not the cardiovascular system.

38. A: Although after puberty males generally have more muscle mass than females, the quality of muscle tissue itself tends to be the same in both sexes. The greater strength and power typically seen in males is due to the increased muscle mass itself and not from a higher quality tissue.

39. B: Understanding normal blood pressure is beneficial to the strength and conditioning professional because it can help the strength and conditioning professional spot dangerous, hypertensive levels and refer the patient to an appropriate medical provider. The upper limits of normal blood pressure are 120/80.

40. C: Since muscles and bones both adapt to external resistance, the tendons and ligaments of the body must do the same to withstand the loads that the muscle and bone can now produce and accommodate. Adaptations of the tendons through the training process to withstand greater loads include increasing fibril diameter, forming more cross-linkages, and the developing new collagen fibers. They do not usually become more flexible; in fact, the adaptations tend to make them stiffer, which is also advantageous for a higher rate of energy return.

41. C: During exercise, especially at higher intensities, the body uses an excessive amount of oxygen to fuel the working muscles and heart. Once the bout of exercise stops, oxygen uptake remains elevated over baseline levels, which is termed excess post-exercise oxygen consumption (EPOC). The function of EPOC is to help restore homeostasis in the different systems of the body that were active during the workload period.

42. D: During the training process, adaptations can occur from the release and storage of certain hormones that promote tissue building. Hormones that promote the tissue building process, especially during protein synthesis, are termed anabolic hormones. Anabolic hormones include testosterone, growth hormone, insulin, and insulin-like growth factor. Cortisol is a catabolic hormone because it signals the body to break down tissues.

43. A: As males undergo puberty, an increase in testosterone can be observed. This increase in testosterone is responsible for increases in muscle mass and bone formation observed during and after puberty.

44. B: Skeletal muscle maintains posture because it is connected to the body's frame, and as such, holds it in place and/or allows it to move. Choice *A* is incorrect because smooth muscle functions to operate internal organs. Choice *C* is incorrect because cardiac muscle is used to pump blood through the circulatory system. Choice *D* is incorrect because dorsal muscles would only include the skeletal muscles of the back; additional skeletal muscles are used to maintain posture.

45. C: Type I muscle fibers (slow-twitch) are most useful for activities that require a lot of endurance, such as a marathon. This is opposed to type II muscle fibers (fast-twitch), which are used to rapidly generate force. Choices *A*, *B*, and *D* are incorrect because they require an athlete to rapidly generate force using type II muscle fibers.

46. D: The throwing motion involves straightening the arm (extension), which is what the triceps muscles do. Choices *A* and *B* are incorrect because they primarily make use of various leg muscles. Choice *C* is incorrect because doing a pull-up makes the arm curl at the elbow (flexion), which is the responsibility of the biceps muscles.

47. A: The pronator teres allows the forearm to rotate and to pronate the hand, hence the name. Choice *B* is incorrect because the brachialis is responsible for helping to flex the elbow. Choice *C* is incorrect because the flexor carpi ulnaris is responsible for flexion and adduction of the hand. Choice *D* is incorrect because the anconeus helps the triceps in extending the forearms.

48. D: The biceps femoris is one of the hamstring muscles, which is responsible for knee flexion. Choices *A*, *B*, and *C* are incorrect because the biceps femoris does not influence movement of the arms or feet.

49. A: Inferior locations are farther away from the head, relative to another body part. The football player's injury would need to be closer to the feet than the right femur, so the right tibia is a possibility. Choice *B* is incorrect because the left femur would be contralateral to the right femur. Choice *C* is incorrect because triceps would be superior (and perhaps contralateral, depending on the side) to the right femur. Choice *D* is incorrect because the coccyx would be superior and medial to the right femur.

50. B: Body parts or injuries that are ipsilateral would be on the same side of the body. Choice *A* is incorrect because lateral simply means away from the body's midline. Choice *C* is incorrect because bilateral means existing on both sides of the body, away from the midline. Choice *D* is incorrect because contralateral means on opposite sides of the body, which is essentially the opposite of ipsilateral.

51. C: The right side of the rib cage meets all of the mentioned qualifications. Choice *A* is incorrect because the ulna would not be medial to the humerus. Choice *B* is incorrect because the ankle would not be superior to the ilium. Choice *D* is incorrect because the scapula is not inferior to the clavicle or anterior to the spine.

52. B: The trapezius muscle is responsible for the shoulder shrug movement. Choice *A* is incorrect because the erector spinae is responsible for back extension. Choice *C* is incorrect because the pectoralis major is used to move the arm toward the chest. Choice *D* is incorrect because the biceps brachii is used for flexion of the elbow.

Sport Psychology

1. B: Attention is the operation of processing environmental, external, and internal cues that enter one's awareness throughout training and competition. It is important for athletes to ensure that their attention and level of focus is based on task-relevant stimuli and keep their attention off of task-irrelevant stimuli.

2. B: Mental imagery involves recreating successful athletic events within the mind of the athlete. This recreation can entail every sensory aspect of the event, such as what might be seen, heard, smelled, and felt. By recreating a successful athletic endeavor, the athlete will increase the desire to experience such events within their athletic career again. The mental image does not need to be limited to competition; it may include a successful practice, or rehearsal, in preparation for the event.

3. D: Somatic anxiety is the negative physical perceptions of anxiety such as increased heart rate, nervous stomach, and sweaty palms. Anxiety is perceived as a negative emotional state characterized by worry, nervousness, apprehension, and fear. The thought process responsible for the perception of arousal as negative is a result of cognitive anxiety, while its counterpart—somatic anxiety—is the perception of physical symptoms.

4. D: Adaptation can occur from any stressor that is placed on the human body, a phenomenon called general adaptation syndrome (GAS). When stress is placed on the body over time, the body will begin to react accordingly and try to build resistance or tolerance to that stress. In the case of exercise as the stressor, the body adapts by increasing neural recruitment of muscle fibers, increasing muscle fiber size and density, increasing mitochondrial density, etc., depending on the specific training program.

5. B: Segmented feedback is not considered a form of feedback during instruction. Throughout training, especially during learning periods, feedback can have a major impact in eliciting the desired movement patterns. Feedback involves providing the athlete with information about their movement patterns or performance of an exercise. This information can then be used to correct any faults in technique or execution. Augmented feedback, knowledge of results, and knowledge of performance are all forms of feedback commonly used in the strength and conditioning profession.

6. B: Positive punishment and negative punishment are considered reinforcement techniques that are utilized within the strength and conditioning profession. When administering punishment reinforcement techniques, the strength and conditioning professional aims to decrease the occurrence of a given undesirable operant; therefore, decreasing the occurrence of the operant can increase the success of the athlete. Positive punishment relates to administering tasks, objects, or events that would likely decrease the occurrence of the negative operant, such as adding sprints to the end of a practice where athletes were continually goofing around.

7. B: Whole practice instruction teaches movements in their entirety. When whole practice teaching occurs, the movements are taught in one fluid movement. Whole practice instruction is best suited for skills that are of low complexity but high organization. Skill complexity relates to the number of components or parts of the task, such that a task of low complexity has just a couple parts whereas one of high complexity has many. A skill that has a higher degree of complexity requires more mental processing to execute, and thus carries a greater cognitive demand. Those that are highly interdependent have high levels of organization. A cartwheel is an example of a skill best taught using whole practice. Choice *A,* skills of high complexity but low organization, are served well by part practice.

8. B: Guided discovery is the term used when specific instructions are given during the learning process but information is limited to allow the athlete to process the movement. Since one of the main drawbacks of explicit instruction is "information overload," guided discovery gives the athlete the main information of the movement, but allows him or her to learn certain aspects independently as the movement is performed. The information given during guided discovery often relates to preventing injury during the movement, but the remaining information is left for the athlete to discover. This technique also allows the athlete to process new material at their own pace and connect more strongly with internal cues.

9. A: There are a variety of signs of overtraining. One of the main signs is poor immunity, which manifests as more frequent sickness or illness. When the stress of training is too significant or constant without ample recovery, the immune system becomes depressed and less able to fend off illnesses. Other symptoms of overtraining can include muscle stiffness and soreness, difficulty sleeping, mood and appetite changes, and an increase in resting heart rate.

10. A: When observing motivation, successful athletes demonstrate both intrinsic and extrinsic motivation. Extrinsic motivation involves the desire for external rewards from successful outcomes of training and competition. Examples include social acceptance, trophies, awards, induction into a hall of fame, and praise. Intrinsic motivation involves the internal desire to be successful, the athlete's love for the sport, and the internal satisfaction gleaned from participation. It is important to note that athletes are usually not solely motivated by extrinsic or intrinsic factors, but from a combination of both.

11. B: For complex movements that require use of multiple muscle groups and joints, part practice instruction may be more conducive to skill acquisition. In part practice instruction, each segment of the movement can be broken down into subcomponents to ensure each segment is taught prior to performing the movement as a whole.

12. A: Self-efficacy refers to the athlete's perception of their ability to perform a situation-specific task successfully. The most significant source of self-efficacy for most athletes is the athlete's past performance experiences. The other choices listed are sources of self-efficacy, but they tend to be less impactful.

13. B: Although higher arousal levels are associated with higher performance outcomes, heightened arousal states are finite and can become detrimental if the arousal level becomes too high. The inverted-U theory describes this phenomenon. It states that arousal levels up to a certain level increase performance, but further increases in arousal are associated with reduced performance.

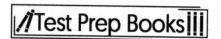

14. A: The intensity and focus of one's effort is a product of motivation. Motivation for competition and training, as well as a desire to be successful, can have major implications to the outcome of one's athletic career. Successful athletes usually possess a combination of both intrinsic and extrinsic motivation.

15. B: Optimal arousal levels are very important in attaining success in athletics. Being able to achieve optimal arousal levels can have a major impact on the outcome and performance of an athletic event. When optimal arousal levels are achieved, increases can be seen in mental activation, positive self-thoughts, and decision-making tasks. Although performance anxiety can be associated with arousal levels, this problem is often observed when the arousal levels rise too high, so they are no longer "optimal."

16. A: Motive to avoid failure is a motive for the athlete to protect their ego, self-worth, and self-esteem. It is important to note that a motive to avoid failure is not to avoid failure per se, but to avoid the perception of shame from one's team, coaches, fans, and family. Athletes with a high motive to avoid failure tend to seek out competitions that are easy and unchallenging to them personally.

17. C: Individuals suffering from bulimia nervosa are often more difficult to identify, as they are more frequently at a normal weight for their height. The binging behavior can prevent weight loss, even when accompanied by purging behaviors.

18. C: Hypertrophy is not a symptom associated with disordered eating. Athletes with disordered eating behaviors often become malnourished, which makes hypertrophy impossible. Furthermore, dehydration, higher body fat composition, and muscle wasting have all been associated with disordered eating patterns.

19. C: It is important for the strength and conditioning professional to recognize symptoms associated with anorexia nervosa. Bradycardia, a slow heart rate, is a common symptom; other symptoms include a decrease in body temperature, hypotension, dull and dry skin, and brittle hair and nails.

20. B: Choice *B* is correct because using imagery techniques is a mental visualization strategy in an attempt to "experience" the sensations of a move before you make it. Choices *A, C,* and *D* have nothing to do with sport psychology.

21. A: Choice *A* is correct because negative reinforcement is the removal of an undesirable experience as a reward. Choice *B* is the addition of a desirable experience as a reward, Choice *C* is the addition of an undesirable experience as punishment, and Choice *D* is the removal of a desirable experience as punishment.

22. C: Choice *C* is correct because positive punishment is the addition of undesirable experiences as a deterrent from unwanted behavior. Choices *A* and *B* are incorrect because they are not in reaction to unwanted behavior. By virtue of Choice *C* being correct, Choice *D* is also incorrect.

23. B: Choice *B* is correct because the primary source of an athlete's self-efficacy is their experience in past performances. Choice *D* is the third source of self-efficacy, and Choices *A* and *C* have little direct relation at all.

Nutrition

1. D: Hypertension, or an elevation in blood pressure, is a common side effect of anabolic steroid abuse. The only other answer choice that pertains to the cardiovascular system is increased myocardial function. Anabolic steroids are known not to increase myocardial function but rather to decrease myocardial function.

2. A: For strength sports, it is recommended that athletes consume 1.4 to 1.7 grams of protein per kilogram of body weight daily. This amount is sufficient to sustain muscle protein synthesis and reduce muscle breakdown from training.

3. B: Post-competition nutrition is vital to recovery. Athletes who compete in sports such as American football, which is primarily strength-based and anaerobic, should consume 20 to 25 grams of protein post-competition to reduce muscle soreness and encourage recovery.

4. C: Creatine is a nitrogenous organic compound that helps supply energy to the cells. It is primarily stored within the skeletal muscle of the human body and some is formed endogenously, while some is consumed with an omnivorous diet. Supplementation is also common in strength sports and is generally considered safe.

5. B: The recommended daily caloric deficit for safe and effective fat loss is roughly 500 calories per day. This amount will ensure that the body still attains enough calories to maintain performance, but the moderate deficit will encourage body fat loss.

6. A: The glycemic index is a ranking system based on how quickly carbohydrates are digested, absorbed, and used as fuel. By using the glycemic index, the athlete can determine the magnitude of the blood glucose level increase from certain carbohydrate-rich foods in the 2-hour post-consumption time period. Foods that score lower on the glycemic index are more slowly digested and absorbed than higher-glycemic foods.

7. C: Athletes who are attempting to increase muscular endurance should consume protein post-exercise. This protein consumption will decrease muscle soreness and damage.

8. D: Erythropoietin, or EPO, stimulates the production of new red blood cells, which carry oxygen to skeletal muscle. When injections of EPO are administered either medically or illegally in athletics, increases in both hematocrit and hemoglobin have been observed. This can translate to improved aerobic capacity and endurance.

9. A: MyPlate is a food guidance tool issued by the United States Department of Agriculture that can help athletes understand their basic nutritional needs based on their age, sex, and physical activity. It is important to note that many of the recommendations are based on the needs of the general population rather than those of competitive athletes. However, the recommendations can form a good starting point for a healthy diet for athletes as well.

10. B: For athletes with a goal of muscle hypertrophy, 30–100 grams of higher-glycemic carbohydrates should be consumed after exercise because this will help replenish glycogen stores and encourage protein synthesis. The recommendation for protein is to consume meals that contain at least 20–30 grams of high-leucine protein every 3–4 hours throughout the day.

11. D: Anabolic steroids have many psychological effects on an individual who is abusing the substance. Increases in aggression, arousal, irritability, and mood swings are common. Athletes have also noted the inability to relax when using anabolic steroids.

12. B: For meals that are consumed 4 or more hours prior to the athletic endeavor, athletes should consume 1 to 4 grams of carbohydrates per kilogram of body weight in a balanced meal containing protein and healthy fats. Hydration is also important.

13. A: MyPlate is a great starting point for athletes to evaluate their current diet and should be used to identify areas within the diet that are lacking. MyPlate categorizes foods into five main components: fruits, vegetables, grains, protein, and dairy. Legumes, although often consumed by athletes, are not a main component of MyPlate. They can provide a good source of protein—especially for vegetarians—and complex carbohydrates.

14. D: The most widely used carbohydrate-loading technique is the three-day loading period protocol. Studies have shown that this timeframe helps increase endurance during aerobic exercise such as marathon running.

15. B: Nutrient-dense foods are foods that have many micronutrients, vitamins, and minerals along with their macronutrients of carbohydrates, fats, and protein. Banana bread is not considered a nutrient-dense food but rather a calorie-dense food.

16. A: Electrolytes lost in sweat need to be replaced to prevent imbalances and deficiencies. The main ones to consider are sodium and chloride, though potassium, magnesium, and calcium are also excreted in sweat and need to be replaced. Iodine is not lost in appreciable levels during exercise.

17. D: Although creatine is widely used, the human body has limits on how much can be used during a certain time period. Skeletal muscle concentrations of approximately 150 to 180 millimoles per kilogram have shown to be the upper limit of the effective concentration during exercise. Once this level is reached, further supplementation will not be beneficial to performance.

18. A: Low iron levels occur in three different stages of increasing severity: depletion, marginal deficiency, and anemia. When anemia is prolonged, red blood production ceases, which reduces oxygen transport throughout the body. Low iron levels can cause difficulty concentrating, fatigue, weakness, decreased exercise and work capacity, and dry mouth.

19. B: Choice *B* is correct because while USDA Food Patterns is a useful nutrition application, the USDA EatRight Health Aide does not exist. Choices *A, C,* and *D* are all real and useful nutrition aid applications.

20. D: Choice *D* is correct because the 2015–2020 Dietary Guidelines has three food patterns: Healthy U.S. Style Eating, Healthy Mediterranean Style Eating, and Healthy Vegetarian Style Eating. Choices *A, B,* and *C* are incorrect values.

Exercise Technique

1. D: Reducing contact time should be the athlete's goal during multiple hops and jumps in plyometric training. During plyometric training, putting attention and focus on the reduction of ground contact time will reduce the amount of time spent on the ground, increase the rate of force development, increase power, and increase the ability of the body to utilize the stretch-shortening cycle.

2. C: If the athlete were to keep their head in an upward position, too much load would be placed on the cervical spine while it was in an unnatural curvature. With an unnatural curvature of the spine, breathing mechanics can become inhibited, decreasing the effectiveness of the metabolic conditioning.

3. A: Accommodating resistance is the technique of using bands or chains in training to increase the force throughout portions of the exercise where resistance is less. While training, attention may be placed on the force-velocity curve of certain exercises. It is important for the strength and conditioning professional to understand different modalities available for the attainment of enhanced performance.

4. B: By slowing down the movement of the drill, strength and conditioning professionals will be able to make the proper adjustments to the athlete's sprint mechanics before increasing the intensity of the run. If the athlete were to perform drills at maximum speed without making corrections to improper technique, it is more likely that improper movement patterns would become further engrained. Technique proficiency should be mastered at lower intensities and slower speeds before performing drills at higher intensities.

5. B: Placing spotters on each end of the barbell ensures a safe environment when performing the front squat exercise. Any other position of a spotter would unbalance the barbell in cases where assistance is needed. If the strength and conditioning professional were to stand in front of the athlete, focus and attention may be lost during the exercise. Furthermore, because the barbell is anterior relative to the athlete, a spotter in the posterior position would not offer enough assistance.

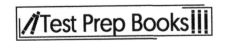

6. A: During midflight, the hip will concentrically contract and flex as it prepares for ground contact. This concentric muscle action of the hip will prepare the athlete for another stride as the opposite leg is beginning to become uncontacted with the ground.

7. C: In the narrow grip, the hands grasp the barbell close to one another while still utilizing the knurling of the barbell. By placing the hands closer together, no knurling would be available and the exercise would not be performed in a safe environment. If, at any time, the knurling is not used, the barbell could slip out of the athlete's hand causing harm or injury.

8. B: While utilizing resistance machines for the attainment of performance enhancement, the tempo—or rate—of the movement should be controlled and performed in one fluid motion. Performing the exercise in a fast and explosive manner would put an excessive amount of stress on the athlete, especially in the eccentric phase of the exercise. Instead, the strength and conditioning professional must ensure that the movement is performed in a controlled manner while the athlete maintains full contact with the pads of the machine. Also, the use of a full range of motion and performing the Valsalva maneuver will increase the effectiveness of the movement.

9. B: By utilizing the stretch-shortening cycle, the athlete will increase force development by engaging the proprioceptors in the muscle bellies and tendons, which can signal the brain to increase force production in the effector muscles. The countermovement, when used in plyometric training, will actively engage muscles that would not be activated if the countermovement were not performed.

10. A: When the athlete becomes fatigued during conditioning exercises, the shoulders tend to start to round forward. This position can decrease the effectiveness of the aerobic system (because the chest cavity, diaphragm, and lungs can be compressed). This can place strain on the tissues and decrease the intake of oxygen. The strength and conditioning professional must ensure proper body alignment is maintained throughout the entire duration of the exercise.

11. D: As the athlete decelerates, the hips should flex, allowing the center of gravity to drop lower as the chest maintains its position over the midfoot. With a lower center of gravity, the athlete will be able to apply maximal force when beginning to accelerate. If the athlete were to keep the hips extended and the center of gravity high, he or she may become unbalanced, and more time would be needed to attain proper position for changing direction.

12. C: By keeping the back flat, the chest up, and the head in a neutral position, the athlete will be performing free-weight exercises in a safe and effective manner. If the back were to round or hyperextend, too much stress could be placed on the spine, and injury could occur. The chest-up position will assist the athlete in maintaining stability throughout the movement, and the neutral head position will ensure the athlete is not placing too much load on the cervical spine during the movement.

13. A: It is important that the strength and conditioning professional ensures that the athlete is stable throughout the entire execution of the barbell bench press. To maintain stability, the five-point position must be employed. First, the right foot must be flat on the ground and pressure must be applied through the foot to ensure that it does not move during the exercise. The second position is that of left foot being in the same position of the right one. The glutes form the third point of contact. They should be in contact with the bench or floor during the entire execution of the exercise. Fourth, the upper back from thoracic spine to cervical spine must stay in contact with the bench or floor during the entire exercise. Lastly, the back of the head, by the occiput, should be in contact with the bench or floor.

14. D: Proper body alignment is critical in plyometric exercises. Any exercise that is performed when the body is not properly aligned will cause improper movement mechanics and place a tremendous amount of stress on the athlete's body. Keeping the shoulders, knees, and mid-feet in line with each other during the movement can ensure that proper body alignment is maintained throughout the exercise. Whether the athlete is performing the countermovement, the concentric extension portion, or the eccentric landing portion of the exercise, it is important to ensure that this body position is maintained for safety.

15. A: Any treadmill used during training should be properly equipped with a safety switch. A treadmill without a safety switch is a safety concern and should not be used. By having working knowledge of a treadmill, the strength and conditioning professional will be properly prepared to conduct safe sessions.

16. B: Agility is defined as the ability to accelerate, decelerate, and rapidly change direction. Although acceleration through changes in direction, the ability to decelerate and hold the body in a static position, and the ability to maintain balance in unstable environments are all components of agility, in isolation, they do not describe agility.

17. B: When training at 85 percent intensity, five repetitions would be considered a maximal-effort repetition range. Therefore, the athlete's focus and arousal levels should both be high. If the focus and arousal levels were lower immediately preceding and during the exercise, it is unlikely that the athlete would have a successful attempt in performing all five repetitions. It is important for the strength and conditioning professional to understand what intensities warrant higher and lower arousal levels and mentally prepare the athlete for the programmed intensities.

18. C: During exercise, faulty movement patterns may occur. It is important that the strength and conditioning professional identify and correct these patterns promptly to prevent such errors from further engraining themselves in the athlete's mind. If the strength and conditioning professional were to wait or not correct the faulty movement pattern, athletes could injure themselves. Less critically, the athlete's performance may also fail to reach its potential.

19. C: Many occasions call for use of a weightlifting belt. Weight belts have the ability, when used correctly, to increase the effectiveness of the Valsalva maneuver by increasing abdominal pressure. This will further enhance the stability of the spine. It is important for the strength and conditioning professional to teach athletes when and how to properly use weight belts while training. Weight belts should be used for movements that place a high load on the spine and during maximal weight training efforts. When movements are not stressing the spine or are at submaximal efforts, the use of a weight belt is not warranted. If the athlete were to use a weightlifting belt on every exercise, proper core strength could be inhibited, and the athlete could start to rely too much on the weightlifting belt.

20. B: Tires have become very popular in non-traditional implement training, and proper technique is vital to ensure that they are used in a safe manner. When using tires for training, it is important for the athlete to be taught the proper movement mechanics because they are different than any other style of training. When flipping a tire, the upper body can be placed onto the tire, increasing the stability of the body. To increase the stability of the body against a tire, the athlete should learn to lean against the tire while performing the Valsalva maneuver. This will increase the safety and effectiveness of the movement.

21. C: As relative loads can be very high during lower-body plyometric training exercises, it is important to ensure that the knees are properly absorbing the loads of the body upon landing. When landing, both knees should flex simultaneously, absorbing the weight of the body in a healthy joint angle. A common cue to give is to have the knees pushed out when performing and landing the jump. If the athlete's knees are caving in upon landing, strengthening exercises should be given to increase the stability of the knee. Failing to do so can increase the likelihood of knee injuries, especially to the ACL.

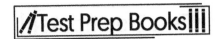

22. D: To ensure proper heel strike, pressure should be placed toward the outside of the foot. By placing the pressure on the outside of the foot, the natural arch will be maintained throughout the exercise and the load will be appropriately dispersed. If the arch becomes flattened through excessive repetitions, biomechanical issues can arise from improper balance and loading from the hips, knees, and ankles.

23. D: While most exercises will require the use of a spotter, it would be very difficult and unsafe to attempt to spot a power clean due to the force and velocity applied to the barbell. The other choices (bench press, back squat, and lying barbell triceps extension) must use a spotter. Although the power clean does not warrant the use of a spotter, it is important to teach the athlete to properly abort the exercise if technique ever becomes faulty.

24. B: The three techniques used for proprioceptive neuromuscular facilitation are the hold-relax technique, the contract-relax technique, and the hold-relax technique with agonist contraction. As PNF stretching is widely used in the strength and conditioning profession, it is important to have a thorough understanding of the terminology and techniques used with PNF stretching.

25. B: While utilizing resistance machines during training, it is important to maintain stability throughout the entire movement. During the use of lower-body resistance machines, the athlete's hands should be placed firmly on the handles of the machine. Any other hand placement could cause the athlete to become unbalanced and unstable when executing the exercise.

26. B: Having a thorough understanding of proper hand placement is advantageous for strength and conditioning professionals and their athletes. A pronated grip is widely used on many exercises in the strength and conditioning profession. The pronated grip is the most common grip when using a barbell or dumbbell. The pronated grip occurs when the athlete looks at their hands and sees the back of the hand where the knuckles are.

27. C: Shoulder and elbow positioning is important to note when utilizing upper-body plyometric exercises. When high forces are placed on the upper body, the elbows will tend to point more anteriorly than is optimal. This is mainly due to the body trying to compensate for the force applied to the upper body. It is important to teach the athlete to keep their elbows closer to the torso, allowing the shoulder to stay within their normal anatomical position. By properly understanding the common faults of upper-body plyometric exercises, the strength and conditioning professional will be more prepared to observe the mistakes and promptly make corrections during training sessions.

28. B: During metabolic conditioning training, it is important to understand the various pieces of equipment. Most equipment will allow the strength and conditioning professional to increase or decrease the resistance of the machine to change the intensity of the work. The rowing machine is equipped with the ability to increase or decrease air flow into the machine. This ability allows the strength and conditioning professional the ability to adjust the intensity of the machine.

29. A: Understanding the reasoning behind a general warmup is important for the strength and conditioning professional. During a general warmup, core temperature increases, circulation to muscles increases, and range of motion about the major joints increases.

30. D: During every exercise, there is a portion of the movement where the force will peak. This portion of the movement is termed the sticking point, and the athlete should learn to exhale during this time. Having a basic understanding of when the sticking point is during each exercise will allow the strength and conditioning professional to accurately cue the athlete through each exercise. Often, faulty movement patterns will occur during the sticking point because this point involves the most force on the athlete's body, so fatigue and compensatory mechanisms are common.

31. D: During plyometric training, after the energy is loaded into the muscle and tendons, there will be a brief period when the body changes direction and the muscle action shifts from eccentric to concentric work. This period is termed the amortization portion of the exercise. Although this could be considered an isometric portion of the exercise, the common terminology in plyometric training is amortization. Once the brief amortization period occurs, the muscles will start concentrically contracting.

32. C: Slight flexion of the knee (around 5–10 degrees) will prevent terminal knee extension and keep the knees in a healthy joint angle range. Although terminal knee extension can sometimes be a safe position during strength training, it is not considered to be safe in a conditioning training session where repetitive fatigue will occur. It is important to adjust the seat according to the athlete's anthropometry.

33. D: The only way to ensure proper breathing mechanics are employed during high-intensity anaerobic conditioning activities is to increase the length or frequency of rest periods when the athlete begins to fatigue. When fatigue occurs, the shoulders will begin to round forward, placing the athlete in a position where the aerobic system will be compromised. Understanding appropriate work-to-rest ratios for the goals of the training session is important when programming anaerobic conditioning activities.

34. C: Although a general warmup is important to perform before any stretching activity, it is not a benefit of static stretching. The main benefits of static stretching include increasing the range of motion of the joints, enhancing recovery, and serving as part of a corrective or rehabilitation program when done properly.

35. C: Knees caving in during hip, knee, and ankle free-weight exercises is a common mistake observed in many training sessions. Having the ability to correct this common flaw is important in ensuring a safe and effective training environment. Although the chest should be high during the entire execution of the movement, this verbal cue would not have any benefit for the stated flaw. By cueing the athlete to maintain outward pressure and ensure proper knee tracking, the hips will stay engaged and the athlete will correct the mistake of having the knees cave in during the movement.

36. D: The segments that comprise lower-limb sprinting mechanics include the eccentric braking period, the concentric propulsive phase, the recovery phase, and the ground preparation phase. Although the acceleration phase is a segment of sprinting mechanics, it is not a phase of the lower-limb mechanics.

37. A: Proper arm action is important during walking, jogging, and running exercises. As the right leg is coming forward, the left arm should be coming forward, and as the left leg is coming forward, the right arm should be coming forward. Natural movement at the shoulder joint is needed when utilizing these types of exercises. Throughout arm action, the elbow should stay flexed around 90 degrees and the hands should be in a relaxed position. The hands should come as high as the chest or sternum during the upward motion and reach back down to the lateral hip during the downward motion. By maintaining the full range of motion at the shoulder joint, the efficiency of the movement will increase.

38. A: When starting, the athlete should either be in an upright position, in a downward position in a three- or four-point stance, or in a downward position set in starting blocks. When the athlete is in any of the downward positions, the lead leg should be flexed to around 90 degrees and the trailing leg should be flexed to around 130 degrees. When starting, the athlete should focus on applying maximum force through the ground with both feet to propel their body forward horizontally. Within the first couple of strides, the athlete will transfer the force from horizontal displacement to gradual vertical displacement.

39. A: Stretches should never be pushed beyond the point of mild discomfort to prevent overstretching, regardless of whether the athlete is warmed up, Choice *B*, or fully relaxed, Choice *C*. Athletes may sometimes try to overstretch themselves, Choice *D*, but this should be discouraged to prevent injury.

40. A: Coaches should make sure that they provide resistance using their hips and trunk. They should not use their extremities, Choice *B*, to apply resistance. They should also remain facing squarely in the direction of movement, as opposed to Choices *C* or *D*, to avoid twisting the spine.

41. C: Muscle hypertrophy typically occurs in approximately four to eight weeks. Choices *A, B*, and *D* are made-up answers.

42. B: The main difference between dumbbells/barbells and free weight training equipment is that dumbbells and barbells are handheld weights, while the training machines are pre-arranged setups designed for specific exercises. Dumbbells and barbells can be used for a variety of exercises rather than just one, Choice *A*. Weights can be added to the machines, Choice *C*, but the movements are predesignated. The machines can be adjusted to accommodate the athlete's height and weight, Choice *D*.

43. A: Performing curls in a standing position engages the body's core muscles to aid in stabilization. This is not necessary when the athlete is in a seated position, Choice *B*, or in a lying-down position, Choices *C* and *D*.

44. C: When doing curls, muscle isolation occurs more intensely during a seated workout. When standing, Choice *B*, the movement is aided by the momentum of the body. Choices *A* and *D* are made-up answers.

45. D: The knees should be flexed to 90 degrees during seated curls. Choices *A, B*, and *C* are made-up answers.

Program Design

1. A: Beginners should begin training by performing three sets of eight to twelve reps of simple exercises using large muscle groups. This amount of total volume will allow strength adaptations, hypertrophy adaptations, and neural activations.

2. C: The mesocycle is a specific time period in periodized training intended to reach a specific goal. It is usually a 21- to 28-day training period that consists of 16 to 23 training days and five days of rest.

3. B: To increase anaerobic capacity, training intensities should remain high. Therefore, 85–90 percent of maximal heart rate should be consistently reached. To maintain a high heart rate, the training should consist of intense movements, followed by short rest periods.

4. D: An antagonist muscle is a muscle that opposes or supports the prime mover of a muscular contraction. The muscle that is involved in the contraction is known as the agonist and is considered the prime mover of the movement. The antagonist, which is the muscle involved in slowing down the contraction or resisting the movement, elongates as the agonist contracts. For every main movement of the human body, there is an agonist and an antagonist. There is also another category of musculature involved in movement: synergists. Synergists are muscles that are not directly involved with the movement but assist by stabilizing the joints involved in the action.

5. B: Total load should be calculated to determine progressive overload and to prevent overtraining volumes. When calculating total load, the number of completed sets multiplied by the number of repetitions per set multiplied by the load used yields an accurate calculation of the total amount of weight lifted in the training session.

6. A: Lower-body free-weight training can be very beneficial to many populations, especially those within athletics. The back squat, power clean, and lunge would all be considered multi-joint, compound, lower-body movements, whereas the barbell thruster would be more of a total body training exercise that is not commonly used for strength-gaining purposes.

7. C: Training for power should allow 3 to 5 minutes of rest between sets. This allotted time will allow the body to fully recover from the previous set so that maximal force can be applied to the next set.

8. D: Overload is the principle of consistently adding resistance to an athlete's training exercises and routines in an effort to improve muscle adaptation and avoid plateaus. With the maintenance of the same resistance, muscle fibers become accustomed to the routine and fail to progress. The ideal goal is to consistently apply forces of increased weight to progress through a program to the next level of performance. With an overload of too much weight or effort, the risk of injury presents itself, so constant awareness and progressive overload should be the focus of this aspect of programming.

9. C: The microcycle is the term used for a 7-day loading period. This usually represents a week's worth of training stimulus that prepares the athlete for more intense activity during the advanced stages of the training program.

10. D: Although flexibility training exercises are often utilized in warm-up sessions and cool-down sessions, the main goal of flexibility training is to increase the range of motion of the major joints of the body.

11. B: Individual considerations should include the specific movement patterns of the given sport, performing power movements first in the training session to prevent fatigue, and selecting exercises based around the predominant muscle fiber type used in the specific sport. Fatiguing exercises should not be performed first within the training session; instead, they should be performed last to prevent fatigue from reducing the technical abilities of the athlete.

12. A: Aerobic endurance refers to the capability of the aerobic metabolic pathway to be activated and engaged throughout a long exercise bout. Long-distance running, cross country skiing, endurance swimming, and triathlons are examples of sports that require highly-developed aerobic endurance.

13. D: Back straight, knees soft, and feet shoulder-width apart reflects the proper biomechanical stance for most bilateral, standing exercises. This position will allow the movement to be performed in a safe and effective manner.

14. A: The athlete's age should be considered prior to incorporating plyometric exercises into a training program. Youth, adolescents, and geriatric populations should be progressed slowly with plyometric training activities in order to allow the body to fully accommodate the stress that is placed on the body.

15. B: Muscular endurance will increase from high-repetition training with short rest periods. This can be very beneficial to many sports since it allows the muscles to continually and reliably perform without premature fatigue. For example, a tennis player with good muscular endurance can stay strong, fast, and effective over a full game without seeing significant declines in swing and serve strength.

16. C: After a musculoskeletal injury, there are generally three phases of tissue healing: the inflammatory phase, the repair phase, and the remodeling phase. By the repair phase, the edema and phagocytosis from the inflammatory phase have resolved. During the repair phase, new tissue replaces the damaged tissue that has been largely removed in the inflammatory phase. Collagen synthesis increases significantly, but as the new collagen fibers aggregate at the injury site, they lay down in a haphazard manner. Instead of being aligned in the optimal arrangement (longitudinally relative to the primary line of stress), many are transversely oriented, though some are going other directions as well. This disorganization decreases the strength and functional capacity of the tissue. During the remodeling phase, the fibers assume a more "normal" and effective arrangement, which restores strength to the tissue and makes it more effective at transmitting force.

17. A: An exercise that is used to exhaust a single muscle group prior to performing a multi-joint exercise is known as pre-fatigue. Pre-fatigue is often used to increase the intensity of a training session, or to specifically target a muscle group. This technique is often used with intermediate and advanced athletes and should be used cautiously with beginners.

18. B: Whether pre- or post-training, protein supplementation has been shown to decrease recovery time after intense bouts of exercise. Other choices would hinder recovery.

19. D. Basic fundamental principles of program design include working large to small muscle groups in a workout, alternating pushing exercises with pulling exercises, and alternating upper-body exercises with lower-body exercises. Performing two pushes for every pull in the training session is not considered a fundamental principle of program design. Doing so may lead to muscle imbalances.

20. C: The rehabilitation phase is not a phase that occurs during the healing process. Instead, the three phases are the inflammation phase, the repair phase, and the remodeling phase. The inflammation phase is characterized by pain, swelling, and redness and occurs within hours of the injury. The repair phase occurs as the number of inflammatory cells decreases and the body begins healing the injury site. Lastly, the remodeling phase is characterized by new tissue growth and strengthening of the muscles, tendons, and ligaments near the site.

21. D: Interval training includes intervals of high-intensity and low-intensity exercises throughout the workout that are alternated to maximize an athlete's cardiovascular, muscular, and overall exercise performance endurance. With consideration of an athlete's age, abilities, restrictions, and health status, an appropriate training program can be designed that implements safe intervals of high- and low-intensity exercises that maximize benefits while minimizing risks.

22. B: Reversibility is the term used for when the body starts to return to pre-training status after the cessation of a training program. When the physical stress is removed, the body responds by regressing back towards an untrained state. The result of this regression is partial or complete loss of the positive adaptations that resulted from the proper and specific training program. For strength and conditioning professionals working in high school and collegiate settings, detraining can occur during academic break periods.

23. A: Increasing lever length, varying the balance demands, and maintaining focus are all strategies that can be used to vary the intensity of exercise. Furthermore, all athletic activities utilize fast concentric muscle action, and slowing down this portion of any exercise could hinder performance.

24. C: General Adaptation Syndrome is considered the first proposed model of periodization. Simply stated, it is the body's ability to adapt to the stress that is placed upon the body during training. Progressive overload takes general adaptation syndrome into consideration when programming for athletic development.

25. A: Adaptations in muscular endurance occur when moderate to high intensities, high volume, and short rest periods are performed. Therefore, 0 to 45 seconds would be the ideal allotted time for rest when intending to improve muscular endurance.

26. B: Adaptation is the principle of the body's natural ability to grow accustomed to certain routines. Whether it be a movement, method, mode, weight, or performance of an exercise, the body will automatically adapt to become more efficient and energy-efficient. In order to avoid adaptation in this sense, the strength and conditioning professional and athlete should work together to consistently restructure the exercises and training program to vary the muscle mechanics and gradually increase intensity and duration.

27. C: Irresponsible loading in program design can produce microtrauma. Overuse injuries are commonly seen in athletes who push the limits too much too often. An aggressive exercise training regimen that incorporates exercises and increases in training volumes and loads is successful only if it gradually increases as an athlete's capabilities increase and improve.

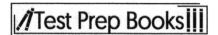

28. D: The athlete should not be able to compete or participate without completing a proper, evidence-based, rehabilitation program. Upon completion of this program, the body should be pain-free and the athlete should be ready.

29. C: Minor ruptures or tears within the muscles, ligaments, or tendons describe a strain. While these injuries seem minimal, ruptures and tears at these specific sites can have serious ramifications and limit the ability to move and function, especially in a pain-free manner.

30. B: The FITT principle is an acronym for frequency, intensity, timing, and type—the four basic keys to designing the most beneficial training program for an athlete. With each of these factors being considered in the design of a fitness training program, the strength and conditioning professional can effectively promote an athlete's successful progression throughout the program to accommodate their ultimate achievement of established goals.

31. A: Power training should occur with lower repetition ranges. Therefore, exercises should be performed within the 1–5 repetition range. Programming low repetition ranges ensures that fatigue will stay minimal and that maximal force can be applied to each repetition.

32. D: Of the choices, kettlebells are the only implement categorized as a free-weight. Free-weights are commonly used in resistance training exercises. Including barbells, dumbbells, kettlebells, and weight plates, these pieces of equipment are convenient, transportable, and versatile in their applications for exercises targeting any major muscle group.

33. D: Barbell curls, triceps extensions, and wrist curls are all considered to be upper-body exercises. Of the potential choices, the barbell bench press is the only choice that is categorized as a multi-joint exercise for the upper body.

34. C: For novice and intermediate athletes, muscular endurance usually occurs at training percentages that fall within the 70–85 percent range.

35. B: An athlete's 1RM, or one-repetition maximum, is defined as the greatest resistance or weight that can be moved through a full range of motion with proper posture and in a controlled manner one time.

36. A: Time under tension, or TUT, is the nomenclature for each phase of the lift and is consistent with the tempo at which the exercise should be performed. Within a training set, tempo is read "eccentric—isometric—concentric" (all in seconds). Furthermore, an exercise with a 4 x 1 x 0 tempo would equate to a 4-second eccentric motion, a 1-second isometric, and an explosive concentric.

37. A: For hypertrophy-based training, the load and volume should both be high. Therefore, the athlete should perform repetitions within the 6 to 12 range to induce adaptations of muscle size and strength.

38. A: The negative or lowering portion of an exercise is an eccentric muscle action. Slow eccentrics consist of slowly lowering the weight, which can cause a lot of muscle damage in a minimal number of sets and repetitions. Reserved for advanced athletes, the recommendation is to keep sets at a load that is 20–50 percent greater than that of 1RM. A slow eccentric usually lasts around 4–10 seconds and requires the strength and conditioning professional to be a spotter for assisting the athlete's concentric portion of the lift since the weight used is greater than the athlete can handle for that portion of the lift.

39. C: Periodization is the general approach to improving fitness benefits and reducing the incidence of injury by systematically staggering "cycles" or periods of training.

40. C: Plyometrics use the stretch-shortening cycle of muscles, which involves a stretch or lengthening of the muscle in the eccentric phase followed by a transition, or amortization, phase and then the concentric phase, in which the muscle shortens or contracts. Choices *A* and *D* are incorrect because they do not list the phases in the correct order. Choice *B* is incorrect because energy is stored when muscles and tendons are stretched in the eccentric phase, and it is released as the muscle shortens in the concentric phase.

41. D: As a beginner in plyometrics, the athlete should be limited to eighty to one hundred repetitions per session; as written, the plan would entail 120 repetitions per session (30 repetitions * 4 exercises). Choice *A* is incorrect because plyometric training is generally safe for older athletes when the program includes no more than five low-to-moderate intensity exercises at a lower volume with three to four recovery days between training sessions. Choice *B* is incorrect because lower-body exercises are not necessary to round out a plyometric program. Choice *C* is incorrect because plyometric sessions should be performed one to three times per week with forty-eight to seventy-two hours of recovery between sessions.

42. C: Sprint training is meant to improve running velocity by producing neurological adaptations that can improve RFD (the amount of force generated divided by the change in time) and impulse generation (the product of force applied to the ground and the amount of force applied). Choice *A* is incorrect because sprint training doesn't set a cap on improvements that may be achieved; 110% refers to the maximum speed that should be achieved in assisted sprint training. Choice *B* is incorrect because range of motion and flexibility are generally improved through mobility drills and appropriate strength and conditioning programs. Choice *D* is incorrect because maximum velocity sprinting is meant to increase impulse generation.

43. B: Resisted sprint training involves adding weight or resistance to enhance acceleration and produce greater propulsive forces using sled/parachute towing, uphill running, weighted vests, wind resistance, and sled pushing. Loads are sport-specific, and a field athlete may use loads between 20-30% of body weight. Choices *A* and *C* are incorrect because braking forces and pulling cords are used in assisted sprint training, which pulls athletes at a faster than normal rate. Choice *D* is incorrect because weighted vests are used with resisted sprint training; downhill running is a training method in assisted sprint training.

Organization and Administration

1. B: During times of overtraining, performance will decrease. The human body can no longer adapt to the increasing stress of the training sessions and begins to gradually decline in performance. The central nervous system will become affected and many other signs and symptoms will begin to show.

2. A: Liability is the legal responsibility to ensure a safe and effective training environment for the athletes and to act appropriately in the event of injury. The other options, although legal terms, do not accurately describe the definition in the question.

3. C: Olympic exercises, plyometric training, and medicine ball exercises require a higher ceiling to allow the exercises to be performed in a safe and effective manner. Ceiling height recommendation is 12 to 14 feet for these types of exercises. It is important to ensure that the recommended height is clear from any obstructions that could get in the way of the exercises being performed. If this recommendation is not met, the training sessions may need to be altered to accommodate for the low ceiling height.

4. B: Prior to purchasing equipment, it is important to research the company and speak to those who have purchased from the company in the past. While doing research, the training and conditioning professional can easily differentiate those who stand behind their products from those who do not. All reliable companies have a thorough liability statement that explains all terms and conditions regarding the liability of their products.

5. A: Ideally, all facilities would be on the ground floor of the building. In reality, this is not always the case, and it is important to understand the flooring capacities when designing or evaluating the facility. Per recommendations, the capacity of the floor should be able to withstand 100 pounds per square foot. When complying with this recommendation, the strength and conditioning professional must ensure that the floor is strong enough to withstand the exercises being performed.

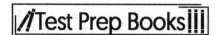

6. A: Placement of equipment is very important to the facility design process. To ensure safe and efficient training sessions, equipment should be organized into groups that coincide with the goals of the equipment.

7. D: Being able to evaluate athletes while performing exercises in extreme temperatures is a responsibility of the strength and conditioning professional. Signs and symptoms of heat-related illnesses include goose bumps, lack of perspiration, cramps, inability to speak clearly, difficulty in standing or walking, dizziness, and nausea. Reduced heart rate is not associated with a heat-related illness, but instead is a symptom of a cold-related illness.

8. B: Although mirrors are not a necessity in the strength and conditioning facility, they are often utilized for aesthetic appeal and as a coaching tool. When designing the facility and installing the mirrors, it is recommended that the bottom of the mirrors are at least 20 inches from the floor. The main reason for this recommendation is to prevent contact from a bouncing piece of free-weight equipment, which could cause damage.

9. C: The first negative phase of overtraining is nonfunctioning overreaching. Therefore, the strength and conditioning professional must understand the signs and symptoms of overreaching and also understand the time that may be needed to fully recover. With nonfunctioning overreaching, this recovery time ranges from weeks to months.

10. D: The recommended temperature is 68–78 degrees for the facility, while 72–78 degrees is usually considered optimal. It is important that the facility has an HVAC system that can accommodate these demands to ensure that these temperatures can be met in any situation.

11. A: Setting the standard of eligibility criteria is important for the strength and conditioning facility. Ensuring that certain criteria are met in terms of the standards of the facility and in terms of those who use it will lessen the likelihood of legal issues since each participant will understand the standards of the facility and be able to act accordingly.

12. B: The strength and conditioning professional has many roles for the attainment of athletic performance. That being said, when it comes to nutrition, strength and conditioning professionals must understand that they are not a registered nutritionist and therefore must refer their athletes to a registered dietician or certified nutrition professional who can create an individualized nutrition plan.

13. D: The facility rules document should outline all rules and regulations of the facility. Although an emergency action plan is a must for any strength and conditioning facility, it should be a separate document that thoroughly describes the actions in any emergency situation.

14. A: Humidity exceeding 60% will not only be uncomfortable and unsafe for those training in the facility but can also lead to the growth of mold and mildew, which can cause health issues in conjunction with damage to the building. Ensuring that the air inside the building is being regularly exchanged at least 8 times per hour will help prevent unpleasant odors due to stagnant air. Placing 2–4 ceiling fans per every 1200 square feet of the facility can achieve this.

15. B: The minimum amount of space for each athlete in the facility should be 100 square feet. It is helpful to pose questions to facility designers such as "How many athletes will use the facility?" and "What are the most likely demographics and training experiences for athletes inside the facility?" so that an adequate amount of space can be planned for and properly executed. A facility with less than 100 square feet per athlete can run into safety issues and problems with overall usage, so it is best to plan to exceed that number.

Testing, Ongoing Monitoring, and Data Evaluation

1. D: Although construct validity is a category within general validity, it is not a subcategory of criterion-referenced validity and is separate from the other options. Criterion-referenced validity refers to the extent to which test scores can be associated with other tests that measure the same athletic ability. Within criterion-referenced validity are three subcategories: concurrent validity, convergent validity, and predictive validity.

2. A: The metabolic energy system that is predominantly used within the specific sport or position should be considered when selecting tests that measure endurance parameters. By utilizing testing protocols that are specific to the energy demands of the athlete, the strength and conditioning professional can ensure the validity and reliability of the administered testing protocols.

3. B: To ensure accurate and valid test results, it is important for the strength and conditioning professional to acquire a thorough understanding of proper procedures when administering 1RM testing. By following the guidelines within the 1RM testing protocol, the strength and conditioning professional should instruct the athlete to warm up with a light resistance that easily allows 5–10 repetitions.

4. C: The Yo-Yo Intermittent Recovery Test measures the aerobic capacity of the athlete. This test is widely used across many sports, especially when an accurate measurement of the athlete's aerobic capacity is desired.

5. B: Body composition and anthropometric testing often use skinfold calipers, bodyweight scales, and height measurement tools. Although stopwatches are used for many testing protocols, they are not used for body composition or anthropometric testing protocols.

6. A: For a given test to be considered reliable and valid, the test must also be selected based on the previous experience and training status of the athlete. If technical proficiency is not yet met for a given exercise, using that exercise as a test would void the reliability and validity of that test. Therefore, the strength and conditioning professional should choose exercises that the athletes have shown to be proficient at.

7. C: Acquiring a thorough understanding of the proper work-to-rest ratios is vital for the testing to be considered valid and reliable. For oxidative-based testing protocols, a 1:1–1:3 work-to-rest ratio should be used.

8. D: The function of such a comparison is to identify specific athletic capabilities that need to be improved upon. Once validity has been established, the strength and conditioning professional can begin to compare the normative results of the test battery to the typical results observed within the sport, position, or population. By doing so, insight will be attained on specific performance parameters as they pertain to an individual or sports team. Furthermore, by comparing the results from the test battery to those often observed in the given sport or athlete, the strength and conditioning professional can determine specific areas that need to be improved upon in future training programs.

9. A: To help support the health and safety of the athletes, athletes should be allowed water and breaks as often as personally needed between maximal bouts of exertion. Allowing water breaks increases the validity of the test and ensures that dehydration or fatigue do not cause any unreliable test results. It also keeps athletes safe.

10. C: Although the 1RM back squat and deadlift are considered maximum power tests, they are also considered low-speed tests. Therefore, the 1RM power clean is the only option that coincides with a maximum high-speed power test. A maximum push-up test would be considered a local muscular endurance test.

11. D: Modifications based on test data aren't always necessary. Modifications and changes to the training program should only be made when a significant capability is not being met with the current program. One flaw that is common within the strength and conditioning profession is changing the program too soon without allowing time for proper adaptation to occur with a given capability.

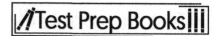

12. B: With the energy systems and proper work-to-rest ratios being accounted for, the strength and conditioning professional should perform high-skill tests and non-fatiguing tests prior to those that require less skill and are more fatiguing. Therefore, within the given options, maximum power tests should be performed first, due to the other options being less skill-dependent and more fatiguing in nature.

13. C: Although the partial curl-up is commonly used within many test batteries in the strength and conditioning profession, it is not tested with a 1RM format. Instead, the partial curl-up is used for local muscular endurance testing. Other options such as the 1RM bench press, back squat, and bench pull are commonly used for testing maximum muscular strength at low speeds.

14. D: The only acceptable option for the use of skinfold calipers is body composition. Body mass index, girth measurements, and anthropometric testing require the use of other specialized testing equipment.

15. B: Prior to test day, athletes should be aware of what tests they are to perform so they can physically and mentally prepare. In the days or week prior to the test, the strength and conditioning professional should fully explain each test, and athletes should be allowed to ask questions about the test.

16. A: Although the appropriate clothing is important for accurate and valid test results, it is not a consideration that falls within the environmental factors of the testing session. Instead, consideration should be given to the specific environmental factors of temperature, humidity, and running surface.

17. A: Selecting and training testing personnel is equally as important as the tests that are chosen. Ensuring that all test administrators are qualified and knowledgeable in each test is vital to the validity and reliability of test results. When possible, athletes should be tested by one tester to reduce the possibility of poor interrater reliability confounding the results.

18. B: On test day, the strength and conditioning professional should make sure all participants engage in a thorough warmup. The warmup should consist of a general warmup to increase body temperature and joint elasticity, followed by a specific warmup that is geared toward the testing that will be performed that day.

19. C: Following the guidelines set forth by the National Strength and Conditioning Association, 3–5 testing sets are ideal when performing 1RM testing. The 3–5 sets will ensure the athletes are given enough attempts, while also preventing fatigue within the testing session.

20. D: Face validity relates to the subjective perception, usually from the athlete, of whether the selected test accurately measures what it is intended to measure. Athletes tend to try harder and perform better on tests with higher face validity, as they believe in the validity and utility of the test.

21. C: BMI is a measure of weight relative to height and not a direct measure of body fat. Skinfolds, DEXA scans, and bioelectrical impedance are common assessments for body fat.

22. D: Practices that strength coaches can implement to foster a safe training environment include clearing loose equipment from the floor, mopping wooden floors, and checking wooden platforms for cracks. Emotional safety is enhanced through encouraging teamwork and positive, supportive attitudes. Weight benches and platforms should not be as close as possible; they require a minimum of 36 inches of clearance for walking around them safely, keeping distance between athletes lifting weights, spotting, and preventing injuring a nearby athlete.

CSCS Practice Tests #3, #4, & #5

To keep the size of this book manageable, save paper, and provide a digital test-taking experience, the 3rd, 4th, and 5th practice tests can be found online. Scan the QR code or go to this link to access it:

testprepbooks.com/bonus/cscs

SCAN ME

The first time you access the tests, you will need to register as a "new user" and verify your email address.

If you have any issues, please email support@testprepbooks.com

Dear CSCS Test Taker,

Thank you for purchasing this study guide for your CSCS exam. We hope that we exceeded your expectations.

Our goal in creating this study guide was to cover all of the topics that you will see on the test. We also strove to make our practice questions as similar as possible to what you will encounter on test day. With that being said, if you found something that you feel was not up to your standards, please send us an email and let us know.

We would also like to let you know about other books in our catalog that may interest you.

ACE

This can be found on Amazon: amazon.com/dp/1628457740

NASM

amazon.com/dp/1637757735

We have study guides in a wide variety of fields. If the one you are looking for isn't listed above, then try searching for it on Amazon or send us an email.

Thanks Again and Happy Testing!
Product Development Team
info@studyguideteam.com

FREE Test Taking Tips Video/DVD Offer

To better serve you, we created videos covering test taking tips that we want to give you for FREE. **These videos cover world-class tips that will help you succeed on your test.**

We just ask that you send us feedback about this product. Please let us know what you thought about it—whether good, bad, or indifferent.

To get your **FREE videos**, you can use the QR code below or email freevideos@studyguideteam.com with "Free Videos" in the subject line and the following information in the body of the email:

a. The title of your product

b. Your product rating on a scale of 1-5, with 5 being the highest

c. Your feedback about the product

If you have any questions or concerns, please don't hesitate to contact us at info@studyguideteam.com.

Thank you!

SCAN HERE

Made in the USA
Middletown, DE
21 October 2024

63062260R00157